D1249035

Adventures in Jewish Cooking

Adventures in Jewish Cooking

The Momele's Ta'am Cookbook

by Rosabelle Edlin and Shushannah Spector

Galahad Books · New York City

Reprinted by Galahad Books by arrangement
with Liveright Publishing Corporation.
Formerly published as *My Jewish Kitchen*.
COPYRIGHT © 1964, BY

LIVERIGHT PUBLISHING CORPORATION

All rights reserved—no part of this book may be repro-
duced in any form without permission in writing from the
publisher, except by a reviewer who wishes to quote brief
passages in connection with a review written for inclusion
in a magazine or newspaper.

ISBN: 0-88365-023-1
Library of Congress Catalog Card No. 73-81658
PRINTED IN THE UNITED STATES OF AMERICA

Contents

"When thou hast eaten and art full,
then thou shalt bless the Lord thy
God for the good land which he hath
given thee."

—Deuteronomy 8-10

Introduction

THROUGH THE CENTURIES THE JEWS HAVE SOJOURNED IN VIR-
tually every corner of the earth, and Jewish cooking has had
the advantage of being able to gather up what was best and
characteristic in cooking from each area.

As a consequence, the recipes in this book have a continental flavor, and in this collection are included recipes
which originated with the Jews who came from Poland and
the depths of Russia, such as the famous strudels (prune, nut,
and fruit-filled) with a flaky crust to tempt the appetite of the
gourmet. From Germany came the puddings and tortes, the
pastries and candies—from Hungary and Roumania came
flavorful stews, "goulashes"—spiced and well-seasoned meats
and vegetables, as well as other delicacies. From the melting
pot of Jews from all over the world, many have found their
haven in Israel and their recipes are included in the Continental Section.

MY JEWISH KITCHEN contains basic Jewish recipes
popular with not only Jewish people, but flavorful enough to
tempt every race and creed.

One of the cornerstones of Judaism is the Laws of Kashruth
which stem from the Mosaic Dietary Laws. For the young
bride or the "seasoned" housewife, the basic rules for keeping
a kosher home and maintaining a kosher kitchen are clearly
described.

Among the highlights of MY JEWISH KITCHEN are the
description of the typical *Shabos* or Friday night dinner in
all its splendor and charm, the ritual and reflection of gracious
living in the Jewish home, and the Biblical background sur-

9

rounding such important holidays as Passover, the High Holy Days and the festival holidays.

I want to express my heartfelt appreciation and gratitude to Mrs. Fannie Goldberg, for her recipes of *Pchai* and Sweet and Sour Eggs, popular in Central Europe and to Mrs. Natalie Friedman, whose succulent recipe for homemade vegetable soup I could not resist. To Mama—a prayerful tribute. My sincere thanks also to N. Mendelson & Sons of Miami and New York, for their courtesy in offering pertinent information concerning popular cuts of Kosher meats and fowl. Special thanks are due too to my co-author, Mrs. Shushannah Spector, for her unusual Israeli recipes and for her cooperation in connection with the book.

May this cookbook bring you luck, health and happiness for many years to come! May it make you famous as a hostess!

ROSABELLE EDLIN

Miami, Florida

Fish .... Why It Is a Favorite

FISH HAS ALWAYS BEEN A GREAT FAVORITE WITH JEWISH PEOPLE. It has been placed on the table as an appetizer, as the main course, and as an added attraction to the festive Sabbath table.

With the abundant variety of lake, river, and ocean fish available, one should make sure it finds a place on the family table every week, for it is rich in iodine and protein and provides vital minerals for the body.

You will find here recipes which are not only palate-tempting, but which may be served attractively with appealing garnishes. There is a fish to meet the budget of every family— one which can be prepared delightfully to suit everyone's taste.

Below is a list of fish found in the vast reservoir of the Atlantic and Pacific Oceans, as well as the delectable fish which inhabit the lakes, rivers and inland waterways. It is natural that some of the fish listed here will not be familiar to those living in certain areas. Those people who live in the central part of America will be more familiar with the fish which come from the lakes and rivers, whereas the people who live near the ocean will recognize the variety to which they have become accustomed.

May we suggest that those of you who have concentrated only on certain types of fish try some of the other varieties listed? You will be agreeably surprised and delighted with the new taste sensations!

FISH

Type	Source	Fat or Lean
Buffalo fish	Fresh Water	Fat
Butterfish	Ocean	Fat
Carp	Fresh Water	Lean
Cod	Ocean	Lean
Drumfish	Ocean	Lean
Flounder	Ocean	Lean
Grouper	Ocean	Lean
Haddock (Finnan Haddie)	Ocean	Lean
Halibut (Have Fat Trimmed)	Ocean	Fat
Herring, Lake	Fresh Water	Fat
Herring, Sea	Ocean	Fat
King Fish	Ocean	Lean
King Mackerel	Ocean	Fat
Mackerel	Ocean	Fat
Mackerel (Spanish)	Ocean	Fat
Ocean Perch (or Rosefish)	Ocean	Lean
Pickerel	Fresh Water	Lean
Pike (Blue)	Fresh Water	Lean
Pike (Sauger)	Fresh Water	Lean
Pike (Yellow)	Fresh Water	Lean
Pompano	Ocean	Fat
Porgy (Scup)	Ocean	Fat
Red Snapper	Ocean	Lean
Salmon (Ocean or Columbia River)	Ocean	Fat
Sea Bass (Black)	Ocean	Fat
Sea Bass (White)	Ocean	Fat
Shad (Seasonal: Dec. to July)	Ocean	Fat
Sheepshead	Ocean	Lean

Type	Source	Fat or Lean
Sheepshead	Fresh Water	Lean
Smelt	Ocean	Lean
Smelt	Fresh Water	Fat
Striped Bass	Ocean	Fat
Sturgeon	Ocean	Lean
Sucker	Fresh Water	Fat
Trout, Sea (Grey)	Ocean	Fat
Trout, Speckled Sea (Nov. to May)	Ocean	Fat
Trout, Lake (White or Pink)	Fresh Water	Fat
Tuna	Ocean	Fat
Whitefish	Fresh Water	Fat
White Perch	Ocean	Lean
Whiting	Ocean	Lean
Yellow Perch	Fresh Water	Lean

HOW TO SELECT FRESH FISH

The flesh of the fish should be firm.
The eyes should be bright.
The gills should be a bright red.
The fins should be moist.

TO FILLET FISH

To fillet means "to separate fish from skin and bone." By cutting in a lengthwise position, the fish remains in one piece. Remove head and tail of fish. Turn fish over and cut other side in lengthwise position. Cut open and remove entrails.

TO CLEAN AND SCALE FISH

Since this procedure can be messy, it is wise to use heavy wrapping paper and perform this task outside the house, with either a fish scaler or grater. Scale or grate from the tail end of fish toward the head. Remove the gills, and cut into the body of fish to remove entrails. Rinse and clean with cold water. Sprinkling salt on fish will help to preserve it.

FOR BAKING

Fish should be cut with skin intact into 2-to-3-in. slices.

FOR BROILING

Fish may be left whole, with head and tail intact (if small).
Fish may be left whole, with head and tail removed.
Fish may be cut into 3-in. pieces with skin intact.
Fish may be filleted.

FROZEN FISH

If purchased in package, read and follow directions carefully.

Fish which is frozen in your freezer should be defrosted at room temperature before using.

HELPFUL HINT: Place a little vinegar or lemon juice in the water while the fish is cooking. Fish will stay firm and retain its flavor.

GEFILTE FISH

3 lbs. whitefish, trout and
pike (or any combination
of fish you prefer)
2 large onions
2 eggs
3 good-sized carrots, sliced
lengthwise

2 tablesp. matzo meal (or 1
slice toast, grated)
1 teasp. pepper
2 teasp. salt
Pinch of sugar
½ cup ice water
1½ qts. water

After the fish has been filleted, the bones and heads are placed in a pot containing 1½ qts. water, 1 teasp. salt and ½ teasp. pepper. Boil this mixture over medium heat while preparing the fish.

Grandmother never resorted to grinders, but you may grind the fish, and then chop the onion in a chopping bowl, adding the ground fish—gradually adding the eggs, sugar, ice water, matzo meal (or bread crumbs), salt and pepper. Mixture must be chopped fine.

Since fish sticks to one's hands, have a bowl of clean water ready so that hands may be moistened to shape the fish mixture into balls.

Reduce the heat on the fish stock from medium to *low heat*. Then, very carefully drop the fish balls into the boiling fish stock, adding the carrots (cut lengthwise). After cooking for 2 hours, remove the cover, season to taste, and cook for another ½ hour.

Cool the fish and remove to platter. Carrots make a lovely garnish when placed around the fish on a lettuce leaf and sliced tomato. Serve with red horse-radish. Serves 8.

HELPFUL HINT: If a little color is desired in the gefilte fish, skins of the onions may be used in the fish stock while cooking. (This will darken the fish.)

carp, pike, salmon, whitefish

SWEET AND SOUR FISH

3 lbs. trout (white or pink)	⅓ teasp. onion juice
or fish of your choice	1 lemon, sliced thin and
1 cup hot fish liquid	seeded
¼ lb. gingersnaps	1 qt. water
½ cup brown sugar	1 carrot, diced
¼ cup seeded raisins	1 tablesp. celery, diced
¼ cup vinegar	1 onion, diced

Slice fish into 2-in. slices. Salt and let stand for several hours. Boil 1 qt. water with carrots, celery, 2 tablesp. vinegar, and onion. Drop fish in, turning the flame to low. Simmer until flesh is firm and leaves the bones. Strain and reserve 1 cup hot fish liquid. Add rest of ingredients, and cook until smooth and thick. This mixture must taste strongly of brown sugar and vinegar. More of either may be added to taste. Serves 6 to 8.

BAKED FISH

¼ lb. butter or ¼ cup	1 teasp. salt
salad oil	1 teasp. sugar
3 lbs. whitefish, trout or pike	½ teasp. paprika
(cut into 1½ in. slices)	2 tablesp. bread crumbs
1 large can whole tomatoes	½ cup diced celery
1 onion, sliced thin	3 large carrots, diced
½ teasp. pepper	

Preheat oven to 350°F. Place butter or salad oil in pan and preheat. Place sliced onion in pan, cover with fish. Add salt, pepper, paprika (covering fish with paprika for color), then place whole tomatoes, celery, carrots in baking pan and sprinkle bread crumbs over fish. Cover. Cook for 45 minutes and uncover baking pan for the last 10 minutes. Serves 6.

HELPFUL HINT: Small whole new potatoes will complement this meal.

SALMON PATTIES

1 can red salmon	*3 tablesp. matzo meal,*
¼ lb. butter, margarine or	*cracker meal, or grated*
salad oil	*toast*
1 small onion, grated	*1 egg*

Remove bones and skin from salmon. Add the egg, and mix until the salmon has been shredded fine. Grate the onion into mixture, add the matzo meal (or alternatives mentioned). When completely mixed, form into oval-shaped patties (flat). Heat butter or oil in large frying pan. Drop patties in one-by-one, and cook until completely browned on one side, over medium flame. This should take approximately 15 minutes. Turn and brown on other side. Garnish with peaches and parsley. Serves 4.

HELPFUL HINT: In order to clean pan more easily after frying fish, place a little vinegar in pan and bring to a boil.

PICKLED HERRING (Marinated)

8 milter herring	*1 lemon, sliced*
2 onions, sliced	*1 tablesp. peppercorn*
1¼ cups vinegar	*1 tablesp. mustard seed*
¾ cup water	*6 bay leaves*
2 tablesp. sugar	

Soak herring in cold water overnight. Cut heads off herrings, drain, remove entrails, but reserve milt. Fillet herrings by running knife between skin and herring, removing the skin. Cut into 2-to-3 in. pieces. Pick out bones which are visible. It is advisable to use an earthen crock deep enough to hold the ingredients. Alternatively add the pieces of herring, lemon slices, bay leaves, mustard seed, peppercorn, and sliced onion. Then, in a pan, boil water, sugar, and vinegar. Mash the milt and add the boiled mixture. Strain through a sieve, and pour over the herring and spices in the crock.

HELPFUL HINT: What is herring without boiled potatoes?

PICKLED HERRING WITH CREAM
(Marinated)

3 milter herring	*1 lemon (juice only)*
1 lemon, sliced	*1 teasp. pickling spices and*
2 tablesp. sugar	*peppercorn*
1 onion, sliced	*1 cup sour cream*

Soak herring in cold water overnight. Follow directions for Pickled Herring (above), except mash milt with lemon juice and add sugar. Cut herring into 2-in. strips, and place in quart or pint glass jars with airtight covers. Add sliced lemon, onion, pickling spices and sour cream. Refrigerate for 2 days before using.

HERRING ROLLS

Follow directions for Pickled Herring (Page 17). Instead of cutting into 2-to-3 in. pieces, take each herring fillet and roll, fastening with either white toothpicks, plastic picks or string. Place in earthen crock for at least 3 to 4 days.

BOILED FISH

4 lbs. fish (trout, pike, carp,	*1 teasp. mixed whole spices*
or any fish you prefer)	*1½ qts. water*
1 onion, diced	*4 tablesp. vinegar*
¼ cup diced celery	*1 teasp. salt*
2 carrots, diced	*¼ teasp. pepper*

Salt fish and let stand for 1 hour. Slice into portion pieces. Cook rest of the ingredients until they come to a boil. Add the fish, and cook over low flame until flesh leaves the bones.

Carefully remove bones, and serve on platter. Garnish with parsley, tomatoes and lettuce. Serves 8.

SMELTS (Fried)

3 lbs. smelts (medium-sized)   *2 teasp. salt*
1 cup flour   *1 teasp. pepper*
           Salad oil (about ½ cup)

Clean smelts, removing heads, tails and entrails (or if you prefer, you may fry them whole). Salt fish, add pepper for flavor. Roll smelts in flour. Heat oil in skillet until hot. Drop fish in skillet and fry over medium-high flame until brown. Turn on other side. When brown, remove from flame and serve hot. Serves 6.

SMELTS (Fried in Batter)

3 lbs. smelts (medium-sized)   *2 teasp. salt*
1½ cups matzo meal   *1 teasp. pepper*
3 eggs   *Salad oil (about ½ cup)*

Clean smelts, removing heads, tails and entrails (or you may fry them whole). Mix eggs, salt and pepper, beating well. Dip smelts into this mixture, then roll in matzo meal. Heat oil in skillet until hot. Drop fish into skillet and fry until brown over medium-high flame. Turn on other side. When brown, remove from flame and serve hot. Garnish with lemon slices. Serves 6.

LEMON SAUCE FOR BOILED FISH

Reserve stock from Boiled Fish (Page 18), and make the following delicious sauce which gives the fish a touch of glamour and a wonderful flavor:

1 large lemon or Persian lime   *3 egg yolks*
   (juice and rind)   *½ teasp. salt*
2 cups fish stock   *3 tablesp. sugar*

Beat egg yolks well, add sugar, lemon juice and grated rind. After mixing thoroughly, add fish stock (which has been strained). Cook over low flame until thick. Add salt to taste. Use hot sauce with cooked fish. This sauce may also be served cold. Garnish with parsley.

SCHARFE FISH (Spicy Fish)

Follow the recipe for Boiled Fish (Page 18). Reserve 2 cups of fish liquid.

2 cups fish liquid	*2 egg yolks*
2 tablesp. flour	*2 tablesp. butter*

Melt butter and add flour as when making a cream sauce. Gradually add the fish stock. Beat egg yolks. Slowly pour batter into egg yolks. While hot, serve with boiled fish. Garnish with parsley and slices of lemon.

TUNA FISH MOLD

Are you having a group of friends in for a snack? The following mold may be prepared in advance so that you will have more time to spend with your guests. It serves 12 people generously and makes an attractive dish.

1 large can white tuna fish, grated or flaked	*¾ cup strained chili sauce*
2 pkges. lemon Jello	*3 tablesp. vinegar*
3 eggs, hard-boiled	*3 cups water (instead of 4 for dissolving Jello)*
¼ cup stuffed olives, sliced	*1 ring mold (to hold 1½ qts.)*
¼ cup diced celery	
¼ cup sweet pickles, diced	

If tuna has been packed in oil, open can and scald fish with hot water to remove the oil. Cut up celery, olives, pickles; slice eggs and strain chili sauce. Boil 1 pint or 2 cups of water and pour over lemon Jello. Add 1 cup cold water and vinegar. Pour strained chili sauce into Jello mixture and chill until it reaches the consistency of raw egg. Place sliced eggs, olives, tuna fish, celery and pickles in ring mold with the Jello. Refrigerate overnight. Serve with Thousand Island Dressing. Serves 12.

HELPFUL HINT: After placing mold on dish, place a mound of cottage cheese in ring of mold and dot with stuffed olives.

THOUSAND ISLAND DRESSING

With the Tuna Fish Mold serve the following dressing. Take the leftover chili sauce which has been strained, add 4 parts mayonnaise and a little cream. Mix thoroughly.

SALMON LOAF

1 large can red Alaska salmon	*½ teasp. salt*
2 eggs, beaten	*½ teasp. pepper*
1 cup grated toast crumbs	*1 small onion, grated*
¼ cup diced green pepper	*½ cup milk*
⅛ teasp. celery salt	*1 teasp. lemon juice*
	½ teasp. baking powder

Drain salmon and discard fish liquid. Flake salmon with fork and bone. Discard bones. Add all ingredients, saving bread crumbs for last. Mix bread crumbs into salmon mixture and place in small buttered loaf pan, 2½ in. high. Bake in moderate oven (350°F.) between 40 and 45 minutes. Remove to hot serving plate. May be served with tomato-cheese sauce (below). Serves 6.

TOMATO-CHEESE SAUCE

1 10½ oz. can condensed tomato purée	*¼ lb. cheddar cheese*
½ teasp. baking soda	*2 tablesp. flour*
1 cup milk	*2 tablesp. butter*
	½ teasp. salt

Heat tomato purée in double boiler. Add baking soda and ½ cup of milk. In a small pan, heat butter, add flour and constantly stir so that there are no lumps. Add ½ cup of milk and stir until smooth, adding cheddar cheese. When all ingredients are smooth and entirely dissolved into one sauce, add to tomato mixture. This makes an excellent garnish for fish.

CREAMED TUNA FISH

1 large can white tuna fish	2½ tablesp. butter or margarine
1 small can pimentos	
1 small can button mushrooms	1½ cups milk
	1 egg yolk, beaten well
2½ tablesp. flour	½ teasp. salt

If tuna fish has been packed in oil, open can and scald with hot water to remove oil. Flake and place in double boiler together with diced pimentos and button mushrooms. Place butter or margarine in small skillet, heat until melted, add flour, stirring constantly. Add milk and salt gradually. Take a tablespoon of this mixture and add to egg yolk; then add egg yolk mixture to cream sauce. When entirely heated, pour into tuna fish in double boiler and allow to blend. Serve hot over toast or cooked rice. Garnish with parsley. Serves 4.

CHOPPED HERRING

3 milter herring	3 eggs, hard-boiled
1 apple	1 large onion, parboiled
3 tablesp. vinegar	2 tablesp. matzo meal or
2 tablesp. sugar	bread crumbs

Soak herring overnight in cold water. Fillet herring and chop or grind. Grate apple after paring. Grind or chop the onion into herring mixture, adding vinegar, sugar, bread crumbs and hard-boiled eggs (chopped fine). Everything in this mixture must be chopped fine so that it is smooth in texture when served. May be served on lettuce leaf with sliced tomatoes. This also makes an excellent appetizer on crackers, melba toast, or small toast squares with a slice of stuffed olive as a garnish. Serves 6.

FINNAN HADDIE (Smoked Cod)

3 lbs. smoked cod   *2 qts. water*

Smoked cod is usually sold in long fillets. Cut into 3 or 4-in. pieces and place in water to boil over medium flame. When water starts to boil, cook for 5 minutes, and remove *hot*. Immediately place a large pat of butter or margarine over each piece and serve. Serves 5.

CREAMED FINNAN HADDIE

Follow direction for Boiled Finnan Haddie. Remove from boiling water and flake. Then prepare the following:

3 lbs. smoked cod (finnan   *3 tablesp. flour*
  haddie)   *1 cup milk*
3 tablesp. butter or mar-   *2 egg yolks*
  garine   *½ teasp. salt*
              Dash of pepper

Melt butter or margarine in small saucepan. Add flour and milk gradually, stirring constantly. Prepare egg yolks beforehand; beat until light. Pour a tablespoon of hot liquid into the egg yolks and add egg yolk mixture to cream sauce. Add salt and pepper and flaked finnan haddie. Heat thoroughly. Remove from stove and serve hot over toast. If a touch of color is desired, dice one slice of canned pimento and place in hot mixture while cooking. Serves 6 to 8.

FRIED HERRING

4 lbs. milter herring   *Cooking oil, margarine or*
4 tablesp. flour   *butter*

Soak herring in cold water overnight. Fillet and leave in
strips. Dip in flour. Place enough oil, margarine or butter in
a deep frying pan, to cover bottom of pan. Heat. Place floured
fillets of herring into hot pan, and fry until brown on one side.
Turn over, and fry on other side until brown. Serves 6.

HELPFUL HINT: An excellent garnish for fried herring is
    fried onions. Slice an onion, and fry until brown. Serve
    with above.

FRENCH FRIED HERRING

4 lbs. milter herring   *Cooking oil, margarine or*
6 tablesp. matzo meal   *butter*
              3 eggs

Soak herring in cold water overnight. Fillet and leave in
strips. Beat 3 eggs thoroughly. Dip herring in egg mixture,
then roll in matzo meal. Heat oil, margarine or butter in deep
frying pan. When hot, drop herring strips in pan, and fry
until brown on one side. Turn on other side, and fry until
brown. Remove to platter. Garnish with spiced peaches and
parsley. Serves 6.

BROILED HALIBUT WITH LEMON SAUCE

3 lbs. halibut   *1 lemon rind (grated)*
1 teasp. salt   *4 tablesp. butter*
½ teasp. pepper   *2 egg yolks*
1 teasp. paprika   *2 tablesp. flour*
              1 cup milk

Cut halibut in 1½ inch slices for broiling. Place in broiling
pan about 2 inches from the flame. Salt, pepper, sprinkle with

paprika and dot with butter. Broil until fish begins to brown, then turn on other side; salt, pepper, sprinkle with paprika and dot with butter. When browned, it is ready to serve.

While broiling fish, in saucepan prepare 2 tablespoons butter and flour, stirring constantly. Gradually add grated lemon rind and milk, continuing to stir. Beat yolks of eggs and add 1 tablespoon hot mixture. Add to cream sauce mixture. When smooth, remove from flame. Garnish with lemon slices and parsley. Serves 4.

BOILED LAKE PERCH

3 lbs. lake perch (whole)   1 teasp. salt
1 large onion, sliced   ¼ teasp. pepper
2 carrots (cut lengthwise)   1 teasp. sugar
              1½ qts. water

Clean perch thoroughly, but do not remove head and tail. Wrap each fish in cheesecloth. Place a large saucepan with 1½ quarts cold water, onion, carrots, sugar, salt and pepper on medium fire. Add perch, and reduce flame to low. Cook for 1 hour. Unwrap fish. Remove to platter. Serve with small whole new potatoes, which have been boiled, buttered, and garnished with parsley. Serves 4.

BROILED MOUNTAIN TROUT

4 whole mountain trout   1 teasp. paprika
2 tablesp. butter or mar-   1 teasp. salt
   garine   Dash of pepper
            ½ cup toasted bread crumbs

Wash fish carefully, but do not remove head or tail. Place in broiling pan, or special aluminum foil broiling pan. Sprinkle with salt, pepper, paprika and dot with butter or margarine. Broil for 15 to 20 minutes on one side. Turn to other side, and sprinkle with salt, pepper, paprika and dot with butter or margarine. Sprinkle with toasted bread crumbs, and broil for 15 minutes. Serve individually with sprig of parsley and sliced lemon. Serves 4.

HELPFUL HINT: Dot the eye of fish with slice of stuffed olive.

FRIED SALT MACKEREL

2 lbs. salt mackerel	Dash of pepper or seasoned
3 tablesp. flour	salt
3 tablesp. oil, margarine or butter	1 large onion, sliced

Soak mackerel overnight in cold water. Clean fish thoroughly and remove head and tail. Roll in flour which has been seasoned. Place frying pan with oil, margarine or butter over medium heat. When hot, drop fish in. Fry until brown on one side. Turn, and fry on other side. While fish is frying, add sliced onions. Brown well. Place on platter. Garnish with pickled pears and cinnamon cloves. Serves 4.

CODFISH PATTIES

2 lbs. salt codfish	3 tablesp. flour
1 small onion, grated	½ cup mashed potatoes
¼ teasp. pepper	Cooking oil, margarine or
2 eggs	butter

Wash fish in cold water. Cut in small pieces, and either mash, or grind fine. Grate in onion, add pepper and before adding the eggs, beat them well. Then blend in mashed potatoes, and form into patties. Roll in flour. Heat either oil, margarine or butter in skillet and *deep* fry until browned, first on one side, and then on the other. Remove to platter. Garnish with parsley, lemon slices and place a small, high dish with applesauce in the center of platter. Serves 5.

SALMON MOUSSE RING MOLD

1 large can red salmon   *3 tablesp. vinegar*
1 cup milk   *1 tablesp. unflavored gelatin*
¼ tablesp. salt   *(with 2 tablespoons cold*
1 tablesp. sugar   *water)*
2 tablesp. butter   *2 egg yolks, beaten well*
                   1 tablesp. cold water

Remove bones from salmon and flake. Scald milk and place in a double boiler. Add salt and sugar to milk. Heat vinegar in separate saucepan. Add melted butter, beaten eggs with 1 tablespoon cold water and hot vinegar to mixture and stir for about 2 minutes. Remove from heat. Soften gelatin in 2 tablespoons cold water. Add to mixture. Last of all, add the flaked salmon. Place in ring mold and chill. Serve with Lemon Sauce (Page 24). Garnish with cottage cheese in center of ring mold dotted with parsley. Serves 6 generously.

MILCHIG AND FLAISHIG (Dairy and Meat)

Rules Governing Waiting Periods Between Meat,
Fowl and Dairy Meals

Under the Mosaic Dietary laws, there are clearly defined waiting periods between meals in which meat and fowl and dairy foods are served. Meats and fowl are classified as "flaishig." Dairy dishes are known as "milchig."

"Milchig" and "flaishig" may not be eaten together. Nor should there be any food product purchased in which meat or fowl and dairy products have been mixed.

The Jewish housewife must maintain separate sets of dishes,

pots and pans, and cutlery—one for "milchig" and one for "flaishig."

Rule 1: One is permitted to eat meat dishes after eating dairy dishes without any specific waiting period.

Exception to Rule 1: The only exception to this rule is when hard cheeses have been served. When this occurs, a waiting period of six hours must be observed.

Rule 2: The waiting period after a meal wherein meat or fowl has been served is six hours. There are certain communities in Western Europe where this waiting period has been reduced to less than six hours.

Rule 3: Two or more people may not sit at the same table when one is eating meat and the other is eating dairy foods without some recognition of this diversity of food. Two tablecloths may be used as a reminder.

Rule 4: The dishes of a meat or poultry dinner must be removed from the table, and a clean tablecloth used with cutlery for dairy dishes after the six hour waiting period, before one may partake of the dairy meal.

Rule 5: Completely separate sets of dishes must be used for meat and dairy meals. They must be kept on separate shelves in the pantry or kitchen cabinets.

Rule 6: "Flaishig" dish towels must be kept apart and used only on dishes serving meat.
   "Milchig" dish towels must be kept separate from "flaishig" dish towels, and used only on dishes serving dairy foods.

Rule 7: Contrary to the belief that "glass" dishes, such as crystal or glassware, may be used for either meat or dairy, *this is definitely forbidden.* A separate set of glass dishes may be used either for meat or dairy dishes.

Rule 8: The washing of meat dishes and dairy dishes must be completely separate and apart. *They may not be washed at the same time.*

Rule 9: If an automatic dishwasher is used, it must be thoroughly cleansed of any food particles and hot water allowed to run through it before placing the dairy dishes in the dishwasher.

Rule 10: Only kosher detergents, soaps and cleansers may be used for cleaning dishes and kitchen sink.

Rule 11: Foods marked "Pareve" may be used with both meat or dairy dishes.

Meats

RULES OF KASHRUTH

The Hebrew word "kosher" means "clean." The Jewish religion makes a distinction between clean and unclean animals or foods which may or may not be eaten. The basis for this selection is to be found in the Bible as well as in later commentaries on the Bible by the rabbis. In interpreting the Biblical prohibitions, the rabbis appear to have incorporated some of the prevailing ideas on health protection.

The Rules of Kashruth state that only animals which are quadrupeds with cloven hooves who chew their cud may be used on the kosher table. They decree that only the forequarters of the cow, goat, sheep and deer are acceptable.

Furthermore, in order to qualify as kosher, the meat must be slaughtered and prepared in accordance with specific provisions. The process of preparing meat is known as "kashering," or soaking and salting the meat to remove the blood. The Bible forbids the consuming of blood because it is "the life of the flesh."

Most kosher butchers today will "kasher" the meat for you, but where the butcher has not previously attended to this ritual, the meat must first be soaked in water for ½ hour and then saturated in medium-coarse salt for 1 hour before it is used. The meat is then washed thoroughly and is ready for cooking, baking or roasting.

METHODS OF KOSHERING MEAT

Step 1: Meat must be soaked in cold water for one-half hour.

Step 2: Remove meat from water and place on a smooth board which is tilted so that the blood may drain freely during the salting process.

Step 3: Meat should be sprinkled generously with a pure salt, which is especially marked "kosher," and allowed to remain for one hour.

Step 4: Completely remove salt from meat by allowing tap water to run freely over the meat, or immerse meat in cold water.

EXCEPTIONS

The Kashruth laws of slaughtering and koshering do not apply to fish.

Where the heart of an animal is used, its tip must be cut off, the remaining portion cut across deeply, and cut across again deeply, so that the accumulated blood may be removed when salting.

BROILING OF LIVER

Since liver contains a lot of blood, the following steps must be taken in the broiling of liver, to make it kosher and acceptable on the kosher table:

Step 1: Liver must be cut in several places before broiling to allow the blood to run out.

Step 2: Rinse with cold water, removing all surface blood.

Step 3: Sprinkle a little koshering salt on the meat before broiling.

Step 4: Place in broiler, and broil until a crust has formed on the meat and there has been a change in the color of the meat.

Step 5: Wash in cold running water after broiling. Meat is now koshered and ready for further preparation.

KOSHER CUTS OF MEAT

For the convenience of everyone using this cookbook, the following is a complete list of the meats one finds in the kosher meat markets throughout this country and the world:

BEEF

STEAKS:

Rib steak
Shoulder steak
Chuck steak (or Fillet steak)
Minute steak (or Chicken steak)
Mush steak (or London broil)
Thick Tenderloin steak (or Hanger)
Thin Tenderloin steak (or Skirt steak)

ROASTS:

Cross Rib roast (or Shoulder roast)
Fillet Chuck roast
Middle Chuck roast
Cholachol roast (lean) Not to be roasted beyond "medium" since it becomes too dry.
French roast
End Steak roast (end of shoulder)
Prime Rib roast

FLANKEN:

Plate flanken (Short rib or top rib)
Breast flanken (boneless)
Long bone flanken (Popular for use in cabbage borscht)

BEEF STEWS:

Boneless Chuck
Cholachol
French Roast
Shoulder Cholachol (People on low cholesterol diets find this
    meat ideal)
Top Rib

HAMBURGER:

Combination of neck meat, tenderloin and chuck

LAMB STEWS:

Shank of lamb
Neck of lamb
Breast of lamb (May also be used for barbecuing)

LAMB CHOPS:

Baby Rib chops (Choicest)
Shoulder Lamb chops (Long bone)
Shoulder Lamb chops (Round bone)

VEAL:

Breast of veal (For potting, roasting and with pocket for
    stuffing)
Shoulder veal (Roast or cutlet)
Rib veal chops
Soft veal (For stews, potting and chow mein)

VARIOUS CUTS OF MEAT KNOWN PARTICULARLY
TO PEOPLE OF THE JEWISH FAITH
THOUGH POPULAR WITH OTHERS

Beef Liver
Calves' Liver
Beef Brains
Calves' Brains
Lamb Brains
Beef Tongues
Calves' Tongues
Lamb Tongues
Beef Cheek (This meat is one of the ingredients of salami.)
Calves' Cheek
Lamb Cheek

Calves' Sweetbreads (Choice and a delicacy; parboil and
   broil.)
Beef Sweetbreads (for potting)

Beef Miltz (This is the spleen.)
Calves' Miltz (This is the spleen.)

Beef Oxtails (Popular if prepared properly.)

Calves' Feet (for *pchai*—more tender, but not as rich as beef.)
Beef Feet (When making *pchai*, you must cook this longer.)

CHOLENT

To most of you, the *Cholent* carries nostalgic memories.
What parent or grandparent who emigrated from Europe to
the United States has not brought with him the story about
the preparation of Cholent in a small village of some Euro-
pean country? The Cholent was prepared on a Friday, and

where the family did not have proper facilities for cooking it at home, it was taken to the village bakery, where it was placed in a huge oven to bake over a slow fire for 24 hours until sundown of the Sabbath. Then the family would return from religious worship in their "Shul" or Synagogue, as it is known here in America, and sit down to a delectable dinner of Cholent—piping hot, well-seasoned and truly palate-tempting.

Today, with our modern ovens, this recipe may be created to grace the table on Friday night, the Sabbath, with much less time in the oven, but with the same flavorful goodness!

4½ lbs. brisket of beef	1¼ cups pearl barley
2 good-sized onions, diced	¼ teasp. cinnamon
2 tablesp. fat (preferably chicken fat)	¼ teasp. ginger
	1 tablesp. paprika
4 carrots (cut lengthwise into halves)	3 tablesp. flour (more or less, depending upon how thick you wish the Cholent)
3 cups lima beans, dried	
12 small round potatoes, peeled	2 teasp. salt
	½ teasp. pepper

Soak the lima beans in water overnight. When ready to use, drain. Brown the beef well in fat with a few onions for flavor. It is best to use a heavy roasting pan or Dutch oven to bake the Cholent. Place beef in either one, season with salt, pepper, cinnamon and ginger. Add the lima beans, barley, carrots, the rest of the diced onions and potatoes. Sprinkle with flour and paprika. Add only enough water to cover about 1 inch of your roasting pan or Dutch oven, and be sure to cover.

Bake in oven at 350°F. for 5 hours. It should be served with a garnish of parsley and with the carrots, beans and barley arranged attractively around slices of meat. Serves 8 with leftovers.

ROASTED BRISKET OF BEEF

5 lbs. brisket of beef (single brisket preferable)	*1 teasp. Season-all*
	1 tablesp. flour
2 carrots, diced	*2 tablesp. fat (for browning)*
2 onions, sliced thin	*6 whole peeled potatoes*
1 clove garlic, minced	*(optional)*
2 teasp. salt	*1 cup water (in roasting pan)*

Brown brisket well on both sides. Place brisket and 1 cup of water in a roasting pan on the bottom of which 2 onions have been sliced. Place diced carrots around the sides of the meat. Sprinkle meat with flour, salt, Season-all and minced garlic. Cover and roast in oven at 325°F. for 3½ hours. One hour before removing from oven, place the whole potatoes in the roasting pan around the meat, and roast until done. Remove to platter, with carrots and potatoes surrounding slices of meat. Spiced peaches make an excellent additional garnish.

SAUERBRATEN
(Sweet and Sour Brisket of Beef)

6 lbs. brisket of beef or chuck roast	*¼ teasp. pepper*
	Equal parts of vinegar and water
1 onion, sliced	
4 bay leaves	*¼ cup brown sugar*
2 teasp. peppercorns	*¼ cup seedless brown raisins*
6 cloves	*6 gingersnaps*
1 teasp. salt	*3 tablesp. flour*

Sprinkle meat with salt and pepper. Slice onions, and place with meat in deep crock, adding peppercorns, cloves, and bay leaves. In a saucepan, heat vinegar and water, adding sugar to taste. While hot, pour over meat to cover. Cover earthen dish and allow to stand for one or two days, turning meat every day, so that it is completely marinated.

Dredge meat with flour and place in small roasting pan.

Add sliced onion and the marinated sauce and brown in 400°F. oven. When browned, cover and cook slowly (300°F.) for about 3 hours, or until soft and tender. Skim fat from liquid and place in saucepan. When hot, add brown sugar, seedless raisins and gingersnaps. When thick and smooth, pour over meat, slice and serve.

BOILED FLANKEN

4 lbs. lean flanken
3 large carrots (cut lengthwise into quarters)
½ cup diced celery
1 large onion, diced

½ teasp. pickling spices
1 teasp. salt
½ teasp. pepper
3 tablesp. fat (for browning
   meat)

1½ qts. water

Brown the flanken in skillet. While preparing the meat, place a good-sized cooking pan over a medium flame, with the water, carrots, onion, celery, pickling spices, ¼ teaspoon salt and pepper. When meat is browned, drop one flanken at a time in the boiling water. Turn the flame down to low, and cook for 2 hours. Remove to platter, arranging carrots around platter, and serve with horse-radish.

FLANKEN-IN-THE-POT

3 lbs. lean flanken
3 carrots, diced
1 stalk celery, diced
6 small onions
1 pkge. frozen peas or 1 lb.
   fresh peas

6 cups boiling water
2 teasp. salt
½ teasp. seasoned salt
½ teasp. pepper
1 beef bouillon cube
   (kosher)

Fat for browning meat

First, brown the flanken well. Place boiling water in large pot with 1 teaspoon salt, carrots, celery and onions. Season flanken with salt, seasoned salt and pepper. Place in boiling water. After it has been cooking over a low flame for 1 hour, skim soup. Place bouillon cube in soup, cover, and allow to cook for at least another hour, or until flanken is tender. Serve in individual casserole with cover, serving portions of flanken in the soup, with vegetables. Excellent garnish: horse-radish, colored with beets. Serves 6.

OLD-FASHIONED BEEF STEW

*3 lbs. chuck (cut into 1½ in.
    squares)
3 carrots, diced
6 potatoes, diced
1 cup fresh or frozen string
    beans
1 cup fresh or frozen peas
1 can whole button mush-
    rooms*

*1 qt. boiling water
1 onion, diced
3 tablesp. flour
1 tablesp. Worcestershire
    sauce
1 teasp. Kitchen Bouquet
2 tablesp. fat (for browning
    meat)
2 teasp. salt*

½ teasp. pepper

Brown chuck cubes well. Place in large pot or Dutch oven, add salt and pepper, diced carrots and onions. Pour enough boiling water to cover over meat and other ingredients. Cook over low heat for 2 hours. If more water is needed, add boiling water. Add Worcestershire sauce and Kitchen Bouquet, mushrooms, potatoes, string beans and peas. Cook another ½ hour. Mix flour with water to make a paste, and thicken the gravy in beef stew. Cook until flour has been completely absorbed into beef stew. For attractive serving, serve in individual small casserole on each plate. Serves 6.

HUNGARIAN GOULASH

2 lbs. chuck (cut into 2-in.   2 tablesp. brown sugar
  squares)   1 teasp. paprika
1 onion, diced   1 teasp. salt
3 carrots, diced   ½ teasp. dry mustard
½ cup diced celery   2 tablesp. flour
½ cup catsup   3 cups hot water
3 tablesp. Worcestershire   1 small clove garlic, grated
  sauce   2 tablesp. fat
2 tablesp. vinegar   4 gingersnaps (optional)

Brown the chuck in fat, adding the onions and garlic for flavor. When browned, set aside. Reserve the carrots and celery. Place the next seven ingredients in a small mixing bowl. Place the meat and onions in a heavy Dutch oven; add the carrots and celery. Pour the hot water over the meat, and place over low flame. Add the balance of the ingredients from small bowl. Mix together. Cover, and allow to simmer for 2 hours. Mix the flour into cold water with fork, and thicken gravy in pot. For added zest, melt 4 gingersnaps into gravy. They give it color and flavor. Garnish with parsley. An excellent supplement to this meal is wide ¾ in. noodles. Place on plate and pour the Hungarian Goulash over the noodles. Serves 6.

SWISS STEAK

3 lbs. boneless chuck (cut in   1 large onion, diced
  portion pieces 1½ in.   ½ cup flour
  thick)   1 large can tomatoes with
1 teasp. salt   juice
½ teasp. pepper   2 tablesp. fat (for browning)

Season meat, sprinkling flour on each side of meat. Then pound meat. Brown onions and remove from pan. Brown meat on both sides and cover with onions. Add tomatoes.

Cook in Dutch oven over low heat for 2 hours or until meat is tender. Garnish with pineapple slices and whole small potatoes. Serves 6.

MEAT AND VEGETABLE PIE

3 lbs. chuck (*cut into cubes and precooked until tender*)
3 tablesp. *flour*
1 *onion, diced*
2 *cups meat stock*
1 *cup cooked carrots, diced*
1 *cup diced celery*

1 *green pepper, sliced and diced*
1 *can small new potatoes*
½ *teasp. salt*
Dash of *pepper*
Paprika
½ recipe Flaky Pastry (*made with pareve margarine*)

Brown onions and add green peppers, celery in meat stock, and balance of ingredients, stirring constantly. When heated through thoroughly and the meat stock has thickened, pour into greased deep baking dish. Roll out Flaky Pastry (Page 358) to ¼-in. thickness and cover baking dish, fluting edges and slitting for steam to come through. Bake in hot oven of 425°F. about 20 minutes until crust is browned.

BEEF SHISH KEBOB

3 lbs. flank steak (*cut in cubes*)
½ cup olive oil
2 tablesp. vinegar
1 teasp. salt
¼ teasp. pepper
1 lb. small whole mushrooms

2 large peppers (*cut in squares*)
1 large can spiced pineapple chunks
3 large onions (*cut in thick slices*)
Kitchen Bouquet

2 lbs. large tomatoes (*cut in wedges*)

Combine olive oil, vinegar, salt and pepper. Pour over meat and vegetables, and let the meat and vegetables remain in cool place for at least 3 hours. Arrange meat, tomato wedge, mushroom, onion slice, green pepper, pineapple chunk, etc. on skewers. Brush meat with Kitchen Bonquet and either place under broiler, turning every 5 minutes, or over charcoal grill, being certain to turn so that it may brown evenly on all sides. Cook until meat is tender. Corn on the cob goes very well with this outdoor type of dish. Another colorful garnish is spiced crab apples. Serves 6.

BUBEH'S GEDEMPTE FLAISH
(Grandmother's Potted Meat)

*5 lbs. chuck or double brisket
   of beef
3 tablesp. fat
1½ teasp. salt
½ teasp. pepper
1 teasp. allspice
1 teasp. Worcestershire
   sauce*

*1 teasp. Kitchen Bouquet
2 cups boiling water
2 large onions, diced
2 large carrots, diced
1 stalk celery, diced (¼
   cup)
1 kernel garlic, cut fine
   (optional)*

Brown the meat well in fat. Place in large Dutch oven or heavy cooking pot and cover until thoroughly browned. Add salt, pepper, allspice, onions, carrots, celery and pour 2 cups of boiling water over meat. Cover and cook over low heat for at least 1 hour. Add Worcestershire sauce and Kitchen Bouquet to meat. Recover and cook for at least 2 more hours, until meat is tender. To thicken gravy, mix 2 tablesp. flour with a little water and salt. Add to the liquid of meat, and cook until thoroughly blended. Apricot and prune compote makes an excellent garnish with sprigs of parsley. Serves 6 with leftovers.

ESSIG FLAISH WITH PRUNES
AND APRICOTS
(Sweet and Sour Meat)

3 lbs. chuck or flank	½ lb. dried prunes
3 large onions, diced	1 teasp. salt
4 tablesp. dark brown sugar	½ teasp. cinnamon
6 gingersnaps, crumbled	3 cups boiling water
½ cup lemon or lime juice	1 tablesp. fat (for browning
or ¼ cup vinegar	meat)
½ lb. dried apricots	

Brown meat in Dutch oven. While browning meat, add onions—but brown lightly. After soaking apricots and prunes in cold water for at least 1 hour, they may be added to the meat. Salt and cinnamon may be added to meat and mixture; then pour boiling water over the meat. Cook over low heat for at least 2 hours with Dutch oven covered. Add the lemon or lime juice or vinegar along with the brown sugar and gingersnaps. Cook for at least 15 minutes longer. An added attractive garnish is pickled pears. Serves 6 with leftovers.

POT ROAST WITH SWEET POTATOES
AND POTATO KNAIDLACH (Dumplings)

3 or 4 lbs. chuck (cut thick so that meat will be smaller in width)	1 teasp. salt
	½ teasp. pepper
	1 tablesp. honey
4 sweet potatoes, peeled and quartered	1 onion, diced
	2 cups boiling water

Brown meat in Dutch oven, adding salt, pepper, onions and water. Cook over low heat for at least 1 hour. Add sweet potatoes and honey. Cover and cook for at least another 2 hours. In the meantime, prepare the following:

POTATO KNAIDLACH
(Dumplings)

2 eggs	2 tablesp. matzo meal
3 cups grated potatoes (with liquid drained)	1/4 cup potato flour
	1 tablesp. grated onion
1 teasp. salt	

Beat egg yolks and whites separately. Add salt and onion to yolks. Stir matzo meal and grated potato into potato flour and add to egg yolks. Fold in egg whites, and form into small round balls. Drop carefully into salted water, and when they rise to top, remove from water. They should be cooked in approximately 20 to 25 minutes.

Place these knaidlach in the Dutch oven for 10 minutes before removing pot roast and sweet potatoes. Serves 6 to 8.

GEDEMPTE FLAISH WITH KISHKE
(Pot Roast with Stuffed Derma)
(Litvok style)

4 to 5 lbs. brisket of beef	1 teasp. salt
1 onion, diced	1/4 teasp. pepper
2 carrots, sliced lengthwise	1 clove garlic, chopped fine
Fat for browning	

KISHKE (Stuffed Derma)

2 feet beef casing	1/4 teasp. pepper
3/4 cup sifted flour	1 teasp. paprika
1/3 cup matzo meal or substitute	1/2 cup chicken fat (include in stuffing)
1 onion, grated	1/4 cup chicken fat for roasting pan
1 teasp. salt	

Brown the brisket in Dutch oven. Season with salt, pepper and clove of garlic. Pour 2 cups boiling water over brisket, add carrots, onions and cover. Cook over low heat for 1 hour.

In the meantime, wash the casing carefully and thoroughly in cold water, scraping the inside clean. Cut in half. Sew the end of each piece. Combine matzo meal with flour, grated onion, salt, pepper and ½ cup chicken fat. Stuff the casings, sew the other end of each piece, and drop in boiling water. Cook for at least 1 hour.

When drained, place in roasting pan with ¼ cup of chicken fat. Sprinkle paprika over the kishke, for added color in roasting, and transfer the beef brisket, carrots and onions from the Dutch oven to roasting pan. Baste kishke while roasting. Set oven at 350°F., and roast at least 1½ hours, or until meat is tender. Remove to platter, and serve while hot. Serves 6.

HAIMISHE HAMBURGERS
(Home-style Hamburgers)

2 lbs. ground chuck	2 eggs
2 tablesp. catsup	¼ cup matzo meal, bread
1 teasp. salt	crumbs or soaked bread
¼ teasp. pepper	1 tablesp. cold water
½ teasp. cinnamon	1 onion, grated

Mix meat with eggs, salt, pepper, and cinnamon. Add water, matzo meal, and catsup. Form into patties and either broil in oven for 10 to 15 minutes on one side, and when browned for 10 to 15 minutes on the other side, or heat fat in skillet and fry patties until brown first on one side and then the other. Garnish with peach halves and parsley. Serves 6 to 8.

SWEET AND SOUR MEAT BALLS

2 lbs. ground beef
2 eggs
1 onion, grated
1½ teasp. salt
Dash of pepper
1 onion, diced
1 cup beef stock
1 lemon, sliced thin

4 tablesp. lemon juice or
  vinegar
4 tablesp. sugar
8 gingersnaps, crumbled
Fat for browning
4 tablesp. cornstarch
2 tablesp. catsup
⅓ cup seedless raisins

Mix meat, grated onion, eggs, salt, and pepper. Form into
1½-in. balls. Roll in cornstarch and brown in heavy skillet in
fat. Add the beef stock, diced onions, lemon juice, raisins,
catsup and sugar. Cover skillet and cook over low fire for
about 1 hour. Uncover and stir in crumbled gingersnaps. Cook
at least another 15 minutes. Remove to serving casserole. This
is excellent with fricassee of chicken, which is an old-time
favorite. Serves 8.

MAMA'S MEAT LOAF

2 lbs. ground chuck
2 eggs
1 cup grated toast crumbs
1 onion, grated
1 small can tomato paste
1 teasp. salt

½ teasp. cinnamon
1 can whole button mush-
  rooms
3 hard-boiled eggs
1 tablesp. Worcestershire
  sauce

¼ teasp. pepper

Mix all ingredients except mushrooms and hard-boiled eggs.
Form into loaf and stuff hard-boiled eggs (shelled) into the
center of meat loaf from either end. Place eggs lengthwise
rather than upright. Place in loaf pan and cover the top of the
meat loaf with the whole mushrooms. Preheat oven to 350°F.

Bake for at least 1¾ hours. Remove to platter. When sliced, the egg provides an attractive variation in color and taste. Serves 8.

STUFFED CABBAGE WITH MEAT

1 cabbage (large head)	*2 eggs*
1 large can tomatoes (No. 3 can)	*2 teasp. salt*
	½ teasp. pepper
1½ lbs. ground beef and beef bones	*⅓ cup lemon juice*
	2 tablesp. honey
1 onion, diced	*2 tablesp. sugar*
2 tablesp. grated onion	*3 tablesp. fat (for browning)*
3 tablesp. matzo meal	*¼ cup seedless raisins*
1 tablesp. catsup	*1 tablesp. cold water*

Pour boiling water over cabbage and let cabbage soak for approximately 20 minutes. Remove leaves carefully so that they do not break. Try to get between 12 to 14 large leaves. (If cabbage is smaller, then leaves are smaller and you may make 18 portions instead of 12 to 14.)

Heat fat in heavy skillet, and brown the sliced onion, adding the tomatoes, a pinch of salt and a dash of pepper. *Add the beef bones.* In a mixing bowl, combine ground beef, eggs, grated onion, cold water, catsup, 1 teaspoon salt, and the rest of the pepper. Using water on hands so that meat may be handled easily, place the equivalent of a small meat patty on each cabbage leaf. Tuck in sides of cabbage leaf, and carefully roll so that leaf remains unbroken. Add each stuffed cabbage portion to the browned onion, tomatoes, and beef bones, also adding the rest of the seasoning to the entire mixture. Cover skillet and cook over low heat, for between 1½ and 2 hours. Add the lemon juice, honey, sugar and raisins. Cook for at least another ½ hour. Add salt and/or sugar to taste. Serve pineapple slices as a garnish. Serves 8.

GEHOCKTE LEBER
(Chopped Liver)

8 to 10 chicken livers	2 tablesp. chicken fat
½ teasp. salt	1 onion, grated
¼ teasp. pepper	2 hard-boiled eggs

Boil chicken livers in just enough water to cover, with a dash of salt. Remove and cool. Chop liver and eggs, season, and then add grated onion. Mix well and combine all with chicken fat. Press entire mixture through sieve for smoothness. Form into mold on lettuce leaves. Garnish with parsley and stuffed olives. Serves 8.

STUFFED PEPPERS
(Sweet and Sour)

8 green peppers	Sauce:
1½ lbs. ground beef	
1 cup bread crumbs or	1 small can tomato purée
cooked rice	3 tablesp. brown sugar
1 onion, grated	2 tablesp. lemon juice
1 teasp. salt	1 tablesp. vinegar
½ teasp. pepper	¼ cup seedless raisins
2 eggs	½ cup water

Combine beef, eggs, salt, pepper, bread crumbs or rice. Mix well. Add grated onion. Cut one end of peppers. Clean and wash thoroughly. Remove seeds and see that pepper is smooth inside. Stuff each pepper with the meat mixture. Place in baking dish with enough water to cover, and cover dish. Bake in oven at 350° for at least 1 hour.

In the meantime, combine the ingredients for the sauce in a small saucepan, and cook over low heat for about 15 minutes. When meat and peppers have been in oven for 1 hour, uncover and add sauce. Bake for at least ½ hour more. Remove to chafing dish. Corn on the cob makes an excellent garnish. Serves 8.

LAMB CHOPS CONTINENTAL

6 shoulder lamb chops	1 green pepper, sliced
1 lemon, sliced	2 cups tomato juice
1 onion, sliced	2 tablesp. fat

Brown lamb chops. Salt and pepper to taste. Top each lamb chop with a slice of lemon, a slice of onion, a slice of green pepper ring. Pour tomato juice over the chops, and place over low flame. Cover and cook for at least one hour. Garnish with parsley, whole small potatoes and pickled peaches. Serves 6.

ROAST SHOULDER OF LAMB

5 lbs. shoulder of lamb (se- lect young lamb)	2 teasp. salt
	½ teasp. pepper
1 teasp. garlic salt	1 teasp. paprika
1 lemon or lime, juice only	1 onion, sliced
1 cup ginger ale	Fat for basting (if lean)

Most people hesitate to roast lamb because the meat has a strong scent. First, take the juice of a lemon or lime, and completely saturate the lamb. This will eliminate any offensive odor. Season with garlic salt, salt and pepper, sprinkling with paprika. Dot the lamb with pareve margarine and pour a cup of ginger ale over the meat in roasting pan. Place sliced onions in roasting pan and roast uncovered at 450°F. for at least 40 minutes. Reduce heat to 325°F. and roast for at least 2½ to 3 hours longer. Baste continually for browning. Garnish with green pickled pears and with cloves which are inserted on top of lamb. Mint jelly is another scintillating garnish. Serves 8 with leftovers.

LAMB SHISH KEBOB

3 lbs. shoulder lamb (cut in cubes)
½ lb. whole button mushrooms
2 lbs. steak tomatoes (cut in wedges)
1 large can spiced pineapple chunks
2 large onions (cut in cubes)
2 green peppers (cut in wedges)
½ cup olive oil
3 tablesp. vinegar
1 teasp. salt
½ teasp. pepper
½ teasp. garlic salt
2 teasp. Kitchen Bouquet

Combine vinegar, oil, salt, pepper, and garlic salt. Pour over meat and vegetables, and let stand in cool place for at least 3 hours. Arrange lamb cubes, tomato wedges, mushrooms, onion, green pepper wedges, and pineapple chunks on skewers. Brush meat with Kitchen Bouquet and either place under broiler, turning every 5 minutes, or over charcoal grill. Turn frequently so that it will brown evenly on all sides and cook until meat is tender. Garnish with green mint jelly. Following barbecue dip is optional. Serves 6:

ORANGE BARBECUE DIP

1 orange, juiced
3 tablesp. brown sugar
1 teasp. Worcestershire sauce
5 tablesp. catsup

Mix ingredients well. Makes an excellent dip for lamb.

MAMA'S BREAST OF VEAL—STUFFED

4 to 5 lb. breast of veal (with
  pocket)
3 tablesp. fat
½ teasp. Kitchen Bouquet
1 teasp. Worcestershire
  sauce
1 teasp. paprika
1 teasp. salt
¼ teasp. pepper

1 cup matzo meal
3 tablesp. cold water
2 eggs, separated
¼ teasp. sage
½ onion, grated
½ onion, sliced
3 carrots, sliced lengthwise
Celery cut into strips (ap-
  proximately 3 stalks)

First, prepare stuffing by beating egg yolks, placing matzo meal in mixing bowl, adding a little salt, sage, grated onion, cold water, and egg yolks. Beat the egg whites and fold them in. Brown meat well, then open pocket and insert stuffing. Seal with skewers or sew end. Brush top of veal breast with Kitchen Bouquet, Worcestershire sauce, salt and pepper. Place onion slices on bottom of roasting pan, putting the breast of veal on top and carrots and celery around the roast. Add 1 cup of water to roasting pan and cover. Roast in oven at 325°F. for 2½ to 3 hours, uncovering pan for the last ½ hour. Baked potatoes or potato pancakes go very well with this meal. Serves 8.

STUFFED BREAST OF VEAL
(With Potato Stuffing)

4 to 6 lbs. breast of veal
  (with pocket)
1½ teasp. salt
½ teasp. pepper

1 teasp. paprika
1 clove garlic, minced
Fat for basting
½ cup water for basting
1 cup water for roasting pan

POTATO STUFFING

1½ cups grated potato	*1 onion, grated*
1 egg	*1 teasp. salt*
3 tablesp. potato flour	*½ teasp. pepper*

Drain the grated potato, and add all ingredients—the potato flour last. Stuff in veal pocket, and use skewers to fasten end or sew open end.

Season breast of veal with salt, pepper, paprika, and sprinkle with minced garlic. Mix a little fat, water and salt, and brush on veal. Brush a little Kitchen Bouquet lightly over top. Place water in roasting pan, slicing onion for bottom. Roast at 325°F. for 2½ to 3 hours, depending upon size of roast. Cover roasting pan for 1 hour; leave uncovered for rest of roasting time. Baste frequently when uncovered. Garnish with spiced crabapples. Serves 6.

MOCK CHICKEN LEGS

1 lb. ground veal	*¼ cup bread crumbs or*
1 lb. ground beef chuck	*matzo meal*
2 eggs	*1 teasp. salt*
1 onion, grated	*¼ teasp. pepper*
½ teasp. cinnamon	*1 tablesp. Worcestershire*
	sauce

For Dipping

2 eggs, beaten	*1 teasp. salt*
1 cup matzo meal	

Mix meat with eggs, onion, cinnamon, salt, pepper and bread crumbs or matzo meal, adding Worcestershire sauce. Form into shapes like the drumstick of chicken. Place stick (as for candied apple) through bottom of drumstick. Beat eggs well and add salt. Roll drumstick in egg mixture, dip in matzo meal. Heat fat in heavy skillet. Drop drumsticks in skillet over medium flame, and brown well, first on one side, then on the other. Place a paper panty on each wooden stick for attractive serving. Serves 6.

FRENCH FRIED VEAL CHOPS

8 rib veal chops
1 cup matzo meal or corn
  flake crumbs

3 eggs
1 teasp. salt
¼ teasp. pepper
2 teasp. garlic salt

Beat the eggs. Salt and season the veal chops, but add garlic salt to eggs. Dip veal chops in egg mixture, then in matzo meal or corn flake crumbs, and repeat. Heat fat in skillet. Place veal chops in skillet, and fry over medium heat until brown, first on one side and then the other. For tender chops, cover skillet and continue cooking over low heat for an added ½ hour. Spiced pineapple chunks, with cloves, are an excellent garnish. Serves 4.

BAKED VEAL CHOPS

6 veal chops
1 teasp. salt
½ teasp. pepper
½ teasp. garlic salt
1 large can tomatoes

2 tablesp. pareve mar-
  garine
2 slices of grated toast
1 small can sliced mush-
  rooms

For Dipping

2 eggs

1 cup matzo meal or bread
  crumbs

Season veal chops and fry in heavy skillet, browning first on one side and then the other. Place in shallow baking pan. Pour large can of tomatoes over veal chops. Place grated toast over chops, together with sliced mushrooms, and bake in oven for 45 minutes at 350°F. Serves 4.

ROAST STUFFED MILTZ

3 lbs. miltz
3 tablesp. bread crumbs
1 tablesp. flour
1 teasp. salt
½ teasp. pepper
½ teasp. paprika

1 onion, diced
Fat for frying
1 onion, sliced
1 stalk celery, diced (½ cup)
2 carrots, diced

1 cup water

Heat fat in skillet. Brown diced onion. Mix bread crumbs and flour, adding a little salt and pepper but reserving most for miltz. Place bread crumb and flour mixture in the onions in skillet. Remove from flame. Do not cut miltz. Fold over. Sew two sides, and fill the pocket with the bread crumb stuffing. Sew the other side of the miltz. Place in roasting pan over sliced onion, celery, carrots and water. Roast in oven at 350°F. for 1 hour. Turn the miltz over, and roast another ½ hour. Serves 6.

BROILED SWEETBREADS

2 lbs. sweetbreads
1 teasp. salt
3 tablesp. bread crumbs
2 tablesp. pareve margarine

1 teasp. salt
½ teasp. pepper
½ teasp. paprika
1 egg, beaten

Sweetbreads must be parboiled. After removing from flame, remove membrane. Dip sweetbreads in egg mixture and then roll in bread crumbs. Place under broiler and dot with margarine, salt and pepper, and sprinkle paprika over each one. Broil until brown first on one side, then on the other. This is a delicacy, if garnished properly. Use spiced peaches with cloves, and a salad with pineapple slices. Serves 6 generously.

CALBENA BRAINS (Calves' Brains)

2 lbs. calves' brains	*1 teasp. salt*
2 eggs, beaten	*¼ teasp. pepper*
1 cup matzo meal	*½ teasp. garlic salt*
Fat for frying	*(optional)*
	1 onion, sliced thin

Calves' brains must be parboiled. Place in pan of salt water, and heat until water boils vigorously. Remove skin. Dip in egg mixture, then roll in matzo meal. Heat fat in skillet. Brown onions, then add calves' brains and fry until brown on both sides. Garnish with applesauce. Serves 6.

PUSTE FISH (Calves' Brains)

2 lbs. calves' brains	*1 onion, diced*
2 eggs	*Shortening for frying*
½ teasp. salt	*Bread crumbs or matzo meal*
¼ teasp. pepper	*(enough to make firm)*

Cook calves' brains until tender. Mash brains and add eggs, seasoning and bread crumbs. Brown onions and add to mixture. Shape into patties and fry until browned. Place in shallow pan and bake at 400°F. for 10 minutes. Serve hot.

PCHAI (Jellied Hoof)

1 beef foot (cow's foot) cut into 4 pieces	*Soup greens*
	2 qts. water
4 beef bones with marrow	*1 teasp. salt*
2 large onions (cut in half)	*½ teasp. pepper*
3 large carrots, sliced lengthwise	*2 hard-boiled eggs, chopped*
	Clove of garlic

Combine beef foot, garlic clove, bones, onions, carrots, soup greens, and seasoning and place in boiling water. Reduce flame and cook over low heat for 3 hours, skimming top often. Remove meat and bones and strain soup stock, pouring it back into pot. Chop meat very fine. If necessary, use a meat grinder so that it is finely chopped. Place in mold, mixing with chopped eggs. Refrigerate until molded and ready to serve. Sprinkle with one hard-cooked egg yolk, which has been pressed through a sieve and garnish with parsley.

STANDING RIB ROAST

6 lbs. rib roast (trimmed so
  that ribs form crown)
¾ cup flour
¾ tablesp. dry mustard
2 teasp. salt
½ teasp. garlic salt
½ cup water
1 onion, sliced
2 carrots, sliced
1 stalk celery, diced

Mix flour, dry mustard, salt, garlic salt and water so that they form a paste. Cover meat with this paste and place in a plastic meat bag in refrigerator overnight. Place sliced onion, carrots and celery in roasting pan with water to cover bottom. Roast meat in uncovered roasting pan at 325°F., allowing ½ hour per pound of meat. An excellent garnish with a crown rib roast is a whole cauliflower placed in the center of your roast, with grated toast browned in pareve margarine. Serves 8 with leftovers.

BAKED SHORT RIBS OF BEEF

4 lbs. beef short ribs
1 onion, diced
2 tablesp. Worcestershire
  sauce
1 teasp. Kitchen Bouquet
2 tablesp. vinegar
2 tablesp. brown sugar
¼ cup lemon juice
1 cup catsup
1 teasp. salt
½ teasp. pepper
1 cup water
Fat for browning meat

Brown meat in skillet. Then brown onions and combine with brown sugar, vinegar, lemon juice, catsup, salt, pepper, and 1 cup of water in pan and simmer for about ¾ of an hour. Brush meat with Worcestershire sauce and Kitchen Bouquet. Place in roasting pan and pour sauce over the top of the meat. Bake in oven at 325°F., allowing ½ hour for each pound of meat, or about 2½ hours when meat will be very tender. Garnish with small whole tomatoes and whole button mushrooms. Serves 8.

SHORT RIBS OF BEEF
(Barbecued)

4 *lbs. short ribs of beef*	1 *teasp. garlic clove, cut up*
1 *teasp. salt*	1 *large onion, diced*
½ *teasp. pepper*	3 *cups boiling water*
1 *teasp. paprika*	*Fat for browning*

BARBECUE SAUCE

1 *orange, juice only*	1 *tablesp. Worcestershire*
4 *tablesp. brown sugar*	*sauce*
	1 *cup catsup*

Brown ribs well in fat. Salt, pepper and sprinkle paprika over them. Place in Dutch oven and add diced onions. Pour boiling water over meat and onions. Cover, and simmer over low heat until meat is tender (or allow 30 minutes per pound). Mix the ingredients for barbecue sauce, and add either sugar or catsup until it is a smooth thick sauce. Remove beef ribs from Dutch oven, brush with barbecue sauce, and place under broiler for 10 minutes on one side and 10 minutes on the other. Place on platter and serve with additional barbecue sauce to cover ribs. An excellent garnish is pineapple wedges and tossed salad. Serves 4 to 6.

PRIME RIBS OF BEEF AU JUS

5 to 6 lbs. standing rib roast	*1 tablesp. Worcestershire*
1 teasp. salt	*sauce*
1 teasp. paprika	*1 large onion, sliced*

After seasoning and brushing Worcestershire sauce all over rib roast, place it in an uncovered roasting pan, fat side up. Place sliced onions in pan with ½ cup of water. Cook at 475°F. for at least ½ hour or until browned. Reduce temperature to 325°F. and roast until meat is completely tender, allowing ½ hour per pound. If rare meat is desired, allow only 18 minutes per pound. If medium meat is desired, allow 24 minutes per pound. Whole cauliflower with browned bread crumbs sprinkled over it makes an excellent garnish. Serves 6 generously.

PRUNE AND SWEET POTATO TZIMMES

3 lbs. brisket of beef	*7 sweet potatoes*
1 teasp. salt	*½ cup sugar*
¼ teasp. pepper	*2 tablesp. honey*
2 cups boiling water	*2 tablesp. lemon juice*
1 lb. prunes	*Fat for browning*

Brown meat well. Season and place in Dutch oven. After soaking prunes overnight in cold water, place in Dutch oven with meat. Pour boiling water over meat and prunes. Cook over low heat until meat is almost tender, which should be about 1½ hours. Remove meat and prunes from gravy. Place peeled sweet potatoes on bottom of pan in gravy, and sprinkle with sugar, honey and lemon juice. Place meat and prunes on top of sweet potatoes. Place covered Dutch oven in 325°F. oven. Bake until potatoes are tender, which should be in about 1 hour. Cranberry sauce makes an excellent garnish. Serves 6 to 8.

CARROT TZIMMES WITH
MATZO MEAL DUMPLINGS

3 lbs. brisket of beef   *¼ teasp. pepper*
4 large carrots, sliced   *1 tablesp. honey*
4 large sweet potatoes, diced   *½ cup brown sugar (firmly*
1 onion, diced   *packed)*
1 tablesp. fat   *2 cups boiling water*
1 teasp. salt   *2 tablesp. flour*
                  ¼ teasp. cinnamon

MATZO MEAL DUMPLINGS

½ cup matzo meal   *½ teasp. salt*
              2 eggs, separated

Brown the beef in Dutch oven, adding diced onions. Season meat with salt, pepper, and cinnamon. Pour boiling water over meat and cover. Cook over low heat for 1½ hours. Add carrots, sweet potatoes, brown sugar and honey. Mix flour with water and add to thicken gravy. Place Dutch oven in the roasting oven and set temperature at 350°F. Bake for at least 1 additional hour.

Meanwhile, mix egg yolks and salt until thick. Next, fold in egg whites and matzo meal gradually. Chill for ½ hour. Shape into 1-in. balls. Drop into boiling salt water for at least 15 to 20 minutes. Remove when they rise to top.

Add to carrot tzimmes about 10 minutes before it is removed from oven. Place on platter—meat in center, carrots and sweet potatoes surrounding it, dotted with matzo meal dumplings. Serves 8.

MOMELE'S TZIMMES
With *Schmaltz Knaidlach*
(With Fat Dumplings)

2 *lbs. beef brisket*
2 *bunches carrots* (*small*)
1 *cup fresh Brussels sprouts*
2 *cups sweet potatoes*
  (*peeled and cut in*
  quarters)

½ *lb. baby lima beans*
1 *teasp. salt*
3 *teasp. sugar or 1 teasp.*
  sugar and 1 tablesp. honey
¼ *teasp. cinnamon*
1 *qt. water*

SCHMALTZ KNAIDLACH
(Fat Dumplings)

1 *cup flour* (*sifted with*
  baking powder)
¼ *cup pieces of chicken fat*
½ *teasp. salt*

¼ *teasp. cinnamon*
2 *tablesp. cold water*
1 *egg*
½ *teasp. baking powder*

Brown beef brisket, and bring water to a boil in Dutch oven. Add brisket, seasoned with salt and cinnamon, saving a little to sprinkle with sugar over other ingredients. Cut carrots into quarters, then slice into small pieces. Wash Brussels sprouts thoroughly. Soak baby lima beans in cold water for about 15 minutes. Drain. Cover brisket with layer of carrots, then Brussels sprouts and beans.

Prepare dumplings in advance by placing flour and baking powder in bowl. Make a well in the flour, adding the seasoning, then the egg; mix and add cold water. Then mix the pieces of chicken fat into the dough, and form into large knaidle. Place on top of the ingredients of the tzimmes.

Place over low flame, and cook about 2 hours. Add the sweet potatoes, and sprinkle with sugar or sugar and honey. Allow to cook for at least another 1½ hours, or until meat is completely tender. Jewish people with parents or grandparents stemming from "Grodna Gebarnia" should find this a familiar recipe. When serving, give a part of the knaidle to each person. Serves 6 generously with leftovers.

PICKLED TONGUE

5 or 6 lbs. tongue   1 cup salt
1½ tablesp. pickling spices 1 tablesp. sugar
8 cloves garlic   ¾ teasp. saltpeter
                1½ qts. water

Combine the pickling spices, garlic, salt, saltpeter, sugar with 1½ qts. of water. Place tongue in a heavy crock. Pour the above ingredients over the tongue, and make sure that additional water is used to cover tongue completely. Use a heavy object to weight meat down. Cover crock with plastic cover. Allow to stand in cool place for at least one week, then remove from crock and keep in refrigerator for 4 to 6 days.

This tongue must now be cooked over low flame in boiling water for 3 to 3½ hours. While still hot, peel outer skin. Serves 6 to 8 with leftovers.

PICKLED CORNED BEEF

5 to 6 lbs. brisket of beef   8 bay leaves
   (single brisket preferred) 1 teasp. saltpeter
10 cloves garlic   1 tablesp. sugar
2 tablesp. pickling spices   1 cup salt
                3½ qts. water

Combine pickling spices, bay leaves, saltpeter, sugar, salt and water (omitting garlic) and boil for less than 10 minutes. Place beef in heavy crock and pour hot liquid over meat. Add garlic cloves. Use heavy object to weight meat down. Cover crock with cheesecloth. Tie securely. Pickle for at least 10 days.

When ready to serve, follow these directions:

Rinse meat thoroughly and place in pot, with two small onions (whole) and diced celery, covering with water. When water comes to a boil, lower flame under beef and cook for at least 3½ hours, until meat is tender. Remove to platter. Cabbage and small, whole, boiled potatoes make an excellent garnish. Serves 6 to 8 with leftovers.

PICKLED TONGUE (Boiled)

Some women prefer not to go through the waiting period of pickling tongue. The modern Jewish butcher usually has pickled tongue ready to be taken home for preparation the same day. Although the preliminary pickling has been accomplished, the following must precede its appearance on the table:

4 to 6 lbs. pickled tongue   3 bay leaves
½ teasp. pickling spices   1 clove garlic
1 onion, whole

Wash tongue, and place in pot with pickling spices, onion, bay leaves and garlic, covering with water. When water boils, place over low flame, and cook at least 3 to 3½ hours, until tender. The water will diminish; add more *boiling water* from time to time. When tender, remove skin and root while still hot, being careful not to burn hands. Wear asbestos gloves for safety. White horse-radish and fruit compote make an excellent garnish. Serves 6 to 8 with leftovers.

PICKLED CORNED BEEF (Boiled)

Follow the same procedure as above, except that there is no skin and root to be removed.

ROAST TONGUE WITH SWEET POTATOES

5 to 6 lbs. fresh tongue   *1 clove garlic (cut up fine)*
1 teasp. salt   *Boiling water to cover*
¼ teasp. pepper   *bottom of roasting pan*
½ teasp. paprika   *6 sweet potatoes*

First cook tongue in boiling water for at least 15 minutes. While hot, remove skin and root. Place sliced onion in roasting pan. After placing tongue in roasting pan, sprinkle with salt, pepper, paprika and garlic. Cover pan and roast in oven for 2 hours at 325°F., and add sweet potatoes. Roast for another 1½ hours or until tongue is tender, and sweet potatoes soft. If a glaze on sweet potatoes is desired, sprinkle brown sugar and a little honey over each potato while in roasting pan. Slice meat and circle with sweet potatoes. Serves 6 to 8 with leftovers.

SALAMI MISH-MOSH
(Western Omelette, Kosher-Style)

8 slices of salami   *4 eggs, separated*
1 small green pepper (cut in   *½ teasp. salt*
*   strips)*   *¼ teasp. pepper*
1 pimento (cut in strips)   *Fat or oil for frying*

Separate eggs. Beat yolks and season with salt and pepper. Cut green pepper and pimento in strips and slice salami. Beat egg whites until they form a stiff peak. Heat skillet. Fold egg whites into yolks carefully, and place salami in skillet. When they curl into cups, add egg mixture into which green pepper and pimento have been added. Cook over medium flame until brown, first on one side, then on the other. Garnish with parsley. Serves 4.

Poultry

SPECIAL RULES OF KASHRUTH

There are certain specific seals or labels to observe if one is to be absolutely satisfied that fowl purchased is governed by the Jewish laws of Kashruth:

1) A "Plumba" (bearing the name of the supervising Rabbi) attached to the wing of kosher dressed or frozen poultry.

2) A special certification (seal) attesting that the fowl has been properly "koshered" and is ready for the oven or pot without further "koshering" by the housewife.

Should the housewife wish to do her own "koshering" of fowl, the following rules should be observed:

1) All claws should be removed from the fowl.

2) The blood vessel in the neck of the fowl should be removed. It may be removed by cutting into the meat, and pulling it out.

3) Fowl should be salted inside and out, and placed on the salting board at an angle, so that open parts face downward, allowing the blood to drain.

4) All inside parts of the fowl which are edible should be removed and salted separately. The gizzard should be cut open and cleaned thoroughly before koshering.

FORBIDDEN

Placing a fowl in boiling water for cleansing before "koshering."

EGGS FOUND INSIDE POULTRY

Many hens have unlaid eggs inside of them, some complete with outer shells. They must be given the same "koshering" as other edible parts found inside the fowl, but placed on the salting board so that none of the blood flowing from the fowl touches them.

These eggs may NOT be eaten with dairy foods, but are considered "flaishig."

DOMESTIC FOWL

According to the Torah, there are twenty-four birds which are forbidden to the Jewish people. Those which are acceptable are:

> Chicken
> Duck
> Geese
> Turkey
> Pigeon
> Squab

In order to strictly observe the Mosaic dietary laws, the eggs of non-kosher birds or fowl may not be eaten.

SLAUGHTERING OF FOWL

Fowl must be slaughtered in accordance with the special laws set forth and required by Jewish law. Any animal, fowl or bird which has died a natural death, which has not been slaughtered in accordance with these laws, may not be eaten and is not acceptable on the Jewish table.

HOW TO IDENTIFY VARIOUS POULTRY

For the convenience of the housewife who is not too familiar with the types of fowl offered by the kosher meat market, here is a list of fowl found in kosher meat markets throughout the country and, for that matter, throughout the world, where the Jewish population is such that special kosher markets are required.

Pullets (Popular because they are young, tender and most choice.)

Yearlings (Known as older chickens—but not too old to maneuver into something palatable.)

Stewing Hens (Oldest of chickens—usually have a lot of fat on them; can be used only for stewing.)

Broilers (Choicest of all chickens because of the little time required to prepare.)

Springs (A little older than broilers; good for frying or roasting, or preparing other types of chicken such as Chicken à la Maryland, etc.)

Ducks (The butcher will give you a choice duck at the weight and quality you desire. Dark meat only.)

Hen Turkeys (Has a greater breast expansion; the white meat is choicer and more succulent.)

Tom Turkey (Can be purchased in large sizes, sometimes
running as big as 28 pounds. More bone structure, leaner
breast, but excellent.)

Geese (Has all dark meat—like the duck. Popular in Jewish
households, particularly the goose liver, the goose fat, etc.)

Cornish Hens (A game fowl—small, with many bones, but
a delicacy when served occasionally.)

Squabs (A delicacy—but so small that one must not consider
a portion less than one whole squab per person.)

There are two types of squab—the broiler and the genuine
broiler. The broiler is the older squab—not as tender and
delectable as the genuine broiler. When buying squab,
question your butcher on this point, making sure that you
secure the genuine broiler.

How many of you can remember the days when you were
a child, when Friday night, "Shabos," was a festive occasion,
when the candles would be lit at sundown? Everyone would
sit down to the savory scent of "gefilte" fish mingled with
the lingering odor of the "challah" that Bubeh baked that
afternoon, and the over-powering odor from the roasting oven,
which foretold the coming of the beautifully browned roast
chicken to be set upon the table after the "broka" with the
sacramental wine and the appetizer had been agreeably dis-
pensed with.

This is the traditional Friday night dinner for Jewish families throughout the land, with varying accompaniments.

But one does not have to wait for Friday night to prepare
these delightful recipes for turkey, chicken, duck, goose and
squab.

ROASTING CHART FOR FOWL

Fowl	Weight in Lbs.	Oven Temperature°F.	Roasting Time-Hrs.
Chicken	3-4	350	2-2½
Chicken	4-5½	325	3-3½
Capon	6-7	325	3½-4
Duck	4-5	325	2½-3
Duck	5-7	325	3-4
Goose	8-10	325	4-5
* Turkey	6-10	325	3-4
* Turkey	10-12	325	4-5
* Turkey	12-16	325	5-6
* Turkey	16-22	300	6-7
* Turkey	Over 22	300	7½-9

* Turkey wrapped in foil may be roasted in the oven at a temperature of 450°F. at ½ the time indicated for other methods. Turkeys roasted in foil should have foil removed from breast during the last ½ hour of roasting.

RENDERING OF FAT
(Known as Griebenes)

Excess fat on a chicken or goose may be rendered by removing it together with skin which is attached to it. This fat should be cut into pieces of about 1 to 1½ inches, placed in heavy pot or skillet and simmered over low flame until all fat has been rendered, and cracklings have turned brown. Dice an onion into this mixture, add a dash of salt and cook until

the onions are golden brown and the cracklings, known as
"griebenes," are brown and crisp. The fat is then drained,
cooled and refrigerated, to be used in cooking other foods.
As for the griebenes, need one add what these may be used
for—or is it not standard procedure for everyone in the family
to want a taste of the griebenes?

GIBLETS OF FOWL
COOKING AND USE

Clean the giblets removed from the fowl carefully. Cover
these giblets with water, salt, pepper and seasoned salt. Simmer over low flame until tender. Add liver about ½ hour
before they are tender and completely done, and then remove
from flame. Water may have to be added in cooking as it
evaporates rapidly. When completely tender, remove and
cool. One of the recipes for stuffing, below, will include these.
Another favorite is giblets cut into small pieces, mixed with
onions and gravy, and served over toast.

ROAST CHICKEN

1 roasting chicken, 4 to 6 lbs.	*½ teasp. paprika*
2 carrots, diced	*Fat for basting and browning*
1 stalk celery, diced	*onions for stuffing*
2 onions (one sliced for	*2 eggs, separated*
roasting pan and one	*6 to 8 slices stale bread*
diced for stuffing)	*½ teasp. celery salt*
1 teasp. salt	*Chicken liver and giblets,*
¼ teasp. pepper	*ground or chopped fine*

Clean chicken thoroughly and salt inside. In the meantime,
dice onion and brown in fat; soak bread, drain the water, and
when almost squeezed dry, place in pan with onions. Add
more fat, brown onions and bread thoroughly, and place in
mixing bowl, beating until blended and until bread is smooth.

Separate egg yolks and beat into mixture with a little salt. Beat egg whites until stiff. Beat bread mixture, adding celery salt, until light and fluffy. Add giblets, ground or chopped, and blend until smooth. Fold in egg whites, which will tend to make the dressing light and fluffy. Stuff and truss with skewers. Heat either chicken fat with salt or pareve margarine, and mix a little warm water with it. Baste fowl. Sprinkle with salt, pepper, paprika. Place diced carrots and sliced onions in bottom of roasting pan, add 1 cup of water, and place chicken, breast side up, in roasting pan. Roast uncovered, allowing 30 minutes per pound at 325°F. After basting continuously, roast 1 hour with breast up and turn to one side allowing ½ hour for each side. Remove to platter. Garnish with carrots and pineapple chunks. Reserve stock for gravy, if desired. Thicken in a separate little pan by adding 2 tablespoons flour with a little water and salt. Cook for at least 10 minutes, until blended.

ROAST CHICKEN
(On Rack)

If the above recipe is used with a rack rather than a regular roasting pan, place chicken on rack breast *down*. Roast at 350°F. for ½ of roasting time. Turn chicken so that the breast is up and roast at 325°F. for the remaining time. Remove to platter.

ROAST CHICKEN
(In Paper Bag)

Prepare chicken as described above, and when completely basted, place chicken in a large brown paper bag, tying the end with strong string. Roast at 325°F. allowing 30 minutes per pound until each pound has had 30 minutes roasting, *including the weight of the dressing*. Remove from the paper bag and find a beautifully browned chicken.

ROAST TURKEY
(With Prune and Apricot Stuffing)

*1 roasting turkey (weight
    you desire)*
1½ tablesp. salt
½ teasp. pepper
1 teasp. paprika
*1 cup bread crumbs or grated
    toast crumbs*

1 tablesp. matzo meal
1 cup diced cooked prunes
1 cup diced cooked apricots
1 tablesp. sugar or honey
½ teasp. cinnamon
2 teasp. lime juice
½ cup water

Mix the bread crumbs, prunes, apricots, sugar or honey, cinnamon, lime juice, and water until blended. Clean turkey. Stuff & truss. Baste with fat or pareve margarine, salt, pepper, and sprinkle with paprika. Cover entire turkey with cheesecloth which has been saturated with margarine or fat. Place in uncovered roasting pan. Set thermostat at 325°F., allowing 30 minutes per pound, and turning first on one side and then on the other until thoroughly browned. Remove cheesecloth after turkey has been removed to platter.

ROASTING DUCK AND GOOSE

A very important thing to remember in the roasting of duck or goose is that these two fowl have the greatest amount of fat, and the roasting process must take care of eliminating this fat, so that when completely roasted and set on the table, they are beautifully browned, but not greasy. In order to master this art, both duck and goose must be roasted in an uncovered roasting pan or on a rack. During the period of roasting (particularly the first half) a fork must be forced through the outer skin, to allow the excess fat to drain from the fowl. Additional basting is not necessary.

Another important thing to bear in mind is that both duck and goose yield ONLY dark meat . . . NO WHITE meat.

ROAST DUCK

1 duck (cleaned and	*2 egg whites*
thoroughly washed)	*1 onion, diced*
2 cups bread crumbs	*2 tablesp. fat*
2 tablesp. matzo meal	*2 tablesp. ice water*
1 orange rind, grated	*1 teasp. salt*
2 egg yolks	*¼ teasp. pepper*

½ teasp. paprika

After salting the inside of the duck and seasoning the outside with salt, pepper, and paprika, prepare the stuffing as follows: Place bread crumbs and grated orange rind in a bowl; brown onions in fat and add them and the fat to the bread crumbs. Beat egg yolks, add a little salt and pepper, and mix with the bread crumbs. Blend all ingredients well. Add matzo meal and water. Beat egg whites until stiff; fold into breadcrumb mixture. Stuff the duck, and either sew end or use skewers. Place in open roasting pan or on rack in oven pan. If the rack is used, place the duck breast *down*. Roast at 450°F. for at least ½ hour. During this period of time, keep sticking a fork into the duck so that the fat will drain more quickly. Reduce temperature to 350°F., allowing 30 minutes per pound for roasting time. Drain fat as it accumulates in roasting pan. When completely brown and tender, remove to platter. An excellent garnish is scooped oranges filled with cranberry sauce (whole berries).

ROAST DUCK (With Orange Glaze)

Following the above recipe, use uncovered roasting pan, and prepare the following:

2 oranges, juice only	*6 tablesp. dark brown sugar*

Blend and use to baste duck frequently—adds an orange flavor and glazes duck as it roasts. Slice another orange thinly and when duck is completely roasted, remove to platter, plac-

ing orange slices around platter. Another attractive garnish is
orange quarters, with a clove in center on the breast of the
duck.

ROAST DUCK
(Filled with Potato Stuffing)

1 duck (thoroughly cleaned	*1 apple, grated*
and washed)	*3 cups drained grated*
1 teasp. salt	*potatoes*
½ teasp. paprika	*1 egg*
1 onion, grated	*¼ teasp. cinnamon*
2 tablesp. potato flour	

Place drained grated potatoes in a large bowl. Add grated
onion, apple and egg. Add cinnamon, a little salt, pepper,
and the 2 tablespoons of potato flour to mixture to hold it
together. Stuff into duck. Sew or skewer end. Place in open
roasting pan; salt and sprinkle duck with paprika. Roast at
450°F. for ½ hour until nicely browned. Keep sticking your
fork into duck to drain fat. Reduce heat to 350°F. and roast
for at least 2½ to 3 hours, depending upon size of duck, allowing 30 minutes per pound roasting time. Remove to platter.
Garnish with spiced crabapples.

ROAST GOOSE
(With Matzo Meal-Goose Liver Stuffing)

1 goose	*½ cup water*
1 large onion, diced	*1 teasp. salt*
Goose liver and giblets	*½ teasp. pepper*
(ground or chopped)	*½ teasp. paprika*
2 cups matzo meal	*½ teasp. garlic salt*
1 cup bread crumbs	*2 eggs*
Fat for browning onion	

Heat fat in skillet and brown onions. Place bread crumbs,
matzo meal, a little salt, pepper, and garlic salt in a bowl.
Add eggs and water. Mix well. Add browned onions and fat

to mixture and combine with ground or chopped goose liver and giblets. Mix well. Salt the goose; sprinkle with paprika. Stuff with goose liver mixture and sew end or use skewers. Place in uncovered roasting pan. Roast at 400°F. for at least 1 hour. Reduce heat to 350°F. and roast for the length of time required by the weight of the goose. Drain fat from roasting pan from time to time.

GEFILTE HELZEL
(Goose Neck with Matzo Meal Stuffing)

1 goose neck	*1 teasp. salt*
2 cups matzo meal	*¼ teasp. pepper*
1 onion, grated	*1 teasp. paprika*
3 tablesp. goose fat	*¼ teasp. garlic salt*

Mix all ingredients, saving a little salt and most of the paprika for sprinkling on outside. Stuff in the carefully removed and cleaned skin from neck of the goose. You can add the neck skin of chickens or duck, sewing these together to make a larger neck skin to fill. After inserting the stuffing, sew ends. Salt and sprinkle paprika on the outer skin. Place in roasting pan with goose, and roast the same length of time as the goose, turning over on each side for thorough browning. Remove to platter when completely browned, and cut in 2-in. slices.

FRIED CHICKEN
(Jewish Style)

1 or 2 fryers (cut into 8 pieces each)	*2 teasp. salt*
	½ teasp. pepper
2 cups matzo meal	*½ teasp. Accent*
4 eggs	*Fat, oil or margarine for*
1 teasp. garlic salt	*frying*

Beat eggs. Add 1 teaspoon salt, the Accent and garlic salt. Dip chicken into egg mixture, then in matzo meal, then in egg mixture, and then in matzo meal again. Heat fat in skillet with whole onion (to add flavor to chicken). When hot, drop chicken in fat until skillet is filled. Brown first on one side, then on the other. Remove chicken and fry the other pieces in the same manner. When completely browned, remove fat from skillet; add a little water, sprinkle salt and pepper in the water and over the chicken, and cover. Place a low flame under skillet, and simmer for at least 1 hour. Remove to platter.

DEEP FRIED CHICKEN
(French Style)

1 or 2 fryers (cut into 8 pieces each)	1 teasp. Accent
	1 teasp. salt
1 cup flour	½ teasp. pepper
½ teasp. paprika	

Salt the chicken and sprinkle on Accent, pepper and paprika. Place 1 cup of flour in a brown paper bag. Take 2 or 3 pieces of chicken and drop them into the bag. Shake the bag so that the flour coats the chicken. Continue until all of the chicken has been coated with flour.

Place polyunsaturated light oil in French deep-fryer and heat. When hot, drop pieces of chicken in fryer. Brown and cook until chicken is tender, but crisp. When frying two chickens, it may be necessary to complete a portion of chicken before placing the balance in the deep-fryer.

Place on platter. An excellent accompaniment to this type of meal is French fried potatoes (in the same deep-fryer), corn on the cob, tossed salad, spiced pineapple chunks and pickled watermelon rind.

CHICKEN FRICASSEE
(With Sweet and Sour Meatballs)

1 chicken, 3 to 4 lbs. (cut up)	½ qt. hot water
	1 teasp. salt
1 onion, sliced	¼ teasp. pepper
½ teasp. Accent	

SWEET AND SOUR MEATBALLS:

1 lb. ground beef	*1 lemon, sliced thin*
1 egg	*2 tablesp. lemon or vinegar*
1 onion, grated	*2 tablesp. sugar*
1 teasp. salt	*4 gingersnaps*
¼ teasp. pepper	*2 tablesp. cornstarch*
¼ teasp. cinnamon	*2 tablesp. catsup*
1 cup chicken stock	*Fat for browning*

¼ cup raisins

First place sliced onions in water in a Dutch oven. Season chicken with salt, pepper and Accent. When water is boiling, place chicken in Dutch oven, and reduce flame to low heat. Cook chicken until tender.

Mix meat, grated onion, egg, salt, cinnamon, and pepper. Form into small meatballs. Roll in cornstarch and brown in heavy skillet in hot fat. Add chicken stock, sliced onions from chicken, lemon juice or vinegar, raisins, catsup and sugar. Cover skillet and cook over low flame for about ¾ of an hour. Uncover and stir in crumbled gingersnaps. Cook for at least another 15 minutes. Remove to serving casserole. When serving, pour sauce and meatballs right over fricassee chicken. Serves 8.

CHICKEN À LA KING

1 chicken, cooked and diced	*3 carrots, diced and boiled*
1 small can pimentos (cut	*until tender*
into thin strips)	*1 teasp. salt*
1 pkge. frozen peas or 1 lb.	*¼ teasp. pepper*
fresh peas (boil and have	*½ teasp. paprika*
ready)	*2 cups chicken stock*
1 lb. fresh mushrooms	*2 tablesp. flour*
(boiled until tender) or	*½ cup water*
1 can mushrooms	*6 sprigs of parsley*

Prepare everything so that it is edible. Then mix the flour with water and a little salt. Heat chicken stock in skillet;

thicken with the flour mixture. Add all of the ingredients mentioned above, except paprika. Heat thoroughly until piping hot. Serve over toast slices or in patty shells. Sprinkle with a little paprika for added color. Use one or two sprigs of parsley. Excellent garnish—steamed rice over which some of the chicken gravy may be poured.

STEWED CHICKEN
(With Potato Dumplings or Knaidlach)

1 stewing chicken, 3 or 4 lbs.	*1 teasp. salt*
1 onion, sliced	*¼ teasp. pepper*
3 carrots, diced	*½ teasp. paprika*
3 cups boiling water	*½ teasp. Accent*

POTATO DUMPLINGS (or Knaidlach)

3 cups drained grated potatoes	*1 teasp. salt*
	¼ cup potato flour
1 medium-sized onion, grated	*2 tablesp. matzo meal*
1 egg	

Place sliced onion at bottom of Dutch oven. Add diced carrots and pieces of chicken. Season with salt, pepper, paprika and Accent. Pour boiling water over contents. Cover and simmer over low flame for about 2½ to 3 hours, or until chicken is tender.

Mix beaten egg with seasoning and onion. Add grated potatoes, matzo meal, potato flour. Shape into 2-in. balls and cook in salted water for about ½ hour, or until the dumplings rise to the top. Use slotted spoon to remove from boiling water and drain.

When chicken is completely tender, place dumplings in the bottom of the Dutch oven around the chicken, and heat together for about 10 minutes. Remove to platter. Serves 6.

STEWED CHICKEN
(With Mushrooms and Rice)

1 stewing chicken, 3 to   *½ teasp. paprika*
3½ lbs.   *1 cup rice*
1 onion, diced   *1 lb. fresh mushrooms*
1 teasp. salt   *2 tablesp. flour (for thick-*
½ teasp. pepper   *ening gravy, optional)*
4 cups boiling water

Boil water with one onion. Season chicken and brown. Place pieces in boiling water over a low flame, and simmer for at least 1 hour. Wash rice. Take 3 cups chicken broth, add rice, and cook until rice is nearly tender. Add the chicken. Cook mushrooms in salted boiling water for 5 minutes, and add to mixture. If thickened gravy is desired, add 2 tablespoons flour.

BARBECUED CHICKEN

There are various ways to achieve popularity, even fame, as a hostess. One way is through barbecue cooking, either indoors or outdoors. Here are two methods:

One is to prepare a marinade, pour it over the chicken, and allow to stand for a few hours before use, thereby ensuring its tenderness and flavor.

The other method is to disjoint the chickens, placing them in a pan of boiling salted water with two whole onions. Cook for at least ½ hour. Remove the chicken, wrap in foil, and refrigerate until time for the barbecue. It requires only about 15 minutes under the broiler or over a charcoal flame for tender, succulent chicken.

MARINADE:

½ cup olive oil   *1 teasp. salt*
2 tablesp. vinegar   *¼ teasp. pepper*

If desired, the quantity may be increased by doubling the recipe. Pour over chicken and allow to stand for at least

3 hours. This is particularly effective when broiling over charcoal.

ORANGE BARBECUE SAUCE:

2 oranges, juice only   6 tablesp. dark brown sugar
1 cup catsup   1 teasp. Worcestershire sauce

CHICKEN-IN-THE POT

2 broiler-type chickens,   10 small onions
  disjointed   1 stalk celery, diced
4 carrots, diced   2 teasp. salt
1 pkge. frozen peas or 1 lb.   ½ teasp. seasoned salt
  fresh peas   1 clove garlic, minced
            6 cups boiling water

Boil water with 1 teaspoon of salt. Add onions, carrots and celery. Season chicken with salt, seasoned salt and minced garlic. Add to boiling water, onions, carrots and celery. Cook over low flame for ¾ of an hour. Add frozen or fresh peas. Remove from flame in another ½ hour, or when chicken is tender. Serve in individual covered casserole with a generous portion of chicken, some carrots, peas and diced celery. Garnish with a piece of parsley. The soup and chicken should be served together with the vegetables. (Please remember to skim the fat from the soup before serving.) Serves 6.

CHICKEN À-LA-MARYLAND

2 broiler-type chickens,   1 teasp. salt
  disjointed   ¼ teasp. pepper
3 eggs, beaten   2 cups crushed corn flakes
½ teasp. garlic salt   or bread crumbs

Season chickens with salt, garlic salt and pepper. Salt beaten eggs and place in shallow bowl. Place corn flake crumbs or bread crumbs in flat dish. Dip chicken pieces first in egg, then in crumbs, in egg mixture and then in crumbs again. Place under the broiler, and brown. Remove to shallow baking pan, and bake in oven at 350°F. for 1 hour, or until chicken is tender. The crust should be golden brown—the juices should remain inside the chicken. Before removing from oven, place peach halves (canned) around chicken, and allow the chicken to remain until the peaches are hot. Remove chicken and peaches to platter. Serves 4 generously.

PÂTÉ DE FOIS GRAS
(Genzen Leber Gehockte)
(Chopped Goose Liver)

Cooked liver from goose (ground fine)

2 tablesp. goose fat and chopped gribenes (put through grinder)

2 hard-boiled eggs (mash to paste)

1 small onion, grated

½ teasp. salt

¼ teasp. pepper

Mix ingredients together until they form a smooth paste, adding more goose fat if required. Makes an excellent spread for hors d'oeuvres on crackers, or for small sandwiches on toasted bread with crusts cut and made into various small shapes.

CHICKEN MOLD

1 fryer (cooked until tender and diced)

½ cup diced sweet pickle and celery

2 hard-boiled eggs, diced

¾ cup strained chili sauce

2 pkges. lemon Jello

2½ cups water

2 tablesp. vinegar

Prepare all diced foods and have ready for mold. Follow directions for dissolving Jello with hot water, but use only the amount of water indicated in this recipe. Other liquids will fill in correct quantity, as indicated above. Strain chili sauce into Jello. Place in large ring mold. Store in refrigerator until it reaches the consistency of raw egg. Place diced chicken in the bottom of mold first, then add eggs, sweet pickle and celery. Refrigerate overnight. When mold is served, garnish with sweet pickles, olives and hard-boiled eggs. Serves 8 generously.

CHICKEN CROQUETTES

1 chicken (boiled and cut into pieces, then ground fine)	*¼ teasp. pepper*
	½ teasp. sage
	2 eggs, beaten
1 onion, grated	*2 eggs, beaten (for batter)*
Parsley (cut fine)	*1 cup matzo meal (for batter)*
1 teasp. salt	

Fat for frying

Mix chicken, grated onion, parsley, salt, pepper, sage, two eggs, and form into croquettes. Dip these croquettes into the egg batter, then in matzo meal, then in egg mixture and matzo meal again. Heat fat in skillet. When hot, drop croquettes in, and brown thoroughly on one side, then on the other. Remove to platter. Small whole boiled potatoes, baked squash, and lettuce and tomato salad with oil and vinegar dressing will complement this meal. Serves 4.

CHICKEN PAPRIKA

1 chicken, 3 to 4 lbs., disjointed	*1 teaspoon salt*
	½ teasp. pepper
1½ teasp. paprika	*2 cups boiling water*
1 cup flour	*Fat for browning*

Mix paprika with flour and place in paper bag. Season chicken with salt and pepper. Drop pieces in paper bag. Shake until thoroughly saturated with flour and paprika. Heat fat in heavy skillet or Dutch oven. Brown chicken thoroughly. Add boiling water to chicken, and add diced onion. Cook over slow fire for 2 to 2½ hours, or until chicken is tender. Gravy should thicken from flour mixture, and color should be golden brown from paprika.

CASSEROLE CHICKEN

1 chicken, 3 to 3½ lbs., disjointed
1 teasp. salt
½ teasp. paprika
¼ teasp. pepper
¼ teasp. ginger
¼ teasp. cinnamon

1 can condensed tomato soup
1 large can whole tomatoes
1 onion, sliced
½ lb. fresh mushrooms (cooked in boiling salt water for 5 min.)
¼ cup flour

Drop pieces of chicken in flour in paper bag, and shake bag until chicken has been dredged with flour. Brown chicken in Dutch oven or heavy casserole. Remove from Dutch oven. Place sliced onions on bottom; add tomato soup, whole tomatoes, and mushrooms. Place pieces of browned chicken over this, and bake in oven in covered Dutch oven or casserole at 325°F. for at least 2 hours, or until chicken is tender. Remove from oven, and serve in individual casserole dishes. Garnish with pickled peaches.

CORNISH HEN (Baked)

3 or 4 Cornish hens
2 teasp. salt
½ teasp. pepper
1 teasp. paprika
1 cup chestnuts, cut and chopped

2 cups bread crumbs
1 orange rind, grated
Giblets of Cornish hens, chopped fine
1 onion, grated
1 cup boiling water

1 egg

Cook the giblets in salt water until tender. Chop fine, add grated onion, orange rind, salt and pepper, bread crumbs, 1 egg. Combine, and stuff Cornish hens. Brown in fat. Add

1 cup boiling water to Dutch oven in which the Cornish hens are placed. Cover, and bake in oven set at 450°F. for ½ hour. Remove cover, and reduce heat to 400°F. Bake for at least another ½ hour, or until tender. Spiced pears, red and green, make an excellent garnish for this platter. Serves 6 generously.

APPLE AND PRUNE STUFFING
FOR GOOSE

1 egg	*1 tablesp. sugar*
2 cups prunes	*½ teasp. salt*
3 large apples (cored, peeled and chopped)	*½ teasp. cinnamon*
	½ cup raisins
½ cup matzo meal	*¼ cup chopped walnuts*

Pour boiling water over prunes and raisins. Cut and chop nuts; peel, core and chop apples. After prunes and raisins have remained in boiling water for 1½ hours, pit the prunes, and cut and chop. Beat egg, add sugar, salt, and the rest of the ingredients. Blend well, and stuff goose.

APPLE AND ORANGE STUFFING
FOR DUCK

1 cup grated bread crumbs	*1 orange rind, grated*
3 apples (peeled and cut in cubes)	*4 pieces of Beef Fry (fried and cut up fine)*
1 onion, diced	*Fat for browning*
2 eggs, beaten	

Mix all ingredients, and stuff duck. Has a delightful flavor.

Soups
and Their Accompaniments

FOR GENERATIONS SOUPS HAVE BEEN A FAVORITE WITH JEWISH people. One of the logical reasons that soup plays such an important role in Jewish menus is the fact that so many of them have been handed down from one generation to the next, with each new generation adding little palate-tempting embellishments. Many of these ancestors, under the stress of the countries from which they came, found it economically easier to substitute soup for the seven-course dinners those few in more fortunate circumstances could afford and enjoy.

Mama would start by boiling a pot of water, looking in her pantry to see what she had on hand . . . a carrot or two . . . one large onion . . . a few potatoes . . . a handful of barley . . . the feet, giblets and wings of a chicken, and she had the start for a pot of soup. If she found a little flour and an extra egg, she thought to herself, "And why not a little *luchshun?*" There it was when dinner time came—good, nourishing soup with freshly baked dark bread to warm a family's heart and fill their tummies, with Papa adding, "A mechayeh!"

With these time-tested recipes as a guide, delight your family and guests with some of these tempting and delicious soups with the assortment of garnishes furnished as an accompaniment. Select the garnish which will go best with the soup being served. Many of them have been a family tradition for centuries.

SOUP STOCK

Soup stock, when prepared, may be stored in jars in the refrigerator, and used when needed to supplement freshly made soup.

Rules to follow:

Use jars which have just been scalded for storing soup stock. Do not skim fat from top until ready to use as it acts as a protective coating. It prevents air from getting into the soup stock and keeps it fresh until ready for use.

3 lbs. soup meat or brisket of beef
1 soup bone (or more)
3½ qts. water
2 teasp. salt

1 onion, diced
1 carrot, diced
1 stalk celery, diced (with leaves)
2 teasp. chopped parsley

½ teasp. pepper

Sprinkle 1 teaspoon salt and a little pepper on meat. Place meat and bones in a pot with 3½ quarts of water over low heat. When water comes to a boil, there will be particles from the meat on top, but DO NOT SKIM. Cover pot, and allow to simmer for at least 3 hours. Add vegetables, and allow to cook for almost another hour. More hot water may be added if some of the water has evaporated. Remove meat from soup when tender. Serve meat, but after soup stock has been allowed to cool, store in scalded jars in refrigerator for future use in making soups.

CONSOMMÉ

1 lb. beef flank (lean)
½ lb. veal bone
1 lb. marrow bone
3 lbs. soup chicken, disjointed
2 teasp. salt
½ teasp. pepper

¼ teasp. celery salt
¼ teasp. nutmeg, grated
3 qts. water
1 onion, diced
2 carrots, diced
1 stalk celery, diced
1 teasp. minced parsley

Place chicken in large pot. Place meat and bones in another smaller pot, and cook until water begins to boil. Skim top and add meat, meat bones and water to chicken. Cover pot and place over low flame for approximately 4 hours. Add vegetables, and allow to simmer until vegetables are tender. Remove vegetables, chicken, meat and bones to platter. Strain soup through sieve until clear. Season to taste. May be served hot in cups. When cooled, it may be stored in refrigerator in scalded jars, and used when desired.

BOUILLON

3 lbs. lean brisket	*1 bay leaf, crushed*
2 lbs. shin bone	*¼ teasp. pepper*
1 onion, sliced	*1 stalk celery, diced*
A few dried onion peels	*½ chicken, disjointed*
2 teasp. salt	*1 cup diced potatoes (raw)*
⅛ teasp. red pepper	*3½ qts. water*

Place meat, bones and chicken in a pot of cold water. Allow them to remain for ½ hour. Season with salt, red pepper, bay leaf, and simmer until it comes to a boil. Cover, and place over low flame for 3 to 3½ hours. Add vegetables and boil until they are completely tender. Remove meat, bones, chicken and vegetables, and strain soup through sieve, skimming fat. Serve hot. Store balance in scalded jars in refrigerator, and serve as required.

BEET BORSCHT
(Cold)

12 large beets, peeled and grated (with one beet sliced thin)	*4 tablesp. sugar*
	1 large onion, grated
	2 teasp. salt
3 qts. water	*3 eggs*
⅓ cup lemon juice	*Sour cream*

Place grated beets and sliced beet, onion and salt in a pot of water. Heat over low flame for 1 hour and 10 minutes.

Mix sugar and lemon juice together and add to mixture. When this has been properly blended (about 15 minutes), remove from flame. Place eggs in a large bowl and beat. Very slowly, add the beet borscht, stirring constantly so that there is no curdling. Cool and place in refrigerator to chill. When serving, place a slice of beet on each portion, and top with sour cream. Some prefer their sour cream blended with the beet borscht. You may fold the sour cream into the beet borscht, if desired.

SCHAV (Sour Grass or Spinach Borscht)
(Cold)

2 lbs. schav (green, sour grass)	2 tablesp. lemon juice
1 onion, grated	6 tablesp. sugar
3 qts. water	2 eggs
	Sour cream
1½ teasp. salt	

Clean schav carefully, first by washing 2 or 3 times with cold water, and then following through with lukewarm water. Combine the schav, onion, water and salt in a large pot. Bring to a boil, then cook over low flame for 1 hour. Mix lemon juice and sugar together and add to schav mixture. Cook for 15 minutes, and taste, adding either sugar or lemon as required. Remove schav from stove. Beat eggs in a large bowl, and slowly add the schav, stirring constantly to avoid curdling. Chill and refrigerate. When serving, garnish with sour cream. If mixing of sour cream with schav is desired, blend before serving. Serves 8.

CABBAGE AND RAISIN SOUP

1 large cabbage, shredded	1½ teasp. salt
1 large onion, minced	¼ teasp. pepper
½ cup seedless raisins	1 small can condensed
2 qts. water	tomato soup
1 large can whole tomatoes	3 tablesp. flour
½ cup sugar	3 tablesp. butter or mar-
¼ cup lemon juice	garine

Pour boiling water over the cabbage in a colander. Combine cabbage and onions in a skillet with butter or margarine. Cook for about 20 minutes. Place in a large pot and sprinkle with 3 tablespoons flour. Stir mixture and add water. Place over medium flame, and cook until mixture comes to a boil. Add seasoning, tomatoes, mixture of sugar and lemon juice and raisins. Reduce flame to low and simmer for about 1 or 1¼ hours. Taste and add either sugar or lemon juice. Serves 8.

MUSHROOM-BARLEY SOUP
(Dairy)

10 dried mushrooms	½ teasp. pepper
4 tablesp. pearl barley	1 onion, diced
3 tablesp. flour	2 tablesp. butter or mar-
2½ qts. water	garine
1 teasp. salt	1 cup milk (optional)

Wash mushrooms and soak in cold water for 15 minutes. Slice mushrooms. Combine barley, mushrooms, and seasoning in a large pot. Add water. Cook over low flame for approximately 1 or 1¼ hours. Brown onions. Add to mixture. If milk is desired, mix flour with a little water and add the milk. Combine with soup mixture and cook for at least another 20 minutes. Serves 8 to 10.

MUSHROOM-BARLEY SOUP
(Meat)

10 *dried mushrooms*
½ *cup pearl barley*
2½ *cups water*
2 *lbs. meat (soup bone at-*
tached)
Parsley, minced

2 *potatoes, diced*
1 *teasp. salt*
½ *teasp. pepper*
1 *onion, diced*
Margarine (for browning
meat and onion)

Brown meat and diced onions well. In the meantime, wash and soak mushrooms in cold water for about 10 minutes. Slice mushrooms. Add mushrooms, barley, salt and pepper to the pot of water. When water comes to a boil, add browned onions and meat, seasoned with salt. Cook over low flame for about 2 to 2½ hours, or until meat is tender. One-half hour before removing, add diced potatoes. Pour into soup tureen and place meat on a platter. Serves 6.

MILCHIG SPLIT PEA SOUP
(Arbe Soup—Dairy)

2½ *cups split peas*
2 *carrots, diced*
1 *large onion, diced*
1 *stalk celery, diced*

1½ *teasp. salt*
½ *teasp. pepper*
4 *diced potatoes or 2 tablesp.*
flour

3 *qts. water*

Wash peas thoroughly. Place in large pot with water, carrots, celery, and onions. Cover pot and bring to a boil. Add seasoning. Reduce heat to low and simmer for at least 2½ to 3 hours.

If potatoes are desired, add potatoes with seasoning and cook for at least another ½ hour, when soup will be fully cooked. If flour is used to thicken soup, mix a little water and salt with flour, stir into soup, and cook another 10 minutes, until flour is thoroughly blended into ingredients. Remove to soup tureen. Garnish with croutons. Serves 8.

MILCHIG VEGETABLE SOUP

3 carrots, diced	(pour boiling water over
2 stalks celery, diced	this before placing in pan)
1 cup fresh peas	1½ teasp. salt
1 cup diced fresh string	½ teasp. pepper
beans	3 potatoes, peeled and diced
1 cup fresh lima beans	1½ qts. water
(baby)	2 cups milk
1 cup fresh shredded cabbage	Butter for browning onion

Brown onion in large saucepan. Add water, seasoning and vegetables. Cover pan and cook over low flame for at least 15 minutes. Add diced potatoes and cook another ½ hour. Add milk and stir. Cook until milk comes to a boil. Serve hot. Garnish with sprigs of parsley. Serves 6.

FLAISHIG VEGETABLE SOUP

2 lbs. soup meat with bone	1½ teasp. salt
1 large onion, diced	1 teasp. seasoned salt
3 carrots, diced	½ teasp. pepper
1 cup lima beans	1 No. 2 can whole tomatoes
1 cup fresh peas	2½ qts. water
1 cup fresh string beans (cut)	

Brown onions and meat well. Heat water in large saucepan, and add meat and onions, carrots, lima beans, string beans, salt, seasoned salt and pepper. Cook over low flame for 1 hour. Skim off meat scum which has accumulated at the top. Cook another hour, and add peas and tomatoes. Cook until peas and meat are tender. Pour into soup tureen and place meat on platter. Serves 6 generously.

MAMA'S SUPREME VEGETABLE SOUP

1½ to 2 lbs. flanken
2 marrow bones
1 large onion
2 carrots
3 stalks of celery
1 parsnip root
2 tablesp. salt
1 teasp. pepper
3 tablesp. pearl barley
½ cup dried lima beans

½ cup dried yellow split peas
1 small can tomato sauce
2 soft tomatoes (optional)
1 pkge. frozen mixed vegetables
4 qts. water
½ cup alphabets, farfel or broken bits of noodles or ¼ cup rice

Place meat, bones, onion and water in 6 quart soup pot. Bring to a boil and permit rolling boil for 15 minutes, skimming surface of soup constantly. In the meantime clean and wash carrots, celery and parsnip (petrushka), and let stand in cold water until the soup is ready for them. Reduce heat under soup to medium and continue cooking for another ½ hour. Add soup greens, lima beans and barley and cook for another ½ hour. Remember to keep clearing the top of the soup. Add the soup greens and the split peas. If you have soft tomatoes, add them at this time, as well as the tomato sauce, and permit this to simmer for another 1½ hours. The meat should be tender by this time. Add the vegetables and the noodle product or rice and cook for another 20 minutes. Lastly, add seasoning. (When you add the seasoning last, the ingredients will not stick to the bottom of the pot.) Soup should be made the day or night before planning to serve it so that it may be placed in refrigerator to permit all the fat to rise to the surface. When cold, this fat should be removed from the surface of the soup; it usually hardens and is easy to remove.

The meat from the soup is particularly tasty and it could make one entire meal along with the soup (and all from one pot, too).

Keep boiled water handy to add to soup if water evaporates while cooking. Also, should you wish to thin soup out the following day (it has a tendency to thicken), tomato juice may be added. Serves 8 generously with leftovers.

SWEET-SOUR CABBAGE AND RAISIN SOUP
(With Beef Flanken) *1 can torn soup.*

3 lbs. flanken	~~*¼ cup seedless raisins*~~
1 large onion, diced	*1 teasp. salt*
1 large cabbage, shredded	*¼ teasp. pepper*
1 large can whole tomatoes	*¼ teasp. ginger*
⅓ cup lemon juice	*2½ qts. water*
	4 tablesp. sugar

Pour boiling water over the shredded cabbage in a colander. Boil flanken in a large pot, and skim when it comes to a boil. Add onions and tomatoes, and cook over low heat for approximately 1 hour. Add cabbage and seasoning, and cook until meat is tender, or approximately another 1¼ hours. Mix lemon juice and sugar and add to cabbage and meat soup, together with raisins. Cook until blended, or about 15 minutes. Taste, and add either lemon juice or sugar. Serves 8.

HOT BEET BORSCHT
(With Beef Brisket)

2 lbs. brisket	*¼ teasp. pepper*
Beef bones	*4 tablesp. brown sugar*
10 beets, grated	*¼ cup lemon juice*
1 large onion, diced	*2 eggs*
1 clove garlic, minced	*2½ qts. water*
	2 teasp. salt

Season meat and beef bones, and place water in large saucepan. When hot, add meat and beef bones. When it comes to a full boil, skim. Add diced onions, beets, garlic and seasoning. Cook over low heat for 2 hours. Mix brown sugar and lemon juice. Add to ingredients. Cook for at least another 20 minutes. Taste and add either sugar or lemon juice. Beat the eggs in a large bowl. Add the borscht, little by little, beating so that it will not curdle. Beat until egg is completely absorbed. Pour into soup tureen, and place meat on platter. Serves 8.

SPLIT-PEA SOUP
(With Beef Flanken—Arbe Soup)

3 lbs. flanken (lean)	*½ teasp. celery salt*
1 ½ cups split peas	*¼ teasp. ginger*
10 cups water	*3 carrots, diced*
2 teasp. salt	*1 onion, diced*
½ teasp. pepper	

Brown flanken and onions. Combine peas and water in a large pot. After cooking over low flame for 1 hour, bring water to a boil and add the flanken, onions, seasoning, and carrots. Cover pot and cook over low flame for approximately 2½ hours, or until meat is tender. Remove meat to platter. Press pea soup through a sieve, until it is like a purée. Place it in soup tureen. When serving, place a few pieces of meat in each serving. Serves 6.

BEAN SOUP
(Beblach Soup)

2 cups lima beans (dried)	*2 teasp. salt*
1 onion, diced	*¼ teasp. pepper*
2 stalks celery, diced	*1 qt. water*
1 carrot, diced	
1 lb. soup meat and bone	Optional:
1 cup soup stock	*2 tablesp. flour*

Soak lima beans overnight in cold water. Brown meat and onions in skillet. Place beans and rest of vegetables, with seasoning, in 1 quart of water. Add meat, soup bone, and soup stock. Place over low flame and allow to cook for at least 3 to 4 hours, until beans and meat are tender. If thicker soup is desired, thicken with a little flour mixed with water. Blend thoroughly into soup, and allow to cook for at least another 20 minutes.

LENTIL OR LINSEN SOUP

2 cups lentils
2 lbs. flanken
1 soup bone
1 cup strained tomatoes
1 stalk celery, diced
1 carrot, diced

2 teasp. salt
2 tablesp. flour
¼ teasp. pepper
¼ teasp. celery salt
1 onion, diced
1½ qts. water

Soak lentils overnight in cold water. Drain. Brown flanken and onions in skillet with a little fat. Place lentils, strained tomatoes, celery, carrot, and seasoning in water. Place over low flame, and cook until water comes to a boil. Add meat, onions, and cover. Continue over low flame for 2 to 3 hours, or until lentils and meat are completely tender. Thicken with flour and water mixture, adding to soup, blending in completely, and cook another 15 to 20 minutes.

SOUP GARNISHES
NOODLES (Luchshun)

2 cups flour (sifted)
½ teasp. salt

2 eggs, beaten
2 tablesp. cold water

Sift flour, adding salt while sifting. Make a well in the center and drop eggs and water into it. Work with flour on the board until dough is formed. Knead well. Roll the dough until it is very thin. Let it dry, and roll it so that it measures about 2 inches in width. Then take a sharp knife and cut into very thin strips (for fine noodles) or ¼ inch strips for thick noodles. After cutting, loosen cut strips and place on a platter to dry further prior to dropping into boiling soup.

Alternate method: Drop into 1 quart of boiling water, into which you place 1 teaspoon salt. Boil over medium flame until noodles rise to the top. Use as a soup garnish or for whatever else you might wish.

KREPLACH (or Pierogi)

Use the same ingredients as those in the recipe for Noodles above. Knead the dough well. Roll the dough with rolling pin until it is about ⅛ inch thick. Take a knife and cut into 2½ inch squares. Place 1 teaspoon of meat (recipe below) on each square, pressing the edges together to form a triangle. These may be dropped into boiling soup, to be served as a garnish, or may be dropped into 1 quart of boiling salted water, and allowed to cook until they rise to the top. They are delicious browned under a broiler. Following is the meat mixture for the Kreplach:

1 lb. cooked meat, chopped fine	*½ teasp. salt*
	¼ teasp. pepper
1 egg	*1 onion, grated*

Mix together thoroughly and place 1 teaspoon of this meat mixture on the 2½-inch square of dough, folding into triangle as described above.

KNAIDLACH (Passover)
(Dumplings)

1 cup matzo meal	*3 egg yolks*
1 teasp. salt	*3 egg whites*

For light, fluffy knaidlach, beat the egg yolks. Fold in the matzo meal and add salt. Chill in refrigerator for at least 1 hour. Use either an electric mixer or rapid stroke beater to beat the whites of the eggs until they are stiff but wet. Fold carefully into matzo meal mixture. Form into about 15 balls. Drop into boiling soup for from 15 to 20 minutes. Alternative: Drop into boiling salted water, and boil briskly until the knaidlach rise to the top. Remove and use when desired.

POTATO KNAIDLACH (Passover)
(Dumplings)

2 cups potatoes, grated and   ¼ cup potato flour
    drained   1 small onion, grated
1 egg   1 teasp. salt
2 tablesp. matzo meal   ¼ teasp. cinnamon

Beat egg, and add potatoes and onions. Add seasoning, and blend in matzo meal and potato flour until you can shape into small balls. Drop into rapidly boiling salted water for about 15 minutes. They will rise to the top when done. These may be used as a garnish for split pea soup, chicken soup, bean soup, vegetable soup (if you omit the potatoes). They may even be used as a side dish for a meal containing meat or fowl. Serves 6 generously.

FARFEL

1½ cups flour   2 eggs, beaten
              ½ teasp. salt

Sift flour and salt. Place on board and make a well in flour. Drop in one egg at a time and work into the flour until dough is formed. Take a small piece of this stiff dough and roll between the hands until a long round strip has been formed. Do this until you have worked all of the dough into long, round strips. Let them dry. When dry enough, chop into small pieces the size of a small pea. After chopping, dry. Placing them in the oven for 10 minutes will help them to dry out.

To use in soup, bring soup to a rolling boil and put farfel in for from 10 to 15 minutes. If preferred, it can be boiled separately in water to which has been added a tablespoon of salt. When drained in a colander it can be used as a cereal with milk, a pat of butter, a pinch of salt and a teaspoon of sugar.

Store uncooked farfel in a tightly covered container and use as needed as a garnish.

MANDLEN (Passover)

3 egg yolks	*Dash of pepper*
3 egg whites, stiffly beaten	*Chicken fat or oil for deep*
¾ cup cake meal	*frying (use French fryer,*
3 tablesp. potato flour	*if possible)*
1 teasp. salt	

Beat egg yolks with cake meal. Add seasoning. Gradually add potato flour. Then fold in beaten egg whites, until completely blended. Heat fat in deep fryer. Drop batter in by the teaspoon, and fry until completely browned. Use slotted spoon to remove from pot and drain until fat has been removed. May be placed in a hot oven for crisping before using as a garnish in soup. Serves 8.

MANDLEN (Flour)

1 cup flour	*½ teasp. salt*
1 egg	*1 tablesp. polyunsaturated*
½ teasp. baking powder	*oil*

Place flour, salt and baking powder in sifter and sift into bowl. Beat egg and oil, blend into flour, kneading. Roll on board into approximately ¼-inch strips. Cut into ½ to ¾-inch pieces and place on greased baking sheet. Preheat oven to 375°F. and bake approximately 20 minutes, or until browned. Shake pan while in oven several times. Serve as soup garnish. Serves 4.

EGG MANDEL

1 egg
2 tablesp. water
½ teasp. salt

4 tablesp. flour
¼ teasp. baking powder

Beat egg. Add water and seasoning. Sift flour and baking powder. Add to egg mixture, blending completely. In a saucepan, bring salted water to a boil. Drop batter from teaspoon into boiling water. When the egg mandel rise to the top, they are done. Use slotted spoon to remove from pan. Use as soup garnish. Goes very well with chicken soup. Serves 4.

AYER KICHEL
(Jewish Egg Drops)

2 eggs
1 cup flour, sifted
½ teasp. baking powder
  (sifted with flour)

1 teasp. sugar
1 tablesp. polyunsaturated
  oil
¼ teasp. salt

Beat eggs. Add sifted flour and baking powder, sugar and salt. Knead on board. Form into small round balls. Brush with oil and place on greased cookie sheet. Bake in preheated oven set at 375°F. approximately ½ hour. When browned, remove from oven. Use as soup garnish. Serves 6.

BASIC RECIPE FOR CREAM SOUPS

Combine flour, butter and milk, the same as when making white sauce (thin or thick as you desire).

Add whatever vegetable you wish to feature.

BASIC RECIPE APPLIES TO:

Cream of Mushroom Soup
Cream of Pea Soup
Cream of Asparagus Soup
Cream of Celery Soup
Cream of Lima Bean Soup

Cream of Onion Soup
Cream of Carrot Soup
Cream of Corn Soup
  (Canned Cream of Corn)

CREAM OF CORN SOUP

1 large can corn (cream-style)	*½ teasp. salt*
	¼ teasp. pepper
1 onion, grated	*3½ cups milk*
2 tablesp. butter	*2 tablesp. flour*

1 teasp. sugar

Blend onion, butter and flour in skillet. Remove to larger pot, and add cream-style corn, milk and seasoning, stirring until the milk comes to a boil. Pour into soup tureen and add croutons, as a garnish. Serves 8.

CREAM OF TOMATO SOUP

This cream soup must be handled a little differently from the above group. When heating the purée of tomato, add a pinch of baking soda so that when the combined flour, butter and milk are added to the tomato mixture, the tomato will not curdle.

POTATO SOUP
(Or Kartoful Soup)

1 carrot, diced	*1 teasp. minced parsley*
2 cups diced raw potatoes	*1 tablesp. Cream of Wheat*
1 large onion, diced	*2 tablesp. butter or mar-*
2 cups water	*garine*
2 cups milk	
1 teasp. salt	Optional:
½ teasp. pepper	*1 teasp. caraway seeds*
¼ teasp. celery salt	

Brown onions in skillet with margarine or butter. Remove to large pot, and add potatoes, carrot, seasoning and water. After mixture comes to a boil, add Cream of Wheat, stirring constantly until completely blended into other ingredients. Add parsley and milk and bring to boiling point. Use a sprig of parsley as a garnish. Serves 6.

The Jewish Festival Holidays and Their Historical Background

FROM THE DAYS OF MOSES, THE FIRST IMPORTANT ADVENT IN the lives of all Jews was the Sabbath, or what is more familiarly known as "Shabos." This day, beginning at sundown on Friday and ending with the appearance of the first three stars on Saturday night, means for the Jew a ritual observance of his religion and abstinence from all labor.

Thus, traditionally at sundown on Friday, Mama would take the polished candelabra and place it on the table. Then, placing a shawl over her head, she would light and bless the Sabbath candles with the following prayer:

> Boruch atto a'donoi,
> E'lohenu melech ho'olom,
> A'sher kidde'shownu,
> Be'mitzvowsov, vetzivonu,
> Le'hadlik nayr shel Shabos.

Sabbath, being different from any other night in the week, calls for a lovely white tablecloth, the best china and silverware. Two challahs (loaves of bread) are placed near the head of the table. Many Jewish families have a special cover, handed down from previous generations, with which to cover the challahs. A decanter with wine and a Kiddish cup are also placed at the head of the table. And "why two challahs?" you ask. To those of you who are unaware of the reason for this, the following story is related so that you will know, and your children will know after you:

This story might be called "Manna from Heaven" for that is exactly what it was when the Israelites were fleeing from Egypt. Under the leadership of Moses, many hardships were suffered by these people, not the least of which was hunger. The people began to grumble with discontent until Aaron, Moses' spokesman, calmed the Israelites by telling them to look toward the wilderness. And behold, the glory of the Lord appeared in the cloud, and He informed Moses that He had heard the murmurings of the children of Israel; and He told Moses to tell them that every morning they would be filled with bread.

On the following morning when the Israelites awakened, lo—there in the fields was a fine scale-like thing, which they were told to gather, each taking only that portion which would take care of his needs for the day only. And each successive day there appeared in the morning this same "manna." Only on Friday were they told to take "two" portions, and they found that there was enough to provide for each and every one on the Sabbath.

This is the reason for the "two" challahs which are found on the Sabbath table.

Papa would take his place at the table, pour some wine in the Kiddish cup, and chant:

> Boruch atto a'donoi,
> E'lohenu melech ho'olom,
> Borei p'ri hagofen.

In this prayer, thanks are given to God for creating the grapes with which the wine has been made.

After the Kiddish, Papa washes his hands and takes a piece of challah, and still another prayer is said:

> Boruch atto a'donoi,
> E'lohenu melech ho'olom,
> Hamotzi lechem
> Min ho'oretz

This prayer gives thanks to the Lord who brings forth bread from the earth.

The traditional Sabbath dinner is as follows:

Gefilte Fish (garnished with horse-radish)
Soup with Matzo Knaidlach
Roast Chicken with Stuffing and Potato Kugel
Prunes and Apricots (compote)
Hot tea

After synagogue, the family comes home to a dinner of Tzimmes with Gedempte Flaish, as follows:

Pickled Herring Appetizer
Tzimmes, made with carrots,
    sweet potatoes, prunes,
    Gedempte flaish
Salad of tomatoes, radishes,
    cucumbers, onions and black olives
Golden brown Kishka, made with
    matzo meal stuffing
Fresh fruit cup
Hot tea in a glass (with a cube of sugar
    held in one's mouth)

ROSH HASHANA

This holiday, known by Jews in every country of the world as part of the "High Holidays," marks the ushering in of the New Year. It is with hope and optimism that the Jew welcomes this holiday. Though festive, it bears a certain solemnity which pervades each and every person endowed with the Jewish heritage.

Rosh Hashana marks the beginning of a new dawn, new hope. With this feeling in his heart, the Jew goes to synagogue or temple to give thanks to the Lord for the blessings of the past and to pray that the future may also be kind to him and his family.

It is traditional to feature something "sweet" on the holiday dinner table. Among these tidbits are: honey, taiglach (a cake-like confectionery concoction rolled in honey with citron and nuts), apple slices dipped in honey, and tzimmes (made with sweet potatoes, carrots, and sugar and spices added to bring out that sweet flavor). As one or more of these items were placed on the table *Bubeh* (Grandma) would say, "For a *zeesa* year," which means "for a sweet year."

A white tablecloth covers the table: the best china and silver are brought forth in deference to this holy of holidays. The table is set with the traditional sacramental wine, with a wine glass at each place setting. Papa takes his usual place at the head of the table, where there is a bread tray of challah. The festive table is laden with a roast turkey with stuffing, a steaming tzimmes with schmaltz knaidlach, taiglach, prune and apricot fruit compote, with the promise of some hot tea to complete a satisfying meal.

Typical Menu for Rosh Hashana *

Appetizer: Gefilte Fish garnished with Beet Horse-radish
Soup: Chicken Soup with Noodles or Farfel
Entree: Roast Turkey, Chicken or Capon (with Stuffing)
Vegetables: Carrot and Sweet Potato Tzimmes
Salad: Tossed Salad of Lettuce, Tomato, Cucumber, Radish
Side Dishes: Taiglach, Apple Slices and Honey, Honey Cake,
    Fruit Compote
Beverage: Tea, Hot or Iced

* The recipes for each of these festive dishes are contained in this book and may be located through the index. The recipe for Taiglach is to be found below.

TAIGLACH

2½ cups flour	1 cup sugar
3 eggs	½ cup honey
2 tablesp. oil	¼ cup almonds, slivered
1 teasp. baking powder	¼ cup mixed citron (in
1 teasp. ginger	small pieces)
½ teasp. cinnamon	

Combine and sift baking powder and flour. Make a well in flour and add eggs, ginger and cinnamon. Knead dough and roll into small balls about ¾ of an inch in circumference. Place sugar, honey and almonds into a saucepan and bring to a boil. Add the small balls of dough, and cook until brown and settled in liquid. Place on wet flour board and sprinkle with mixed citron. If a pyramid of taiglach is desired, use a double portion of honey. When taiglach are brown, place on plate in graduated layers until they come to a point. Then sprinkle citron over the entire cluster.

YOM KIPPUR

Yom Kippur is one of the High Holidays. It follows Rosh Hashana, falling on the tenth day of Tishri. This holiday is the most solemn of the year, since it is a day when Jews atone for their past sins and ask the Lord for forgiveness. Thus it is a day of fasting, which means that sundown of the evening before Yom Kippur must mark the beginning of repentance.

Unlike Rosh Hashana, the menu for Yom Kippur omits anything which is highly seasoned or salted. Because of the 24-hour fasting period, during which no food or water may pass the lips, it is unwise to have food on the menu which would tend to make one thirsty.

The entirety of this High Holiday is spent in the synagogue or temple, and its end is heralded by the symbolic "blowing of the Shofar" or ram's horn, signifying that everyone may depart from the house of worship and partake of food.

Typical Menu for Erev-Yom Kippur
(Food served at sundown at the beginning of the holiday)

Appetizer: Fresh Fruit Cup or Honeydew Melon
Soup: Schav (served with sprig of parsley)
Entree: Brisket of Beef (with very little seasoning)
Vegetables: Potato Kugel and Peas
Salad: Orange Gelatin Mold with carrots
Beverage: Hot Tea and Kichel and a pitcher of ice water

After the "blowing of the Shofar," everyone looks forward
to his first glass of water with fervor, and often with impa-
tience. Mama has the traditional table setting for the holiday
on hand, with the challah and the wine for the "broka."
Everyone sits down at the table, thankful that he has had the
strength to last through the trying fast day and looking forward to partaking of Mama's good, wholesome food.

Mama is not unmindful of the fact that if she has a heavy
dinner for her family after a day of fasting, the body might
not be in the proper condition to handle it.

Typical Menu for Yom Kippur Evening

Appetizer: Melon Balls (Honeydew, Cantaloupe, and Apple
   slices)
Soup: Beet Borscht (cold) with Sour Cream
Entree: Fried or Broiled Lake Superior Whitefish
Vegetables: Mixed Carrots, Turnips, and Peas, Mashed
   Potatoes
Salad: Lettuce Leaf with canned peaches
Dessert: Old-Fashioned Apple Pie with Raisins
Beverage: Coffee or Tea

SUKKOTH

This joyful holiday marks the gathering of the harvest. It
is a favorite with children because many Jewish families who
own their own home and have the facilities allow their chil-

dren to help in the building of a "Sukka," which is an out-side hut with a roof decorated with fruit and vegetables usually gathered at harvest time, such as apples, grapes, pears, corn, squash, pumpkin, etc. Synagogues and temples also build "Sukkas" where children and parents alike celebrate the joyful occasion and eat their dinner. The holiday lasts one whole week, beginning on the 15th day of Tishri.

The foods generally popular for this holiday are those containing fruits and vegetables which would normally be gathered in the harvest. Among the favorites on this holiday are:

Strudels: (containing apples, nuts, citron, raisins)
Stuffed Cabbage: traditionally known as Holeskes (See recipe for Stuffed Cabbage on Page 46)

STRUDEL (Mixed Fruit)

3 cups flour	*¼ teasp. salt*
2 tablesp. sugar	*2 tablesp. oil (and 2 tablesp.*
1 egg	*oil to brush on stretched*
¾ cup ice water	*dough)*
	1 teasp. baking powder

FILLING

1 cup toasted, grated bread crumbs	*½ cup sugar*
	1 teasp. cinnamon
1 cup chopped nuts	*½ cup mixed citron (in*
1 orange rind, grated	*small pieces)*
1 lemon rind, grated	*¼ cup citron cherries*
2 tablesp. lemon juice	*(cut up)*
	¼ cup seedless raisins

Combine sifted flour, baking powder and sugar in a large bowl. Add salt. Make a well and drop egg in center; then add oil. Add ice water gradually until dough is manageable.

Work dough and knead until it is elastic. Roll out to thin
sheaf and brush with oil. Sprinkle the bread crumbs over half
the sheaf. Mix the filling together with the exception of the
sugar and cinnamon. Spread the filling over the half sheaf
with the bread crumbs, and sprinkle with sugar and cinnamon. Roll up, and brush with oil. Place on cookie sheet, in
moderate oven of 350°F. Bake for 50 minutes. When brown,
remove, and cut in desired lengths while hot. Makes about
3 dozen strudels.

CHANUKAH
(The Festival of Lights)

Truth is sometimes stranger than fiction. In the instance
of Chanukah and its history, it seems more like a fascinating
tale out of Arabian Nights.... But the legend has withstood
the test of time, and the miracle of the burning golden candelabra in the recaptured Temple, with its one-day supply of
oil which lasted for eight days, shall ever burn in the hearts of
generation after generation of Jews.

Chanukah brings with it joy unconfined. Coming as it does
at a time when not only Jews but Christians as well are
celebrating a holiday, the modern Jew has made a holiday of
Chanukah which is most popular with the children.

The Menorah with its eight candleholders and one
"Shamus" is brought forth, polished and set in the window
for all to gaze upon, and each night of the eight days of
Chanukah, another candle is lit until the final night, when
all eight candles are aflame. Traditionally, each night of
Chanukah when the candle or candles are lit, presents are
dispersed among the family, to celebrate the dedication of
the recaptured Temple and the right of all Jews to worship
God in their Temple.

Chanukah celebrates the 25th day of Kislev, 165 B.C.,
when the brave Maccabees, led by Judah Maccabee, over-
threw the yoke of Antiochus Epiphanes, the Greek king who

tried to force upon the Jews the religion of the Greeks. This is perhaps the only holiday celebrated by the Jews which was inspired by military rather than spiritual strength, but without this military might, the Jews might have been completely obliterated.

Since it is a most festive holiday, it brings with it a menu of potato latkes and potato kugel, and songs reminiscent of soldiers and swords and conquering heroes. Also there are the "dreidls" which are very similar to a top, and are spun in a game played by the children to determine who might get the most choice tidbits of sweets offered on this festive occasion.

CHANUKAH POTATO LATKES

6 large potatoes	½ teasp. cinnamon
1 large apple	1 teasp. salt
2 tablesp. flour	Oil for frying
3 eggs	1 onion, grated

Grate potatoes, apple and onion. Break in eggs, and beat into mixture. Add seasoning and flour. Shape into oval pancakes. Place oil in skillet. When hot, drop latkes one at a time in hot oil. When brown on one side, turn over. When crisp and brown on the other side, remove from skillet to platter. Serve with raspberry applesauce or sprinkled sugar.

POTATO KUGEL

2 cups potatoes, grated and drained	1 teasp. salt
	Dash of pepper
2 eggs	3 tablesp. melted margarine
1 onion, grated	or chicken fat
3 tablesp. potato flour	½ teasp. baking powder

Beat eggs well. Gradually add grated potatoes, potato flour, onion, salt, pepper, baking powder and melted margarine or chicken fat. Place in well-greased casserole, and bake in uncovered casserole in moderate oven at 350°F. for about 1 hour. Excellent garnish: applesauce. Serves 6.

PURIM

How often have you watched children perform in the pageantry of the days of Esther, Mordecai and Haman? One in the costume of Queen Esther, the regal, beautiful queen of a non-Jewish King; another in the costume of the hangman, and yet another who, in the tri-cornered hat and garb of Haman, the wicked man who tried to undermine the favor of the Jews in the eyes of the King, receives "boos" from everyone. Finally . . . the triumphant victory for the Jews and their beloved Queen Esther. The Feast of Esther, known as "Purim," occurs on the 14th day of Adar.

Rejoicing can best describe this holiday. With it comes the delectable "hamantaschen," which are a pastry delicacy, filled with a poppy seed combination that is truly delightful. Usually these "hamantaschen" are shaped like tri-cornered hats, such as the ones Haman wore:

DOUGH FOR HAMANTASCHEN

2 cups flour (sifted)	*½ cup melted margarine or*
1½ teasp. baking powder	*butter*
½ teasp. salt	*½ cup sugar*
2 eggs	*1 lemon rind, grated*

1 lemon, juice only

Beat eggs and shortening; add sugar and lemon rind and juice. Combine flour (sifted with baking powder) and salt, and work until a dough is formed. Place on board, and roll until ¼-inch thick. Either use biscuit cutter or a glass to make round pieces of dough. Place the following poppy seed filling in each round piece of dough, turning up edges to form tri-corners. Pinch edges together, and brush with melted shortening and egg yolk mixed with cold water. Bake at 375°F, for 30 to 40 minutes.

POPPY SEED FILLING

1 cup poppy seed	*1 tablesp. lemon juice*
½ cup honey	*1 tablesp. fine cake crumbs*
1 egg	*¼ cup chopped walnuts*

Mix ingredients well and place one heaping tablespoon of filling in each round of dough, to complete Hamantaschen as explained above.

The Passover Festival Holiday

THE OBSERVANCE OF THE PASSOVER BEGINS ON THE 14TH DAY of Nisan and continues to sundown of the 22nd day of Nisan. The name of the holiday is derived from the Biblical account of the "passing over" of the homes of the Jews when the first-born sons of the Egyptian homes were being taken by the Angel of Death. Passover marks the flight of the Jewish people from bondage in Egypt after the death of Joseph.

When Joseph was second in command to the ruling Hyksos (Shepherd) king, the Kingdom was very favorable to the Jews. The Hyksos kings belonged to an Asiatic dynasty whose rule in Egypt commenced centuries before Joseph. It is believed by historians as well as theologians that the dynasty following the rule of the Hyksos kings was that of Rameses, and that Rameses II ruled at the time of the Israelites' flight from Egypt.

This particular dynasty was a cruel and ruthless one (which is the reason for reference to the rulers of that era as "the cruel Pharaohs"). The only hope of the Jews under Rameses II lay in following their leader, Moses, into the desert in an effort to reach Israel, the Promised Land.

At the outset of their flight, they dared not risk apprehension by the Egyptian soldiers. They could spend no time preparing food. They therefore rolled a thin unleavened pancake-style sheath, placed this on flat boards, and continued their flight. The hot sun baked it into what is known today as "matzos," the substitute for bread which has since then been used for the eight-day holiday known as "Passover" or "Pesach."

Hardships were plentiful during the forty-year period of flight. Weary and discouraged, the first generation of wanderers communicated their discontent to Moses, who, in turn, asked the Lord to help him restore the faith of the Israelites. The Lord did not fail the Israelites or Moses, and dropped "manna" from Heaven so that they would have food in those disconsolate days. This miracle from Heaven carried them through a trying period, and gave them faith and courage with which to carry on their flight. At the end of forty years, after many trials and tribulations, Moses guided the strongest of the ensuing generation into Israel, the Promised Land, though Moses himself did not enter Israel. Thus, the prophecy set forth in the Bible held true:

"And I will bring back the captivity of my people of Israel, and they shall build the waste cities, and inhabit them; and they shall plant vineyards, and drink the wine thereof; they shall also make gardens, and eat the fruit of them. (15) And I will plant them upon their land, and they shall no more be pulled up out of their land which I have given them, saith the Lord thy God."

—Amos, 9-14

HOW TO PREPARE FOR THE PASSOVER

The house must be prepared in compliance with tradition, for the Passover. A complete cleaning must be undergone, with every crack and crevice being inspected.

DISHES

All dishes which have been used throughout the year must be taken from the shelves in cabinet or pantry, and removed from the house for the duration of the Passover holiday. All pots and pans must be replaced with pots and pans reserved for this special holiday.

EXCEPTION:

Silverware may be made usable for the Passover by tying it with string, and dropping it into boiling water.

TABLECLOTHS

Special Passover tablecloths and napkins should be used to replace those on which bread has been served.

SHOPPING

All foods purchased for Passover use must bear a special seal or be marked "Kosher for Passover." Stores stock supplies such as matzos, matzo meal, potato flour, matzo cake meal, and other canned goods or food in glass jars, especially prepared for the Passover. Dairies enjoying a Jewish clientele do their "spring cleaning" in honor of Passover, and so mark their milk, cream, butter, and other dairy products "Kosher for Passover."

RITUAL OF RIDDING
THE HOUSE OF "KOMETZ"

In addition to the actual cleaning of the home in preparation for Passover, there is a ritual performed which represents a symbolic cleansing. Pieces of bread are placed in every room of the house so that on the evening preceding the 14th day of Nisan, when Papa comes home, he may search for the bread and gather it together on a large wooden spoon with a feather. The bread, spoon, and feather are carefully wrapped and then burned on the following morning before noon, so that when the Passover is ushered in, everything in the house is "Pesakdek." Should Passover, the 14th day of Nisan, fall on a Saturday, this traditional search is made on the 13th, and the bread is burned before noon on Friday.

THE SEDER

The first two nights of Passover are usually spent in family gatherings known as the "Seder" at which a service, which is essentially the story of the Exodus retold with food, ritual and song, is performed by the father. Many families spend Seder night at a Temple or at a kosher dining room in a hotel where group services are conducted by a rabbi and cantor.

The word "Seder" means "order" and refers to the traditional order of the Passover ritual. The tablecloth, as on other holidays, should be white, and is accompanied by your best china and silver. Each place is set with a wine goblet, for on Seder nights, everyone is obliged to drink wine at intervals proscribed in the service.

A large, round, decorative plate—the traditional seder platter—is placed at the head of the table. On it are hard-boiled eggs, charoses (a mixture of apples, nuts and honey), radishes, bitter herbs, shank bone (of lamb), a dish of salt water and some parsley to be dipped into the water, and the Kiddish cup or goblet. All of these items have a symbolic meaning which is explained as the service proceeds. Through the eating of these foods, the Jews recall and pay tribute to the memory of that historic occasion.

Encompassed in the services are the "Feer Kashas" or the four questions concerning the reasons for the various traditions, such as the eating of matzos. These questions are usually asked in Hebrew and in English by the youngest male child present, and answered by the father or rabbi. Another ritual centering around the children is the hiding of the matzos or "affakamon." The child who finds the hidden matzos is rewarded with a gift or money.

Many variations of traditional foods have found their way to the modern table. All are made from matzo meal and other substitutes for foods which cannot be eaten during this holiday. The following recipes are all appropriate for Passover.

MATZO MEAL PANCAKES

4 egg yolks	*½ teasp. salt*
4 egg whites, stiffly beaten	*1 tablesp. melted butter or*
1 cup matzo meal	*margarine*
¾ cup ice water	*Fat or oil for deep frying*

Beat the egg yolks, adding water and salt. Melt butter or margarine, allow to cool, and add to mixture. Beat egg whites, add the matzo meal to the egg yolk mixture, and carefully fold in egg whites so that mixture remains light and fluffy. Heat the fat or oil in a large skillet, and when hot, drop in batter with a tablespoon. If you plan to serve with meat, omit butter and use pareve margarine. Serve with strawberry preserves, stewed strawberries, or plain or raspberry applesauce. Serves 4 to 6.

MATZO MEAL SPONGE CAKE

9 egg yolks	*½ lemon or Persian lime,*
9 egg whites (stiffly beaten,	*juice only*
but not dry)	*1½ cups sugar*
1 lemon or Persian lime rind,	*1 cup matzo cake meal*
grated	*(sifted) with pinch of salt*
1 tablesp. potato flour	

Beat egg yolks well and add sugar, continuing to beat mixture. Add the matzo cake meal, potato flour, grated rind of lemon or lime, and juice. Fold in egg whites very thoroughly and carefully so that the cake will be light. Place in tube pan in a preheated oven at 350°F. for 45 to 50 minutes. When removing from oven, place tube over neck of bottle until the cake cools, then remove from pan onto cake plate. Sprinkle powdered sugar over the top of the sponge cake.

PESACH APPLE PUDDING

6 apples, peeled and grated   ¾ cup sugar
3 egg yolks   ¾ teasp. cinnamon
3 egg whites   ¼ cup seedless raisins
1 cup matzo meal   ¼ teasp. salt

Place grated apples and raisins in large bowl. Add beaten egg yolks, matzo meal, sugar, cinnamon and salt, and blend. Beat egg whites until stiff, and fold into mixture. Bake in greased casserole (without cover) in 350°F. oven for 30 minutes. Serves 6.

MATZO BRIE (Fried Matzos and Eggs)

4 eggs   4 matzos
1 teasp. grated onion or   ½ teasp. salt
  1 onion, diced or sliced   ¼ teasp. pepper
  (if onion is desired)   Fat for frying

Beat eggs, mix in grated onion (if used) and seasoning. If diced or sliced onion is desired, do not mix this into eggs but heat fat in skillet, and place diced or sliced onions in hot fat. Place matzos in bowl of cold water. Squeeze and drain. Crumble into egg mixture, and when fat is hot in skillet, turn this mixture into pan. Brown first on one side, then turn on the other side. Added garnish: strawberry jam. Serves 4.

PESAKDEK OVEN ROLLS
(Passover Oven Rolls)

1 cup matzo meal   3 egg whites
¼ cup cake meal   ½ cup milk
3 egg yolks   2 tablesp. melted butter

Beat egg yolks. Cool melted butter and add to mixture. Alternately add mixture of matzo meal and cake meal with

milk into the egg yolk mixture. Beat egg whites until stiff.
Fold into mixture. Grease 12 roll muffin tin. Fill, leaving
½ inch from top of each muffin mold. Bake in preheated
moderate oven of 360°F. for 35 to 40 minutes, or until brown.
Remove and cool. Delightful variation during Passover. Serve
with dairy foods. Serves 6.

FRIED MATZOS

3 matzos   ¼ teasp. salt
3 eggs, beaten   Fat for frying

Dampen matzos by letting cold water from the tap run
over them. Take mixture of beaten eggs and salt, and drip
matzos into it. Heat fat in skillet, and drop matzos into skillet.
Brown on both sides. Serves 3 to 4.

PESAKDEK CHEESE BLINTZES
(Passover Cheese Blintzes)

4 eggs   ¼ teasp. salt
1 cup matzo meal cake flour   Butter for frying
              1 ¾ cups cold water

Cheese Filling

2 cups dry cottage cheese   1 teasp. sugar
2 eggs   ¼ teasp. cinnamon

Beat eggs and add cake flour and water alternately, adding
salt. This should make a thin batter. Use a round skillet,
about 8-to-9 inches in circumference, grease lightly and heat.
Drop in about 3 tablespoons batter, allowing it to cover bottom of pan by tilting on all sides. Brown well on the one side.
Turn skillet over a tea towel and drop batter, browned side
up, on tea towel or foil.
    Mix cheese filling. Spread 2 tablespoons of filling in center

of batter. Tuck ends in, and start rolling until you have a square-shaped blintze.

Place butter in large skillet. Heat, and when hot, drop blintzes into butter, browning on both sides. Serve with sour cream. Serves 4.

PESAKDEK EGG NOODLES
(Passover Egg Noodles)

3 eggs	1 tablesp. matzo cake flour
3 tablesp. cold water	¼ teasp. salt
(ice water preferred)	Dash of pepper

Beat eggs, and add cake flour, salt and pepper. Add water to make a thin batter. When smooth, grease a 9-inch skillet, and pour 3 tablespoons of batter into pan, tilting until the batter covers the bottom of the pan. Place over moderate heat on stove, and when browned, turn over on either a tea towel or foil. When cool, roll up pancake. Heat oven and when all pancakes are rolled up, place on cookie sheet in oven for 2 minutes, or until dry. Cut into strips, thin or thick, and store in glass jar until ready for use in soups when noodles are desired.

PESAKDEK PUFFS
(Passover Puffs)

1 cup water	½ teasp. salt
⅓ cup butter	1½ tablesp. sugar
1¼ cups matzo meal	3 eggs

Place water, butter and seasoning in saucepan. Bring to a boil. Slowly stir in the matzo meal and sugar until the mixture forms a ball in saucepan. Remove from flame, and let cool. Add eggs, one at a time, beating vigorously until mixture is smooth and shiny. Grease cookie sheet, and drop by tablespoon onto cookie sheet. Preheat oven to 350°F. Bake from

35 to 45 minutes. They will turn brown quickly but be certain to allow them to remain in oven for at least 35 to 40 minutes, to insure their being done. Should make 12 puffs. Fill with lemon filling below.

LEMON FILLING FOR PUFFS

1 lemon, juice only	*1½ tablesp. potato flour*
1 lemon rind, grated	*(with a little water to*
¼ cup sugar	*moisten)*
¾ cup water	*2 egg whites (beat until stiff,*
2 egg yolks	*use pinch of salt)*

¼ cup sugar

Using double boiler, bring lemon juice, grated lemon rind, ¼ cup sugar and ¾ cup water to boil. Cream egg yolks with ¼ cup sugar, and when mixture comes to boil, stir in this egg mixture. Blend in potato flour, and stir until complete mixture is smooth and thick. Remove from heat and cool. Beat egg whites until stiff, and fold into the above combination after it has cooled. Use as filling for puffs.

MATZO CHARLOTTE

4 matzos	*1 lemon rind, grated*
5 eggs, separated	*¼ cup almonds, chopped*
1 large apple, grated	*¼ cup seedless raisins*
1 lemon, juice only	*¼ teasp. cinnamon*

Soak matzos in water. Squeeze dry. Beat yolk of eggs, and mix with matzos. Add rest of ingredients, except egg whites. Beat egg whites until stiff. Fold into mixture carefully. Grease casserole, and preheat oven to 350°F. Bake for 30 to 35 minutes. Remove from oven. Place pieces of glazed fruit on top with almonds as a garnish. Serves 6.

MATZO KNAIDLACH (Matzo Dumplings)

2 egg yolks   ½ cup matzo meal
2 egg whites, beaten   ½ teasp. salt

Beat egg yolks, adding salt. Blend matzo meal into mixture.
Place in refrigerator and chill. When ready to cook, beat egg
whites until stiff but not dry. Fold into mixture carefully.
Form into balls, and drop into boiling salted water. Cook for
about 20 minutes, or until balls rise to the top. Remove from
pan. Use in soup, or brown in oven with meat dishes.

MATZO KNAIDLACH
(Matzo Dumplings with Fat)

2 eggs   ¼ cup water
2 tablesp. chicken fat   ⅔ cup matzo meal
     ½ teasp. salt

Beat eggs and chicken fat vigorously. Add seasoning, water
and blend in matzo meal. It should form a thick batter. More
matzo meal may be added if desired. Chill in refrigerator for
one hour. Shape into balls, and drop into boiling salted water.
Cook for 30 to 35 minutes in a covered saucepan. Remove
from water, and store to serve in soups.

PASSOVER CHOCOLATE SPONGE CAKE

8 egg yolks   ¼ cup chopped walnuts
8 egg whites   (optional)
½ cup matzo cake meal   1 lemon, juice only
¼ cup cocoa (pareve for   1 lemon rind, grated
     Passover)   1 cup sugar
     1 tablesp. potato flour

Beat yolks well. Add grated lemon rind, cake meal and
sifted flour, alternately with lemon juice and cocoa. Add nuts.

Beat egg whites until stiff. Fold into mixture carefully. Place in ungreased tube pan, and bake in moderate oven (350°F) for 45 minutes, or until brown. Remove from oven, and place tube over bottle neck until cool. Remove cake from pan. May be decorated with fruit citron and almonds.

PASSOVER CHREMZLACH
(Fruit and Nut Filled Pancakes)

2 cups matzo meal	*2 tablesp. butter or chicken*
2 egg yolks	*fat*
2 egg whites (beaten until	*1 lemon, juice only*
stiff)	*1 lemon rind, grated*
¼ teasp. salt	*½ cup sugar*
2½ tablesp. hot water	*Fat for frying*

FILLING

1 cup strawberry or cherry	*¼ cup chopped nuts*
preserves	*2 tablesp. matzo meal*

Using large mixing bowl, combine chicken fat or butter, lemon juice and rind. Slowly stir the matzo meal and water into this mixture, making a stiff batter that is smooth. Beat egg yolks and cream with sugar, adding to the mixture. Beat egg whites until stiff, adding salt. When batter is cool enough, fold in egg whites. If batter needs a little more moisture, add a little more water. Allow batter to stand for about 20 to 25 minutes.

In the meantime, mix filling ingredients. Form balls of the batter, making an indenture in the center, into which one tablespoon of filling is placed, and covered. Flatten ball into oval pancake. Heat fat in skillet, and fry until brown first on one side and then on the other. Garnish with sugar and cinnamon, or honey. Yields 7 to 8 pancakes.

PASSOVER APPLE KUGEL

3 apples, grated
1 lemon, juice only
1 lemon rind, grated
3 matzos, soaked and
   squeezed dry
¾ cup matzo meal
3 egg whites (beaten until
   stiff)

3 egg yolks
¼ teasp. cinnamon
¼ cup fat
¼ cup seedless raisins
   (optional)
¼ cup chopped walnuts
   (optional)
Pinch of salt

Beat egg yolks, and add crumbled pieces of matzos. Add lemon juice, rind, salt, apple and cinnamon. Then add matzo meal. Beat egg whites until stiff. Preheat oven to 375°F. Fold in egg whites, and place in greased casserole. Pour fat over top, and bake in uncovered dish for 35 to 40 minutes. Raisins may be added, as well as chopped walnuts, if desired. Serves 4.

ALMOND FLAVORED
COCONUT MACAROONS

1 lb. almond paste (You may
make your own by blanch-
ing almonds, and grinding
into paste)

1 lb. sugar
Whites of 8 eggs
½ cup cocoanut, chopped
fine

Cream almond paste and sugar. Gradually add unbeaten egg whites to this mixture, and work into mixture until it is smooth. When it is stiff enough to hold its shape, add shredded cocoanut, and place wax paper or foil on cookie sheet. Preheat oven to 325°F. Drop from spoon at least 1 inch apart. Bake 20 to 25 minutes. Remove from oven, and cool. Remove from cookie sheet and store. Yields about 24 macaroons.

CHOCOLATE, ALMOND FLAVORED MACAROONS

¾ cup sugar
3 oz. grated baking chocolate (pareve)

3 oz. blanched, ground
  almonds
Whites of 3 eggs

Mix almonds into a paste with sugar and chocolate. Fold in stiffly beaten egg whites. Place wax paper or foil on cookie sheet. Drop by teaspoon about 1 inch apart and bake in preheated oven at 325°F. for 30 minutes. Yields about 16 macaroons.

MANDELCHEN

1½ cups almonds (blanched
  and dried overnight, grated
  and then ground)

Up to 2 tablesp. butter
  (enough to knead paste)
½ cup sugar

To the almond mixture, ground fine, add butter and sugar, and knead into a stiff paste. Roll thin and cut into different shapes for cookies. Place on cookie sheet and bake in preheated oven at 350°F. for ½ hour. Remove from oven, and roll in chopped nuts and sugar.

PESACH BANANA NUT CAKE
(Passover Banana Nut Cake)

8 egg yolks
8 egg whites (beaten until
  stiff)
1 cup sugar
½ cup bananas, mashed

½ cup walnuts, chopped fine
⅔ cup matzo meal cake
  flour (sifted)
⅓ cup potato flour
Dash of salt

Cream egg yolks and sugar until creamy. Sift flour into mixture, and add bananas. Blend in nuts, folding in egg whites last. Grease tube pan and bake in moderate oven of 350°F. for 35 to 40 minutes, or until brown. Place tube on neck of bottle to cool cake. Garnish cake with citron pieces.

COTTAGE CHEESE KNAIDLACH

4 egg yolks
4 egg whites (beaten until stiff)
4 tablesp. melted butter
4 tablesp. milk
½ teasp. salt
1¼ cups cottage cheese
1 tablesp. sugar
¼ teasp. cinnamon
1 cup matzo meal

Beat egg yolks, adding melted butter, milk and salt. Beat egg whites until stiff. Add matzo meal to egg yolk mixture. Combine in a separate bowl cottage cheese, sugar and cinnamon. Fold egg whites into egg yolk and matzo meal mixture. Form into matzo balls, making a dent in the center. Drop about 1 teaspoon cottage cheese mixture into dent, and cover over, so that none will come out in boiling. Heat salted water in saucepan. When it is boiling briskly, drop matzo balls into water. When they rise to top, use slotted spoon to remove to platter. May be served hot. Garnish with either sour cream or applesauce. Yield: 15 to 18.

PESAKDEK CITRINE
(Passover Lemon Pie)

1 cup matzo meal cake flour
⅓ cup margarine
1 tablesp. sugar
¼ teasp. salt
1 tablesp. cold water
1 tablesp. potato flour

Combine all the ingredients. Roll on board, and make into one pie crust. Place in either glass pie plate or regular aluminum one. Flute edges. Bake in moderate oven of 375°F. for 15 minutes, or until brown.

LEMON PIE FILLING

Juice of 1 large lemon or
2 small lemons
1 lemon rind, grated
½ cup sugar
1¼ cups water
4 egg yolks

4 egg whites (beaten until
stiff)
2½ tablesp. potato flour
(moistened with a little
water)
½ cup sugar

Using double boiler, combine lemon juice, rind, sugar and water. Bring to a boil. Cream egg yolks and ¼ cup sugar, and add to mixture. Blend in potato flour, and stir until entire mixture is smooth. Remove from stove and cool. When cool enough, pour into pie crust. Beat egg whites and add remaining sugar, beating until it forms into peaks. Top lemon filling with this, and place under broiler until brown.

MATZO AYER KICHEL
(Egg Cookies)

6 egg yolks
6 egg whites (beaten until
stiff)

⅓ cup matzo meal
¾ cup cold water
½ teasp. salt

Soak matzo meal in water. Beat egg yolks and add to mixture. Season with salt, and let stand about 10 minutes, or until egg whites are beaten. Fold egg whites into mixture. Grease cookie sheet or griddle and when hot, drop by spoonfuls, browning first on one side and then on the other. Sprinkle with sugar. Serve with preserves. Yield: 12 to 14.

BAKED MATZOS

6 matzos
4 eggs, beaten well

Mixture of cinnamon, ground
nutmeg, ginger and sugar

Beat egg yolks and add a pinch of salt. Dip matzo into mixture, and sprinkle with spice and sugar mixture. Bake in moderate oven (325°F. to 350°F.) for 15 minutes or until crisp. Makes an excellent companion to coffee or tea for a snack. Serves 6 generously.

MATZOS (Fried Like French Toast)

6 matzos (broken in quar-
  ters)
3 eggs (beaten well)

¼ cup milk
½ teasp. cinnamon
1 tablesp. sugar

Beat eggs well, adding milk, cinnamon and sugar. Dip matzos into mixture. Heat butter, margarine or oil in skillet and when hot, drop in each matzo. Brown first on one side, then on the other. Serve hot, with honey and preserves or sprinkled with sugar. Serves 3.

KARTOFUL KNAIDLACH
(Potato Dumplings)

6 medium-sized potatoes
  (pared and grated)
⅓ cup chicken fat or pareve
  margarine

4 eggs
¾ cup cold water
2 cups matzo meal
1 teasp. salt

Combine ingredients, mixing thoroughly. Allow to stand for about ½ hour. Form into balls. Drop either into boiling salted water, cooking about 1 hour, or into boiling soup.

MOCK OATMEAL COOKIES

1 cup matzo meal
1 cup matzo farfel
2 eggs
½ cup oil (polyunsaturated-
  vegetable oil)

1 cup sugar
½ cup raisins
½ cup chopped walnuts
½ teasp. cinnamon
½ teasp. salt

Beat eggs. Combine all dry ingredients, and add eggs and oil. Mix well. Grease cookie sheet. Drop by teaspoonfuls on

cookie sheet. Bake in 350°F. oven for 30 to 35 minutes. Yields
about two dozen cookies.

PASSOVER MUFFINS
(Potato Muffins)

5 eggs, separated   *3 tablesp. ice water*
1 cup potato flour   *1 lemon rind, grated*
3 tablesp. sugar   *Dash of salt*

Cream egg yolks and sugar and combine with ice water
and lemon rind. Gradually sift potato flour into mixture. Beat
egg whites until stiff, adding a pinch of salt. Fold into batter
gently. Half fill muffin tin. Preheat oven to 350°F. Bake in
oven for 30 minutes or until brown. May be served with meat
or fowl dishes. Yields about 12 potato muffins.

MED OR MEAD

This amber liquid used to be a tradition during Passover.
In the past two decades, it has gradually disappeared so that
the present generation is almost completely unaware of its
existence. To revive this tradition, the following recipe is
included, in the hope that it will again find its place among
the favorites of the Hebrew people during Passover.

First, you must purchase a small wooden keg or barrel, with
a spigot, and at least one yard of cheesecloth.

½ oz. hops   Optional:
½ gallon honey (pure   *½ cup caramelized sugar to*
honey)   *be added to med (after fer-*
2 gallons water   *mentation) to darken the*
1 lemon, sliced thin   *color*

Combine water and honey in a large pot, adding lemon
and hops (tie hops in a piece of cheesecloth). Stir frequently
and bring to a boil. Reduce heat to low, and cook for at least
½ hour. Skim frequently. Remove from heat. Let cool. When
cool enough, strain through cheesecloth. If possible, strain

directly into the wooden keg or barrel, being very careful to leave at least one quarter of the keg or barrel empty, to allow for fermentation. Store in a cool, dark place for at least 3 weeks. The liquid may then be removed from the keg into bottles, or left in the keg, as you wish. Remember: if a darker color is desired, caramelized sugar may be added to the med *AFTER FERMENTATION.*

GRAPE WINE (Concord)
(Sacramental Wine)

At the turn of the twentieth century, the "bubeh" or grandmother was still preparing for the holidays as her mother and her mother's mother used to do. One of the most important steps when one moved into one's own home was to immediately plant a grape arbor, so that the wine for the Kiddish cup could be made from these grapes. This, too, is a lost art since wines adequate for use in the traditional ceremonies during the Passover and other festival holidays may be purchased.

20 lbs. of dark blue Concord grapes (washed and stemmed)

For each cup of mashed grapes add 1 cup sugar

Keep in a large, covered jar in a warm storage place for at least 2 weeks. Put through a strainer, and bring strained fluid to a boil. Purchase and sterilize at least 6 quart-sized bottles. Pour wine into bottles and seal. Store in cool place. Yields about 2 gallons.

PASSOVER BEET PRESERVES

1½ lbs. beets
1½ lbs. sugar
1 teasp. ginger

½ cup chopped blanched almonds
½ cup water
1 lemon, sliced thin

Boil whole beets until tender. Drain, cool and peel. Slice into thin strips. Bring sugar and water to a boil. Add beets, and cook for at least 1 hour. Add lemon slices and cook over low heat for another hour, or until beets are jellied. Add nuts and ginger, and continue cooking for at least another 20 minutes. Cool. Store in covered earthen jar to preserve color.

PASSOVER NUT CAKE

1 cup matzo meal cake flour	*2 cups sugar (mix 1 cup*
½ cup potato flour	*with egg yolks and 1 cup*
¼ teasp. cinnamon	*with egg whites)*
10 egg yolks	*¼ cup sacramental grape*
10 egg whites	*wine*
¾ cup ground walnuts	

Sift cake flour and potato flour. Beat egg yolks and cream with 1 cup sugar. Add cinnamon and ground nuts to this mixture. Add flour alternately with wine into egg yolk mixture. Beat whites, adding a pinch of salt and 1 cup of sugar gradually, until it forms stiff peaks. Fold into mixture. Grease a tube pan and pour mixture into pan. Bake in moderate oven of 375°F. for 1 hour. Invert pan and cool. Place on cake platter. Sprinkle with powdered sugar.

PIE CRUST (Matzo)

3 matzos	*½ teasp. salt*
1¼ cups matzo meal	*2 eggs*
1 lemon rind, grated	*Yolk of one hard-cooked egg,*
1 cup sugar	*mashed*
¼ teasp. cinnamon	*½ cup shortening*
¼ teasp. nutmeg	

Soak matzos for about 15 minutes, and squeeze dry. Cream shortening with matzos and stir. Add hard-cooked egg yolk, sugar, seasoning and eggs, well beaten. When everything is thoroughly blended, add matzo meal. Place in oven of 400°F. and bake for about 15 minutes. (Save part of batter for top crust.) Prepare filling as follows:

APPLE FILLING

8 apples (pared and cored, and cut into sections)	*1 cup sugar*
¾ teasp. cinnamon	*(Dot with butter when placed in pie crust)*
½ teasp. nutmeg	*1 teasp. lemon juice*

Cook apples with seasoning, saving ¼ teaspoon cinnamon, ¼ cup sugar, butter and lemon juice until placed in pie crust. Cook until tender, but not crumbly. Remove from heat and cool. Place mixture into matzo pie crust, sprinkling with sugar, cinnamon, butter and lemon juice. Drop spoonfuls of batter on top of apples before baking. Bake in hot oven of 400°F. for 20 to 25 minutes, or until crust is completely brown.

SHAVUOTH
(Feast of Weeks—Torah Festival)

This most important holiday, commemorating the giving of the Torah by God to Moses on the Mount, and also joyously proclaiming the fruits of the harvest, falls on the sixth day of Sivan, exactly seven weeks after the second day of Passover.

It was traditional for every farmer, rich or poor, to place the first ripe fruit into baskets—gold, silver or wicker—and bring it into the Temple as a "hag habikkurim," as it is known in Hebrew, or offering to the Lord, thanking Him for His bounty.

On the eve of Shavuoth, it is customary to go to Synagogue or Temple, after the traditional festival candles have been lit in the home.

Among the customs followed on this holiday are:

The reading of the story of Ruth, since it embraces not only the harvesting in Palestine, but also Ruth's acceptance of Judaism as her religion.

Decorating the house with plants, flowers and even potted trees to remind one of the green mountains of Sinai and the harvest festival of ancient times.

To impress deeply on the minds of the young the giving of the Ten Commandments by God to Moses, many boys and girls who have studied Hebrew in the Temples are confirmed on the morning of Shavuoth.

The meals most popular on this holiday are composed of dairy foods, including cheese blintzes, cheesecake, and other light, frothy and delectable foods.

LIGHT FLUFFY CHEESECAKE

1½ lbs. dry cottage cheese
½ lb. cream cheese
1 pint sour cream
1 cup sugar
2½ tablesp. flour
1 lemon rind, grated
1 teasp. vanilla

7 eggs, separated
2¼ cups graham cracker crumbs
1 teasp. cinnamon
½ cup sugar
1 stick margarine or butter, softened

Use spring-form pan. Roll graham crackers into crumbs. Mix with sugar, cinnamon and butter, lining the spring-form pan, but leaving a little of the mixture for the top of the cheese cake. Rub cottage cheese through sieve, and cream with cream cheese and sugar, mixing thoroughly. Add egg yolks, one at a time, and sour cream, following through with sifted flour and grated lemon rind, and vanilla last. Beat egg whites until stiff and add a little sugar, beating until it forms into stiff peaks. Fold egg whites into mixture carefully and well. Preheat oven to 350°F. Bake for 50 minutes and remove from stove. Cool. Sprinkle graham cracker mixture, left for this purpose, over the top of the cheesecake.

SEE OTHER DAIRY DISHES APPROPRIATE FOR THIS HOLIDAY IN THE "DAIRY DISHES" section of our cookbook.

Dairy Dishes

MEALS WHICH CONSIST OF ONLY DAIRY DISHES ARE CALLED "milchig," and they can be just as tempting as the meals prepared for dinners and lunches which contain meats and fowl or "flaishig." There is nothing to match the fragrance of cheese blintzes, or the scent of rice pudding or the various soufflés which may be prepared from eggs and cheese, not to mention the accompaniments and side dishes which have been handed down from family to family.

The recipes below consist of those dishes which are strictly dairy dishes. However, they may be combined with other milchig recipes contained in this book to make a most enjoyable and delightful lunch or dinner. These meals are usually light and easily digested as well as palate-tempting and attractive.

FARMER'S CHOP SUEY

1 pint sour cream
3 tomatoes, quartered
1 cucumber, diced and pared
3 strands fresh green onion (cut into ½ in. pieces)
6 radishes, washed and sliced thin
¼ head lettuce (cut in small wedges)
1 teasp. salt
½ teasp. pepper

Combine all ingredients. Serve in individual small bowls. Serves 4 generously.

CHEESE BLINTZES
(Polish)

6 eggs, beaten
½ cup water
1 tablesp. potato flour

Filling

1 lb. Farmer's cheese (pot cheese)	*2 egg yolks*
	½ teasp. cinnamon
½ lb. cottage cheese (drained of liquid)	*¼ cup seedless yellow raisins*
	3 tablesp. sugar

Combine flour and water. Add 6 eggs, beaten well. Mix thoroughly. Place oil in a skillet. When hot, drop in one ladle of batter, turning pan so that batter spreads all over skillet. When brown on one side, turn out on tea towel with browned side up.

Combine Farmer's cheese and cottage cheese, adding 2 egg yolks, cinnamon, yellow raisins and sugar. Place 2 tablespoons of this mixture on each round pancake, rolling ends in at once, and then rolling the balance securely. Heat oil, margarine or butter in skillet until hot. Place blintzes in skillet, browning first on one side, then on the other. Remove to platter. Serve with sour cream. Another excellent garnish is applesauce. Serves 6.

CHEESE BLINTZES
(Litvok)

4 eggs	*3 tablesp. melted margarine or butter*
1 cup water	
¾ cup flour (sifted)	*½ teasp. salt*
	Butter for frying

Filling

1 lb. cottage cheese (drained of liquid)	*1 tablesp. melted butter or margarine*
2 egg yolks	*½ teasp. cinnamon*
	2 tablesp. sugar

Combine ingredients of batter, sifting the flour in last. Heat butter in skillet. Be certain that skillet is round and about 9 inches in circumference. Using a ladle, pour in one ladle of batter or 2 tablespoons, tilting the skillet until a round pancake is formed. Keep over flame until only the underside is brown. Remove to tea towel with browned side up.

Beat cottage cheese and egg yolks, adding melted butter, cinnamon and sugar. Place 2 tablespoons of this mixture on round pancake batter. Fold side in first, and roll into a square blintze. Heat butter in skillet. Drop blintzes in, browning first on one side and then on the other. Serve with sour cream. Serves 4.

APPLE BLINTZES

4 apples, peeled and sliced	2 tablesp. granulated sugar
4 tablesp. bread crumbs or cracker crumbs	½ teasp. cinnamon
	2 tablesp. melted margarine
4 tablesp. brown sugar	or butter

Place ingredients in saucepan and cook over low flame for about 15 minutes, stirring continuously. Cool sufficiently and use to fill pancakes (recipe above).

DAIRY FRITTERS

1 onion, diced	1 teasp. salt
½ cup celery, diced	¼ teasp. pepper
2 carrots, grated	3½ tablesp. matzo meal
4 eggs	3 tablesp. butter or mar-
1 cup cooked string beans, chopped	garine
	Fat, oil or margarine for
½ cup cooked peas	frying

Combine onion, celery and carrots in small skillet with butter. Stew until soft. Add peas, beans, seasoning and 2 eggs, stirring in matzo meal last, cooking until all the ingredients are thoroughly warmed through. Cool and form into round fritters. Dip into batter made from the remaining 2 eggs and fry in hot fat until well-browned on both sides. Serves 4.

LOX, EGGS AND ONION

¼ *lb. lox (or Nova Scotia*	*Butter or margarine for*
smoked salmon)	*frying*
4 eggs, beaten well	*Diced green peppers may be*
1 onion, diced	*added, if desired*

¼ *teasp. pepper*

First, dice lox or Nova Scotia. Beat eggs well. Combine eggs, diced onions and lox and pour into hot fat in skillet. Cook over medium flame until brown on one side. Turn over and brown on other side. Serve with bagels! Serves 2 to 3.

CORN FRITTERS

2 cups cream of corn	½ *teasp. baking powder*
4 egg yolks	*Salad oil or margarine for*
4 egg whites (beaten until	*frying*
stiff)	½ *teasp. salt*

3 tablesp. flour

Combine beaten egg yolks, cream of corn, salt, flour and baking powder. Fold in beaten egg whites. Heat oil or margarine in skillet, and drop in batter by tablespoon. Brown on both sides. Serve with either maple syrup or powdered sugar. Serves 6.

MILCHIG TZIMMES

1 lb. apricots	*2 tablesp. butter*
1 lb. prunes	*1½ tablesp. lemon juice*
1½ cups farfel (uncooked)	*5 cups boiling water*
¾ *cup honey*	*2 tablesp. brown sugar*

Wash prunes and apricots and soak in cold water for at least 1 hour. Bring them to a boil in 5 cups of boiling water. Add the rest of the ingredients and again bring to a boil.

Place in casserole, cover, and bake for 30 to 35 minutes in 400°F. oven. Remove and serve hot. An excellent garnish for boiled fish or salmon patties. Serves 8 generously.

CHEESE SOUFFLÉ

1 cup grated American or cheddar cheese	*5 egg yolks*
	5 egg whites
2¼ cups bread crumbs	*1 stick butter or margarine*
1¼ cups milk	*¾ teasp. salt*

Using double boiler, combine cheese, bread crumbs, milk, butter and salt. Beat egg yolks well while cheese is melting. When ingredients have melted and blended, remove from fire and cool. Add egg yolks; then carefully fold in egg whites. Place in greased casserole or baking dish. Bake in moderate oven of 350°F. for 30 to 35 minutes or until firm. Excellent garnish: asparagus tips with hollandaise sauce. Serves 6.

WELSH RAREBIT

1 cup grated American cheese	*2 tablesp. butter*
	¼ teasp. pepper
½ cup milk	*¼ teasp. salt*
2 eggs	*⅛ teasp. mustard*

Using small skillet, melt butter, and add cheese. Season with salt and pepper. Beat eggs into milk, and when cheese is melted, add these ingredients and mustard. Serve over triangular toast pieces or toasted English muffins. Serves 6.

FLUFFY OMELETTE

5 eggs, separated	*Butter or margarine for frying*
½ cup milk	
½ teasp. salt	

Beat egg yolks. Add seasoning and milk. Beat egg whites until stiff. Fold gently into mixture. Heat butter or margarine in skillet. Pour in batter. Brown well on one side, then on the other. Excellent garnish: strawberry jam. Serves 2.

TOMATO MUSHROOM OMELETTE

Follow recipe above for Omelette, *omitting* milk. Then prepare the following:

1½ cups canned tomatoes   *2 tablesp. sliced mushrooms*
(whole)   *Dash of salt*
1 onion, diced   *Dash of pepper*
Butter for frying

Heat butter in skillet, adding the combined ingredients. When cooked through, particularly the onions, have omelette ready in another larger skillet. Place the combined ingredients on ½ of omelette and fold it over.

MAMALIGA (Corn Meal Pudding)

1½ cups yellow corn meal   *1 tablesp. sugar*
1 teasp. salt   *1 tablesp. butter*
3 cups boiling water

Bring water and salt to boiling point in double boiler. Add corn meal. Stir continually, to prevent lumps, and cook over low heat for at least 30 minutes. Serve hot, placing a pat of butter on each serving, with a little milk (for cereal) and sugar.

To serve fried: allow to get cold and then fry in butter or margarine.

To serve baked: place in a greased casserole (after cooking) and spread grated American or cheddar cheese over top. Bake in moderate oven for 15 minutes.

CHEESE AND RICE SOUFFLÉ

⅓ cup grated American or   1 cup cooked rice
  cheddar cheese   3 egg yolks
1 cup cream sauce   3 egg whites (beaten until
  (Made with 1 tablesp. flour,   stiff)
  1 tablesp. butter, ¼ teasp.   1 cup cottage cheese
  salt, ¾ cup hot milk)   ¼ teasp. salt
                    Dash of pepper

Combine ingredients, and fold in egg whites last. Place in greased casserole, and bake in moderate oven (350°F.) for 45 minutes. Serves 6.

ISRAELI CROQUETTES

8 eggs   ½ teasp. salt
3 tablesp. flour   Dash pepper
3 tablesp. water   Butter or margarine for
1 onion, diced and fried   frying

Beat 4 eggs well, adding flour and water. Fry, forming 2 thin omelettes. Boil 4 eggs until hard-boiled. Brown onions well. Place all these ingredients through grinder. Season with salt and pepper. Form into patties and fry in butter or margarine. Excellent garnish: lox, cream cheese and bagels. Serves 3.

COTTAGE CHEESE SOUFFLÉ

2½ cups cottage cheese   3 egg yolks
1 lemon rind, grated   3 egg whites (beaten until
2 tablesp. sugar   stiff)
2 tablesp. butter   2 tablesp. flour

Press cottage cheese through sieve. Melt butter, add flour, and blend well. Cool. Place in mixing bowl. Add beaten egg yolks, lemon rind and cottage cheese, and beat until thoroughly blended. Beat egg whites, adding sugar, and beating until stiff. Grease casserole or baking dish. Fold egg whites into mixture, and place in baking dish. Bake in moderate oven of 350°F. for 45 to 50 minutes. Excellent garnish: sour cream. Serves 8.

SOUR CREAM RING

4 cups sour cream (thick)   *½ cup cold water*
2 tablesp. chives, chopped   *½ cup hot water*
1 cucumber, sliced thin   *2 tablesp. vinegar*
2 tablesp. unflavored gelatin   *2 tablesp. sugar*

Soak gelatin in cold water; add boiling water and stir until completely dissolved. Cool. Whip sour cream until stiff. Add rest of ingredients, placing the slices of cucumbers around the bottom of the mold. Add gelatin to sour cream and chives, plus vinegar and sugar. Place in ring mold and refrigerate. Goes well with any dairy meal. Mayonnaise thinned with cream makes an excellent dressing. Serves 8.

AMERICAN CHEESE RING

1 cup grated American   *¼ cup chopped chives and*
* cheese*   * green peppers*
¼ cup cold water   *2 cups whipping cream*
¼ cup hot water   * (whipped)*
            1 tablesp. gelatin

Soak gelatin in cold water. Add hot water and stir until dissolved. Cool. Combine all ingredients and beat until light. Fold whipping cream into mixture and place in ring mold. Refrigerate. Garnish with candied cherries over top of mold. Place potato salad dotted with pimentos in center of ring. Serves 8.

STRAWBERRY CHEESE BLINTZES

Use recipe for Cheese Filling (Page 132).

1 cup preserved strawberries

To preserve strawberries:

1 qt. fresh strawberries   *½ cup water*
1 cup sugar

Wash berries well and place them in a saucepan along with sugar and water. Bring to a boil, and cook for 15 minutes, or until berries are completely soft.

Mix preserved strawberries and cheese filling. Place 2 tablespoons of this mixture on batter when turned out of frying pan. Fold, roll and fry as in cheese blintzes. The sauce of the preserved strawberries may be reserved to pour over hot blintzes. Serves 6.

BLUEBERRY CHEESE BLINTZES

Use recipe for Cheese Filling (Page 132).

1 cup preserved blueberries

To preserve blueberries:

1 qt. fresh blueberries   *½ cup water*
1 cup sugar

Wash berries well and bring them to a boil with the sugar and water. Cook for another 20 to 25 minutes. Pour off excess liquid and reserve for use as a sauce over hot blintzes.

Proceed the same as in Strawberry Cheese Blintzes (above). Serves 6.

CHERRY CHEESE BLINTZES

Use recipe for Cheese Filling (Page 132).

1 cup frozen cherries (pitted and preserved)

Defrost and reserve liquid. Proceed the same as in Strawberry Cheese Blintzes (above). Serves 6.

PANCAKES

1 cup flour	*2 tablesp. melted shortening*
1 teasp. baking powder	*(butter or margarine)*
1 egg	*½ teasp. salt*
	1 cup milk

Sift flour and baking powder; add salt. Beat yolk of egg, adding shortening and milk. Beat egg white separately. After adding egg yolk and milk mixture to flour (beating until batter is smooth), fold in egg white. Drop batter on hot griddle or skillet, which has been greased with a piece of fat or butter. When griddle cakes are full of bubbles, turn over with spatula, and brown other side. Follow this procedure until all griddle cakes are done.

BUTTERMILK PANCAKES

1 cup flour	*2 tablesp. melted butter*
1 teasp. baking powder	*2 eggs*
½ teasp. baking soda	*¼ teasp. salt*
	1½ cups buttermilk

Sift flour, baking powder and baking soda into a bowl. Beat eggs, adding buttermilk and melted butter. Using paper funnel, gradually sift dry ingredients into buttermilk mixture. Mix ingredients until batter is smooth. Heat griddle until very hot, grease with butter, and drop batter on griddle with a cooking spoon. When surface of pancake is covered with bubbles, turn over with a spatula and brown on other side. Serve hot.

CORN MEAL PANCAKES

1 cup white flour	*1½ cups milk*
1 cup corn meal	*1 teasp. salt*
1½ teasp. baking powder	*1 teasp. molasses (for color;*
2 eggs	*optional)*

Beat egg yolks and add milk and salt. Sift dry ingredients into a separate bowl. Combine the two mixtures, stirring constantly until smooth. Beat egg whites until stiff and fold in. Cook pancakes according to above directions.

FRENCH PANCAKES

This batter is a little richer than the batter used for pancakes or that used in rolling cheese for cheese blintzes, but it may be preferred for variety:

1½ cups flour	*2 tablesp. melted butter*
2 cups milk	*½ teasp. salt*
4 eggs	*1 teasp. sugar*

Sift flour and salt. Beat eggs well, adding milk. Using a funnel, pour flour into egg mixture, beating well. Use skillet which has rounded sides for better results. Place 1 teaspoon of butter at least in skillet, so that it will cover the sides as well as the bottom. Using a pitcher, pour batter into skillet, and tilt as you pour, so that batter will spread over entire skillet. Be certain that skillet is hot when you pour in batter.

Brown on one side, then turn over, or if you feel confident, flip the pancake over on the other side. Spread with either strawberry, cherry or blueberry preserves; roll pancake so that it will be about 2 to 3 inches in width and a little longer in length. Serve with powdered sugar and, if desired, with sauce from the fruit preserves.

CONTINENTAL PANCAKES

Use the same batter as above, making small-sized round
pancakes, and serve with a variation of side dishes, such as
sour cream, creamed fillet of herring, or pickled lox.

BLINI PANCAKES
(Russian in Origin)

1 cup flour   *½ teasp. salt*
½ teasp. baking powder   *2 eggs*
                   ¾ cup milk

Sift flour and dry ingredients. Beat eggs and add milk alternately with dry ingredients. Grease griddle, and drop batter
by the tablespoon, so that pancakes are small and thin. Turn
over, and brown on other side. Serve with sour cream.

AS TO EGGS...

What can be done in cooking without eggs? They play an
important role in every family's menu—as a snack, as an
accompaniment, or as a meal in themselves. There are so
many ways to present eggs on the table attractively and temptingly, and with all the value of their protein content retained.
Many times eggs have saved the day for a busy mother when
shopping for and cooking an elaborate meal was too time-
consuming.

There are certain rules to be followed in the pre-cooking
and preparation of eggs. One fundamental rule, which came
in prior to the days of refrigeration, is that eggs should be
taken out of the cold the night before they are going to be
used and allowed to remain at room temperature for better
results.

Another rule to follow is that with boiled, poached, fried,
scrambled and baked eggs, remember always to use a moderate

rather than a high flame. Eggs can become tough and leathery unless this rule is observed.

POACHED EGGS

You may either use a small skillet or a poacher.

If you use a skillet, fill three-quarters full with water. Sprinkle salt in water and bring to a boil. Place one egg at a time in a saucer, sliding gently into the briskly boiling water. Allow to remain in water, which will boil over eggs, hardening them a little at a time. When eggs have reached desired consistency, remove with slotted spoon or pancake turner. Serve on toast or in a sauce dish.

If you use an egg poacher, put a little butter in each poacher, and place the saucepan container on the fire, half filled with water. When the water has come to a boil, drop one egg in a saucer, then slide into poacher, until you have from two to four eggs in the poachers. Allow to simmer over boiling water until they reach the desired consistency. Serve on toast or in a dish.

CODDLED EGGS

With coddled eggs, water must come to the boiling point before eggs (in the shell) are dropped in carefully. Remove pan from fire, covering pan so that the steam will cook the eggs. Depending upon how you desire them, allow them to remain in covered pan for from 4 to 8 minutes. Remove, and serve while hot.

SOFT-BOILED EGGS

Place eggs (in the shell) in cold water in a small saucepan. Be certain that the water covers the eggs. Cook over slow flame until it comes to a boil. Remove from pan and serve in egg cup, slicing the top with a knife, or break into a larger egg cup, scooping out egg and serving without shell. An egg-timer may be used to serve 2, 3 or 4-minute eggs, as desired.

HARD-BOILED EGGS

Cover eggs with water in saucepan. Simmer for 10 to 15 minutes. Turn flame off, and allow to stand in covered pan for another 10 minutes. Remove eggs from pan, and plunge into cold water.

SCRAMBLED EGGS

6 eggs
⅓ cup milk or cream
¾ teasp. salt

¼ teasp. pepper
Butter or margarine for
    frying

Beat eggs, adding seasoning and milk or cream. Heat butter or margarine in skillet. Add eggs, and stir constantly with a fork until mixture reaches a creamy consistency. Remove from flame, serving hot on a hot plate. Serves 3.

SCRAMBLED EGGS (In Double Boiler)

Using the same ingredients as above, place egg mixture into top of double boiler, and place over boiling water, stirring constantly until it reaches a creamy consistency. Be certain to place a little butter in top of double boiler before pouring in egg mixture. These eggs are more easily digested than the above.

LIGHT, FLUFFY SCRAMBLED EGGS

6 egg yolks
6 egg whites
¾ teasp. salt

¼ teasp. pepper
Butter or margarine for
    frying
¼ cup cream

Beat egg yolks, mixing with cream and seasoning. Beat egg whites until stiff, adding a pinch of salt. Fold into egg yolk and cream mixture. Heat butter or margarine. Add egg mixture, stirring constantly until it reaches a creamy consistency. Serve while hot. Excellent garnish: strawberry jam. Serves 3.

FRIED EGGS

2 to 4 eggs　　　　　　*Butter or margarine for*
½ teasp. salt　　　　　　　*frying*
　　　　Dash of pepper

Heat a little butter or margarine in a skillet. If two eggs are going to be fried, use smaller skillet. Over low heat, drop one egg at a time into a saucer, sliding into skillet gently. Fry until white of egg is firm, and yellow is loose. If an "over" egg is desired, when white of egg is firm, use pancake turner or spatula and turn over gently, removing when egg is the same as on other side. Season with salt and pepper.

DEVILED EGGS

5 hard-boiled eggs　　　　*¼ teasp. Worcestershire*
1 teasp. grated onion　　　　*sauce*
¼ teasp. vinegar　　　　　*Paprika*
½ teasp. prepared mustard　*Sliced pimento strips*
¼ teasp. sugar　　　　　　*Stuffed olive, sliced thin*
　　　1 tablesp. mayonnaise

After removing hard-boiled eggs from saucepan, cool. When cool enough, slice lengthwise, removing yolks. Force egg yolks through sieve, and add the ingredients listed above, *except* paprika, pimento strips and sliced stuffed olives. Whip until smooth. Heap into egg whites. Sprinkle with paprika and place two thin strips of pimento on top with a slice of stuffed olive. Excellent garnish: lettuce and cherry tomatoes.

CREAMED EGGS AND ASPARAGUS
ON TOAST

6 hard-boiled eggs	2 tablesp. flour
1 lb. cooked fresh or frozen	1⅔ cups milk
asparagus or canned	1 teasp. salt
asparagus tips	Dash of pepper
2 tablesp. butter	

Slice eggs and set aside. Using double boiler, melt butter, blending in flour gradually and adding milk. Prepare asparagus in advance; have cooked asparagus ready and drained of liquid. When cream sauce has thickened, add asparagus, salt, pepper and eggs. Heat thoroughly, and serve hot over toast. Excellent garnish: spinach, mashed potatoes and peach halves.

CREAMED EGGS AND MUSHROOMS
ON TOAST

5 hard-boiled eggs, diced	mushroom pieces (with
2 tablesp. butter	liquid included)
2 tablesp. flour	1 teasp. salt
2 cups milk	Dash of pepper
1 pt. fresh button mush-	Parsley, chopped
rooms, cooked or 2 cans	¼ cup grated cheddar
button mushrooms and	cheese (if desired)

Have diced eggs and cooked mushrooms ready. Using double boiler, melt butter, adding flour, stirring constantly and adding milk gradually until thick and smooth. Add seasoning and chopped parsley. Last, add mushrooms and diced eggs. (If grated cheese is desired, sprinkle over cream sauce before eggs and mushrooms are added.)

Use one slice of toast on which to serve the piping hot eggs and mushrooms, and cut another slice of toast into a triangle, using as garnish on plate. Excellent garnish: fresh green onions and sliced cucumbers.

EGGS AS A GARNISH

Eggs may be sliced thin lengthwise, and used as an excellent garnish when serving a plain casserole dish, such as potatoes au gratin, by placing a ring of sliced eggs in the center and filling the small center with sprigs of crisp parsley.

FINEKOCHEN WITH FRIED POTATOES AND ONIONS

2 potatoes (pre-cooked and   4 eggs, beaten
  sliced)   1 onion, diced
                 Seasoning to taste

Heat skillet, adding butter or margarine. Brown onions and sliced potatoes. Add beaten eggs and brown on one side, using pancake turner to turn. When brown on other side, remove to platter. Excellent garnish: mint jelly. Serves 3.

APPLE FINEKOCHEN SUPREME

4 large eggs   ½ cup thinly sliced apple
3 tablesp. butter or mar-   ⅓ cup milk
  garine   ¼ cup flour
                 ½ teasp. salt

Beat eggs. Add a little milk and flour alternately, with the seasoning. Beat with rotary or electric beater until mixture is smooth. Use a 10-inch heavy skillet, brushing the sides with butter or margarine. Turn egg mixture into hot skillet, and sprinkle apple slices over the surface. Preheat oven to 400°F. Bake in hot oven for 20 to 25 minutes. Finekochen should rise up in puffed rims. Serve hot, sprinkling powdered sugar over the top. Excellent garnish: strawberry jam. Serves 2 generously.

EGG SALAD

6 *hard-boiled eggs (sliced,*   3 *tablesp. mayonnaise*
  then diced)   1 *teasp. salt*
1 *stalk celery, diced*   ¼ *teasp. pepper*
        2 *stalks scallions, diced*

Combine ingredients and mix with mayonnaise. Save a few slices of egg for garnishing. Sprinkle with paprika and dot with parsley.

EGG SALAD
(Variation)

6 *hard-boiled eggs (sliced,*   3 *tablesp. mayonnaise*
  then diced)   ½ *teasp. mustard*
1 *stalk celery, diced*   Paprika
4 *super sweet pickles,*   1 *teasp. salt*
  chopped   ¼ *teasp. pepper*

Combine all ingredients except mustard, mayonnaise and paprika. Mix mustard and mayonnaise and combine with balance of ingredients. Salvage a few slices of egg to use as a garnish, sprinkled with paprika and dotted with parsley.

SWEET AND SOUR EGGS

6 *eggs*   ½ *teasp. pepper*
2 *carrots, sliced thin*   ½ *teasp. salt*
1 *medium-sized onion, sliced* ½ *cup vinegar*
¼ *cup yellow raisins*   ½ *cup sugar*
        2 *cups water*

Combine carrots, onion, raisins, water, pepper and salt. Place in small saucepan over low flame. Cook ½ hour. Add vinegar and sugar, and cook for another ½ hour. Break one egg at a time into a dish and carefully slide into saucepan containing other ingredients. Remove cover and cook for 5 minutes. Replace cover on saucepan and cook for another 15 minutes.

Vegetables

THE ART OF COOKING VEGETABLES IS PERHAPS THE MOST IMPOR-
tant one for the housewife to master, since the vitamins and
minerals contained in vegetables play a vital role in keeping
the family healthy.

There are definite rules to follow in cooking vegetables
if the housewife is to derive the greatest benefit for her family.
Different rules apply to different vegetables, depending upon
their color:

Green vegetables derive their attractive shade of green in
both leaves and stems from the substance known as
"chlorophyll." (The word is derived from two Greek words
meaning "light green leaf.") Because of the presence of
chlorophyll, caution must be taken in the cooking of these
vegetables so that they do not lose their vivid color. Green
vegetables should be cooked in an *uncovered* pan as quickly
as possible. It is better to cook them just until tender rather
than overcook them. They should be served with all of their
natural juices.

Yellow vegetables derive their bright color from the pigment
known as "carotene." (This chemical substance is the
source of the orange hues, as well as certain light shades of
red, in vegetable and plant life.) There is not much danger
that this color will change in cooking. The only caution
which must be observed is not to overcook these vegetables,
since there is a tendency for the pigmentation to color the
liquid in which the vegetable is cooked, leaving the vegetable looking pale. Although there is no rule against cook-

ing squash, carrots, sweet potatoes, or yellow corn in an uncovered pan, it is suggested that these vegetables be cooked in a covered pan in order to shorten the length of cooking time. Some types of squash, such as acorn squash, are more attractively served if baked.

Red vegetables. The chemical substance known as "anthocyanin" is the one responsible for the deep reds and purples in plant life and in such vegetables as beets, radishes, and red cabbage. Also included in this category is rhubarb, the red rhubarb which should definitely be cooked with the skin. Cooking rhubarb with strawberries will enhance both the color and the flavor.

Red vegetables should always be cooked tightly covered. The addition of a little lemon juice, vinegar, or cooking apples (tart in flavor) preserves the color and improves the flavor. Particular care should be taken in preparing red beets: keep the tap root intact, avoid breaking the skin, and leave the stems intact when cooking.

White vegetables. It is most important when cooking cauliflower, turnips, broccoli and Brussels sprouts that they not be exposed to the iron which may be present in the water in which they are cooked. (Although broccoli and Brussels sprouts are not white in color, they are considered in the same family as cauliflower.) Therefore, do not cook any of these vegetables in an iron pan. Do cook them as quickly as possible in ample water in an uncovered pan. Be careful not to overcook since the substance "flavones" contained in these vegetables can be affected, with the result that the vegetables may emerge unattractive in color.

Pot liquor. This is not an intoxicating beverage but rather an invigorating liquid. It is the leftover juices from the vegetables and its valuable mineral content should not be wasted. Retain these juices and use for sauces, soups, or chill them and consume.

ASPARAGUS

1 lb. asparagus	*Water to cover (boiling,*
2 tablesp. butter or mar-	*with 1 teasp. salt)*
garine	

Wash asparagus thoroughly (they have a tendency to be very sandy), cutting scales off sides and the pulpy stalks, so that the tender top half is left. Cook rapidly in enough boiling salted water to cover asparagus for 15 to 20 minutes at most. Test with fork, and when tender, remove from flame onto platter, placing butter over the asparagus. Excellent garnish: vegetable platter of cauliflower in center, surrounded by glazed carrots and asparagus. Use round platter. Serves 4.

HOLLANDAISE SAUCE

Another very tasty manner to serve asparagus is with Hollandaise Sauce:

1 stick margarine or ¼ lb.	*½ teasp. salt*
butter	*Dash of pepper*
2 teasp. lemon juice	*½ cup boiling water*
	3 egg yolks

Cream margarine or butter by softening it and then whipping with a cooking spoon. Add egg yolks and continue to beat. Add lemon juice and seasoning. When you are ready to serve the sauce, add the boiling water, stirring constantly. It is wise to place Hollandaise sauce in a double boiler. Continue to stir constantly until it reaches the desired consistency. When pouring Hollandaise sauce over asparagus, dot with pieces of parsley.

STEAMED RICE

An important factor to bear in mind is that rice increases at least three times in quantity when cooked. Also, be certain to wash rice carefully, placing it in a strainer and letting cold water run through the strainer until the rice is clean. The basic recipe for rice is as follows:

1½ cups rice   *1 teasp. salt*
                2½ qts. boiling water

Add salt to water and bring to a brisk boil. Slowly add rice, stirring constantly, and allow rice to boil briskly for at least 30 minutes. Drain rice by placing rice in a strainer and pouring boiling water over it. Keep rice hot in double boiler until you wish to serve it.

RICE RING

Use rice above   *¼ cup yellow raisins*
                ⅓ cup melted butter

Mix ingredients and place in well-greased ring mold. Place in pan of hot water and bake in 350°F. oven for 30 to 35 minutes. To serve: heat a large round platter, loosen edges of ring mold with a spatula, and turn onto the hot platter. Broccoli, green string beans with blanched almonds, or Brussels sprouts placed in the center of the mold will provide a delicious and attractive color contrast to the white rice.

RICE RING WITH TOMATOES

1½ cups cooked steamed rice   *1 teasp. salt*
1½ cups strained tomatoes   *2 tablesp. melted butter*
1 green pepper, chopped   *1 teasp. paprika*
                1 onion, chopped fine

Mix ingredients and place in well-greased ring mold. Place in pan of hot water and bake in 350°F. oven for 30 to 35 minutes. Heat a round platter and loosen edges all around ring mold with a spatula or knife. Turn onto hot platter. Buttered baby lima beans make an excellent garnish in the center.

KASHA (Buckwheat Groats)

Kasha may be purchased either fine, medium or coarse, according to individual taste. It is very easy to prepare:

3 cups boiling water   *1 ¾ cups buckwheat groats*
1 teasp. salt   *1 egg, beaten well*

Mix groats and egg in saucepan over low heat. When grains separate, pour boiling water (to which salt has been added) into the pan and cover. Cook over low heat for 20 to 25 minutes or until all of the water has been absorbed. A tablespoon of butter may be added when served.

NOODLES, SPAGHETTI, AND MACARONI

All three of these items are cooked in the same manner. Remember that they increase at least twice in quantity when cooked.

1 8-oz. pkge. of macaroni,   *2 qts. boiling salted water*
spaghetti or noodles   *1 tablesp. salt*

Drop the macaroni, spaghetti or noodles into the briskly boiling (salted) water gradually, so that the water continues to boil briskly. Keep stirring until tender or from 10 to 15 minutes. Drain in colander, and *be certain to pour boiling water over it.* This will take some of the starch content out of macaroni product.

MACARONI AND CHEESE CASSEROLE

1 8-oz. pkge. macaroni
1 teasp. onion juice
⅓ cup buttered toast crumbs
   (grated)

⅓ cup grated American
   cheese
1½ cups cream sauce
   (recipe below)
1 teasp. paprika

Prepare macaroni according to the basic recipe above. Drain, and pour boiling water over it. Rinse. Add onion juice and half of the grated cheese to the cream sauce (below). Place macaroni in a well-greased casserole, pouring in cream sauce. Sprinkle remaining grated cheese and the buttered toast crumbs over the top, and lastly, sprinkle with paprika. Bake in uncovered casserole in moderate oven of 375°F. for 30 minutes, when cheese and bread crumbs will be browned. Serves 6 generously.

CREAM SAUCE

2 tablesp. butter
2 tablesp. flour

1¼ cups milk
2 egg yolks

Heat butter in skillet and add flour, mixing constantly. Then add milk gradually, stirring until it thickens. Gradually add egg yolks, heating and stirring until completely absorbed.

SPAGHETTI SUPREME

1 8-oz. pkge. spaghetti
1 large onion, diced
1 green pepper, diced
1 can tomato paste

1 large can whole tomatoes
½ lb. button mushrooms
2½ qts. boiling water
2 teasp. salt

Slowly drop spaghetti in briskly boiling (salted) water so that it continues to boil briskly. Boil for 15 to 20 minutes or until tender. In the meantime, brown onions in a hot skillet, adding green pepper. When spaghetti is tender, drain in colander, pouring cold water over it. Place in large saucepan, adding the browned onions, green pepper, cooked mushrooms, tomato paste and whole tomatoes, and heat thoroughly. Place sprigs of parsley on platter as garnish. Serves 6 generously.

NOODLE RAISIN RING

1 8-oz. pkge. broad noodles	*2 egg yolks*
¼ cup seedless raisins	*2 egg whites*
1 stick margarine or butter	*1 teasp. cinnamon*
1 cup toasted bread crumbs	*2 tablesp. sugar*
	1 cup milk

Cook noodles in briskly boiling (salted) water, dropping in gradually so that water continues to boil briskly. Cook for 15 to 20 minutes until tender. Pour cold water over noodles in colander, and drain. Heat milk, but do not boil. Beat egg yolks, and gradually add warm milk to egg yolks; add cinnamon and sugar. Beat egg whites last, and drop raisins into the noodles, folding egg whites into entire mixture, placing in greased ring mold. (Add butter alternately in layers.) Sprinkle toasted bread crumbs over the top of the ring mold. Place in pan of hot water, and bake in moderate oven of 350°F. for 1 hour. Remove from mold onto hot platter. Place round small dish of raspberry applesauce in the center of the ring mold for contrast in color. Garnish also with spiced crabapples—bright red.

JERUSALEM ARTICHOKES

12 Jerusalem artichokes	*3 tablesp. melted butter*

Soak artichokes in cold water, adding a little vinegar, for about 1 hour. Drop artichokes in pan of boiling salted water and cook until tender. Peel immediately, and serve with hot melted butter.

ARTICHOKES

8 small artichokes　　　　2 teasp. salt
3 qts. boiling water　　　　3 tablesp. vinegar

Cut about 1 inch off points of artichokes before cooking.
Add vinegar to boiling salted water, and cook artichokes for
30 to 40 minutes or until the leaf may be pulled out easily
with prongs. Small artichokes may be left whole and served
individually. Serve with melted butter, lemon juice or Hollandaise sauce. (Be certain to remove white fiber before
serving.) Serves 8.

STRING BEANS AND MANDLEN
(String Beans and Blanched Almonds)

1 lb. string beans　　　　　2 tablesp. vinegar
½ cup blanched almonds　　1 tablesp. corn starch
　(slivered)　　　　　　　　1 tablesp. prepared mustard
1 small onion, diced　　　　1 teasp. prepared horse-
2 tablesp. butter or mar-　　　radish
　garine　　　　　　　　　　¼ cup pimentos (sliced
1 cup water　　　　　　　　　thin)
　　　　　3 tablesp. sugar

Wash beans carefully, removing strings by snapping tip
and pulling down to the end of the string bean. Break in two,
so that size is appropriate for serving. Place about 1 cup of
water in saucepan with string beans, and cook until tender.
Reserve ½ cup of this liquid. Brown the diced onion in butter
or margarine. Combine the bean liquid with the last six ingredients, and cook with the onions, stirring constantly until
sauce thickens. Pour this over the hot string beans, adding
the slivered blanched almonds. Excellent garnish: cooked
noodles. Serves 6.

STRING BEANS AND MUSHROOMS

1 lb. string beans
1 box fresh mushrooms (or
* canned button mushrooms)*

1 onion, diced
1 cup water
2 tablesp. flour
1 teasp. salt

Wash string beans, remove strings, and cut beans in half. Using 1 cup water, cook string beans until tender. Remove ½ cup of this liquid. Brown onion in margarine, adding bean liquid, flour, and salt and mixing until thickened. Then add to string beans. Add mushrooms, cooking if fresh. Excellent garnish: spiced apple rings. Serves 6.

BAKED BEANS

4 cups Navy beans
2 lbs. brisket of beef
2 teasp. salt

2 tablesp. honey
2 cups boiling water
1½ teasp. prepared mustard
3 tablesp. molasses

Wash beans and soak overnight in cold water. Drain, cover with water in saucepan, and cook slowly until beans start to burst. Brown brisket of beef, and when beans are ready, place in covered casserole or baking dish. Combine rest of ingredients, and pour over beans and beef. Bake in moderate oven of 325°F. for 5 to 6 hours. Excellent garnish: baked potatoes and spiced crabapples. Serves 8 generously.

CORN ON THE COB

6 ears corn

1 teasp. sugar
1 qt. water

Cook corn on the cob for 20 to 25 minutes in boiling water to which sugar has been added. Remove from saucepan, piping hot, to platter. Serve with melted butter and use corn holders. Excellent garnish for broiled whitefish or lake trout, fruit cocktail, escalloped potatoes, tossed salad.

CREAM-STYLED CORN RING MOLD

2 *No. 10 cans cream-style*   3 *eggs, separated*
  corn   1 *teasp. sugar*
1 *cup milk*   ¼ *teasp. pepper*

Combine cream-style corn and milk. Add beaten egg yolks, and fold stiffly beaten egg whites into mixture, placing in large ring mold. Place in pan of hot water, and bake in moderate oven of 325°F. for 30 to 35 minutes. Remove to platter, and serve hot. Place in center: salmon salad dotted with stuffed olives. Added garnish: spiced pineapple spears.

STEWED TOMATOES

3 *lbs. large firm tomatoes*   1 *tablesp. corn starch*
2 *tablesp. butter*   1 *tablesp. sugar*
1 *cup bread crumbs*   1 *teasp. salt*
1 *green pepper, diced*   1 *cup water*
              1 *onion, diced*

Cut green pepper into small squares. Cook tomatoes in 1 cup of water, adding green peppers and salt. When tomatoes are thoroughly cooked and tender, heat a skillet with butter and brown onion. Add bread crumbs, sugar and corn starch, stirring slowly. Combine with stewed tomatoes, stirring until completely blended. Remove to vegetable serving dish. Serve hot. As an added garnish, sprinkle bread crumbs over top with sprigs of parsley. Suggestion for menu: Finekochen with apple slices, sweet pickles and black olives, home-fried potatoes and fruit Jello. Serves 6.

BEETS

1 *bunch fresh beets*   ¼ *teasp. pepper*
3 *tablesp. butter*   ½ *cup vinegar*
              1 *teasp. salt*

Wash beets thoroughly, leaving at least 1 to 2 inches of the stem and root, so that color will remain after cooking.

Place in enough water to cover, steam cooking in a heavy, covered saucepan. After beets are cooked, skin may be scraped off. Slice beets. Combine butter, salt, pepper and vinegar, and heat in saucepan. Pour over beets and heat until thoroughly blended. Excellent garnish for herring and boiled potatoes (with jackets on). Added garnish: sauerkraut sprinkled with sugar. Serves 4.

SWEET AND SOUR RED CABBAGE

1 large head red cabbage	*¼ teasp. pepper*
3 cooking apples (tart)	*3 tablesp. margarine or*
½ cup brown sugar	*butter*
2½ tablesp. vinegar	*3 tablesp. flour*
	½ teasp. salt

Shred cabbage and pour boiling water over it 3 or 4 times. Slice apples and combine with cabbage. Heat skillet and melt butter or margarine. Add shredded cabbage and apples. Pour boiling water over, and cook until tender. Sprinkle with flour. Combine brown sugar, vinegar, salt and pepper. Add to cabbage and apple mixture. Cook until thoroughly blended. Serve hot in vegetable serving dish. Excellent garnish for pickled tongue or corned beef and boiled new potatoes with parsley. Serves 6.

SPICED CARROTS

1 bunch carrots	*2 tablesp. honey*
3 tablesp. butter or pareve	*1 tablesp. cloves*
margarine	*½ teasp. ground ginger*
2 tablesp. brown sugar	*Juice of one orange*
	Pinch of salt

Wash, scrape, and slice carrots. Place all ingredients in saucepan, except the cloves and ginger. Cook over low heat for 20 minutes. Add cloves and ginger and cook another 15

minutes. Be certain that *saucepan is covered*. If carrots are
to be served with meat, use pareve margarine instead of butter.
Serving suggestion: Place carrots in decorative bowl in center
of round vegetable platter with asparagus in a ring surrounding carrots, and string beans in a ring surrounding asparagus.
Place stalks of celery in-between string beans and asparagus.
Serves 6.

PEAS AND CARROTS (Creamed)

1 pkge. fresh or frozen peas	*1 cup water*
1 cup diced carrots	*2 tablesp. flour*
½ teasp. salt	*1 cup milk*
¼ teasp. pepper	*2 tablesp. butter*

Cook peas in separate saucepan from the carrots. Carrots
take longer than peas. Be certain that the carrots are completely done. Then with very little water cook peas until
tender, 20 to 25 minutes. When both carrots and peas are
ready, combine them in one saucepan. Make a cream sauce
by melting butter in a small skillet, and adding flour, and
then the milk, stirring constantly. Drain peas and carrots, and
use a portion of the liquid in the cream sauce. Pour cream
sauce over peas and carrots, and serve hot in vegetable serving
dish. Excellent garnish: pieces of parsley over top of each
portion. Serves 6.

BAKED LIMA BEANS WITH BEEF FRY

2 cups dried lima beans	*¼ cup honey*
1 teasp. whole spices	*6 slices Beef Fry (cut into*
1 bay leaf	*2-inch pieces)*
½ cup catsup	*2 teasp. salt*
½ cup chili sauce	

Soak beans overnight in cold water to cover. Drain when
ready to prepare. Cover lima beans with water in saucepan,

and bring to a boil. Add salt to water, and continue cooking over low heat for at least 1½ hours. Drain. Using casserole or baking dish, combine beans, catsup, chili sauce, honey, bay leaf, spices, beef fry, and pareve margarine. Bake in moderate oven of 350°F. for 1 hour and 15 minutes. Remove from oven, and serve hot. Excellent garnish: fresh fruit cup in scooped honeydew melon. Serves 6 generously.

BAKED ACORN SQUASH

3 acorn squash (cut in halves)	2 tablesp. brown sugar
	2 tablesp. honey
1 stick butter or margarine	¼ teasp. salt

Remove seeds and fibers from inside of squash, and bake in shallow pan, cut-side down first. Bake in oven of 375°F. for 30 minutes, then turn upright. Place melted butter and a little salt on each half. Bake another 30 minutes. Remove from oven, leaving oven on. Place flesh of tender squash in mixing bowl. Add mixture of brown sugar, honey and butter, and mash and beat until completely soft and pliable. Place back in skins of squash, and return to oven, sprinkling a little brown sugar over each half. Bake for about 5 minutes. Serve hot. Excellent garnish: preserved or canned dark cherries. Serves 6.

MASHED YELLOW SQUASH

2 lbs. yellow squash	2 tablesp. butter
½ teasp. salt	½ cup milk
2 tablesp. sugar	

Peel squash, and slice thin. Cook the squash in very little salted water, until tender or about 1½ hours. If water is absorbed, add more hot water while cooking. Remove, and mash squash, adding sugar, butter and milk. If necessary to reheat, do so in double boiler, serving while hot. When ready to serve, some toasted bread crumbs may be sprinkled over top. Serves 4 generously.

BROCCOLI

1 bunch brocolli   *2 tablesp. butter or mar-*
1 teasp. salt   *garine*

Wash broccoli thoroughly, cutting off tough ends of stalks. Leave flowerets intact. Place a saucepan of salted water over flame, and bring to a rapid boil. Place broccoli upright in water for the first 10 to 15 minutes. Then, cover with water, and cook until tender. Serve with melted butter or pareve margarine. A round platter with broccoli in the center, surrounded by glazed carrots or corn on the cob, when in season, is most attractive.

BRUSSELS SPROUTS

1 qt. box Brussels sprouts   *1 cup white sauce*
                ½ cup toasted bread crumbs

Wash Brussels sprouts thoroughly, cutting away the top leaves, and soak in cold water for about 15 minutes. Cook in boiling salted water until tender—about 20 to 25 minutes. Serve with white sauce (Page 174), sprinkling toasted bread crumbs over top.

TURNIPS OR RUTABAGAS

4 or 5 (either yellow or   *2 tablesp. butter or mar-*
  white) turnips or rutabagas   *garine*
1 tablesp. sugar   *Dash of pepper*

Wash, peel, and cut lengthwise. Bring saucepan of water to which sugar has been added to a boil, and drop turnips or rutabagas in. Cook over moderate flame for 25 to 30 minutes, or until tender. Save some of the liquid, and use to mash turnips or rutabagas, adding butter and a dash of pepper.

BAKED HUBBARD SQUASH

2 squash   ½ stick of butter or mar-
2 tablep. brown sugar   garine

Cut squash lengthwise, and remove seeds and strings. Cut into squares, and place in shallow pan. Add a pat of butter and sprinkle with brown sugar. Bake in moderate oven of 350°F. for approximately 1 hour. When serving squash with meats or fowl, use pareve margarine instead of butter.

TOMATO ASPIC

6 large tomatoes   1 lemon, juice only
2 teasp. allspice (whole)   2½ tablesp. vinegar
1 envelope (2 tablesp.)   1 teasp. salt
  unflavored gelatin   ¼ teasp. pepper
1 lemon rind, grated   1 onion, diced
                ½ cup cold water

Boil tomatoes with onion and spices, pepper and salt. When tomatoes are soft, push through sieve or colander, straining tomatoes so that there are no seeds in juice. If you do not have at least 2 cups of juice, add a little condensed tomato soup to mixture. Bring to boiling point. Soften gelatin in ½ cup cold water, and when dissolved, pour in boiling tomato juice. Add lemon, vinegar, and grated rind. Pour into proper sized mold and chill in refrigerator. Excellent garnish for salads of any type. Serve with either mayonnaise or thousand island dressing.

BEETS AND PINEAPPLE

2 cups diced cooked beets   3 tablesp. brown sugar
  (drained)   ½ cup orange juice
½ cup crushed pineapple   ½ cup seedless raisins
  (drained)   2 tablesp. flour
              2 tablesp. butter

Melt butter in skillet, adding brown sugar, flour, orange
juice and raisins. Blend, and cook until mixture thickens. Add
beets and pineapple, and heat thoroughly. Excellent garnish:
cottage cheese, sour cream and potato puffs. Serves 6 to 8.

RICE PILAF

2 cups rice   1 teasp. salt
½ cup vegetable shortening   ¼ teasp. pepper
2 cups tomato juice   ¼ teasp. cinnamon
2 cups chicken broth   Sprigs of parsley

Sauté rice in Dutch oven or heavy skillet with shortening.
Keep stirring until rice has completely absorbed shortening.
Add seasoning, tomato juice and chicken broth, blending
thoroughly. Place mixture in covered casserole and bake in
oven at 375°F. for 1 hour, or until rice is completely tender.
Fluff rice with fork. Garnish with parsley and peach halves.
Serves 8.

QUICK TZIMMES

1 large can sweet potatoes   2 tablesp. butter
1 large can diced carrots   3 tablesp. brown sugar
1 large jar or can of un-   ½ teasp. salt
  sweetened prunes   ¼ teasp. pepper
½ cup juice from each of   ¼ teasp. cinnamon
  above (1½ cups in all)

Combine sweet potatoes, carrots, prunes and juice. Heat
thoroughly. Add butter, brown sugar, and seasoning. To give

it the semblance of slow-cooked tzimmes, add potato knaidles
as follows:

3 potatoes, grated and	*1 teasp. salt*
drained	*Dash of pepper*
1 egg	*3 tablesp. flour*
	2 tablesp. butter

Mix all ingredients, and drop by spoonfuls into tzimmes.
Cook until potato knaidles are completely tender.

KASHA WITH VEGETABLES

1½ cups kasha	*1 onion, diced*
1 egg	*1 cup fresh mushrooms,*
1 teasp. salt	*cooked*
½ teasp. pepper	*3 tablesp. chicken fat or*
2½ cups boiling water	*suitable substitute*
	1 8-oz. pkge. broad noodles

Using heavy skillet, brown kasha with a little fat. Scramble
egg with kasha. Cover with boiling water, and simmer until
water is absorbed and kasha is cooked. Boil noodles until
tender. Sauté mushrooms in onion. Combine noodles, mushrooms and onion with kasha. Season. Place in uncovered casserole and bake in moderate oven of 350°F. for 30 minutes.
Excellent garnish for sliced roast beef, lettuce and tomato
salad, pineapple tidbits. Serves 8.

BAKED ZUCCHINI SQUASH

1 zucchini squash	*¼ teasp. pepper*
1 cup bread crumbs	*½ teasp. onion powder*
1 teasp. salt	*2 tablesp. butter*

Cut squash into ¼-in. round slices. Grease a casserole, and
put in a layer of squash, then bread crumbs with seasoning,
another layer of squash, and then bread crumbs and season-

ing, until casserole is filled. Dot with butter, and bake in moderate oven of 375°F. for about 1 hour or until tender. Garnish with lettuce and tomatoes. Serves 6.

BEETS AND SOUR CREAM

2 cups cooked beets (grated)	*3 tablesp. sugar*
3 tablesp. melted butter	*1½ tablesp. flour*
2 tablesp. vinegar	*Sour cream*

Place grated beets in double boiler, adding butter, vinegar, sugar and flour and stirring continually until mixture thickens slightly. Serve as a side dish topped with sour cream.

PEPPERS STUFFED WITH CHEESE

2 cups cottage cheese	*½ teasp. salt*
1 egg	*¼ teasp. pepper*
½ cup matzo meal	*1 tablesp. sugar*
4 green peppers	*1 tablesp. melted butter*
	Paprika

Cut tops of green peppers, and clean out seeds and pulp. Mix cottage cheese, egg, seasoning, sugar, matzo meal, and melted butter. Fill peppers. Place in shallow baking pan in moderate oven of 350°F. for 1 hour. Garnish with peach halves and sticks of clove. Serves 4.

FRENCH FRIED GREEN TOMATOES

4 green tomatoes, sliced	*¼ teasp. pepper*
2 eggs	*¼ teasp. onion salt*
1 teasp. salt	*½ cup matzo meal*
	Fat for frying

Beat eggs, adding seasoning. Dip tomato slices into egg, then in matzo meal. Heat fat in skillet, and fry tomatoes, first on one side, then the other, until batter is brown. Garnish with lettuce leaf and slices of red tomatoes. Serves 4.

FRENCH FRIED EGGPLANT

1 eggplant   *1 teasp. salt*
2 eggs   *¼ teasp. pepper*
1 tablesp. lemon juice   *¼ teasp. onion salt*
1 cup matzo meal   *Fat for frying*

After peeling eggplant, cut into ¼ to ½-inch slices. Season and sprinkle with lemon juice. Beat eggs. Dip eggplant into batter, then into matzo meal. Heat fat in skillet, and fry eggplant, first on one side until brown, then on the other side. Serve hot. An excellent garnish for broiled chicken, cucumbers in vinegar and sugar, iced tea with mint leaves, cookies. Serves 4 generously.

COOKED OKRA

1 lb. okra   *3 tablesp. butter*
1 teasp. salt   *1 pt. boiling water*
             ¼ teasp. onion salt

If okra is large, cut pods into small pieces. Cut pods from stems. Cook in boiling salted water for at least ½ hour, or until okra is tender. Drain and add seasoning, if desired. Serve hot with melted butter. Some people prefer to add other vegetables, such as rice, tomatoes, etc. This may be done, if desired. Excellent garnish: rice and carrots. Serves 6.

FRENCH FRIED ONION RINGS

3 large Bermuda onions   *Fat for deep frying*
2 eggs   *1 teasp. salt*
Matzo meal   *¼ teasp. pepper*

Cut into slices at least ¼-inch in width, and separate one from the other. Beat eggs and season. Dip onions into eggs, then into matzo meal, then into eggs, and matzo meal again, to be certain that batter is thick. Heat fat in deep fryer. Drop onion rings in about ten at a time. Fry until golden brown. Remove, and replace with ten other onion rings, until they are all done. Be certain to place on paper toweling on platter so that fat may be absorbed. Serves 6 generously.

RHUBARB SAUCE

Most people searching for recipes on rhubarb automatically think of it as a vegetable, even though it is generally classified under "Fruits." Therefore, for your convenience, it is being included in the vegetable section.

2 lbs. rhubarb   *Rind of 1 lemon, grated*
                              2 cups sugar

Cut leaves and ends of stems on rhubarb. Purchase young, red rhubarb for best results. Cut in 1-inch pieces, and place in saucepan with very little water. When water reaches boiling point, add sugar and grated lemon rind. Cook until soft, and stir occasionally. When it dissolves into a sauce, remove from flame and pour into serving bowl. It should be a rich, red color.

RHUBARB AND STRAWBERRIES

1 lb. rhubarb (young and   *1½ cups sugar*
  red)   *Rind of one orange, grated*
                      1 pt. strawberries

Cut leaves and ends of stems on rhubarb. Wash thoroughly, but *be certain to leave the skins on the rhubarb.* Cut in 1-inch pieces. Clean strawberries, removing hulls and washing carefully to remove sand. Place in saucepan with rhubarb with very little water. When water comes to a boil, add sugar and grated orange rind. Continue cooking over low heat until rhubarb dissolves into a sauce. Pour into serving bowl. It will be a beautiful red, and the strawberries will greatly enhance the flavor of the rhubarb.

SAUCES FOR FISH, MEAT, FOWL, AND VEGETABLES

MUSTARD BUTTER SAUCE

½ *stick butter* ½ *teasp. prepared mustard*

Place in small saucepan and stirring continually, cook over low heat until butter is melted. Serve hot over vegetables, fish, or if pareve margarine is used, over meats.

MEUNIERE BUTTER SAUCE

½ *stick butter* *1 tablesp. lemon juice*
1 tablesp. chopped parsley

Melt butter, cooking until brown. Cook slowly so that butter will not burn. Add lemon juice and parsley. Excellent sauce for fish.

PUNGENT SWEET-SOUR SAUCE
(For Meat and Fowl)

2 tablesp. cornstarch *1 tablesp. lemon juice*
Drippings from roasting pan *1 cup water*
2 tablesp. brown sugar

Blend cornstarch with gravy from meat or fowl. Add water, continuing to stir. When mixture thickens, boil about 3 minutes. Stir in brown sugar and lemon juice. Strain into serving dish. Pour over meat or fowl.

Potatoes

THE POTATO IS PROBABLY THE MOST UNDERESTIMATED VEGE-table. It is available in great variety—from home-grown cooking potatoes to fancy Idaho baking potatoes—and abundance.

It is believed that the potato originated in South America, having been found to exist in Peru and Bolivia by Spanish explorers. They, in turn, introduced the potato into Spain, Italy, England, and Ireland. These countries began growing them in 1500's, and they found their way into North America sometime during the following century.

Contained in the potato are many important food elements, and it is important in the making of alcohol as well as flour and starch. In Europe today, potato starch is used almost exclusively for thickening soups and puddings. Potatoes provide such vital minerals as iron and niacin (nicotinic acid), and such vitamins as B-1, B-2 and C. Actually, a medium-sized potato has only 70 calories in it; it is the butter and other ingredients with which potatoes are prepared that add the calories.

Varieties of potatoes include:

White potato (known as the Irish potato)
Red potato (known as the Bliss potato)
Baking potato (known as Idahos or Maine, taking their name from the states which produce them)

POTATO LATKES
(Potato Pancakes)

6 *large potatoes, grated*   *1 teasp. salt*
1 *large apple, grated*   *Oil for frying (or suitable*
2 *tablesp. flour*   *substitute)*
3 *eggs*   *1 onion, grated*
½ *teasp. cinnamon*

Grate potatoes, apple and onion. Break in eggs and beat into mixture. Add seasoning and flour. Shape into oval pancakes. Place oil in skillet. When hot drop latkes, one at a time, into hot oil. When brown and crisp on one side turn. When brown and crisp on other side, remove from skillet to platter. Serve with sour cream, applesauce, or sprinkle with sugar.

POTATO LATKES
(Potato Pancakes)
Variation

6 *large potatoes, grated and*   3 *eggs*
  drained   1 *teasp. salt*
1 *large apple, grated and*   1 *onion, grated and drained*
  drained   *Oil or chicken fat for frying*

Grate potatoes, apple and onion, and drain. Break in eggs and beat into mixture. Add seasoning. Place oil or chicken fat into skillet. When hot, drop 2 tablespoons batter for each latke into skillet. When brown and crisp on one side, turn. When brown and crisp on other side, remove from skillet to platter. Serve with plain or raspberry applesauce or preserves. If preferred, sprinkle with sugar.

POTATO KUGEL

2 cups potatoes, grated and   1 teasp. salt
   drained   Dash of pepper
2 eggs   3 tablesp. chicken fat or
1 onion, grated   melted margarine
3 tablesp. potato flour   ½ teasp. baking powder

Beat eggs well. Gradually add grated potatoes, potato flour, onion, salt, pepper, baking powder and melted chicken fat or margarine. Place in well-greased casserole, and bake uncovered in moderate oven at 350°F. for about 1 hour. Excellent garnish: spiced crabapples. Serves 6.

SWEET POTATO BALLS

3 cups mashed, cooked   ⅓ cup honey
   sweet potatoes   1 cup chopped pecans
1 teasp. salt   Butter for heating honey and
¼ teasp. pepper   greasing baking dish
2 tablesp. melted butter   3 egg whites (beaten until
1 teasp. sugar   stiff)

Combine mashed sweet potatoes (after chilling) with seasoning and melted butter. Beat egg whites and add sugar, beating until very stiff. Fold egg whites into mashed sweet potatoes. Shape into balls. Heat 1 tablespoon butter with honey in skillet. When honey is hot, roll one potato ball at a time quickly, coating with glaze. Then roll in chopped nuts. Proceed in this manner with balance of potato balls. Place in greased, shallow baking dish about 1½ inches apart. Bake in moderate oven at 350°F. for 25 minutes. Excellent garnish: fluffy apple finekochen pancake and sliced pineapple. Serves approximately 12.

BOILED POTATOES WITH JACKETS

10 small new potatoes   *1 teasp. salt*
Water to cover

Scrub potatoes and place in saucepan with cold water. Bring to a boil and add salt. Cook for about 20 to 25 minutes. Drain. Remove to platter. Peel, salt and pour melted butter over them.

BOILED POTATOES WITH ONIONS

6 medium-sized potatoes   *1 teasp. salt*
1 onion, diced   *¼ teasp. pepper*

Pare potatoes, and cut into small pieces. Add diced onions and seasoning and place enough water in pan to cover. Boil in covered pan until potatoes are tender and soft. Drain water. Melted butter and a little more salt and pepper may be added before serving. Excellent garnish: pickled herring and sauerkraut sprinkled with sugar.

POTATOES AU GRATIN

3 cups boiled potatoes (cold)   *1 cup bread crumbs*
1½ teasp. salt   *2 tablesp. butter*
¼ teasp. pepper   *1 cup white sauce*
⅓ cup grated cheddar   *(see recipe below)*
cheese   *½ cup chopped parsley*

Cut potatoes into slices about ¼ inch thick. Season and sprinkle with chopped parsley. Grease casserole or baking dish. Place one layer of potatoes on the bottom, sprinkle with grated cheddar cheese, then place another layer of potatoes, and another layer of cheese. Prepare the following white sauce and pour over the top of the potatoes and sprinkle with bread crumbs and cheese. Bake in a moderate oven of 325°F. until golden brown.

WHITE SAUCE

1 cup milk   *2 tablesp. flour*
2 tablesp. butter   *¼ teasp. salt*
Dash of pepper

Melt butter in skillet, add flour, and gradually add milk and seasoning, stirring constantly, until mixture thickens.

BAKED POTATOES

4 large baking potatoes

Scrub potatoes thoroughly. Grease lightly with either margarine or butter, depending upon whether the meal consists of dairy or meat dishes. Bake in hot oven of 500°F. for at least 1 hour or 1 hour and 10 minutes. Remove to platter, and slit top first lengthwise and then across. Pinch both ends of potato, until slits give way to an opening at top. Dot with butter or margarine and paprika. Serves 4.

BAKED POTATOES
Variation

4 large baking potatoes   *¼ teasp. pepper*
1 teasp. salt

Bake potatoes as directed above. Remove from oven to platter, and cut lengthwise. Scoop insides and using rotary or electric beater, mash potatoes with salt, pepper, a little milk and butter (if dairy is being served) or omit and use pareve margarine. Refill halves, sprinkle with paprika, and place in oven for 10 minutes to brown crust. Garnish with sprigs of parsley. Serves 4 with two halves.

SCALLOPED POTATOES

6 large potatoes   1 teasp. salt
1 onion, sliced   1 cup white sauce
1 cup toasted bread crumbs   (see recipe, Page 174)

Pare potatoes, and cut into slices between ¼ and ½ inch thick. Slice onion thin. Place a layer of potatoes in greased baking dish or casserole, sprinkle some sliced onions on top, and add another layer of potatoes, and sprinkle some sliced onions over them. Pour white sauce over top of potatoes and onions, sprinkle with salt and pepper and a dash of paprika. Cover with toasted bread crumbs. Bake in moderate oven of 350°F. for at least 1 hour and 15 minutes, or until browned. Serve hot. Garnish: flaked red salmon with lemon slices and salad of lettuce, avocado, grapefruit and French dressing.

MASHED POTATOES

6 large potatoes   2 tablesp. butter or mar-
½ cup hot milk (if dairy   garine
  meal is served; otherwise   1 teasp. salt
  omit)   ¼ teasp. pepper

Pare potatoes, and cut into small pieces. Place in saucepan and add water to cover. Bring water to a boil, then add salt and pepper. Cook until potatoes are soft. Drain, and mash with fork until there are no lumps. Use rotary or electric beater until potatoes are smooth and fluffy. Add hot milk and butter or margarine and whip with cooking spoon. Place in vegetable bowl, and dot with sprigs of parsley and paprika. Excellent garnish: a green vegetable, such as asparagus, string beans, or peas and an orange vegetable, such as carrots. Serves 6 to 8.

LYONNAISE POTATOES

3 cups boiled potatoes (cold)   Dash of paprika
1 teasp. salt   1 tablesp. chopped parsley
½ teasp. pepper   Oil or shortening for frying
                1 onion, diced

Cut potatoes across into slices. Season (except paprika), and brown onions lightly. Add the sliced potatoes and brown thoroughly first on one side, and then on the other. Sprinkle with paprika, and chopped parsley. Serve hot. Excellent garnish for French fried veal chops, pickled beets and lettuce and tomato salad with oil and vinegar dressing and lemon. Serves 6 to 8.

POTATO CHIPS (British Style)

3 large potatoes (sliced   1 ½ teasp. salt
  thin)   Decanter of malt vinegar
            Oil in deep fryer

Pare and slice potatoes. Heat oil in deep fryer. Soak potatoes in cold salted water, and drain between towels until dry. Fry about 10 slices at a time until brown and crisp. Remove from deep fryer onto paper toweling in platter. Continue this procedure until all are brown and crisp. Serve with salt and sprinkle with malt vinegar. Excellent garnish: deep French fried whitefish or trout and iced tea with mint leaf.

SWEET POTATO & APPLE CASSEROLE

2 lbs. cooked sweet potatoes   2 tablesp. butter
4 tart apples   ⅛ teasp. grated nutmeg
Rind of 1 orange, grated   ⅓ cup brown sugar
Juice of 1 orange   ¼ cup white sugar
            ½ teasp. cinnamon

After cooking sweet potatoes in jackets, cool. Peel and slice potatoes. Pare and slice apples. With very little water, cook in saucepan for 20 minutes. Reserve liquid, and mix balance of ingredients: orange rind and juice, cinnamon, nutmeg, brown sugar and white sugar (everything except butter). Place sweet potatoes and apples in alternate layers, pouring juice of apple mixed with rest of ingredients over the sweet potatoes and apples. Dot with butter, and bake in an uncovered casserole in moderate oven of 350°F. for at least 1 hour. Serve hot. Excellent garnish: cheese blintzes. Serves 6.

CANDIED SWEET POTATOES

2 lbs. sweet potatoes
¼ cup honey
¼ cup corn syrup (dark)
2 tablesp. butter or margarine
¼ cup orange juice
⅓ cup brown sugar

Cook sweet potatoes (with skins) in boiling water for 20 to 25 minutes. Cool. In the meantime, heat butter in saucepan, adding honey, corn syrup, sugar and juice. Cut sweet potatoes lengthwise (after peeling) and place in baking dish, uncovered. Pour mixture from saucepan over sweet potatoes, and bake in moderate oven (350°F.) for at least 40 minutes, continually basting potatoes with sauce. Garnish with sprigs of parsley and kumquats. Serves 6 generously.

FRENCH FRIED POTATOES

6 large potatoes
Oil for deep frying
1 teasp. salt
Dash of pepper

Peel potatoes, and cut lengthwise into strips about ½-inch thick. Using deep French fryer, heat oil. Wash potatoes, and dry thoroughly. Drop into French fryer and remove when completely brown. Place on paper towel on platter, so that extra oil is absorbed. Season and serve. Excellent garnish for broiled hamburgers or frankfurters, with tossed salad of lettuce, tomatoes, cucumbers, radishes, scallions, with an oil and vinegar dressing, sweetened with a pinch of sugar. Serves 4 to 6.

CARAMEL SWEET POTATO RING

8 sweet potatoes　　　　　*⅓ cup chopped pecans*
⅓ cup butter　　　　　　　*or walnuts*
　　　　1 scant cup of brown sugar

Cook sweet potatoes (unpeeled). Peel and mash. Melt butter and place on bottom of a ring mold, brushing some on the sides. Sprinkle sugar on bottom of mold and on sides also. Place nuts around the bottom of the mold. Allow to stand in cold place for about 10 minutes. Carefully fill mold with mashed sweet potatoes, and placing mold in pan of hot water, bake in moderate oven of 350°F. for 40 to 50 minutes. While hot, turn onto serving platter, with caramelized top upright. Excellent garnish for broiled fish, broccoli and fruit cocktail.

POTATO PUFFS

1½ cups boiled potatoes　　*¾ teasp. salt*
¾ cup flour　　　　　　　*Oil or margarine for frying*
　　　　½ cup buttermilk

Place boiled potatoes through ricer or grater. Mix with flour and buttermilk, adding salt. Heat oil or margarine in heavy skillet or deep fryer. Knead potato and flour mixture, and roll out about ½-in. thick. Cut with biscuit cutter, and drop into hot oil or margarine. When brown, serve hot. Excellent garnish for dairy meal, with green vegetable, topped with fresh fruit dessert. Serves 4 to 6.

HASH BROWNED POTATOES

2 cups boiled potatoes　　*¼ teasp. pepper*
(cut in cubes)　　　　　　*Butter or margarine for*
½ teasp. salt　　　　　　*frying*

Blend fat in skillet with potatoes. Using a spatula, press potatoes firmly down in skillet forming a pancake. Cook until browned on both sides. Sprinkle with paprika. Remove onto platter.

NEW POTATOES WITH CARAWAY SEEDS

10 small, new potatoes	1 teasp. salt
1 tablesp. butter	¼ teasp. pepper
1½ teasp. caraway seeds	Sprigs of parsley

Boil potatoes in jackets. Peel, sprinkle with melted butter, salt, pepper, and caraway seeds. Place on platter. Garnish with parsley.

ORANGE BASKETS OF SWEET POTATOES

10 sweet potatoes	from the halfway mark of
4 tablesp. brown sugar	orange and removing the
2 tablesp. butter	pulp; reserve juice from
4 orange baskets (made by	pulp)
cutting a ¾-inch handle	

Boil sweet potatoes in jackets. Heat butter, adding juice from orange and brown sugar, for sauce. Mash sweet potatoes, and add sauce, blending thoroughly. Fill orange baskets, sprinkling each basket with a little brown sugar and a pat of butter, and bake in moderate oven (350°F.) for about 10 minutes. Serve hot. Garnish with sprigs of parsley. Serves 4 (with some mashed sweet potatoes left over).

BAKED SWEET POTATOES
(In Half Shell)

4 large sweet potatoes	Juice of 1 orange
¼ cup brown sugar	2 tablesp. butter

Bake sweet potatoes in hot oven of 450°F. for 1 hour and 15 minutes. Remove from oven, and cut lengthwise. Scoop

and mash potatoes with butter. Blend in orange juice and
place back into half shells. Place a pat of butter on each and
sprinkle with brown sugar. Return to oven for 10 minutes.
Serve hot. Excellent garnish: canned green pears. Serves 4
generously, or more if only a half shell is served to each person.

Kishke and Knishes

KISHKE
(With Matzo Meal Filling)

2 feet of beef casing
¾ cup sifted flour
⅓ cup matzo meal
1 teasp. salt
¼ teasp. pepper

1 teasp. paprika
½ cup chicken fat (for stuffing)
¼ cup chicken fat (for roasting pan)
1 onion, grated

Casing should be washed carefully and thoroughly in cold water, and scraped inside until clean. Cut in half and sew one end of each piece. Combine matzo meal with flour, grated onion, salt, pepper and ½ cup chicken fat. Stuff the casings with this filling, sew the other end of each piece, and drop into boiling water. Cook for at least 1 hour.

Drain and place along with ¼ cup of chicken fat and slices of onion in roasting pan. Sprinkle paprika over the kishke for added color in roasting. Baste kishke while roasting, so that casing becomes brown and crisp. Roast in moderate oven of 350°F., for at least 1½ hours.

It is generally understood that kishke is never roasted alone. Usually, there is a brisket of beef in the roasting pan, or a chicken, duck or goose. Always another entrée shares space in the oven with kishke.

KISHKE
(With Potato Filling)

2 feet of beef casing	¼ teasp. pepper
1½ cups grated potato	½ cup chicken fat (for
1 egg	stuffing)
3 tablesp. potato flour	¼ cup chicken fat (for
1 onion, grated	roasting pan)
1 teasp. salt	1 teasp. paprika

Follow directions above for matzo meal filling and kishke.

KISHKE
(With Corn Meal Filling)

Follow the ingredients and directions for Matzo Meal Filling, but substitute ⅓ cup of corn meal for matzo meal.

KNISHES

2 cups flour, sifted	½ cup salad oil
2 eggs	1½ tablesp. ice water
1 teasp. baking powder	½ teasp. salt

Sift flour, baking powder and salt directly into a large bowl. Make a well and drop eggs, oil and water into well. Work mixture and knead until smooth. Roll dough as thin as possible, after dividing it into two equal parts. Brush with oil. Place the filling (see recipes below) on each sheath of dough, and roll up like jelly roll. Cut into 2-inch strips, place on greased baking sheet and bake in moderate oven at 375°F. for approximately 40 minutes or until browned.

POTATO FILLING

3 cups mashed potatoes
2 onions, diced
½ cup chicken fat

1 teasp. salt
½ teasp. pepper
1 egg

Brown onions in fat. Remove from flame, and beat in potatoes, seasoning, and egg. Beat well until mixture is fluffy. Use this filling for above dough.

MEAT FILLING

2 cups ground meat
1 onion, grated
3 tablesp. chicken fat

1 tablesp. matzo meal
1 teasp. salt
¼ teasp. pepper

1 egg

Combine and mix meat, egg, and matzo meal. Brown meat well, adding onion, chicken fat and seasoning. Blend until smooth. (Have the butcher put meat through the grinder three times as meat used in making knishes should be ground very fine.) Use as a filling for knishes, and follow above directions for baking.

LIVER FILLING

1 lb. chicken livers
1 onion, diced

1 teasp. salt
¼ teasp. pepper

2 tablesp. chicken fat

Brown onion, add seasoning and then sauté chicken livers until done. Place onions and liver through grinder. Mix with chicken fat. When smooth, place on greased knishe dough, roll, and follow above directions for baking.

CHICKEN FILLING

2 cups cooked chicken   1 teasp. salt
  (remove skin and grind)   Dash of pepper
1 egg   Dash of onion salt
              ½ cup mashed potatoes

Mix ingredients. Place on greased knishe dough, roll, and follow above directions for baking.

CHEESE FILLING

2½ cups dry cottage cheese   1 teasp. salt
  or pot cheese   ¼ teasp. pepper
2 eggs   1 large onion, diced
3 tablesp. butter   Sour cream

Brown onion in skillet with butter. Remove from flame, and add rest of ingredients. Beat until smooth. Place on greased knishe dough, roll and follow above directions for baking.

DEEP FRIED GRIMSLACH

2 cups bread crumbs   ¼ cup chopped figs and
2 egg yolks   seedless raisins
2 egg whites (beaten until   ½ teasp. cinnamon
  stiff)   2 tablesp. ground blanched
¾ cup sugar   almonds
              ¼ teasp. nutmeg

.After soaking bread crumbs in water and squeezing out moisture, add egg yolks, raisins, chopped figs, sugar, cinnamon, nutmeg and almonds. Blend with mixing spoon. Lastly, fold in egg whites. In a deep fryer, heat oil. Drop mixture by tablespoon and brown. Drain before serving on paper toweling on platter. It is delicious served with fruit sauce. Serves 4 to 6.

PIROSHKI
(Stuffed with Potato or Liver)

1 cup flour	*2 tablesp. ice water*
½ teasp. baking powder	*½ teasp. salt*
1 egg	*½ cup butter or margarine*

Sift dry ingredients into bowl. Cut in butter or margarine with pastry blender. Beat egg, adding water and then combine with flour mixture, using hands to form dough. Chill in refrigerator. Then roll dough into sheath about ¼-inch thick, on board sprinkled with flour. You may make small circles of dough, or squares, whichever you desire. Fill with either the potato or liver filling below or both, placing 1 or 2 teaspoonful on each round or square, folding dough over to encase it securely. Using a flat well-greased baking sheet, place in hot oven (400°F.) for 25 to 30 minutes or until browned.

POTATO FILLING

1½ cups mashed potatoes	*1 large onion, diced*
3 tablesp. margarine or	*½ teasp. salt*
butter	*¼ teasp. pepper*

Heat shortening in skillet, and brown onion. Add potatoes and seasoning. Mix well. Cool before placing on piroshki dough.

LIVER FILLING

½ lb. chicken livers, cooked	*1 onion, diced*
and ground	*½ teasp. salt*
2 tablesp. margarine	*¼ teasp. pepper*
(pareve)	*¼ teasp. garlic salt*

Sauté onion in shortening, adding chicken livers until blended, and seasoning. Cool. Place on piroshki dough. Excellent for appetizers.

Salads

THE MOST REFRESHING DISH, IF PROPERLY SERVED, IS A SALAD. There are the usual in salads—the old standbys, such as lettuce and tomatoes with various salad dressings of one's choosing. However, it is those salads which combine the unusual or with that little touch of something different which make a hostess famous.

The most artistic salads may be produced with fruits arranged in basket containers made of fruits or vegetables.

FRUIT SALAD—MELON BALLS

1 cantaloupe   *1 honeydew melon*
¼ watermelon   *¼ cup seedless green grapes*
¼ cup Bing cherries

Cut cantaloupe and honeydew melon in half. With melon ball scoop, extract fruit from both melons, placing the balls in a large bowl. Use melon ball scoop to make watermelon balls, and place in bowl. With a sharp knife, scallop the edges of the 4 melon halves.

Wash grapes and cherries. Mix with melon balls. Place in fancy melon containers, arranging fruit so that the colors blend on the top.

FRUIT CUP (Melon Balls)

Place the melon balls from above in sherbet glasses with a small scoop of lime, tangerine or lemon sherbet.

FRUIT SALAD IN SCOOPED
HALF WATERMELON

3 oranges	1 cup strawberries (or
3 grapefruits	berries in season)
1 pineapple (cut in cubes)	1 cup seedless green grapes
1 cup Bing cherries	1 cup cantaloupe balls
1 cup blueberries	2 cups watermelon balls

Scoop watermelon balls from half a melon. Section oranges and grapefruits. Cut pineapple lengthwise, and cut into cubes. Distribute other fruits so that there is a myriad of color in the scooped watermelon, which may be scalloped with pointed or rounded edges. Most decorative, it is used as a serving dish for fruit cocktails. Helpful suggestion: To make blueberries and grapes look "frosty," wash carefully, then dip in sugar.

WALDORF SALAD

This salad must be made just prior to serving, since apples turn brown if allowed to stand for any length of time.

1 cup diced celery	Lettuce leaves
3 apples (cored, peeled and diced)	Mayonnaise (about 3 tablesp.)
1 cup pecans or walnuts (cut in large pieces)	1 teasp. sugar
	2 teasp. sweet cream

Mix cream, sugar and mayonnaise. Stir in celery and diced apples and then fold in nuts. Serve on lettuce leaf. For a touch of color, save a small piece of apple with skin to place on the top of each portion.

CANDLELIGHT SALAD

This salad must be made just prior to serving, since bananas do not keep their freshness for any great length of time.

4 bananas (or more, depending on how many people are being served)
4 maraschino cherries (whole, with stem if possible)
4 whole slices canned pineapple
4 canned half pears (pickled green ones, if possible)
Toothpicks
Lettuce leaves

Place slice of pineapple on lettuce leaf. Peel banana and stand upright, securing in the center hole of pineapple by sticking toothpicks underneath. On the right side of the banana, place the half pear, with the broad side resting on the pineapple slice and the narrow part leaning on the banana. Secure with toothpick in inconspicuous place. Place cherry with stem on top of the banana, securing with toothpick.

HAWAIIAN SALAD

1 fresh pineapple, sliced lengthwise
2 grapefruits, sectioned
2 avocados (½-inch slices)
3 tangerines, sectioned
Blueberries, frosted
Pineapple (cut in cubes)

Cut pineapple into cubes. Combine with grapefruit and tangerines, and place in scooped out pineapple. Frost blueberries by washing and dipping in sugar; sprinkle them over fruit. Arrange avocado strips attractively.

FRUIT SALAD PLATE
(With Cottage Cheese)

4 pears (canned halves)
4 peaches (canned halves)
4 cooked whole prunes
  (without liquid)

4 heaping tablesp. cottage
  cheese
1 cup pineapple chunks
Lettuce leaves

1 whole maraschino cherry

Arrange pears, peaches, pineapple chunks, and prunes alternately around 2 tablespoons cottage cheese on lettuce leaves, placing 1 cherry in center of cottage cheese.

FRUIT SALAD PLATE
(Variation)

Substitute lime, orange or lemon sherbet for the cottage cheese in recipe above.

STUFFED PRUNE SALAD

1 lb. cooked prunes
Philadelphia cream cheese

Chopped walnuts
Lettuce leaves

Drain prunes and cool. Pit, and fill with mashed Philadelphia cream cheese and nuts. Serve attractively on lettuce leaf. Allow the cream cheese to show at the opening of the prune. Or, prunes may be split and cream cheese spread placed in the cavity.

PATRIOTIC SALAD

1 lb. cherries
Cottage cheese

1 lb. blueberries

On a salad platter place a mound of cottage cheese. Arrange cherries around the cottage cheese, and the blueberries around the cherries. Place a small silk American flag in the middle of the mound of cottage cheese.

DAIRY SALAD

1 large cucumber, diced   2 cups sour cream
3 tomatoes (1 halved, 1 quar-   1 teasp. salt
  tered, 1 cut into eighths)   ¼ teasp. pepper
1 small bunch scallions,   ¼ cup thinly sliced radishes
  sliced   4 or 5 whole radishes (for
1 cup cottage cheese   rosebuds)

Combine all ingredients, except sour cream and whole
radishes. When thoroughly mixed, serve on lettuce leaf in
round individual salad bowls with 1 tablespoon of sour cream
on top, garnished with a rosebud made from radish.

POTATO SALAD

4 cups cubed, cooked   1 large onion, chopped or
  potatoes   grated
3 hard-boiled eggs, diced   1 tablesp. mustard
1 green pepper, diced   3 tablesp. mayonnaise

Combine ingredients and place in an attractive bowl. Garnish with sprigs of parsley and strips of pimento, and scallions.
(Scallions may also be substituted for grated onion.)

CARROT AND PINEAPPLE MOLD

2 pkges. orange Jello   (Substitute pineapple juice
1 cup crushed pineapple,   for 1 cup of liquid in pre-
  drained   paring Jello)
                2 cups grated carrots

First prepare the Jello in a ring mold and chill. Place grated
carrots on bottom of mold, following with crushed pineapple.
Refrigerate overnight. Serve on lettuce leaf, with mayonnaise
and a slice of orange peel on the mayonnaise.

HOT POTATO SALAD
(To be Served with Meat Dishes)

2 lbs. boiled potatoes
4 hard-boiled eggs
½ cup diced celery
1 onion, diced
1 teasp. prepared mustard
2½ tablesp. vinegar
2 teasp. sugar
1 teasp. salt
¼ teasp. pepper

1½ tablesp. flour
6 strips of Beef Fry
¼ cup chopped parsley
½ cup water
½ teasp. paprika
Pimento, sliced lengthwise
   (optional)
Green pepper, diced
   (optional)

Prepare potatoes freshly boiled in jackets. Peel, and cut in ½-inch slices, then cut in half again. Prepare hard-boiled eggs freshly boiled. Reserve for last. Meanwhile, fry Beef Fry, reserving liquid in skillet. Combine prepared mustard, sugar, seasoning, water and finally mix in flour, stirring, so mixture is smooth. Carefully add potatoes, celery, onion, and see that liquid covers these ingredients completely. Add vinegar, heating through. When hot, remove from skillet. Place in bowl, mixing with salad fork and spoon, so that chopped parsley is evenly distributed. Slice hard-boiled eggs, and use as garnish with additional sprigs of parsley; also use small size pieces of Beef Fry. If desired, a green sweet pepper may be diced and added to potato salad for additional color and flavor, as well as a pimento (sliced in long strips). Sprinkle with paprika.

COLE SLAW

1 cabbage, shredded
   (about 1 lb.)
3 tablesp. sugar

3 tablesp. malt vinegar
¼ teasp. pepper
1 teasp. salt

1 small onion, grated

Shred cabbage and soak in cold water for ½ hour. Drain. Combine other ingredients in bowl. Mix in cabbage, being certain that it is completely saturated with vinegar and sugar combination. If more sugar or malt vinegar is desired, it may be added. Place with sliced onion, pimento and green pepper on serving dish.

COLE SLAW
(To be Served with Dairy Dishes)

1 small new cabbage,	*2 tablesp. cream*
shredded	*½ teasp. salt*
2 tablesp. vinegar	*⅛ teasp. pepper*
2 tablesp. sugar	*½ cup mayonnaise or salad*
1½ teasp. prepared mustard	*dressing*

Shred cabbage and soak in cold water. Drain. Combine other ingredients in bowl. Mix in cabbage and make sure that it is coated with dressing. Use serving bowl, and place thin strips of green pepper over top as a garnish.

CABBAGE AND CARROT SALAD

2 cups shredded cabbage	*¼ cup sweet pickles, diced*
1 cup grated carrot	*1 teasp. onion juice*
¼ cup green pepper, diced	*½ cup mayonnaise or salad*
1 teasp. sugar	*dressing*

Juice of 1 lemon

Mix mayonnaise with onion juice, sweet pickles, lemon juice and sugar, and set aside. Combine cabbage, carrots and green pepper. Pour dressing over cabbage and carrots. Mix until blended. Serve in salad bowls.

STUFFED TOMATO SALAD

Many attractive and delicious salads may be made by scooping out the inside of a tomato and filling the tomato with a surprise filling, such as cottage cheese, tuna fish, egg salad, salmon salad, chicken salad, etc.

COTTAGE CHEESE STUFFED TOMATO

Large firm tomatoes   *1 lb. cottage cheese*
2 tablesp. chopped stuffed   *3 tablesp. mayonnaise or*
  olives   *salad dressing*
              2 tablesp. chopped chives

Combine all ingredients, saving a stuffed olive as a garnish, and fill as many tomatoes as required.

TOMATO FILLED TUNA FISH SALAD

Large firm tomatoes   *¼ cup celery, diced small*
1 family-size can of tuna fish   *¼ teasp. pepper*
1 onion, grated   *1 teasp. lemon juice*
¼ cup sweet pickles, diced   *½ teasp. salt*
  small   *2 tablesp. mayonnaise*
              2 hard-boiled eggs, diced

If tuna fish has been packed in oil, scald with hot water to remove oil. Mash tuna fish with fork; mix in a little mayonnaise, and it will be easier to manage. Combine with all other ingredients, and fill tomatoes. Garnish with sprig of parsley or stuffed olive and potato chips.

TOMATO FILLED SALMON SALAD

Large firm tomatoes   *¼ cup sweet pickles, diced*
1 large can salmon (Red   *2 hard-boiled eggs, diced*
  Alaska)   *¼ teasp. pepper*
1 onion, grated or ¼ cup   *3 tablesp. mayonnaise*
  chopped chives   *1 teasp. lemon juice*

Be certain to remove all bones from salmon and drain. Combine all ingredients, mashing salmon until smooth. Fill tomatoes, garnishing with a slice of egg, a sprig of parsley or stuffed olive. Spiced apple rings make an excellent accompaniment.

TOMATO FILLED CHICKEN SALAD

3 cups diced cooked chicken
2 tablesp. diced onions or
finely chopped scallions
¼ cup finely chopped sweet
pickles
½ cup diced celery

1 teasp. prepared mustard
2 tablesp. malt vinegar
½ teasp. salt
¼ cup of diced apples for
added flavor (optional)

Mix prepared mustard, salt and vinegar together. Pour over rest of ingredients. Mix well, and stuff tomatoes. Garnish with a piece of apple (with skin) for color and pineapple slices.

EGG SALAD IN STUFFED TOMATO

6 hard-boiled eggs, diced
2 tablesp. chopped chives
¼ cup diced celery
¼ cup finely diced sweet
pickles

3 tablesp. mayonnaise or
salad dressing
1 teasp. paprika
1 teasp. salt
Dash of pepper

Mix ingredients, stuff into tomatoes, sprinkle with paprika and garnish with stuffed olive. French fried potatoes go well with this salad.

AVOCADO, GRAPEFRUIT AND MANGO SALAD

3 large avocados
3 grapefruits (sections)
2 bananas

4 large mangos
¼ cup dark seedless raisins

Peel avocados, grapefruit, and mangos, saving bananas until last, since they spoil quickly. Cut avocado lengthwise into strips, grapefruit in sections, mangos lengthwise in about 1-inch wide slices. Cut bananas in half, then quarters. Arrange attractively on plate, sprinkling with raisins, and serving a choice of French or thousand island dressing.

SARDINE SALAD

2 cans boneless sardines
  (drain)
6 hard-boiled eggs (yolks
  only)

1 teasp. onion juice
1 teasp. lemon juice
1 tablesp. salad dressing
¼ teasp. prepared mustard

Remove tails from sardines. Mash, and push hard-boiled egg yolks through ricer, adding onion and lemon juice. Mix salad dressing with prepared mustard, then combine with other ingredients. Place portion on tomato slice on lettuce leaf. Garnish with crumbled egg yolks and a slice of pimento on top and serve with canned pear halves and potato chips.

TONGUE AND SALAMI SALAD

4 cups shredded lettuce
2 cucumbers, sliced thin
  and soaked in vinegar and
  sugar
3 stalks scallions (cut—
  including tops)
6 radishes, sliced thin
1 green pepper, diced

¼ lb. pickled tongue
  Julienne
¼ lb. salami Julienne
6 to 8 finger tomatoes
  (whole)
2 tablesp. vinegar
3 tablesp. salad oil
1 tablesp. sugar

1 teasp. lemon juice

Combine vinegar, oil, sugar and lemon juice. Dice, slice and shred other ingredients. Prepare the meats, so that they are in long strips. Toss salad together. Pour salad dressing over entire salad and mix. Garnish with finger tomatoes or cherry tomatoes (whichever is in season) and slices of cucumber with bits of the tongue and salami.

STUFFED CELERY SALAD

1 pkge. Philadelphia cream   *2 tablesp. cream*
*   cheese*   *2 teasp. anchovy paste*
*   6 stalks of celery*

Wash and cut stalks of celery into 3-inch pieces. Mix cream cheese, cream and anchovy paste. Stuff each piece of celery with mixture. Garnish with red pickled pears and place on lettuce leaf.

SALMON MOLD

1 large can Red Alaska   *2 tablesp. vinegar*
*   salmon*   *¾ cup strained chili sauce*
3 hard-boiled eggs, diced   *2 pkges. lemon Jello*
¼ cup diced sweet pickles   *(Reduce amount of liquid*
*   and stuffed olives*   *to include chili sauce and*
¼ cup diced celery   *vinegar)*

Bone and drain salmon. Flake. Using ring mold or large fish mold, place salmon around the bottom of mold. Follow with diced eggs and then pickles and olives and celery. Mix lemon Jello with strained chili sauce and vinegar. Place in mold and chill in refrigerator. Garnish with sprigs of parsley and thousand island dressing. (This may be made by mixing mayonnaise and the remaining strained chili sauce.)

SALAD DRESSING

Many housewives prefer to make their own salad dressings to fit the particular meal and salad at hand. You will find below many salad dressing variations you might wish to try. Surprise your family with one which has a slightly new or different flavor. There are two types of dressings: those which may be mixed and served over salads and those which must be boiled and properly cooled before serving. You will find both types below.

BOILED SALAD DRESSING

2 eggs	¾ teasp. salt
⅓ cup cream	⅓ cup sugar
2½ tablesp. butter	2 tablesp. flour
⅓ cup cider vinegar	Dash of pepper
½ teasp. dry mustard	

Beat eggs in top of double boiler. Mix sugar, dry mustard, salt, pepper and flour together, and combine with eggs. Add vinegar to mixture, stirring constantly until completely blended. After removing from heat, add butter and cream (or evaporated milk may be substituted, if desired). Cool. Place in refrigerator for chilling before serving. Variation: include the juice of 1 lemon.

ROQUEFORT CHEESE DRESSING

⅓ cup Roquefort cheese	¼ teasp. salt
⅓ cup cream	Dash of pepper
¼ cup salad oil	½ teasp. paprika
¼ teasp. dry mustard	Juice of 1 lemon

Mash cheese, adding cream, and seasoning. Slowly add salad oil, and blend; then add lemon juice and stir until all ingredients are mixed well. Chill in refrigerator until ready to serve.

MAYONNAISE DRESSING (Boiled)

5 egg yolks	½ teasp. dry prepared
1½ tablesp. butter	mustard
4 tablesp. sugar	¼ teasp. pepper
½ cup vinegar	1½ tablesp. flour
½ cup water	1 teasp. salt

Mix flour, sugar and seasoning. Place in the top of a double boiler, adding butter, water and vinegar. Beat egg yolks, and add a small portion of the mixture from double boiler, stirring and blending thoroughly. Add egg yolks to top of double boiler, stirring until completely blended. *Do not allow to come to boiling point.* When serving, use a little lemon juice, if it needs thinning.

MAYONNAISE DRESSING (Boiled)
(Variation)

5 whole eggs, beaten　　　　½ *teasp. salt*
¾ *cup oil*　　　　　　　　*Dash of pepper*
2 teasp. sugar　　　　　　½ *teasp. dry mustard*
3 tablesp. vinegar　　　　½ *to* ¾ *cup sour cream*
　　　　　2 teasp. lemon juice

Using double boiler, mix sugar and seasoning, adding eggs. While stirring add oil, vinegar and lemon juice. When ready to serve add sour cream to mixture, blending thoroughly.

HORSE-RADISH DRESSING

3 tablesp. grated horse-　　*1 cup sour cream*
　radish (either plain or　　½ *teasp. salt*
　with beets)　　　　　　*Dash of pepper*
　　　　*3*½ *tablesp. vinegar*

Add vinegar gradually to sour cream, stirring. Add seasoning, and fold in horse-radish last.

FRENCH DRESSING

¾ *cup salad oil (or olive oil,*　*1 teasp. salt*
　if preferred)　　　　　¼ *teasp. pepper*
¼ *cup tarragon vinegar*　　*1 teasp. paprika*
2 tablesp. lemon juice　　*1 teasp. onion juice*
½ *cup catsup*　　　　　*1 clove of garlic (cut in half)*
　　　　　¼ *cup sugar*

Combine dry ingredients and add oil, lemon juice, vinegar, onion juice, and catsup. Place in mason jar, and add more vinegar to taste, if desired. Place clove of garlic in dressing, but remove garlic in a day or so.

THOUSAND ISLAND DRESSING

1 hard-boiled egg, chopped
½ green pepper, chopped fine
2 teasp. onion juice
Dash of Worcestershire sauce
½ teasp. paprika
2 tablesp. catsup
2 tablesp. chili sauce
1 cup mayonnaise
1 cup whipped cream
1 tablesp. pimento, chopped
½ teasp. salt

Combine all ingredients except mayonnaise and whipping cream. Blend thoroughly with mayonnaise. Whip cream, and fold into mixture. A delightful dressing for frozen salad molds.

QUICK THOUSAND ISLAND

1 cup mayonnaise
3 tablesp. chili sauce

Combine ingredients and serve.

SOUR CREAM SALAD DRESSING

5 egg yolks, beaten
3 tablesp. butter
¾ cup water
¾ cup sugar
1 teasp. salt
Dash of pepper
½ teasp. paprika
2½ tablesp. lemon juice or orange juice
1 cup sour cream

Using double boiler combine egg yolks with dry ingredients, adding lemon or orange juice and water, stirring continually. Add butter, continuing to stir. Cook until mixture is thick. Cool and store. When ready to use, fold in sour cream. Excellent for use on salad molds of all types.

HONEY SALAD DRESSING

½ cup honey   ¼ teasp. nutmeg
½ cup lemon juice   ¼ teasp. paprika

Blend ingredients until thoroughly mixed. An excellent dressing for fruits.

SOUR CREAM AND BEET DRESSING

½ cup mayonnaise   ½ cup finely chopped beets
           ¾ cup sour cream

Fold mayonnaise into sour cream, adding chopped beets. This dressing makes an excellent garnish for vegetable salads of all types.

OIL AND VINEGAR DRESSING

1 cup salad oil   ½ teasp. paprika
½ cup vinegar (tarragon   ½ teasp. salt
   or malt)   Dash of pepper
2 teasp. sugar   1 teasp. lemon juice

Combine and chill. When ready, pour over salads. A wonderful dressing for vegetable salads.

Beverages

THERE IS NOTHING THAT WHETS THE APPETITE LIKE THE AROMA of freshly brewed coffee wafting through the house. Following the rules below for making coffee will ensure a perfect cup of coffee to set before your family and guests.

COFFEE BREWED AT ITS BEST

Measuring: 2 level tablespoons to each cup of water.

Cleanliness: Keep coffee-maker immaculate, washing and airing parts after each use.

Grind: Be certain that you use the right type of coffee grind for your coffee-maker. There is a "percolator" grind and a "drip" grind depending upon whether you are using a percolator or a dripolator. There is also an instant coffee which is made merely by the addition of boiling water.

PERCOLATOR COFFEE

Step 1: Measure cold water from the tap according to the number of cups desired. Measure 2 tablespoons of coffee for each cup of cold water into basket and set in water in percolator.

Step 2: Place over medium flame. When water boils, it will begin to percolate. Allow coffee to percolate for at least 5 to 7 minutes before removing from heat.

Step 3: Remove coffee grounds from percolator. Serve fresh and hot.

DRIP COFFEE

Step 1: Measure 2 tablespoons of coffee for each cup of water. Place it in the middle section of dripolator which fastens onto the top section.

Step 2: Measure boiling water, according to the number of cups desired, in upper portion of dripolator.

Step 3: When water has dripped through coffee into the bottom of the dripolator, remove top (containing coffee mid-section) and stir coffee so that its strength is evenly distributed.

VACUUM METHOD

Step 1: Drip grind is used for this type of coffee. It is made in a container that has twin glass or stainless steel sections, the bottom one with a spout, the top one with a long tubular stem which is inserted through the mouth of the bottom section.

Step 2: Measure 2 tablespoons drip grind coffee for each cup of cold water. Place coffee in little container which snaps in the middle of the two glass sections. Place water in the bottom. Snap coffee container in place, and place top in position.

Step 3: When water comes to a boil, it will be sucked into a vacuum which takes it into the top section. Then it slowly drips into the bottom.

Step 4: When all the water has seeped through, remove the top with coffee container, and stir coffee. Serve while fresh and hot.

IF STRONGER COFFEE IS DESIRED

Should 2 level tablespoons not provide coffee strong enough for your needs, increase to 2½ level tablespoons per cup of water.

IF WEAKER COFFEE IS DESIRED

Should 2 level tablespoons prove too strong for your needs, reduce to 1½ level tablespoons of coffee per cup of water.

SERVING LARGE GROUPS

Coffee may be prepared for large groups in any large vessel containing the amount of water required. In this case boil water first. Using a fine cheesecloth and percolator grind coffee, place the amount of coffee required in cheesecloth, and tie securely. Place cheesecloth in boiling water. In order to obtain clear, good coffee by this method, place carefully washed egg shells in the cheesecloth bag along with the coffee. Remove bag when coffee has been brewed. Using a funnel, pour coffee in regular coffee urn for serving.

VIENNESE COFFEE

This coffee was extremely popular during the colorful era of the 1900's and through to the 1920's. Since then it has diminished in popularity, but it is hard to image why a beverage so delicious and dramatically served should fall from public favor. Perhaps its inclusion here will contribute to its revival.

Use 2½ level tablespoons of coffee to each cup of water. Brew as usual and serve with freshly whipped cream and sugar.

This same flavorful Viennese coffee may be served iced. Brew coffee that is strong, and fill half of a tall glass with ice cubes. Use confectioners' sugar so that it will melt without difficulty and pour hot coffee over ice. Top with a generous serving of whipped cream. Serve mint patties of various colors as a garnish.

CAFÉ AU LAIT

This coffee, garnered from the French, is a refreshingly satisfying beverage particularly in the morning. Serve with miniature prune and cheese danish.

*2½ tablesp. coffee for each
cup of water, brewed
as usual*

Mix coffee in equal portions to milk, and serve hot. Or, if weaker *café au lait* is desired, mix 1 part coffee to 3 parts milk. Top with whipped cream. Serve with sugar.

AFTER-DINNER COFFEE
(Café Noir)

In drawing room circles *Café Noir* is a "must." Properly, coffee served after dinner should be served in demitasse cups (small-sized coffee cups), accompanied by demitasse spoons. The coffee should be extra-strong, usually double strength, and black. Sugar is optional.

ICED DRINKS

Iced Coffee: Brew coffee double-strength, so that it does not lose its flavor when hot coffee is poured over ice cubes. Use powered sugar and cream.

Iced Coffee: Brew coffee in regular way (2 level tablespoons coffee to each cup of water). Pour into ice cube trays and freeze. When ready to serve, brew fresh coffee and pour over coffee ice cubes. Serve with powdered sugar, cream, and top with whipped cream.

Iced Tea: Prepare boiling water. Place one teaspoon tea leaves or one tea bag for every cup of water prepared in china or earthenware teapot. Pour in boiling water in the

amount desired for specified number of cups of tea. Allow
to steep for five minutes. Remove tea leaves or tea bags.
Fill half a tall glass with ice cubes. Pour hot tea over ice
cubes. Serve with powdered sugar, lemon slices, and a sprig
of mint leaf for color; also, a candied cherry with stem
intact may be placed on top for color.

Iced Tea: Prepare hot tea as above, and pour into ice cube
trays and freeze. When ready to serve iced tea, place these
ice cubes in tall glass, pouring freshly brewed hot tea over
the ice cubes. Serve with powdered sugar, lemon and garnish with mint leaf or candied cherries.

Mocha Iced Coffee: Prepare double-strength coffee. Prepare
cocoa, made with 4 tablespoons cocoa, 1 cup water, 1 tablespoon sugar, 3 cups milk. Boil water, mix water with cocoa,
bring to a boil again, reduce flame and add milk. Bring to
a boil. Remove from heat and cool. Combine equal parts
of coffee and cocoa. Fill half of a tall glass with ice, pour
this mixture over the ice, using powdered sugar and serving
cream. Top with whipped cream.

Mint-Flavored Iced Tea: Prepare iced tea as directed above,
and add a few drops of mint. Also use a sprig of mint leaf
to garnish, as well as lemon slice.

HOT TEA

Allowing one teaspoon tea leaves or one tea bag for each
cup of tea, place in china or earthenware pot, pouring boiling
water to top and covering. Allow to steep for five minutes.
Remove tea bags or tea leaves (which usually are encased in
a tea strainer). Pour into cup, adding the desired quantity of
hot water to produce the strength of tea each one desires.
Garnish with slices of lemon. Serve a divided dish containing
honey, preserves, and orange peel (sugared). Also serve sugar
and cream, if desired.

RUSSIAN TEA

Russian tea is prepared in the same manner as the above, except that it must be double-strength. Use two teaspoons of tea leaves or two bags for each cup of hot water. Serve in a glass with a slice of lemon and lump sugar.

MOCHA

Prepare double-strength coffee and cocoa, as directed in Iced Mocha Coffee. Blend equal parts of both, and serve hot with cream and sugar. Top with whipped cream.

HOT CHOCOLATE

Substituting chocolate syrup for cocoa, allow 2 tablespoons syrup for each cup of milk. Heat until it comes to a boil. Remove from heat. Serve with whipped cream topping.

COCOA

Using 1 tablespoon cocoa to each cup of milk, place cocoa, water (1 cup water to every 4 cups of milk) and sugar to taste in saucepan. Bring to a boil. Add milk, and bring to a boil again. Serve with whipped cream topping and wafers or crackers.

ICED FLOATS

Beverages used: Either root beer, ginger ale or carbonized fruit drink may be used.

1st Step: Fill a tall glass half full with any carbonated beverage of your choice. Place two scoops of either vanilla, chocolate or strawberry ice cream in glass, and stir with an iced tea spoon. May be topped with whipped cream.

Alternate: Fruit ices, such as pineapple, lime, orange, lemon or tangerine sherbet, may be substituted for ice cream.

Decoration: If it is a special occasion, and it is desired that these floats be more decorative, secure a package or two of the little paper umbrellas, and place one on top of the ice cream in each glass.

MALTED MILKS

If you have a malted milk shaker (electric or manual) or an electric mixer, preparation is a little easier, but a rotary beater may be used.

Allow 2 tablespoons of malted milk for each glass of milk. Add ½ teaspoon vanilla flavoring and 1 scoop of ice cream, and whip until smooth, using electric or manual equipment or a rotary beater.

FLAVORED MALTED MILKS

The desired flavor may be achieved through the addition of the appropriate syrup, such as chocolate, pineapple, strawberry or cherry.

MILK SHAKES

A milk shake is made with milk, fruit flavor, and 2 scoops of ice cream (vanilla, chocolate, strawberry or coffee). A teaspoon of vanilla extract may be added for additional flavor.

Variation: In addition to the ice cream of various flavors, the fruit syrup from canned fruit may be extracted and added, to enhance flavor.

Variation: Frozen fruits in and out of season, such as strawberries, cherries, blueberries or blackberries, may be whipped into the milk shakes.

Topping: Whipped cream, decorated with cherry, strawberry, pineapple, etc.

EGGNOG (Basic Recipe)

2 cups milk	½ teasp. vanilla extract
2 eggs, separated	Dash of nutmeg
	2 tablesp. sugar

Separate egg yolks and beat well, adding milk and vanilla extract. Fold in stiffly beaten egg whites (with sugar added). Sprinkle nutmeg on top of each serving. It may also be made with warm milk.

ORANGE EGGNOG

Follow basic recipe for eggnog, but also include ¾ cup orange juice (for each 2 cups milk). Do not mix orange juice with milk first: substitute honey for sugar, and mix honey with orange juice (½ cup). Omit vanilla extract. Garnish with nutmeg and a slice of orange, splitting it so that it may be placed on edge of glass.

LEMONADE

5 lemons	1 banana
1 cup corn syrup (light)	Candied cherries with stems
	6 cups of water

Juice lemons. Add corn syrup and water. When ready to serve, slice bananas, and place several slices on each glass of lemonade, along with a candied cherry. Serve ice cold.

FRUIT PUNCH

1 cup orange juice	1 cup lemon juice
1 cup grape juice	1 cup blackberry juice
1 cup pineapple juice	½ to 1 cup light corn syrup
1 cup raspberry juice	(optional)
	2 cups water

Combine juices. If not sweet enough, add ½ to 1 cup of light corn syrup. Use large punch bowl for serving. This recipe is designed to serve a large group of people, though quantities may either be increased or decreased according to the number of guests expected. Garnish with slices of orange, cut in half.

SWEET APPLE CIDER

Purchase at least a bushel of apples, for only the juice of the apple is used to make Sweet Apple Cider. Using a press, crush apples and extract juice. Place in large preserving kettle and boil juice down to half its original amount, skimming often to keep clear. Have sterilized jars ready and hot. Pour sweet cider into jars and seal.

CIDER VINEGAR

Place amount of cider desired to turn into vinegar in an open jug. Cover mouth of jug with a piece of cheesecloth and allow to stand for about one month. It will turn into vinegar.

RASPBERRY JUICE CONCENTRATE

3 qts. raspberries   *4 lbs. sugar*
                    4 qts. water

Wash fruit and place in preserving kettle. Cover with water and boil until fruit is soft. Strain in jelly bag or through cheesecloth. Measure juice and for every quart of juice, add one cup of sugar. Heat to boiling point and boil for one minute. Pour liquid into sterilized, hot jars and seal.

May be used for making raspberry drinks by adding cold water and ice.

May be mixed with orange juice for added flavor.

BLACK COW

A refreshing combination of root beer and vanilla or chocolate ice cream. Place one or two scoops of ice cream in a tall
glass. Pour root beer over the ice cream, and stir until the
beverage threatens to flow over the top of the glass. Serve
with iced tea spoon and straw.

Kugels and Charlottes

RICE KUGEL
(Rice Pudding)

2½ cups cooked rice
2 tablesp. butter
2½ cups milk
2 eggs, separated
¾ cup sugar

Grated rind of Persian lime
  or lemon
¼ cup seedless raisins (dark)
¼ teasp. salt
½ teasp. cinnamon

Beat egg yolks well. Add all other ingredients except egg whites, butter and cinnamon. Beat egg whites until stiff. Melt butter, and add to mixture. Fold in egg whites last. Place in buttered baking dish, sprinkle with cinnamon and bake in moderate oven (350°F.) for 20 to 25 minutes.

RICE KUGEL
(Variation)

½ cup rice
4 cups milk, scalded
⅓ cup sugar
¼ cup seedless raisins
  (light)

3 tablesp. butter
¼ teasp. cinnamon
1 teasp. nutmeg (sprinkle
  over top)

Combine rice, sugar, seasoning and raisins. Place in baking dish. Pour in scalded milk and add butter. Sprinkle with nutmeg, and bake in oven of 325°F. for about 2 hours, or until rice is tender and the scalded milk has formed into a thick creamy substance. At intervals stir with fork, and stir under any crusty substance which forms around the edges. However, do not disturb during the last 45 minutes of baking. Serve hot.

BREAD PUDDING
(With Vanilla Sauce)

3 cups bread crumbs   ½ cup brown sugar
5 cups milk   5 egg yolks
1 lemon rind, grated   5 egg whites
½ cup chopped walnuts   Extra brown sugar for
1 cup white sugar   topping
             ½ teasp. cinnamon

While soaking bread crumbs in milk, beat egg yolks well, and cream with sugar (both white and brown). Add bread crumbs, milk, grated lemon rind and walnuts. Fold egg whites into mixture last. Sprinkle top with brown sugar and cinnamon and dot with butter. Place in greased casserole or baking dish, and bake in moderate oven (350°F.) for 35 to 40 minutes.

VANILLA SAUCE
(Hot)

1 cup boiling water   2 tablesp. flour
3 tablesp. butter   1 teasp. vanilla
             3 tablesp. sugar

Melt butter in saucepan, add flour and stir until it reaches the consistency of white sauce. Add boiling water and sugar, continuing to stir. When well blended, remove from flame. Add vanilla, and serve hot with bread pudding.

APPLE CHARLOTTE

4 cups diced apples   Grated rind of 1 lemon
1 cup sugar   ¼ cup currants
¾ cup seedless raisins   ¾ teasp. cinnamon
Juice of 1 lemon   ¼ cup almonds, blanched
⅓ cup grape juice   and slivered

Mix ingredients, place in lined baking pan (see below), and bake in 425 to 450°F. oven at least 1 hour.

To Line Baking Pan: Cream 1 stick of margarine or butter with 2 tablespoons sugar. Combine 1 scant cup flour and a pinch of salt. Beat 1 egg yolk and add it to creamed butter and sugar. Blend in flour. Place this mixture into baking pan in ¼ to ½-in. thickness. Chill in refrigerator overnight. There should be enough left to cover baking pan or at least to form criss-cross strips over Apple Charlotte.

MATZO CHARLOTTE (Apple)

3 cups sliced apples	4 egg whites
½ cup sugar	¼ cup seedless raisins (dark)
1 stick margarine (pareve)	½ teasp. cinnamon
3 whole matzos	¼ cup grated blanched
4 egg yolks	almonds

Soak matzos in water and squeeze dry. Beat egg yolks, melt margarine, and combine balance of ingredients, folding in stiffly beaten egg whites last. Place in baking dish or casserole in moderate oven of 350°F., and bake for about 1 hour and 10 to 15 minutes.

NOODLE KUGEL
(Noodle Pudding)
(Serve with Meat Dishes)

6 cups broad noodles, cooked	2 tablesp. lemon juice
½ cup chicken fat	1 tablesp. grated lemon rind
½ cup firmly packed brown sugar	¼ cup toasted bread crumbs
	½ teasp. cinnamon
4 eggs	¼ teasp. nutmeg
¾ cup seedless raisins (light)	

Cream eggs and sugar either in electric mixer or with rotary beater. Add noodles, sugar, raisins, lemon juice and rind, seasoning and chicken fat. Sprinkle toasted bread crumbs over top. Grease casserole (uncovered) and bake in oven of 375°F. for about an hour, or until browned. May be served with any meat dish.

NOODLE KUGEL
(Noodle Pudding)
(Serve with Dairy Dishes)

Using same ingredients as above, substitute butter for chicken fat. Bake in oven at 375°F. for about an hour, or until browned. Serve with dairy meals.

NOODLE RING

Using same ingredients as either of the above recipes, place in well-greased ring mold. Place in pan of hot water, and bake in oven for about an hour or until browned. Unmold and serve with either dairy or meat dishes, depending upon which recipe you use.

CARROT AND POTATO CHARLOTTE

Important Note: If this is to be served with meat dishes, use chicken fat; if served with dairy dishes, use butter.

1½ cups grated carrots	1 tablesp. sugar
4 cups grated potatoes, drained	¼ teasp. cinnamon
	⅛ teasp. ginger
½ cup chicken fat or butter (see note above)	1 teasp. salt
	4 egg whites (beaten until stiff)
½ cup bread crumbs or cracker meal	1 cup water

4 egg yolks, beaten

Using 1 cup of water in a saucepan, cook carrots for about 20 to 25 minutes. Do not drain. Combine potatoes, egg yolks, bread crumbs, seasoning (except sugar), butter or chicken fat; then add the carrots with juice. Beat egg whites and add sugar, and when it forms a peak, fold into mixture. Grease a casserole or baking dish, pour ingredients in and bake in a moderate oven of 350°F. for about an hour.

MUSHROOM-BARLEY KUGEL

1 cup chopped mushrooms
2 cups pearl barley
3 eggs, beaten
1 teasp. salt
¼ teasp. pepper
¼ cup chicken fat or margarine
5 cups boiling water
1 onion, diced

Stir barley into boiling water, and bring to a boil again. Add salt, cover and cook over low heat for about an hour. When barley is soft, drain. Have mushrooms and onions ready after having browned them in chicken fat or margarine. Add to barley, together with pepper and beaten eggs. Grease casserole or baking dish and bake in moderate oven of 350°F. for about another hour. Makes an excellent substitute for a vegetable served with dinner.

FISH AND POTATO KUGEL

2 lbs. smoked finnan haddie
3 cups sliced potatoes
2 large onions, sliced
½ teasp. pepper
1 teasp. salt
2 cups white sauce (see Page 174)
1 cup toasted bread crumbs

Cook finnan haddie in water; let it come to a boil, and then cook the finnan haddie for 10 minutes. Remove from fire, and flake. Slice the potatoes and onions thinly. Grease baking dish or casserole and arrange potatoes, onions and fish alternately until you reach top. Pour white sauce over top, and sprinkle with toasted bread crumbs. Bake in moderate oven of 350°F. for an hour.

Cereals and Favorite Breakfast Varieties

THERE ARE TWO DIFFERENT VARIETIES OF HOT CEREAL: ROLLED oats or rolled wheat and the granular-type cereals such as grits, farina, and corn meal. Either of two methods may be used to cook these cereals. One is by *direct heat*, which consists of bringing salted water to a rapid boil in saucepan, adding required amount of cereal and stirring continually until cereal is completely cooked. (The time will depend upon whether it is a slow or quick-cooking type of cereal.)

The other method of cooking is by using a *double boiler*. This is cooking in the top pan of the double boiler, over direct heat, bringing water to the boiling point, and then adding required amount of cereal, stirring until it thickens, placing the cereal over the lower part of the double boiler and cooking until done. All cereal boxes contain instructions as to the length of time required for cooking. Following these directions is important.

The addition of an extra tablespoonful of butter towards the end of required cooking time will improve the flavor of the cereal.

Honey comes in a variety of flavors, any one of which may be added, during the last part of cooking, to enhance the flavor of the cereal. The addition of molasses, for instance, in corn meal will enhance the flavor considerably.

Though not listed among the hot cereals served in this country, many other countries tend to rely on cereals derived from rice rather than on the wheat variety. Rice in these other countries does not resemble the type of rice with which we are familiar. Rather, it is the unpolished rice which is served or rice with hull. Nutritional experts have found that rice in its unpolished state contains the most valuable vitamins and is the most nutritious.

Most appropriate for serving attractive eye-appealing bowls of dry cereals are fruits of various kinds, such as sliced fresh peaches in season, blueberries, blackberries, raspberries, strawberries, bananas (sliced), pitted prunes, pitted cherries or a heaping teaspoon of some colorful preserve.

CORN MEAL MUSH

1 part corn meal *1 ½ to 2 teasp. salt*
5 parts water

Using methods described above, this may be cooked and then stored in refrigerator, if desired. Later, it may be taken out, dipped in corn meal and fried in deep fat in skillet until crisp and brown.

FRENCH TOAST

4 thick slices bread (white) *½ teasp. vanilla extract*
2 eggs *Butter for frying*
½ cup flour *1 teasp. cinnamon mixed*
½ teasp. salt *with sugar*
1 ½ cups milk

Sift flour and salt into mixing bowl. Add mixture of cinnamon and sugar, well-beaten eggs, milk and extract; then add to flour, beating well. Soak each slice of bread in this batter, and after heating butter in skillet, fry until brown, first on one side and then on the other. Sprinkle with powdered sugar and serve with hot maple syrup.

MILK TOAST WITH EGG IN MIDDLE

Can you remember your mother when you were a child, pampering you when you were ill, trying to tempt your appetite with something that would be nutritious? This is one of those palate-tempting recipes. It will pay dividends to bring a tray containing this delicious repast to your little one:

4 thick slices bread (*white*)   *4 eggs*
1 cup of milk   *Butter for frying*
                 ½ teasp. salt

Combine milk and seasoning. Cut a square in the center of each slice of bread. Dip slice of bread (with hole in center) into milk. Heat butter in skillet, place slice of bread in skillet, and brown on one side. Turn over carefully with spatula; place a little butter in the center of slice of bread and drop 1 egg into this space. When egg is done to your satisfaction, use pancake turner to remove to plate. You may dip the centers of bread in milk and fry until brown on both sides, and serve with this delightfully different breakfast delicacy. If desired, serve a little hot maple syrup with this, or sprinkle with powered sugar.

OMELETTE (Mock Crepe Suzettes)

3 eggs   *Dash of pepper*
½ cup milk   *Butter for frying*
              ½ teasp. salt

Whip eggs well, adding milk and seasoning. After heating butter in 9-in. skillet, drop in mixture, turning skillet until omelette is thinly spread. Brown on one side, and turn over to brown on other side. When ready to remove from heat, spread strawberry preserves over entire top of omelette, sparingly. With a fork on one side of the omelette, fold over and over again until it is rolled and strawberry preserves are entirely encased in omelette. Remove to serving dish—sprinkle with powdered sugar.

FRENCH PANCAKES
(Same idea as above—only with batter)

1½ cups flour	Strawberry or other fruit
½ teasp. salt	preserves
4 eggs	Powdered sugar
2 cups milk	

Sift flour and seasoning, add milk with well-beaten eggs, and beat until thoroughly blended. Heat lightly-greased, rounded skillet about 8-in. in circumference, and when hot, pour in sufficient batter so that when tilted, the pancake will spread around the edges of the skillet. Brown on one side; turn and brown on other side. Spread with strawberry or other fruit preserve, roll up and sprinkle with powdered sugar. Serve hot with hot maple or other flavored syrup.

SOUR CREAM PANCAKES

2 cups sour cream	1 cup flour
1½ teasp. baking soda	Butter for frying
4 eggs	

Mix sour cream and baking soda. Beat eggs well and add sour cream mixture to eggs, stirring in flour. Use butter for griddle or skillet, heat, and drop 1 tablespoon batter on griddle for each pancake. Brown well on each side. Serve with blueberries or jelly and hot maple syrup, or sprinkle with powdered sugar.

WAFFLES

Every manufacturer of waffle irons gives specific instructions regarding the use of his waffle iron. Follow these directions carefully. As to the waffle batter itself, enough fat must be included so that the waffle will not stick to the waffle iron.

The recipes below will be a boon to your breakfast table or
at snack time.

PLAIN WAFFLE

1½ cups flour   5 tablesp. melted shortening
1½ teasp. baking powder   (butter preferred)
2 egg yolks   Pinch of salt
2 egg whites   1½ cups milk
1 tablesp. sugar   ½ teasp. vanilla extract

Using triple sifter, sift flour, baking powder, sugar and salt.
Beat egg yolks well, adding milk and melted butter, and blend
with dry ingredients. Beat egg whites until stiff, adding a little
sugar. Fold egg whites into other combined ingredients. Add
vanilla. Bake in waffle iron, following directions of manufacturer as to cooking time. Serve hot with any hot syrup you
wish.

SOUR CREAM WAFFLES

2½ cups sour cream   4 egg yolks
1¼ teasp. baking soda   4 egg whites
1½ cups flour   ¾ teasp. salt
1 teasp. baking powder   4 tablesp. butter

Using triple sifter, sift flour, baking powder, baking soda
and salt. Beat egg yolks well, adding melted butter and sour
cream, and blend with dry ingredients. Beat egg whites, adding a pinch of salt. Fold egg whites into combined mixture.
Bake in waffle iron, following directions of manufacturer.
Serve hot with syrup or with orange-flavored hard sauce below:

ORANGE-FLAVORED HARD SAUCE

1 cup confectioners' sugar   2 tablesp. candied orange
¼ cup butter   peel (chopped fine)
              1 tablesp. orange juice

Cream sugar with butter, and add orange juice and orange
peel. Press into small mold, and refrigerate. Unmold, and

serve a portion with each waffle. Prepare yourself for a new taste sensation.

PECAN WAFFLES

Using recipe for plain waffles, add ¼ cup chopped pecans. Follow same directions for mixing and baking. The pecans add zest to a plain waffle.

CHOCOLATE-FLAVORED WAFFLES

1 sq. chocolate, melted	*4 egg yolks*
1 cup sugar	*4 egg whites*
2 cups flour	*3½ teasp. baking powder*
1¾ cups milk	*Pinch of salt*
5 tablesp. butter	*1 teasp. vanilla*

Cream sugar and butter; add melted chocolate. Beat egg yolks well. Add to mixture. Add flour and milk alternately, and fold in stiffly beaten egg whites (adding pinch of salt to egg whites) last. Flavor with vanilla extract. Bake in waffle iron until done. Serve hot with powdered sugar or maple syrup.

MAMALIGA WAFFLES

1 cup corn meal	*2 egg whites*
1 cup cake flour	*1 cup milk*
4 teasp. baking powder	*3 tablesp. melted butter*
2 tablesp. sugar	*½ teasp. salt*
2 egg yolks	*½ teasp. lemon extract*

Using triple sifter, sift flour, baking powder, sugar and salt. Beat egg yolks well, adding milk and melted butter. Combine with flour mixture. Fold in egg whites, stiffly beaten, and add lemon extract. Be sure that waffle iron is hot. Serve with confectionery sugar or orange hard sauce (see Page 220).

SPICED WAFFLES

½ *cup sour cream*   *1 teasp. ginger*
1 ½ cups flour   ¼ *cup melted butter*
½ *teasp. baking soda*   ½ *cup molasses*
1 teasp. baking powder   *2 eggs*
                  ½ *cup sugar*

Beat eggs. Add sugar and blend with molasses and sour
cream. Sift dry ingredients into mixture, stirring until completely blended and smooth. Stir in melted butter. Bake in
waffle iron. Sprinkle with cinnamon and sugar combination
and serve with a scoop of vanilla ice cream.

QUICK FRENCH TOAST

3 eggs, beaten well with   *Butter for frying*
½ *cup cream*   *4 thick slices bread (white)*
            1 teasp. cinnamon and sugar

Heat skillet with butter. Dip bread into egg mixture. Fry
in hot skillet until brown, first on one side, then on the other.
Sprinkle with confectionery sugar and serve with hot maple
syrup.

BANANA ORANGE FRENCH TOAST

1 cup milk
4 eggs
1 small banana
2 tbsp frozen o.j. concentrate, thawed
6 slices bread
butter

Buttery Orange Marmalade Sauce

½ cup butter   } Combine
½ cup orange marmalade   } saucepan
                           heat at
                           slow

Combine milk, eggs, banana & orange
in blender till smooth. Dip bread & refr
till all absorbed. Fry in butter.

Bread and Rolls

BREAD IS THE STAFF OF LIFE. IS THERE AN ODOR AS PUNGENT and appetizing as that of brown crusty loaves of bread baking in the oven? Customary in the Jewish household on Friday morning is the sight of large containers covered with towels— of dough rising and ready for Mama to put it into the oven. But, before this can happen, the flour board must be ready and waiting, so that Mama can braid the dough for that wonderful "challah" which everyone anticipates for Friday night! Enough bread is baked to take care of the household for the entire weekend. Three loaves will be plain, but the other loaf—the one served on Friday night—will have lightly colored raisins throughout.

Today, with modern bakeries having attained the art of baking in the manner of Mama and Grandmother, it is rare indeed to find the young housewife baking bread. There is an old wiseman's saying: "Even if you do not have to do anything . . . possess the knowledge, for you never know when it will prove invaluable." That is the reason this cookbook contains those time-tested, delicious recipes for yeast breads and quick breads. Use them when it suits your fancy and taste. Give your family a special treat; show them that the younger generation can walk in the footsteps of the past generation and that the "apple does not usually fall far from the tree."

There are two categories of breads: *yeast breads or those leavened with yeast* which require additional time for rising; *quick breads* or breads and rolls which may be mixed and

223

prepared immediately before a meal and served with no additional waiting.

Popular on the modern table are the freshly baked popovers, baking powder biscuits, continental French rolls—the hard-crusted roll so delicious in the morning served with pats of butter and a steaming urn of hot coffee, as well as the favorite bagels—sometimes lovingly referred to as "petrified doughnuts." Also popular with people of the Jewish faith are the hard rolls with the four mounds or peaks and poppy seeds on top and the savory onion pockets or onion rolls as well as the poppy seed twists of different dimensions, usually served in miniature form. There is a special onion roll called "Bialystok," which does not have a shiny exterior but is browned well, with a cluster of onions in the center.

There are little suggestions and specific rules which should be followed when baking bread at home. It is also important when you go to the market to purchase flour, to be well informed as to the variety you are seeking.

Below is a guide for baking breads in your home.

FLOURS USED IN BAKING OF BREADS

Wheat flour, or white flour, which is sold:
   Bleached
   Unbleached
   Vitamin Enriched

Cake flour is a specially refined flour, which is white in color and fine in texture. This type of flour is usually boxed and clearly marked "Cake Flour."

Graham flour and whole-wheat flour are usually blended with white flour in the baking of certain types of breads, such as whole-wheat, dark rye, etc.

Corn meal is also used in the baking of breads combined with other flour, mainly white. Other flours, such as potato, rice, rye, etc. are also combined with white flour to produce wonderful results.

Of the two types of breads, yeast breads require a lot more patience and, of course, knowledge of exactly what to do, but once bread-baking with yeast is practiced, one may become an expert. Quick breads are baked with baking powder and/or baking soda, and the term "quick" is used because one may prepare this type of bread within a short time, placing it on the table from the flour board within a matter of a little less than an hour.

Baking soda has a definite place in baking, particularly when sour milk, sour cream or buttermilk are used in the baking of biscuits, pancakes or breads, coffee cakes, sweet rolls, etc. (*The ratio is ½ teaspoon per cup.*)

Using scalded milk and boiling water in formulas for breads is suggested and called for in most recipes because it prevents the multiplying of bacteria while dough rises in warm temperatures.

YEAST BREADS

CHALLAH
(White Braided Bread)

7½ cups sifted flour	2½ tablesp. sugar
6¼ tablesp. shortening	2 teasp. salt
(pareve margarine pre-	2 cakes yeast (compressed)
ferred)	¾ cup lukewarm water
1¾ cups boiling water	4 eggs

Dissolve yeast in the ¾ cup of lukewarm water. Allow to stand about 15 minutes. Mix in 3 eggs and the white of the fourth, of which the yolk is reserved for the top of the bread. Meanwhile, melt margarine in boiling water in large mixing bowl. Add sugar and seasoning and allow to cool. When just lukewarm, add yeast and egg mixture. Mix well, and as you mix, gradually stir in flour.

Using well-floured board, knead dough until smooth; this should take about 5 to 7 minutes. Grease larger bowl, one in which dough can rise to twice its bulk. Place dough in this bowl, oiling the top of the dough with a little melted margarine so that it will not dry out. Leave in warm place; place a tea towel over the top of the bowl or pan, and allow to attain twice its bulk—about 2 to 2½ hours.

When dough is ready, knead by punching down bulk. Then divide into three equal sections. Take each section, and again divide into three sections, braiding each loaf. There should be three loaves of bread in all. Beat egg yolk which had been reserved for this purpose, and mix with a little cold water. Using pastry brush, brush egg yolk mixture on each loaf which has been placed in bread loaf pan. Sprinkle with poppy seeds or sesame seeds or leave plain. Bake in oven of 375°F. for 1 hour. They should be well browned.

Variation: For added flavor, ¼ cup seedless yellow raisins may be added to one or more of the loaves above.

Important Note: There are three types of yeast:

1) Compressed yeast (Perishable—keep refrigerated and use supply immediately. Get fresh supply for each using.)

2) Granular yeast (Dry yeast—is less perishable. Keeps well, particularly in a cool place.)

3) Granular yeast in cake form (Keeps for several weeks or longer if kept in a cool place; takes about 30 minutes to soften, as against 5 to 10 minutes for the above.)

WHITE BREAD

8 cups sifted flour	*3 tablesp. sugar*
3 cups boiling water	*2 teasp. salt*
1½ tablesp. margarine	*1 cake compressed yeast*
(pareve)	*¼ cup lukewarm water*

Scald water and melt shortening in it, combining with sugar and salt. Cool while adding yeast to ¼ cup lukewarm water. When softened and the scalded liquid has cooled to point where it is lukewarm, add yeast. Add flour gradually, and when completely blended, mix thoroughly. Turn onto floured board, and knead until smooth and glossy. Place rounded dough into large greased bowl to allow it to rise. Cover with tea towel, and allow to remain in warm place, at least 80°F. or more, until it doubles its bulk. Knead and punch down, and place in bowl again to allow it to rise. Divide into three equal portions. Form each into ball, and let it remain for about 10 minutes. Place in well-greased loaf pans. When it doubles its bulk again, bake in hot oven of 400°F. for 1 hour or until browned.

USING YARDSTICK OF STANDARD RECIPE FOR WHITE BREAD:

RYE BREAD

Substitute: half rye flour and half white flour
substitute molasses for sugar
add 2 to 3 tablespoons of caraway seeds during kneading process.

WHOLE-WHEAT BREAD

Substitute: half whole-wheat and half white flour
substitute molasses for sugar.

OATMEAL BREAD

Substitute: half oatmeal (uncooked oats) and half white flour.

DARK RYE BREAD

2 cups rye flour
1 cup sifted white flour
1 cake compressed yeast
½ cup lukewarm water
1 egg white and water for glaze

1 tablesp. margarine (pareve)
1 cup boiling water
1 tablesp. molasses
1 teasp. salt
1 tablesp. melted shortening

Add molasses and salt to boiling water. Cool to lukewarm. Dissolve yeast in lukewarm water. Allow 5 to 10 minutes. Add to molasses mixture. Mix flours and sift. Add about half the flour mixture to other mixture in large bowl. Mix until smooth. Add melted shortening and remaining flour and when dough may be handled, knead on floured board for about 5 or 6 minutes. Place in large greased pan or bowl, covering with tea towel. Let it stand in a warm place until it rises about double in bulk. This should take between 2 and 3 hours. Shape into long loaf and place into shallow greased pan sprinkled with flour. Cover and let rise again. Glaze with egg white mixed with a little water. Bake in oven of 400°F. for about 30 minutes; increase to 425°F. and bake for 20 minutes longer.

If more loaves are desired, double recipe. If caraway seeds are desired, these may be added to dough when kneading.

SALT-RISING BREAD
(Use With Dairy Only)

3 cups sifted white flour
3 tablesp. white corn meal
¾ cup scalded milk
½ teasp. salt

1 tablesp. melted margarine or butter
1 tablesp. sugar
½ cup lukewarm water

Scald milk and add corn meal, sugar and salt. Blend thoroughly and place in large bowl or container. Cover and set in a pan of hot water; store in warm place and allow it to ferment—from 6 to 8 hours. When it is light and bubbly, stir in lukewarm water, half the flour and a little sugar. Return to lukewarm water pan. Let it rise again, and add remaining flour, stirring. Knead dough until it is smooth and has a satin gloss. Cover for about 10 to 15 minutes. Place in greased loaf pan. Using pastry brush, brush with shortening. Cover again and let it rise to at least double its bulk. Bake at 375°F. for 40 minutes or until brown. Yield: one loaf. If two loaves are desired, double the recipe.

BASIC DOUGH FOR ROLLS

4 cups sifted white flour	*⅔ cup lukewarm water*
2 tablesp. margarine (pareve)	*⅔ cup boiling water*
1 egg	*4 tablesp. sugar*
1 cake compressed yeast	*1 teasp. salt*

Dissolve yeast in lukewarm water. Add sugar, salt and margarine to boiling water. Cool, and when lukewarm, add 1 cup flour, then add beaten egg and softened yeast. Add enough flour to make a soft dough. Using floured board, add the balance of the flour, and work by kneading until smooth and glossy. Place in greased bowl and cover. When it has doubled in bulk, punch down. Cover again and allow to rise again— about 15 minutes. Shape into rolls and place into greased pans. Allow to rise again until doubled. Bake in oven of 425°F. for 20 minutes or until well browned.

SHAPING OF ROLLS

Bagel-shaped: Roll dough into 6-in. rolls and fold over, leaving hole in middle.

Crescents: Roll dough into circle about ¼ inch thick, like a pie crust. Cut into 6 pieces. Start rolling from the widest end to the narrow end. Shape into crescent and place on greased sheet.

Cloverleaf Rolls: Form dough into three balls. Brush with melted butter, and place the three balls together in each section of muffin tin.

Salt Sticks: Roll dough into circle about ¼ inch thick, like a pie crust. Cut into 6 pieces. Start rolling from the widest end to the narrow end. Sprinkle with caraway seeds and coarse salt.

Twists: Roll dough ¼ inch thick. Cut into 7-in. strips. With hands roll and stretch into longer strips. Fold each strip in half lengthwise. Pinch ends. Twist and tuck ends under.

Bowknots: Roll dough to ¼ inch thickness. Cut off ½ inch wide strips, 4 to 5 inches long. Roll, and stretch into longer strips. Twist, and tie into single or double bow knots. Place on greased baking sheet.

Swirls: Roll dough to ¼ inch thickness. Cut off ½ inch wide strips, about 5 inches long. Roll and stretch into longer strips. Holding index finger on one end, coil the strip around. Doing this on greased baking sheet is more convenient than trying to do it on a floured board and then transfer it to the baking sheet.

Clothespins: Roll dough to ¼ inch thickness. Cut off 7-in. strips. Roll and stretch strips. Wrap around greased clothespins (wooden type). Tuck in ends. When baked, twist out clothespins.

Fantans: Roll dough into long strip 2 inches wide and ¼ inch thick. Cut into 1-in. strips, stacking seven strips. Brush with butter and place on end in muffin tin. When baked, they have the markings of the cut every ¼ inch.

Butterflies: Roll dough into rectangle 6 inches wide and ¼ inch thick. Brush with melted butter or margarine. Roll, starting with long side. Cut roll into 2-in. pieces. Press knife handle across center of rolls. Bake on greased baking sheet.

BREAKFAST ROLLS

Use basic recipe for Challah, cutting it in half. Form into small round rolls. Take dough, and roll into ½ inch wide and 4-in. long rolls. Place these from end to end down center of each round roll. Brush with egg yolk and water mixture. Sprinkle with poppy seeds. Bake in oven of 375°F. for ½ hour.

WHOLE-WHEAT BREAD
(Serve With Dairy Meals Only)

2 cups whole-wheat flour	2 tablesp. butter
1 cup sifted white flour	4 tablesp. brown sugar
1 cake compressed yeast	½ cup water
1 egg	2 teasp. salt
½ cup milk	

Scald milk and add butter, salt and sugar. Cool with ½ cup water. When lukewarm, add yeast and blend thoroughly. Add egg, and gradually stir in whole-wheat flour, following with white flour. Mix until thoroughly blended. Using large bowl, grease well, and place dough in bowl. Cover bowl and place in cold place for between 2 to 3 hours. Shape into loaf on floured board. Place in well-greased pan, cover and let rise in warm place. When double in bulk, bake in oven of 375°F. for about 1 hour or until brown.

PUMPERNICKEL BREAD

This bread is one of the most popular with Jewish people. It is a dark brown color, usually has caraway seeds in it, and when fresh, is positively the most satisfying bread in the world.

3 cups rye flour	1 tablesp. shortening
3 cups white flour	2 tablesp. caramelized sugar
1 cake compressed yeast	1½ tablesp. caraway seed
¼ cup lukewarm water	Pinch of salt
1 cup boiling water	

Dissolve yeast in lukewarm water. Add sugar, shortening, salt, and caraway seeds to boiling water. When cooled to lukewarm, add yeast mixture. Add rye flour and white flour, and turn out on lightly floured board. Knead until smooth and easily handled. Place in well-greased bowl, greasing the top so that it will remain moist, and allow to stand in a warm place until double in bulk. Divide into two portions, and form into balls. Then roll until it is twice the width and length of the loaf pan, doubling or folding the ends in so that they overlap in the center of the bottom. Place in greased pan with seam at the bottom. Again grease top and allow to double in bulk. Bake in oven of 375°F. for a little over 1 hour.

POTATO ROLLS (Basic Recipe)
(Serve With Dairy Dishes)

4 cups sifted white flour	*¼ cup sugar*
1 cake compressed yeast	*1 stick margarine or ¼ lb.*
¼ cup lukewarm water	*butter*
1 egg, beaten well	*¾ cup mashed potatoes*
¾ cup milk, scalded	*1 teasp. salt*

Combine scalded milk with sugar, butter, mashed potatoes and salt, and allow to stand until cool. In the meantime, dissolve yeast in lukewarm water. When milk mixture is lukewarm, add yeast mixture and beaten egg. Add half the flour, and blend thoroughly, beating well. Cover, and allow to remain in warm place until it begins to get full of bubbles. Stir in balance of flour, and knead on floured board until smooth and pliable. Return to greased bowl, and grease top of dough. Cover and place in refrigerator to chill. About an hour or so before you wish to serve rolls, shape number of rolls desired, place in greased pan, and allow time for the rolls to double in bulk before placing in oven of 400°F. for 20 to 25 minutes.

An additional amount of the above basic recipe may be

prepared and placed in the refrigerator for other types of rolls, such as the following:

Date and nut rolls (adding chopped dates, nuts and brown sugar instead of the white sugar)

Prune and nut rolls (chop pitted cooked prunes, nuts, add ½ teaspoon baking powder and sprinkle with cinnamon and brown sugar)

BRIOCHES

1 cake compressed yeast	*½ cup scalded milk*
¼ cup warm water	*Melted butter for brushing*
4 cups sifted white flour	*dough*
3 eggs (reserving one egg yolk)	*¾ cup softened butter*
4 egg yolks	*¼ cup sugar*
	¼ teasp. salt

Set 2 twelve-cup muffin tins aside to accommodate brioches. Dissolve yeast in lukewarm water. Blend softened butter, sugar and salt. Pour scalded milk over this mixture; blend. Allow mixture to cool. Blend in half the flour with yeast mixture. Beat well. Add the eggs, one at a time, reserving 1 egg yolk. Add balance of the flour, and beat thoroughly until you can turn into greased bowl large enough for the bulk to double. Brush top with melted butter.

Cover with waxed paper, and then with tea towel. Set in warm place and allow to rise. When doubled in size, punch down, butter surface again and recover. Place in refrigerator overnight. Punch down several times when it rises.

Grease muffin tins and remove dough from refrigerator. Place dough on floured board. Shape ⅔ of dough into 2-in. balls. Form an equal number of smaller balls out of balance of dough, and shape into cones. With finger make a little hole in each of the bigger balls in the muffin tin. Insert tip of cone in each one. These cones form hats when baked. Cover

gently with light towel, and set in warm place to double its
bulk. Brush with mixture of egg yolk and a little milk. Bake
at 425°F. for 20 minutes.

BAGELS

BAGELS, the so-called "petrified doughnut" as bagel en-
thusiasts so lovingly call them, typify a Jewish delicacy in rolls.
Served plain or buttered, there is nothing like it. Served with
whipped cream cheese, it has no peer. But a bagel, cream
cheese and Nova Scotia . . . well, this is the nearest thing to
a taste sensation this side of heaven!

At first there was just the water bagel. Now, there are
bakeries which bake NOTHING BUT BAGELS! And these bakeries
turn out a variety which leaves nothing to the imagination
. . . water bagels, egg bagels, onion bagels, rye bagels, pumpernickel bagels, etc.

Although there is machinery now for making bagels, many
bakers still make them "by hand." To attempt to bake them
individually is quite a project, but if one has the time and
patience, here are the instructions:

WATER BAGELS

6 cups flour	2 eggs
1 cake compressed yeast	3 tablesp. sugar
1 cup lukewarm water	6 tablesp. salad oil
2 teasp. salt	5 qts. boiling water

Dissolve yeast in ¼ cup of lukewarm water. Combine oil
with balance of lukewarm water and mix with yeast. Sift dry
ingredients into large bowl. Make a well and drop two eggs
into well, adding balance of liquid mixture. Stir and form into
dough. Knead on floured board. Then return to mixing bowl
and punch down several times. Cover and let rise at room
temperature for about 20 minutes. When dough has risen,

knead again and divide into two dozen equal portions. Form into 6-in. pieces, about ¾ inch thick, and pinch ends together. Sprinkle baking sheet with flour, and place these forms under broiler flame for about 3 to 4 minutes.

In the meantime, fill a large pot with briskly boiling water. Drop each bagel into water. Cook over medium heat for about 20 to 25 minutes. Using strainer, take each bagel out of water, and place on baking sheet in oven at 375°F. for 15 minutes, then increase heat to 400°F. for another 10 minutes or until bagels are brown and crusty.

ONION ZEMMELS

4 cups white sifted flour	*1 tablesp. sugar*
1 pkge. yeast	*1½ cups of water*
¼ cup lukewarm water	*1 cup chopped onions*
1 teasp. sugar	*Coarse salt to sprinkle on top*
1 teasp. salt	*Melted shortening to spread*
1 tablesp. shortening	*over top of dough*

1 egg yolk

Follow the directions for regular bread dough. After kneading and allowing the bread to rise, shape into round balls and flatten to about 1-in. thickness. Place on a greased baking sheet about 3 inches apart, and press crease in center. Allow to rise in warm place. Brush with egg yolk and water mixture, sprinkle with coarse salt and chopped onions. Bake in moderate oven of 350°F. for about 25 minutes or until onions are browned.

Variation: Instead of onions and coarse salt, sprinkle with poppy seeds or sesame seeds, or prepare round strips of dough about ½-in. in width and 4 inches in length and place the strips down the center of each roll. Or, rolls may be braided, like a small challah.

QUICK BREADS

The basic difference between yeast breads and quick breads is that quick breads may be prepared within a short time and placed before the family without time-consuming preparation. The dough may be prepared within minutes and placed in the oven for baking. These breads have, in a sense, replaced the yeast breads in the home. Generally, the housewife will purchase the yeast breads from the baker, but will, in many instances, prepare the quick breads for her family at home, giving her family that home-baked flavor in rolls. That way she can also fit the bread to the particular meal being served.

BISCUITS (Basic Recipe)

3 cups flour
4 teasp. baking powder
1¼ cups ice water

1 stick pareve margarine or
butter (if dairy dishes are
being served)
1 teasp. salt

Sift flour and baking powder, adding salt. Cut in shortening until the flour and shortening mixture form crumbs. Add liquid gradually, handling dough as little as possible until a stiff dough is formed. On floured board, roll out to a thickness of about ½ inch. Using various shaped biscuit cutters, cut into biscuits and brush with melted margarine or butter. Bake in hot oven of 400°F. for approximately 15 minutes or until browned.

Important Note: Whenever making sour milk, buttermilk, or sour cream biscuits or when using these ingredients in baking, be sure to add ½ teaspoon baking soda for every cup used.

SOUR CREAM BISCUITS

3 cups flour   *1 stick butter*
1 ½ cups sour cream   *½ teasp. salt*
¾ teasp. baking soda

Sift flour and salt, and cut in shortening. Combine sour cream and baking soda, and add to mixture, making a soft dough. Turn onto floured board, and roll to about ½ inch thickness. Using biscuit cutter, place shapes on baking sheet and bake in hot oven of 400 to 425°F. for approximately 20 minutes or until browned. These biscuits must be served with a milchig meal.

CINNAMON RAISIN BISCUITS

Using basic recipe for biscuits, add ¼ cup seedless raisins to dough, and roll out in strips 6 to 7 inches long, about 3 inches wide. Sprinkle with cinnamon and sugar, roll up and place in round cake tins, brush with melted shortening, and sprinkle top with cinnamon and sugar. Bake in oven at 375°F. for about 15 minutes or until browned.

POPOVERS

1 ½ cups sifted flour   *1 ¼ cups milk*
½ teasp. salt   *2 tablesp. melted butter*
3 eggs

Grease muffin tin and preheat in oven for about 10 minutes or until hot. In the meantime, prepare the above ingredients by sifting flour and salt. Beat eggs well, and add milk and melted butter. Place flour in bowl, and make a well. Pour liquid ingredients into well, and beat with electric mixer or rotary beater until batter is smooth. Fill hot muffin tin half-full with batter, and bake at 450°F. for about 10 minutes.

Reduce temperature of oven to 375°F. and bake about 30 minutes more. Yield: about 11 or 12.

BRAN MUFFINS

1 cup bran	*¼ teasp. salt*
½ cup white flour	*1 tablesp. melted margarine*
1 egg	*1 cup buttermilk*
2 tablesp. molasses	*½ teasp. baking soda*

Combine flour and bran. Combine buttermilk and soda, and stir in beaten egg. Add molasses, seasoning and shortening to buttermilk mixture. Combine with flour and bran, beating until smooth. Grease muffin tin, and fill half-full with batter. Preheat oven to 375°F. and bake from 25 to 30 minutes.

Variation: ¼ cup seedless raisins, chopped and rolled in white flour, may be added just before placing in muffin tins.

CORN MEAL NUT MUFFINS

1½ cups corn meal	*6 teasp. baking powder*
1½ cups white flour	*4 tablesp. melted margarine*
3 tablesp. sugar	*or butter*
2 eggs	*½ cup coarsely chopped*
1½ cups milk	*walnuts*
½ teasp. salt	

Sift white flour and corn meal baking powder, salt and sugar. Beat eggs and add liquid and shortening. Combine until flour is completely blended. Grease muffin tins, and before pouring batter in, fold in nuts. Then fill tins a little over half-full, and bake in hot oven of 400°F. for between 25 and 30 minutes.

BLUEBERRY MUFFINS

1 cup flour	*2 tablesp. butter*
2 teasp. baking powder	*4 tablesp. sugar*
½ cup milk	*¼ teasp. salt*
1 egg	*1 cup blueberries*

Roll blueberries in a little flour. Cream butter and sugar, adding well-beaten egg. Sift flour, baking powder and salt and add alternately with milk. Add blueberries and place batter in well-greased muffin tins. Bake in hot oven of 425°F. for 30 to 35 minutes. Serve hot.

HONEY, NUT AND BRAN MUFFINS

1¼ cups flour	*1½ cups bran*
½ teasp. soda	*1 tablesp. melted butter*
1½ cups milk	*1 cup walnuts, chopped*
½ cup honey	*¼ teasp. salt*

Sift flour, baking soda, salt, bran and blend in other ingredients well. Grease muffin tin, pour in batter, and bake in oven of 425°F. for 30 to 35 minutes. Serve hot with melted butter and honey.

BANANA AND NUT BREAD

2 cups flour	*1 teasp. lime juice*
2 teasp. baking powder	*1 cup chopped walnuts or*
¾ cup sugar	*pecans*
1 cup mashed bananas	*2 eggs*
½ teasp. salt	*¼ cup butter*

Cream butter and sugar, add well-beaten eggs, bananas and lime juice. Sift flour, baking soda and salt. Combine mixtures, blending well. Grease loaf pan well. Fill loaf pan a little over half-full, and bake in oven of 375°F. for about a little more than 1 hour.

BAKING POWDER BISCUITS

1 ½ cups flour	2 tablesp. butter or marga-
3 teasp. baking powder	rine, softened
½ cup milk	½ teasp. salt

Sift flour with baking powder and salt. Blend flour and softened butter or margarine. Make a well, and pour milk into center of flour. Stir only until flour has been moistened. Turn onto floured board, and knead or roll with floured rolling pin until about ½ inch thick. Place on baking sheet, and bake in hot oven of 425°F. about 20 minutes or until browned.

BISCUITS FOR FRUIT SHORTCAKES

2 ¼ cups flour	1 stick butter or margarine
1 cup milk	½ teasp. salt
4 teasp. baking powder	3 tablesp. sugar

Sift dry ingredients and work in shortening with fork or blender. Add milk, and turn onto floured board. Roll to about ¾-in. thickness. Using larger biscuit cutter than used for regular biscuits, shape into large biscuits, place on floured baking sheet and bake in hot oven of 425°F. for about 15 to 18 minutes. For strawberry shortcake, split into 2 layers, placing berries over one half and covering with the other. Top with whipped cream.

Coffee Cakes, Sweet Rolls, and Kuchen

COFFEE CAKE
(Basic Recipe)

2 cups sifted white flour	½ teasp. salt
3 teasp. baking powder	1 cup milk
¾ cup sugar	¼ cup melted margarine or
2 eggs	butter

Sift dry ingredients. Beat eggs, and add melted shortening and milk. Add to flour mixture, but do not mix too much. Grease a square-type cake tin and pour in batter. The most popular topping for this cake is streusel topping (listed below):

STREUSEL TOPPING

1 stick butter or margarine	½ teasp. cinnamon
3 tablesp. sugar	½ cup toasted bread crumbs

4 tablesp. flour

Cream butter and sugar and add flour, cinnamon and toasted bread crumbs. Mix until it resembles cookie crumbles. Sprinkle over coffee cake. Bake in hot oven of 425°F. for 30 minutes.

Variation: Roll ¼ cup seedless raisins in flour and include in coffee cake to improve flavor.

Variation: In addition to the raisins, 3 cups of sliced apples may be placed over the cake and sprinkled with cinnamon, butter and brown sugar. The baking time, however, must be increased to about 45 minutes at 425°F.

Variation: The above coffee cake with raisins, may be iced with the following:

2 *tablesp. butter*	¼ *teasp. vanilla extract*
1 *cup confectionery sugar*	*A bit of candied fruits*
2 *tablesp. cream*	*A bit of chopped pecans*

Cream sugar and butter, and add cream and vanilla extract. Spread over top of coffee cake when cooled, and sprinkle with candied fruits and chopped pecans.

HAMANTASCHEN (Pareve)

3 *cups sifted white flour*	*Grated rind of 1 lemon*
2 *teasp. baking powder*	*Pinch of salt*
½ *cup sugar*	3 *eggs*
¼ *cup margarine (pareve)*	

Sift all dry ingredients and add eggs, margarine (melted) and lemon rind. Mix and blend thoroughly. Knead until smooth. Turn out on floured board and roll to about ⅛-in. thickness. Using cutter, cut into 3½-in. rounds. Place 1 tablespoon of poppy seed filling (below) in the center, and bring edges together, forming a triangle, and pinch securely. Place on greased baking sheet in moderate oven of 375°F. for about 30 to 40 minutes or until brown.

Variation: Double amount of sugar, double margarine, and add 1 teaspoon vanilla extract. This dough is a little sweeter.

POPPY SEED FILLING (For Hamantaschen)

2½ *cups poppy seeds*	1 *cup water*
¾ *cup honey*	⅓ *cup sugar*
1 *egg, beaten*	*Pinch of salt*

Pour boiling water over poppy seeds, and allow to stand until poppy seeds have settled. After draining, put through grinder at least twice, so that seeds are finely ground. Combine in saucepan with honey, sugar, a pinch of salt and water and cook over a low flame, stirring continually until mixture thickens. When cool, add egg and blend thoroughly. It is now ready for the Hamantaschen dough.

Variation: For prune filling, cook prunes with sugar to sweeten, pit, and either put through grinder or chop fine, adding a little lemon juice and grated rind of lemon.

Variation: Chopped raisins and nuts may be added to the poppy seed filling.

Variation: Using Hamantaschen filling and basic recipe for coffee cake, roll to about ¼ to ½-in. thickness, spread filling over dough, roll up and bake in hot oven of 425°F. for about 30 to 35 minutes. Sprinkle top with chopped nuts.

HAMANTASCHEN KUCHEN

2 *cups white flour, sifted*	1 *lemon rind, grated*
1 *teasp. baking powder*	2 *egg yolks, beaten well*
¼ *teasp. salt*	½ *cup sugar*
	1 *cup milk*

Sift dry ingredients and blend thoroughly with egg and milk mixture. Let stand while you prepare poppy seed filling (above). Roll out dough to about ¼ to ½-in. thickness, spread with poppy seed filling, roll dough so that it is like jelly roll. Brush top with egg yolk and a little water for sheen. Bake in moderate oven of 375°F. for about 30 to 35 minutes.

APPLE COFFEE CAKE

2½ cups sifted white flour   ¾ cup milk
3 teasp. baking powder   1½ teasp. cinnamon
1 stick margarine   2 cups sliced apples
½ cup sugar   Pinch of salt
      1 egg, beaten

Sift flour and baking powder and a pinch of salt together. Cut in shortening and add well-beaten egg and milk together, and then add to flour mixture, stirring to form dough. Place in greased, shallow baking pan and pat to about ½ to ¾-in. thickness. Sprinkle mixture of sugar and cinnamon over dough, reserving half to sprinkle over apples after arranging on top of dough. Top with Streusel (see Page 241) and bake in moderate oven of 350°F. for about 35 to 40 minutes. Increase heat to 400°F. last 10 minutes.

CINNAMON ROLLS

2½ cups flour   ½ cup seedless raisins,
4 teasp. baking powder   chopped fine
3 tablesp. sugar   Pinch of salt
3 tablesp. butter   ¾ teasp. cinnamon
      1 cup milk

Sift dry ingredients, cut in shortening, and add milk gradually, handling very little. Roll out into strips about ¼ to ½-in. in thickness and 6 inches in length. Combine sugar and cinnamon; roll raisins in flour and combine with cinnamon and sugar mixture. Sprinkle this mixture on each strip, and roll like a jelly roll. Butter a pan well and sprinkle generously with brown sugar. Place in the cinnamon rolls and bake in hot oven of 425°F. for about 35 to 40 minutes or until browned. Remove and serve caramel side up.

ORANGE NUT ROLLS

Using same ingredients as in Cinnamon Rolls, except cinnamon and raisins, substitute:

1 cup orange juice	*3 tablesp. butter*
Grated rind of 1 orange	*¾ cup sugar*
and Add:	*½ cup chopped pecans*

Sift dry ingredients, cut in shortening, and add milk gradually, handling very little. Roll out into strips of ¼-in. thickness and about 6-in. length. Brush with butter and a little orange juice, sprinkle with a little sugar. Bring orange juice, grated rind, butter and sugar above to a boil, and boil for about 2 minutes. Grease a pan and pour in this liquid. Sprinkle nuts on. Place rolls in this mixture and bake in hot oven of 425°F. for about 30 to 35 minutes. Serve orange side up.

UPSIDE-DOWN FRUIT COFFEE CAKE

Using basic recipe for Coffee Cake (see Page 241), prepare the following drained fruits: crushed pineapple, canned cherries, frozen sweetened strawberries, canned blueberries.

Using deep cake pan, oblong shape preferred, melt about 3 tablespoons butter in bottom of pan, sprinkle with about ⅓ cup of brown sugar, and cover bottom with drained canned fruit of your preference. Cover fruit with coffee cake dough (basic recipe) and bake in hot oven of 425°F. for between 20 to 30 minutes.

KUCHEN

Using basic recipe for Coffee Cake (see Page 241), add the following ingredients to batter:

½ cup honey   ¼ cup seedless raisins
            ½ teasp. cinnamon

Bake in hot oven for approximately 30 minutes. When cool, top with glazed confectionery icing (see Page 300) and sprinkle nuts and candied citron over top.

BEATEN BATTER (Basic Recipe)

1 cake compressed yeast   4 tablesp. butter or marga-
¼ cup lukewarm water   rine
1 cup scalded milk   3 cups white flour, sifted
Pinch of salt   2 eggs
            ⅓ cup sugar

Soften yeast in lukewarm water. Scald milk and add shortening, sugar and salt. When cool, add half the flour and beat. Combine softened yeast and eggs. Beat and blend thoroughly, then add remaining flour and beat until smooth. Cover and let rise until doubled in bulk, or about an hour. This dough would make one coffee cake and about one dozen sweet rolls, which could be iced and topped with chopped nuts and citron.

Variation: Using half the dough, top it with streusel topping (see Page 241).

Variation: Add ½ cup raisins to coffee cake and top with confectionery sugar icing and chopped nuts.

Variation: Add currants, raisins and chopped nuts and top with streusel topping.

APPLE KUCHEN

½ recipe for beaten batter   ¾ teasp. cinnamon
  (above)   ¼ cup seedless raisins (dark)
½ cup sugar (half white   2 tablesp. currants
  sugar and half dark brown)   Melted butter
3 to 4 tart apples

Shape dough to a ¾ inch thickness in either a round or oblong baking pan. Brush dough with melted butter. Arrange apple slices in pan: in round pan, start from the center and place slices in circles until they have completely covered the dough; in oblong pan, arrange slices in straight rows until dough has been covered. Mix the sugar, cinnamon, currants and raisins, and sprinkle this mixture over apples until entire surface is covered. Dot with pieces of butter, cover, and allow to rise to double its bulk. Bake in oven of 375°F. for about 30 to 40 minutes.

HONEY NUT BUNDT

½ beaten batter recipe   ¾ cup chopped walnuts
½ cup melted butter   ½ cup raisins

HONEY GLAZE

¾ cup honey   ¾ teasp. cinnamon
½ cup brown sugar   2 tablesp. flour
2 tablesp. melted butter

Make small balls from the dough. Brush with melted butter, then roll in chopped nuts and arrange in well-greased tube pan about ½-in. apart. Sprinkle with raisins. Place a second layer of round balls brushed with butter and dipped in chopped nuts on top of first layer and sprinkle with raisins. Press down so that the two layers become fused.

Combine honey, brown sugar, flour, butter and cinnamon

and spoon mixture over dough. Allow to rise until doubled in bulk. Bake in preheated oven of 375°F. for 40 to 45 minutes. Let cool for about 5 minutes before removing from pan.

SCHNECKEN

½ *beaten batter recipe*
¾ *cup melted butter*
1 cup brown sugar
½ *cup seedless raisins*

1 cup coarsely chopped pecans
¼ *cup currants*
1½ teasp. cinnamon

Lightly grease wells of 2 muffin tins (24 wells in all). Place about 1 teaspoon of melted butter in each well. Mix chopped nuts, brown sugar, currants, raisins and cinnamon. Place about 2 teaspoons of this mixture into each well, with at least 1 or 2 whole pecans in the center of mixture. Divide dough into 2 sections and roll each into a ball, shaping each ball into a piece about 6 inches wide and 12 inches long. Brush with melted butter, and sprinkle with remainder of brown sugar mixture. Roll each section of dough tightly into a long roll. Press edges and seal. Cut each of the two rolls into 12 slices, and place one slice in each of the muffin wells. Cover with towel, and let rise until doubled in bulk. Bake in 375°F. oven for 20 to 30 minutes. Leave Schnecken in pan for 5 minutes, then remove, glazed side up.

DANISH PASTRY

3½ cups white flour, sifted
2 cakes compressed yeast
½ *cup lukewarm water*
½ *cup scalded milk*
2 eggs (reserve 1 egg white)
Dash of salt

½ *cup sugar and* ½ *cup butter (creamed)*
½ *teasp. lemon extract*
½ *teasp. almond extract*
1 stick butter (for finished dough)

Dissolve yeast in lukewarm water, adding 2 tablespoons sugar to mixture. Allow scalded milk to cool, then add half the flour and beat with cooled milk and yeast mixture, until smooth. Cream butter and sugar, and beat eggs (reserving white) until light. Add salt and eggs to creamed mixture. Add this mixture to flour mixture, and gradually add the balance of the flour, making a stiff dough. Knead on floured board, and place ball of dough in greased bowl. Cover and let rise to about one-half its size more in bulk. Roll into long oval piece, about ½ to ¾-in. in thickness. Place pieces of butter over top, and roll over, so that this is encased inside; repeat, rolling dough until butter has been evenly distributed inside dough. Chill in refrigerator for about 1 hour.

Roll on floured board to a thickness of about ½ inch and form into various shapes—crescents, round-type rolls, triangles, etc.—leaving a little space in the middle which will be filled with either prune, cherry, or some other filling. Place on greased baking sheet and let it stand in a warm spot for about 1 hour. Fill the dough and fold it over. Brush with a mixture of egg white and water. Bake in very hot oven of 450°F. for about 10 minutes. Reduce heat to 400°F. and bake for about 30 minutes more, until well-browned. The various fillings are listed below.

FILLINGS FOR DANISH PASTRY

APPLE: Pare and slice 3 to 4 apples. Place a little water in pan and cook until tender. Add ½ teaspoon cinnamon, ½ cup sugar and ½ cup butter. Chill.

CHEESE: 1 cup dry cottage cheese, 1 beaten egg, 2 tablespoons sugar, 2 tablespoons melted butter, ¼ teaspoon cinnamon, ¼ teaspoon nutmeg. Beat until smooth.

PRUNE: Cook about 1 lb. prunes in water until tender. Remove pits, drain and put through food grinder. Add ½ teaspoon cinnamon, liquid sweetener and 1 tablespoon melted butter, as well as ½ teaspoon vanilla extract. Chill.

PINEAPPLE: Mix 1 cup drained crushed pineapple with
1 tablespoon sugar, ½ teaspoon lemon extract. Top Danish
with chopped nuts.

CHERRY: Either use cherry preserves or make your own by
washing and pitting cherries. Add about ¾ the amount of
sugar as you have cherries and cook with very little water.
When thick and clear, remove from flame. Chill.

The Spice Shelf

A SELECTION OF SPICES
FROM ALL OVER THE WORLD

FOR THE CONVENIENCE OF HOUSEWIVES, HERE IS A LIST OF SPICES easily secured in any supermarket or gourmet shop, which may be used in the preparation of kosher foods.

For kosher purposes, spices containing meats, derivatives of broths, poultry, etc., have been purposely omitted.

GROUND SPICES

Allspice, Ground Jamaica
Cardamom, Ground
   Decorticated
Chili Powder
Cinnamon, Saigon
Cloves, Ground Zanzibar
Cream of Tartar
Cumin (Comino) Ground
Curry Powder, Indian
Ginger, Ground Jamaica
Mace, East Indian
Marjoram, Ground French

Mustard, DSF
Nutmeg, Ground East
   Indian
Oregano, Ground Italian
Paprika, Fancy Imported
Poultry Seasoning
Pumpkin Pie Spice
Sage, Rubbed Dalmatian
Savory, Powdered
Thyme, Ground French
Turmeric, Ground Alleppy

PEPPERS

Black, Java
Black, Coarse Ground
Cayenne (Red)

Crushed Red
White Muntok

WHOLE SPICES

Allspice, Whole Jamaica
Anise Seed, Spanish
Basil Leaves, Sweet
Bay Leaves, Turk (Laurel)
Caraway Seed, Dutch
Cardamom, Fancy
Celery Seed, French
Cinnamon, Fancy Stick
Cloves, Whole Zanzibar
Coriander Seed
Cumin Seed (Comino)
Dill Seed, Indian
Dill Weed
Fennel Seed, Light
Ginger, Whole Jamaica

Marjoram, Whole French
Mustard Seed, Yellow
Nutmeg, Whole, East
   Indian
Oregano Leaves, Italian
Pepper, Black Java
Pickling Spice, Fancy
Poppy Seed, Dutch
Rosemary Leaves, French
Saffron, Spanish
Sage Leaves, Dalmatian
Sesame Seed, Hulled
Tarragon
Thyme, Whole, French

FLAKES

Celery Flakes
Garlic Flakes
Green Bell Pepper Flakes
Mint Flakes

Onion Flakes
Parsley Flakes
Vegetable Flakes

SALTS

Celery Salt
Garlic Salt

Hickory Smoked Salt
Onion Salt

GARLIC AND ONION (In Various Forms)

Garlic Chips
Garlic, Instant Powder
Onion, Instant Minced

Onion, Instant Powder
Onion, Sauté Style
Onion, Shredded Green

MISCELLANEOUS SEASONINGS

Barbecue Spice

Bon Appetit

Charcoal Seasoning

Chervil Leaves

Chives

Cinnamon-Sugar

Herb Seasoning

Horse-Radish Powder

Italian Seasoning

Lemon Peel

Monosodium Glutamate

Mushroom Powder

Salad Herbs

Season-All

Desserts and Puddings

PEACH MELBA

THIS DESSERT ORIGINATED IN FRANCE IN THE 1890's. IT WAS created by the fabulous Escoffier. Those of you who have parents or grandparents who emigrated from France are no doubt familiar with peach melba . . . luscious, attractive, and most delightful to any palate.

4 large ripe peaches   ½ *teasp. vanilla extract*
¾ cup sugar   *Lime or lemon juice*
                  ¾ cup water

Just before serving, peel and cut the 4 peaches into halves. Pit them. Rub either lime or lemon juice over peaches so that they will retain their yellow color. Blend sugar and water in saucepan and bring to a boil. Cover and boil for 3 minutes. Add vanilla extract and peach halves to saucepan and cook for about 3 minutes, or until peaches have been thoroughly warmed.

To serve peach melba: In individual deep dessert sherbets place the following:

1. A large scoop of vanilla ice cream
2. A warm peach-half over ice cream
3. Cold raspberry sauce over peach-half (see recipe below)
4. Topping of whipped cream

RASPBERRY SAUCE (For Peach Melba)

1½ cups fresh or frozen   2 teasp. water
raspberries   1 teasp. cornstarch
                 ½ cup sugar

Press berries through sieve. Blend together cornstarch and water, making a smooth paste. Place berries, sugar and cornstarch paste in saucepan, and blend thoroughly. Cook over low flame, stirring constantly, and bring to a boil. Cool. Place in covered dish and chill in refrigerator until ready for use.

FLOATING ISLAND

3½ cups milk   2 teasp. cornstarch
3 egg yolks   Pinch of salt
3 egg whites   ½ teasp. vanilla extract
          ½ cup sugar

Heat milk. Beat egg yolks and add sugar, salt and cornstarch. Beat egg whites until stiff, adding 1 tablespoon sugar (beating until it forms a peak). Drop 1 tablespoon of this meringue at a time into the hot milk, and continue cooking for about 3 minutes, or until firm. Set these meringue forms on a plate and pour hot milk on beaten egg yolk mixture. Place mixture in double boiler and stir constantly. Remove when thickened and cool. Add vanilla extract. Serve in sherbet glasses, filling bottom with thickened mixture and placing one meringue floating island on top. Dot with candied cherry.

BAKED CUSTARD

3 cups hot milk   ¼ cup sugar
3 eggs   ¼ teasp. salt
          ½ teasp. vanilla extract

Beat eggs, adding salt and sugar. When sugar dissolves, add· hot milk gradually to egg mixture. Add vanilla extract. Pour into individual dessert cups and place in a pan of hot water. Bake at 325°F. for 30 to 40 minutes, or until custard is firm in center. Test with knife. If knife comes out clean, custard is ready to remove from oven.

CHOCOLATE CUSTARD

3 cups scalded milk	½ teasp. vanilla extract
1 oz. square bitter chocolate	1 egg
⅓ cup sugar	1 tablesp. cornstarch
Pinch of salt	

Mix slightly beaten egg with cornstarch, salt and sugar. Add scalded milk gradually, stirring constantly. Add melted chocolate to mixture, placing in top of double boiler. When it thickens, remove from flame and cool. Add vanilla extract. Serve in individual sherbet glasses.

BLANC MANGE

3 cups scalded milk	3 tablesp. sugar
3 egg whites	Pinch of salt
3 tablesp. cornstarch	¼ cup cold milk
½ teasp. vanilla extract	

Mix cornstarch, sugar and salt and add cold milk. Add mixture to scalded milk in top of double boiler. Stir constantly over low flame until mixture thickens. Cool to lukewarm. Fold in stiffly beaten egg whites. Add vanilla extract. Place in individual molds. May be served with fruit sauce over it.

CARAMEL CUSTARD

3 cups scalded milk	⅓ cup sugar
4 eggs, slightly beaten	½ teasp. vanilla extract

Caramelize sugar by placing it in a small skillet over a low flame, until it becomes completely melted. Add milk very gradually, making certain that it does not bubble over. Add this mixture to eggs, along with flavoring. Place in greased individual molds in a pan of hot water and bake at 325°F. from 35 to 40 minutes, or until firm. Chill and serve with a topping of whipped cream, flavored with a little vanilla extract.

CHOCOLATE PUDDING

1 pt. milk	*½ cup sugar*
1 oz. square bitter chocolate	*2½ tablesp. cornstarch*

Melt chocolate in double boiler. Mix cornstarch with ½ cup of milk and set aside. Add sugar and balance of milk to chocolate mixture and cook until it reaches the boiling point. Add cornstarch in ½ cup milk to mixture, stirring until blended. Cook until mixture thickens. Place in sherbet glasses and chill. Top with whipping cream and candied cherry.

CHOCOLATE PUDDING (Variation)

2 sqs. unsweetened chocolate	*Pinch of salt*
3 egg yolks	*1 tablesp. flour*
¾ cup sugar	*½ teasp. vanilla*
1½ cups scalded milk	

Beat egg yolks. Melt chocolate in top of double boiler. Combine flour, sugar and pinch of salt, and stir into chocolate. Gradually stir in ½ scalded milk, beating mixture until smooth. Mix balance of scalded milk with well-beaten egg yolks. When completely blended, add to chocolate mixture, stirring continually. Cook for at least 5 minutes in double boiler. When you remove from heat, add vanilla. Place in sherbet glasses and cool. Serve with topping of whipping cream.

CORN MEAL PUDDING
(Vilna Pudding)

½ cup yellow corn meal   ½ teasp. ginger
1 qt. milk, scalded   ½ teasp. salt
Grated rind of 1 lemon   ½ cup molasses

In top of double boiler, pour scalded milk over corn meal, and cook for at least ½ hour. Add molasses, seasoning and lemon rind. Grease baking dish, and bake in oven of 325°F. for 1½ hours. May be served with rich cream or sprinkled with brown sugar.

CORN MEAL PUDDING
(Odessa Pudding)

3 cups milk, scalded   3 tablesp. tapioca (minute
⅓ cup yellow corn meal   type)
½ teasp. ginger   2 tablesp. butter
¼ teasp. cinnamon   1 cup cold milk
                ½ cup brown sugar

Scald milk in double boiler, adding corn meal and tapioca. Stir continually until mixture is smooth and thickened. Add seasoning, sugar and butter. Add cold milk last and cover. Cook slowly for another 2 hours. May be served hot with a fruit sauce.

TAPIOCA CREAM PUDDING

½ cup quick tapioca   Pinch of salt
½ cup sugar   2½ cups milk
2 egg whites (beaten until   ½ teasp. vanilla extract
stiff)   2 egg yolks

Combine tapioca and milk in top of double boiler. Cook until tapioca is clear. Beat egg yolks, add to the tapioca with sugar and salt and cook until it thickens. Remove from fire. Cool. When cool enough, fold in stiffly beaten egg whites and flavor with vanilla extract. Top with whipped cream and maraschino cherry.

DATE AND NUT PUDDING

1 cup sifted white flour	½ cup pecans, chopped
¾ cup brown sugar	1½ cups boiling water
2 teasp. baking powder	½ cup milk
1 cup dates (cut in small pieces)	2 tablesp. butter
	¼ teasp. salt
½ teasp. vanilla extract	

Sift flour 3 times into mixing bowl. Add dates and milk, stirring until blended. Grease casserole and preheat oven to 375°F. Pour batter into casserole and add rest of ingredients. Pour boiling water over batter in casserole, stirring until sugar is completely dissolved. Bake 30 to 35 minutes. Serve hot.

BAKED ALASKA

Ready-made sponge cake	6 egg whites
1 qt. ice cream in brick form	¾ cup sugar

This dessert must be prepared just before it is served. Sponge cake should be 2 inches thick and cut so that it is a little longer and wider than a quart brick of ice cream. Place cake in a shallow baking pan. Beat egg whites, adding sugar gradually, so that when stiffly beaten, the mixture is smooth and has a glossy look. Place brick of ice cream over sponge cake. Spread meringue over sides and top of ice cream. Place in hot oven of 500°F. and bake from 3 to 4 minutes, or until meringue is golden brown. Use spatula to remove Baked Alaska from baking pan, and serve at once, so that ice cream does not melt. Cut into 1 inch slices.

APRICOT WHIP

2 cups cooked apricots,   3 egg whites
    ground   ½ cup sugar
Juice of 1 lemon   1 cup whipping cream

Combine ground apricots and lemon juice. Whip cream
until stiff, and fold into apricot mixture. Beat egg whites
until stiff, adding sugar gradually. The mixture should be
smooth and glossy. Fold into apricot mixture. Pour into
greased casserole. Bake in shallow pan of hot water at 325°F.
for 40 minutes.

PRUNE WHIP

1 lb. prunes   ¾ cup sugar
¼ cup chopped walnuts   1 teasp. lemon juice
6 egg whites   Pinch of salt

Cook prunes and when soft, pit. Grind in food chopper
and add sugar. Cook until thoroughly blended, or about 6
or 7 minutes. Remove from heat and chill. Beat egg whites
until stiff, adding a pinch of salt when almost done. Add
lemon juice and nuts to prune mixture, and fold in egg whites
last. Place in greased casserole and bake in moderate oven of
300°F. for about 15 to 20 minutes. Chill. Serve individually
in sherbet glasses topped with whipping cream.

PRUNE WHIP (Baked)

2 cups prunes, cooked and   ½ cup sugar
    ground   1 lemon rind, grated
5 egg whites (beaten until   ⅓ cup chopped walnuts
    stiff)   ¼ teasp. salt

Beat egg whites until stiff, adding salt. Add sugar gradually
to egg whites until it forms peaks and is smooth and glossy.
Fold into prunes, adding chopped nuts and grated lemon
rind. Turn into greased casserole, which has been placed in
shallow pan of hot water, and bake at 300°F. for an hour.

FRUIT WHIP

3 cups dried prunes, apricots   1½ cups whipping cream
    and pears   ¾ cup sugar
2 cups water   1 tablesp. lemon juice

Simmer dried fruits in 2 cups of water over low flame for ½ to ¾ hour (after soaking in cold water overnight). Place these fruits through sieve with liquid. Stir in sugar and lemon juice and chill. Whip cream until stiff. Fold into fruit mixture and place in dessert sherbets. Chill in refrigerator.

SCHAUM TORTE

You must follow the directions precisely when preparing this torte, since it is made entirely without flour and its success depends upon how you handle the mixture of meringue and addition of other ingredients.

2 cups refined sugar (sifted)   Sweetened strawberries, rasp-
2½ teasp. water   berries or blueberries
2½ teasp. vanilla   1 cup whipping cream (fla-
2½ teasp. vinegar   vored with ¾ teasp. of the
7 egg whites   fruit juice used in layer of
½ teasp. baking powder   torte)
            Dash of salt

Beat egg whites until stiff, adding baking powder and salt. Separately combine vinegar, water and vanilla. Add 1 teaspoon of sugar and a little of the vinegar mixture, alternately, to egg whites, continually beating as these ingredients are added. After all ingredients have been added, beat for an additional 2 or 3 minutes, or until mixture is stiff. Place in 2 spring forms (10-in. type preferably), well-greased and sprinkled with a little flour. Bake in oven of 275°F. for about 1 hour and 40 minutes. Remove from oven and cool. Fill layers with sweetened fruit, and top with whipping cream.

APPLE BROWN BETTY

This dessert may be served with variations and is most acceptable with whatever fruit is substituted for the above. Try this in its various forms to top one of Mama's lavish dinners.

2½ cups apples (cored and   1 stick melted butter
   sliced)   ⅓ cup sugar
Juice of 1 lemon   ½ teasp. cinnamon
Grated rind of 1 lemon   ¼ teasp. nutmeg (ground)
½ cup water   ¼ cup chopped pecans
        1½ cups soft bread crumbs

Combine sugar, cinnamon and nutmeg and set aside. Mix melted butter and bread crumbs. Grease a baking dish and place a layer of buttered bread crumbs on the bottom, then a layer of apples. Sprinkle with the sugar-cinnamon-nutmeg combination and repeat layers, sprinkling with chopped nuts and topping with bread crumbs. Then pour lemon juice, rind and water over top and sprinkle with a few chopped nuts. Bake in moderate oven of 350°F. for 45 to 50 minutes. Serve with a topping of whipped cream.

Variations: Fruits which may be substituted for apples:

Cherries (pitted)   Stewed prunes
Blueberries   Stewed apricots
Peaches   Sliced bananas
Canned pineapple (chunks or
   slices, diced)

BAVARIAN CREAM PUDDING
(Refrigerated Mold)

6 egg yolks   ½ cup hot milk
1 tablesp. unflavored gelatin   6 tablesp. sugar
¼ cup cold water   1 cup whipping cream
        1 teasp. vanilla

Beat egg yolks and add sugar, beating until light. Soften gelatin in water and hot milk. Using top of double boiler, heat these 5 ingredients in saucepan, stirring constantly until mixture thickens. Cool. Whip cream until thick, add vanilla to pudding mixture, then fold in whipping cream. Place in mold and refrigerate. When serving, place lady fingers in sherbet glasses, then the Bavarian pudding, and top with whipped cream and maraschino cherry.

BAVARIAN CREAM PUDDING (Butterscotch)

6 egg yolks	*1 cup whipping cream*
1 tablesp. unflavored gelatin	*1 teasp. vanilla*
¼ cup cold water	*2 tablesp. brown sugar*
½ cup hot milk	*(sprinkle on whipped*
½ cup firmly packed brown	*cream topping on each*
sugar	*serving)*

Follow directions for Bavarian Cream Pudding. Serve in sherbets, topped with whipping cream and sprinkled with brown sugar.

BAVARIAN CREAM PUDDING (With Berries)

Use either strawberries, blueberries, raspberries, or canned, pitted cherries.

2 cups berries	*Pinch of salt*
1 tablesp. unflavored gelatin	*1 cup whipping cream*
½ cup sugar (or more, ac-	*¼ cup cold water*
cording to taste)	*¼ cup boiling water*

Saturate berries in sugar, before crushing. Leave as many whole berries as needed to garnish each serving. Dissolve gelatin in cold water, pour boiling water over it in top of double boiler. Cool and add crushed fruit and salt. When it starts to jell, fold in whipping cream, placing in wet mold. Refrigerate. Serve in sherbets, topping with whole berries or whipped cream dotted with whole berries. Bavarian pudding may be used to make a beautiful parfait. Place some lady fingers in parfait sherbets, follow with a layer of Bavarian pudding or cream, a layer of crushed fruit and sauce, and a layer of Bavarian cream, etc. Top with whipped cream and whole berries.

FRUIT MOLD

30 to 40 vanilla wafers
2 cups fresh or frozen straw-
   berries or raspberries
   (If frozen berries are used,
   use only 2 tablesp. sugar)

1 pkge. unflavored gelatin
¼ cup cold water
2 cups whipping cream
½ cup sugar

Wash berries and sprinkle ½ portion of sugar over them. Soften gelatin in cold water and place in top of double boiler to dissolve. Cool. Whip cream, adding sugar, and bring to a thick glossy consistency. Place vanilla wafers in bottom of mold, spread whipped cream over, then berries, then whipped cream and top with vanilla wafers. Refrigerate overnight. Serve, garnishing with whole berries and a dab of whipping cream.

STRAWBERRY SHORTCAKE (Old-Fashioned)
(Basic Shortcake Recipe)

1½ cups sifted white flour
3 teasp. baking powder
¼ teasp. salt

1½ tablesp. sugar
3 tablesp. butter, margarine
   or other shortening
½ cup milk

Mix and sift dry ingredients and cut in shortening with knife. Gradually add milk until dough can be handled. Place on floured board and roll out to ½ inch thickness. Cut with a large biscuit cutter, place on baking sheet, and bake in hot oven of 425°F. for 15 minutes or until browned. Split in half, covering bottom half with crushed fruit. Replace top half of biscuit. Cover with whole berries and top with whipped cream.

Those prefering to use prepared biscuit dough, frozen biscuit dough, or prepared biscuit ready for the oven, should follow directions for baking given by the manufacturer.

Strawberries: Crush 2 cups of strawberries with ¾ cup of sugar. Refrigerate for several hours before using. Wash 2 cups of whole berries and sprinkle with sugar. Set aside in refrigerator until ready to use.

APPLE PAN DOWDY

2½ cups apples, cored and
    sliced
Rind of lemon, grated
1 cup sifted white flour
1 teasp. baking powder
2 eggs

½ cup firmly packed brown
    sugar
¼ teasp. cinnamon
⅓ cup milk
⅓ cup shortening, softened
½ cup granulated sugar

½ teasp. salt

Grease the bottom and sides of baking dish and cover bottom with apple slices and grated rind of lemon. Sprinkle with cinnamon and brown sugar. Sift flour and baking powder. Cream shortening and granulated sugar, adding eggs and combining with flour. Add the milk little by little, and beat until smooth. Pour batter over apples and bake in moderate oven of 350°F. for between 40 and 45 minutes. Carefully use sharp knife to loosen batter from sides of pan and invert onto cake platter for serving, so that apples are on top. Garnish with vanilla ice cream or top with whipping cream.

AUF LAUF

6 egg yolks
6 egg whites (beaten until
    stiff)

½ teasp. salt
2 cups milk
1 cup sifted white flour

Bring milk to a boil and stir in flour. Cook until thick, stirring continually. Remove from heat and beat in egg yolks one at a time. Then beat the egg whites stiffly, add salt, and beat until they form a stiff peak. Fold carefully into batter and pour into greased baking dish or casserole. Bake in hot oven of 400°F. for about 25 minutes, or until brown. Serve hot with strawberry preserves or stewed blueberries with sauce.

AUF LAUF WITH APPLES

4 egg whites	*1 teasp. baking powder*
4 egg yolks	*2 cups apples, peeled and*
4½ tablesp. butter	*cored **
½ cup brown sugar *	*¼ cup almonds, blanched*
¾ cup white sugar	*and ground*
1 cup flour	*1 teasp. vanilla extract*

2 tablesp. ice water

Grease a 2 to 2½ quart casserole on bottom and sides. Place brown sugar over bottom, arrange apples in layers on the bottom of casserole and sprinkle with brown sugar, dotting with a few pats of butter and a sprinkle of cinnamon. Bake in oven of 350°F. for about 15 minutes. Remove from oven and allow to cool.

Beat egg yolks, adding sugar, butter and ice water, and continue beating until light and fluffy. Sift flour, baking powder, measure and sift again. Add to mixture, including ground almonds and vanilla extract, and blend thoroughly. Beat egg whites until stiff, but not dry, and fold them into mixture carefully, so that batter will be light and fluffy. Pour batter over apples (which should be cool) in casserole and bake in preheated oven for 35 to 40 minutes. Serve hot, sprinkling with a little confectionery sugar and cinnamon.

* Look for instructions on this before making batter.

LEMON SPONGE

1 tablesp. unflavored gelatin	*Juice of 2 lemons*
¼ cup cold water	*4 egg whites (beaten until*
1¼ cups sugar	*stiff)*
1¼ cups boiling water	

Dissolve gelatin in cold water for about 5 minutes. Add boiling water, strained lemon juice and sugar. When mixture begins to thicken, fold in stiffly beaten egg whites, blending thoroughly. Pour into mold and refrigerate. Serve with favorite fruit sauce, custard sauce or vanilla sauce, or top with whipping cream and a slice of lemon.

MOUSSES

There are two different varieties of the so-called "mousse" in the dessert family. One type is made with gelatin and the other without. Listed here are the mousses prepared with gelatin; they are not quite as rich as the other type which may be considered the "true" dessert. The latter type of mousse is made with whipping cream, sometimes egg yolks, and confectionery or granulated sugar, chocolate, maple or fresh fruit flavoring. This variety is actually superfine ice cream; thus, you will find them in the section on ICE CREAM AND FROZEN DESSERTS.

VANILLA MOUSSE
(Basic Recipe)

1 teasp. unflavored gelatin	*3 egg whites*
1 cup of milk	*⅓ cup sugar*
1 cup of whipping cream	*½ teasp. vanilla*
Dash of salt	

Dissolve gelatin in ¼ cup of milk. Heat balance of milk and pour over gelatin. Add sugar and salt. Chill. Allow gelatin mixture to thicken slightly, then beat. Add vanilla and beaten whipped cream. Beat egg whites stiffly and fold into gelatin mixture. Freeze.

Maple Mousse may be made by substituting ⅓ cup of maple syrup for the sugar.

Chocolate Mousse: 1½ squares of chocolate—heat in top of double boiler with a little of the hot milk. Add ½ cup sugar instead of ⅓ cup sugar. Beat with rotary beater. Chill, and fold into balance of mixture, folding in whipped cream and stiffly beaten egg whites carefully.

Peppermint Mousse: Crush 6 to 8 peppermint stick canes (red and white striped). Omit sugar.

Strawberry Mousse: Add 1 cup of crushed strawberries and 2 teasp. lemon juice with whipped cream.

Raspberry Mousse: Add 1 cup of crushed raspberries and 2 teasp. lemon juice with whipped cream.

APRICOT MOUSSE

2 cups dried apricots	*2 tablesp. lemon juice*
1 cup sugar	*1½ cups whipping cream*

After soaking in cold water, cook apricots slowly until tender. Press through a sieve. Mix with sugar until sugar is dissolved, using a little lemon juice to aid this process. Whip cream, fold in lemon juice and then apricot mixture. Freeze either in freezing trays or mold which is placed in freezing compartment.

VANILLA CUSTARD MOUSSE

2 egg yolks	*⅓ cup sugar*
2 egg whites	*1 cup whipping cream*
½ teasp. vanilla extract	

Beat egg yolks, adding sugar and vanilla extract. Using rotary beater, beat until sugar is completely blended. Fold stiffly beaten egg whites into mixture. Whip cream until thick. Fold into mixture and place in freezing trays or mold, placing in freezing compartment until firm.

Chocolate Custard: Melt 1½ squares unsweetened chocolate in top of double boiler. Increase sugar to ½ cup. Blend in double boiler, beating with rotary beater. Chill. Add beaten egg yolks to mixture. Fold in whipped cream and freeze in trays or mold.

Chocolate Chip: Shave or grate semi-sweet chocolate, and add to vanilla custard mousse recipe. Freeze in trays or mold.

Lemon: Add grated rind of lemon and juice of 1 lemon to whipped cream before folding into egg mixture. Freeze in trays or mold.

BAKED APPLES
(With Orange Sauce)

4 to 6 apples	*2 tablesp. butter*
1 cup orange juice	*1 cup seedless raisins (light)*
⅓ cup sugar	*½ teasp. cinnamon*

Pare and core apples. Place in salted cold water to prevent them from discoloring. Cook orange juice, sugar and butter together until clear. Remove apples from salted water and wipe dry. Fill centers with raisins sprinkled with cinnamon. Stick a clove of cinnamon in center of each apple. Place in greased shallow baking dish. Pour orange mixture over each apple and bake in moderate oven of 350°F. for 1 hour. Baste frequently with orange sauce.

CUP CUSTARD

1 cup milk (scalded)	*Dash of salt*
3 tablesp. sugar	*2 egg yolks*

Scald milk in top of double boiler, adding sugar and dash of salt. Beat egg yolks until light, and stir in hot milk gradually, blending well. Pour into custard cups. Place in pan of hot water and bake in moderate oven of 325°F. for about 40 to 45 minutes or until set. May be served hot or cold with cream.

CARAMEL CUP CUSTARD

Caramelize custard in small pan, and pour into each cup-custard mold, tilting so that caramel will spread over entire bottom. Pour regular custard (recipe above) in each cup while hot. Bake as instructed for Cup Custard.

MAPLE CUP CUSTARD

Substitute maple syrup for the sugar called for in Cup Custard and add ¼ cup chopped nuts, or if desired, just garnish each cup with a whole pecan.

APPLE DUMPLINGS

Biscuit dough: 1½ cups flour, 3 teaspoons baking powder, 2 tablespoons shortening, ⅔ cup milk, ½ teaspoon salt, 2 tablespoons sugar. Sift flour, baking powder, salt and sugar. Cut in shortening until crumbs are formed. Combine with liquid, to make a stiff dough. Roll on floured board to ¼ inch thickness and cut in squares large enough to encompass an apple, cored and pared, with enough dough left over to tuck edges in tightly.

Apples: Pare and core 6 apples. Fill apples with a mixture of 1 cup brown sugar, ½ teaspoon cinnamon, ½ teaspoon nutmeg and dot with butter. Cut straight line gash on apple in four different places. Cover with square of biscuit dough, pinching together at top and pinching seams of dough on sides. Brush with milk, place in baking pan with ¼ inch hot water, and bake in oven of 425°F. for 45 to 50 minutes, or until crust is browned. Thicken fruit juice which comes through seams and blends with hot water, with 2 tablespoons cornstarch, 3 tablespoons sugar, a little vanilla extract and serve as a hot sauce over dumplings.

Variation: Peaches may be pitted and substituted for apples. Serve garnished with whipped cream or sour cream.

CHOCOLATE ICEBOX CAKE

2 cups milk	½ cup sugar
1 square unsweetened chocolate	2½ tablesp. cornstarch
	24 lady fingers

Melt chocolate in top of double boiler, adding sugar and half the milk. Mix cornstarch with rest of milk and add to chocolate mixture. Line glass pie plate with lady fingers, bottom and sides. Pour thickened chocolate mixture into glass pie plate filled with lady fingers and chill in refrigerator. When ready to serve, top with whipped cream garnished with shaved, semi-sweet chocolate bits.

RICE CUSTARD PUDDING

¾ cup uncooked rice	¼ teasp. nutmeg, ground
3½ cups milk	½ cup seedless raisins
4 tablesp. butter or margarine	(light)
4 eggs	Combined cinnamon-sugar
⅔ cup sugar	(for sprinkling on top)
½ teasp. salt	1 teaspoon vanilla extract

Cook rice, following directions on label of package. Pour into generously buttered baking dish. Scald milk with butter or margarine. Separately, in mixing bowl, beat eggs slightly with sugar, salt, nutmeg and vanilla extract. Gradually stir this mixture into scalded milk mixture, adding raisins. Strain over rice in baking dish and sprinkle with cinnamon-sugar.

Place baking dish in shallow pan of hot water in oven and bake at 325°F. for 1 hour, until almost set but soft in center.

As mixture cools, custard will set. Serve either warm or chilled.
May be served with topping of whipped cream, if desired.

NESSELRODE PUDDING

1 pkge. unflavored gelatin
½ cup cold water
6 egg yolks
6 egg whites
½ cup sugar

½ cup raisins
¼ cup blanched almonds
¼ cup citron (cut in small
*   pieces)*
2 cups hot milk
1 teasp. vanilla

Dissolve gelatin in cold water. Beat egg yolks with sugar
and heat milk in top of double boiler. When hot, add egg
yolk mixture and dissolved gelatin. Keep stirring until blended
thoroughly. Add nuts, citron and raisins. Chill. When cool,
add vanilla and fold in egg whites (beaten until stiff). Place
in mold and chill in refrigerator until firm. Serve with topping
of whipped cream and maraschino cherry.

STEAMED APRICOT PUDDING

2¼ cups sifted flour
2 cans (1 lb. each) apricot
*   halves*
3 teasp. baking powder
½ teasp. salt
1 teasp. ground cardamon

2 eggs
1 cup sugar
5 tablesp. butter or
*   margarine*
¾ cup milk
½ teasp. lemon extract

Grease an 8 cup tube mold and sprinkle with sugar; set
aside. Reserving juice from canned apricots and 7 perfect
halves, drain balance of apricots; cut up to measure about
¾ cup. Cream butter and sugar and beat in eggs. Sift flour,
baking powder, salt, and cardamon several times. Then add
to creamed butter and sugar, stirring until well-blended. Stir
in apricots and lemon extract. Pour into prepared mold. Cover
with foil and tie tightly with string. Place on rack in large

kettle or steamer with water (boiling hot) to half the depth of mold. Cover kettle and steam for about 2 hours, or until long skewer placed in center of mold comes out clean. Cool on wire rack for 5 to 10 minutes. Loosen edges of mold with a knife and invert onto serving platter. When ready to serve, place 7 perfect apricot halves around top of mold and pour hot apricot sauce over top.

APRICOT SAUCE

Apricots (whatever is left
  from pudding)
4 tablesp. butter or
  margarine

¼ teasp. salt
Juice (from canned apricots
  above)
½ cup honey

Beat syrup and apricots not used in above pudding until smooth. Either use a blender or press through a sieve. Pour into saucepan. Stir in honey, butter or margarine, and salt. Heat to the boiling point. Cook uncovered and stir continually for 20 to 25 minutes, or until thick. Use ½ cup to pour over top of apricot pudding, and the rest to serve over individual portions.

CHOCOLATE CRÊME DESSERT

2 tablesp. sugar
1 tablesp. cornstarch
     2 cups prepared eggnog

2 squares semi-sweet
  chocolate

Combine sugar and cornstarch with a little eggnog in top of double boiler. Stir in balance of eggnog and add chocolate. Heat over boiling water until chocolate melts and mixture thickens. Pour into dessert dishes and chill. Serve with whipped cream and garnish with grated semi-sweet chocolate.

Ice Cream and Frozen Desserts

Parfaits, ice cream of a variety of flavors, frozen desserts which are eye appealing and appetite teasing delight the junior members of the family, but very often intrigue adults as well. Most important in the preparation of these delightful desserts, snacks, or party fare, is to bear in mind the manner in which they are served. Parfaits, in order to carry their message to the palate, must be served in suitable parfait taller-type glasses, preferably with stems. Ice cream should be served in sherbet glasses with stems. There are also dessert dishes, bowl-shaped, which have accompanying small plates which may be used when iced cakes or cookies are served with ice cream.

PARFAIT (Basic Recipe)
(Vanilla Flavor)

1¼ cups sugar	3 egg whites
1 cup water	1¾ cups whipping cream
¼ teasp. salt	1 teasp. vanilla extract

Combine sugar and water and boil until threads are formed. Beat egg whites and add salt, beating until stiff, although moist. Pour sugar mixture over egg whites, continually beating until cool. Add vanilla flavoring and carefully fold in whipped cream. Chill in freezer trays. Serve with topping of whipped cream, maraschino cherries and chopped nuts.

Raspberry parfait: 1 cup crushed berries, reserving juice if frozen. Add 1 tablespoon lemon juice with whipped cream and omit vanilla extract. Pour juice over parfait when serving, with whipped cream and berry.

Strawberry parfait: 1 cup crushed berries, reserving the juice if frozen. Add 1 tablespoon lemon juice with whipped cream and omit vanilla extract. Serve, pouring juice over parfait, topping with whipped cream and whole strawberry.

Chocolate parfait: Add ½ cup grated or shaved unsweetened chocolate to sugar and water mixture, continually beating until chocolate has been completely blended. Follow basic recipe for vanilla parfait for balance of ingredients and instructions for serving.

Pineapple parfait: Add 1 cup drained, crushed pineapple and 1 tablespoon lemon juice to whipped cream, omitting vanilla extract. Reserve juice and use it in serving parfait, plus a little of the crushed pineapple on top.

Maple parfait: Heat 1 cup of maple syrup, and substitute for both sugar and water in the basic recipe for vanilla parfait. Top with whipped cream and chopped nuts.

Coffee parfait: Combine sugar with 1 cup strong black coffee instead of water in the basic recipe for vanilla parfait.

CHOCOLATE MOUSSE

2 squares unsweetened chocolate	Dash of salt
	½ cup sugar
1 cup milk	1 cup whipping cream
3 egg whites	¼ teasp. vanilla extract

Melt chocolate in top of double boiler, adding milk and sugar and beating with rotary beater. When thoroughly blended, remove and cool. Fold in whipped cream and well-beaten egg whites, after adding vanilla extract. Freeze in refrigerator trays. Serve with topping of whipped cream with shavings of chocolate.

MAPLE MOUSSE

1 ¼ cups maple syrup   5 egg whites
5 egg yolks   1 teasp. vanilla extract
            2 ¼ cups whipping cream

Beat egg yolks until light and fluffy. Add maple syrup and place in top of double boiler, stirring constantly until it thickens and coats spoon. Cool quickly by placing in pan of ice. Beat until mixture is creamy. Add vanilla extract, and carefully fold in stiffly beaten egg whites and whipped cream. Place in refrigerator trays and freeze until firm. Serve with topping of whipped cream with maraschino cherry.

PISTACHIO MOUSSE

½ cup shelled pistachio nuts,   ¼ teasp. vanilla extract
   chopped   3 drops of green coloring
⅓ cup confectionery sugar   (vegetable)
            1 cup whipping cream

Whip cream. Fold ingredients into cream, blending. Refrigerate in freezing trays. When firm, serve with topping of whipped cream and candied green cherry.

STRAWBERRY MOUSSE

2 cups strawberries   1 teasp. vanilla extract
¾ cup confectionery sugar   1 cup whipping cream
            Dash of salt

Let strawberries and sugar stand for about 1 hour. Place through sieve. Whip cream, adding vanilla extract and a dash of salt. Fold into strawberry mixture and place in refrigerator trays or mold in freezing compartment until firm. Raspberries may also be handled in this manner.

ORANGE ICE

1 ¼ cups corn syrup
1 ¾ cups water
⅓ cup sugar
¼ teasp. salt

2 orange rinds, grated
1 lemon rind, grated
1 ¾ cups orange juice
1 tablesp. lemon juice

Combine corn syrup, water, salt and sugar and boil for about 5 to 7 minutes. Add grated orange and lemon rinds. Cool and add fruit juices. Freeze in refrigerator trays at coldest temperature.

LIME ICE

1 cup lime juice (strained)
3 cups water
1 ¼ cups sugar

4 egg whites
Few drops of green food
    coloring

Dash of salt

Cook sugar and water over low flame for 8 to 10 minutes. Add to lime juice and cool. Place a few drops of green food coloring in mixture and place in refrigerator trays. Freeze until firm. Return to ice-cold bowl and beat until light. Beat egg whites until stiff, adding pinch of salt. Fold into lime ice mixture and place in refrigerator trays. Freeze until ready to serve.

RASPBERRY ICE

2 cups fresh raspberries
1 cup sugar
½ cup water

2 tablesp. lemon juice
2 teasp. unflavored gelatin
3 egg whites

Soak gelatin in water. Cook berries and sugar, crushing berries, over low flame for 5 to 7 minutes. Strain through sieve, adding gelatin and lemon juice. Cool, then place in refrigerator trays until mushy. Remove to ice-cold bowl and beat until very light. Fold in stiffly beaten egg whites. Place in refrigerator trays and freeze until ready to serve. Save a few whole berries with which to garnish top.

STRAWBERRY ICE

2 cups strawberries   1 cup sugar
2 egg whites   2 tablesp. lemon juice

Press strawberries through sieve or strainer. Mix juices and remaining pulp with sugar and lemon juice. Fold in stiffly beaten egg whites. Place in refrigerator trays and when almost frozen, remove to ice-cold bowl, beating until smooth. Place in refrigerator trays until ready to serve. Garnish with whole strawberries.

LEMON ICE

2 cups water   1 egg white (beaten until
1 cup sugar   stiff)
             ½ cup lemon juice

Boil sugar and water until syrupy—approximately 5 to 7 minutes. Cool. Add lemon juice, and fold in stiffly beaten egg white. Freeze in refrigerator trays.

PINEAPPLE ICE

1½ cups crushed pineapple   2½ cups water
   (canned)   3 egg whites (beaten until
1½ cups sugar   stiff)
             ¼ cup lemon juice

Boil sugar and water for between 5 to 7 minutes, or until syrupy. Cool. Combine pineapple and lemon juice and add to sugar mixture. Freeze until slightly thickened. Remove to ice-cold bowl and fold in stiffly beaten egg whites. Return to refrigerator trays, stirring occasionally until frozen.

RASPBERRY BOMBE GLACÉ

Raspberry ice (sufficient to   2 egg whites (beaten until
line a mold)   stiff)
⅓ cup confectionery sugar   1 cup whipping cream
                1 teasp. vanilla extract

After lining mold with raspberry ice, beat egg whites, gradually adding confectionery sugar. Beat whipping cream and add vanilla extract. Fold egg whites into whipping cream and fill center of mold with this mixture. Freeze until ready to serve.

VANILLA ICE CREAM (Basic Recipe)

2½ cups heavy cream   1 cup confectionery sugar
½ cup whipping cream   1¼ teasp. vanilla extract

Combine sugar with heavy cream, stirring until dissolved. Freeze in refrigerator tray until mushy. Place in ice-cold bowl and beat until light. Add vanilla extract and fold in whipped cream. Return to refrigerator tray and freeze until ready to serve.

Coffee Ice Cream: Add ½ teaspoon instant coffee.

Chocolate Ice Cream: Add 1 square chocolate, melted and blended with heavy cream and sugar.

Fruit flavoring: Add 1 cup of whatever fruit pulp desired—in the case of pineapple, crushed, canned pineapple—strained.

MOCHA ICE CREAM

2 cups heavy cream   ½ cup strong black coffee
3 egg yolks   2 squares sweet chocolate
                ½ cup sugar

Melt chocolate in top of double boiler with about ½ cup of cream. Gradually add sugar and coffee, stirring continually.

Beat egg yolks and mix with a little of the cream. Add to chocolate mixture. Cook and stir constantly until mixture thickens. Cool. Whip remaining cream and fold into mixture. Place in refrigerator trays.

FRENCH ICE CREAM

2½ cups heavy cream	1¼ cups water
4 egg yolks	1 teasp. vanilla
1¼ cups sugar	¼ teasp. salt

Boil water and sugar over low heat for between 5 to 7 minutes. Beat egg yolks, adding salt and place in top of double boiler. Gradually stir the sugar mixture into eggs, stirring continually and cooking for about 5 minutes. Place top of double boiler in pan with ice cubes, continually beating mixture. When cool, add vanilla extract and fold in whipped cream. Freeze in refrigerator trays or place in mold and freeze.

Variation: If several refrigerator trays of French ice cream are made, and a smooth ice cream with crushed berries is desired, add crushed and sweetened strawberries to one of the trays when partially frozen.

PEPPERMINT ICE CREAM

6 to 8 peppermint candy	1½ cups cream
canes	2½ cups heavy cream
1 cup sugar	(whipped)

Crush candy canes and add sugar. Pour plain cream over this mixture and allow to stand until both sugar and peppermint candy have dissolved. Whip cream and fold into candy mixture. Place in refrigerator trays and freeze or use mold and freeze.

MAPLE ICE CREAM

1½ cups maple syrup
6 egg yolks

2 egg whites (beaten until stiff)

3 cups whipping cream

Heat maple syrup in saucepan, bringing to boiling point. Beat egg yolks, placing in top of double boiler and pour maple syrup over egg yolks gradually, stirring constantly. Keep stirring until mixture becomes thick enough to coat spoon. Cool. Place top of double boiler in pan of ice cubes and fold in combined whipped cream and egg white mixture. Freeze in refrigerator trays or mold.

CARAMEL ICE CREAM

½ cup caramelized sugar
1 cup hot milk
1 tablesp. cornstarch

1 egg yolk
1 egg white
2 cups whipping cream

1 teasp. vanilla

Combine sugar, hot milk, cornstarch and beaten egg yolk, making a custard. Using heavy skillet, melt sugar until it becomes a brown liquid. Slowly and gradually pour this liquid into the hot custard. Cool and add the vanilla extract. Beat egg white and fold into mixture. Whip cream and fold into mixture. Freeze in refrigerator trays or mold until ready to serve.

COFFEE ICE CREAM

½ cup strong coffee
2 egg yolks

¾ cup sugar
Pinch of salt

2 cups whipping cream

Beat egg yolks and combine with sugar and salt. Add coffee and 1 cup of cream, placing all these ingredients in top of double boiler. Cook slowly until mixture is thick. Whip balance of cream and when mixture has cooled, fold in. Place in refrigerator trays or mold and freeze until ready for serving.

NEW YORK ICE CREAM

2 egg yolks   *¾ cup sugar*
2 egg whites   *2 cups whipping cream*
                1 teasp. vanilla extract

Place 1 cup whipping cream in top of double boiler. Scald cream. Beat egg yolks and combine with sugar, beating until thoroughly blended. Fold stiffly beaten egg whites into egg yolk mixture, and blend thoroughly. Mix gradually into scalded cream, stirring continually until thick enough to coat spoon. Cool and fold in whipped cream, adding vanilla extract last. Freeze in refrigerator trays.

PHILADELPHIA ICE CREAM

3 cups whipping cream   *¾ cup sugar*
                1 teasp. vanilla extract

In top of double boiler, bring one cup of cream to boiling point. Add sugar. When sugar dissolves thoroughly and completely, remove from heat. Cool, fold in balance of cream which has been whipped, adding extract. Freeze in refrigerator trays until ready to serve.

LEMON SHERBET (Made With Milk)

1 lemon rind, grated   *2 cups milk*
¼ cup lemon juice   *1½ cups sugar*

Combine sugar with grated lemon rind and lemon juice, then adding milk. Place in refrigerator trays and freeze until ready to serve.

MINT SHERBET

Juice of 3 lemons
Grated rind of 1 lemon
Juice of 1 orange
1 tablesp. freshly cut fresh
  mint (chopped fine)

3 or 4 drops of green
  coloring (vegetable)
1 egg white (beaten until
  stiff)
1 cup sugar

Combine sugar, water and rind. Boil for about 5 to 7 minutes. Pour boiling mixture over chopped mint leaves. Steep for an hour, covered, as with tea. Strain this mixture over fruit juices and add green coloring. Fold in beaten egg white and place in refrigerator trays and freeze. Serve with sprig of mint leaf.

NESSELRODE PUDDING (Frozen)

¾ cup sugar
2 cups whipping cream
½ cup water
1 cup candied fruit
  (cut fine)

½ cup blanched almonds
  (chopped fine)
1 tablesp. maraschino
cherries
2 egg yolks

Combine sugar and water and boil until syrupy. Beat egg yolks well, and pour sugar mixture into egg yolks, cooking and stirring until smooth. Cool and add nuts, candied fruits and maraschinos. Whip cream and fold into mixture, placing in refrigerator trays or mold, and freeze. Decorate with candied cherries.

SAUCES FOR ICE CREAM AND DESSERTS

Here are some long established favorites among sauces and garnishes for ice cream, parfaits, ices (when desired). They take very little time to prepare and add so much to your family's pleasure in desserts. When planning the menu to include ice cream, be certain to purchase the additional requirements for the sauce. In many instances, some of these sauces are made up of ingredients which are among the staples stored for use in cooking in almost every home.

BUTTERSCOTCH SAUCE

⅓ cup milk
1¼ cups brown sugar
  (light)

2½ tablesp. corn syrup
3 tablesp. butter

Combine sugar, milk and syrup and cook over low heat, stirring frequently until it forms a soft ball when tested by dropping a little in cold water. Add butter, stirring into mixture, and serve hot over ice cream.

CHOCOLATE FUDGE SAUCE

1 cup semi-sweet chocolate
  chips

½ cup sugar
½ cup hot milk

Melt chocolate in top of double boiler, stirring until completely dissolved. Add hot milk and sugar and continue stirring until smooth. Serve hot over ice cream.

CHOCOLATE SAUCE

1 square unsweetened
  chocolate
1 cup sugar

2 cups water
1 tablesp. cornstarch
½ teasp. vanilla extract

Combine sugar and water and boil until syrupy. Add chocolate, stirring until completely dissolved. Then add cornstarch, which has been dissolved in a little water, to mixture with a dash of salt. Cook over low flame and stir continually until mixture is completely smooth. Cool and add vanilla extract. Serve over ice cream, or use on certain types of puddings.

BASIC SAUCE
(To which flavoring may be added)

½ cup miniature
  marshmallows

1 egg white
⅓ cup sugar
¼ cup water

Combine sugar and water and boil for between 5 and 7 minutes. Add marshallows, which will melt immediately. Remove from flame and pour into stiffly beaten egg white, beating until smooth.

Mocha sauce: In the above recipe, substitute strong black coffee and 1 teaspoon cocoa for water.

Mint sauce: Add ½ teaspoon peppermint extract to above, and garnish with mint leaf.

MAPLE SAUCE

1 ½ cups maple syrup   *2 tablesp. butter*

Combine over low heat, stirring until it forms threads. Serve hot over ice cream. Garnish with candy maple leaf.

STRAWBERRY SAUCE

1 cup strawberries   *1 cup sugar*
½ cup water

Combine sugar and water and boil over low heat for about 5 minutes. Add strawberries, reserving a number of large ones as a garnish. Cook until soft. Cool. Serve over ice cream, garnishing with whole strawberry.

BLUEBERRY SAUCE

1 cup blueberries   *1 cup sugar*
½ cup water

Combine sugar and water and boil for about 5 minutes. Add blueberries, reserving enough of them to serve as a garnish, and boil slowly until blueberries are soft. Remove and cool. Serve over ice cream, parfaits or ices.

RASPBERRY SAUCE

2 cups raspberries   *1 cup sugar*
                         ¾ cup water

Combine sugar and water and boil for about 5 minutes. Add raspberries, reserving enough whole raspberries to garnish ice cream. Press through sieve or strainer. Cool. Serve over ice cream, parfaits or ices.

LEMON SAUCE

Juice of 1 lemon   *1½ cups boiling water*
Grated rind of 1 lemon   *Pinch of salt*
1 cup sugar   *2 tablesp. cornstarch*
                   2 tablesp. butter

Combine cornstarch, sugar and salt. Add boiling water and cook over low flame, bringing to boiling point. Stir constantly until thick and clear. Add lemon juice and lemon rind and last of all, add butter. May be served hot over desserts and puddings.

Lime sauce: Use same ingredients, substituting lime for lemon.

HARD SAUCE

This sauce is generally used with plum or fig or other rich puddings. It is unusually rich in vitamins and calories.

1½ cups confectionery   *2 tablesp. cream*
  sugar   *1 teasp. vanilla extract*
                   ½ cup butter

Cream butter and confectionery sugar until smooth by adding, little by little, the cream and vanilla extract. Beat until smooth and fluffy. Place in mold and chill until it can be served in mold form. A small amount on each serving goes a long way. The following sauce may be used over the hard sauce.

HOT SPICED SAUCE

1½ cups hot water   10 whole cloves
½ cup sugar   2 tablesp. butter
1 stick cinnamon   ¼ teasp. salt
              1 tablesp. cornstarch

Combine sugar, salt and cornstarch, slowly pouring hot water over mixture in saucepan. Cook over slow flame until clear, stirring continually. Add butter, cinnamon and cloves and cook another 10 minutes or until flavor of spices has been completely blended. Serve hot over hard sauce on puddings or desserts.

CUSTARD SAUCE

2½ cups milk   4 egg yolks
½ cup sugar   ½ teaspoon vanilla

Combine milk and sugar in top of double boiler. Add beaten egg yolks, stirring continually. When mixture coats spoon, remove from flame. Add vanilla extract and cool. Serve over puddings or desserts.

MINT FLAVORED CHOCOLATE SAUCE

½ cup heavy cream   ½ cup sugar
1 square unsweetened   4 tablesp. corn syrup (light)
   chocolate   2 drops oil of peppermint
              ½ cup water

Combine syrup, water and sugar and cook over low flame until it forms a soft ball when tested in cold water. Remove from flame, adding chocolate. Stir continually until chocolate has melted. Add oil of peppermint and heavy cream, stirring. Cool by placing in pan with ice cubes. May be served hot, if desired.

Fruits, Compotes, and Stewed Fruits

WHAT IS MORE REFRESHING THAN TO WALK INTO A ROOM where a bowl of fruit is temptingly arranged, chilled to perfection, in Mama's inimitable style with colorful fruit plates and small ivory handled knives waiting to be utilized for this palatable feast?

Fruit is on almost every menu in Jewish families, whether it be fresh fruit, compotes, stewed fruit, canned fruits or preserves; it appears on the table during festive holidays, on Shabos, or as an appetizer, dessert, or after dinner snack. It adds color and dramatic zest to any occasion, particularly in a frozen mold, on a buffet table, as an individual salad, or as a garnish for the main entrée.

When serving fresh fruit, make use of the outer shells as serving dishes for fruit salads. Baskets may be cut from canteloupe and honeydew skins. A watermelon half may be scooped out and the rind used for serving decorative fruit salads at large buffets, parties, or cook-outs. Pineapples should be cut lengthwise and cubed internally in order for the hull to be usable as a decorative platter.

There are many fresh fruits, such as blackberries, blueberries, pineapple, mangos, strawberries, and raspberries, which, when in season, are best served with a sprinkling of sugar, or added to fruit cups or salads. For those who cannot eat fresh fruits, they may be stewed lightly, for digestibility, and strained where required.

For glazing fruit, water and sugar are combined in a saucepan and brought to a boil, until syrupy. Fruit is dipped into this mixture, when cooled, and glazed. Glazed grapes or cherries are particularly decorative.

FRUIT COMPOTE

1 cup prunes	*3 or 4 stick cloves of*
1 cup dried apricots	*cinnamon (½ teasp.*
1 cup dried pears	*cinnamon or ¼ teasp.*
¾ cup sugar	*nutmeg may be*
½ cup seedless raisins	*substituted)*

½ lemon, sliced thin

Soak prunes, apricots and pears overnight in cold water. Cook over low fire, adding sugar, raisins, lemon slices for about 1 hour. Add sticks of cinnamon during the last ½ hour of cooking. Remove, cool, and serve cold. Garnish with lemon slice.

FRUIT COMPOTE
(With Nuts)

4 cups assorted dried fruits	*¾ teasp. cinnamon*
(prunes, apricots, pears)	*1 lemon, sliced*
1¼ cups water	*¾ cup sugar*

¼ cup blanched almonds

Soak dried fruits in cold water overnight. Place in saucepan with water, sugar, cinnamon, lemon slices and cook over low heat until tender and soft. Add blanched almonds and cook until completely heated and blended. Chill and serve.

Note: If more spice is desired, about 6 whole cloves may be added with the cinnamon.

FRUIT TZIMMES

4 cups dried prunes, apricots	*¾ teasp. cinnamon*
and pears	*6 whole cloves*
2½ cups water	*¼ cup brown sugar*
½ tablesp. cornstarch	*Pinch of salt*
3 tablesp. honey	*Rind of 1 lemon, grated*

Soak dried fruits overnight. Combine dried fruits and water. When this comes to boiling point, add honey, brown sugar, cinnamon and cloves and pinch of salt. Add lemon rind and allow to cook over low flame for about 20 to 25 minutes.

Mix cornstarch with a little cold water and pour into liquid of fruit tzimmes. When completely absorbed and thoroughly blended, remove. Chill and serve.

REFRIGERATED FRUIT COMPOTE

4 cups dried prunes, apricots, pears	Grated rind of 1 lemon
2 sticks cinnamon	Juice of 1 lemon
8 whole cloves	¾ cup brown sugar
	4 or 5 thin slices of lemon

Place in casserole with space allowed for fruit expansion. Pour boiling water over fruit to cover. Add grated rind of lemon, lemon juice, lemon slices and sugar with cinnamon sticks and cloves. Place in refrigerator for between 24 to 48 hours, until fruit is tender and spices have blended. Stir occasionally to blend flavors of fruits and spices. Serve cold.

SNOW PEAKED APPLES (Baked)

4 to 6 firm apples	sprinkling of red cinnamon candies
Juice of 1 orange	
1 cup brown sugar	2 tablesp. butter
2 teasp. cinnamon and	4 egg whites
2 teasp. confectionery sugar	

Core apples but do not pare. Peel one-fourth way down around top section. Place in ½ inch water in casserole. Fill core center with mixture of orange juice, brown sugar and cinnamon, topping with a few cinnamon candies and dotting with butter. Bake in covered casserole for about an hour (basting) at 350°F. Uncover, baste with liquid, and bake uncovered for about 5 to 7 minutes. Beat egg whites until stiff, adding confectionery sugar and beating until thoroughly blended. Place mound of meringue on top of each apple.

Place in oven again in uncovered casserole at 425°F. until meringue browns.

CRANBERRY SAUCE

4 cups cranberries
2 cups water
2 cups sugar
Grated rind of 1 orange
Juice of 1 orange

Boil cranberries and water, orange rind and orange juice until cranberries start bursting. Add sugar and cook until all of the cranberries have burst, and sugar has completely blended. Remove from fire. Using cranberry hand press, crush cranberries so that seeds and hulls of berries are eliminated. Place strained cranberries in mold and freeze in refrigerator (not in freezer). When ready to serve, invert on decorative platter.

Variation: If desired, cranberries may be served hot. Strain and serve in bowl.

Variation: Cranberries may be served whole; do not strain.

STRAWBERRIES HADERA

1 qt. strawberries
½ cup brown sugar
2 cups sour cream

Serve washed strawberries in dessert dish, top with sour cream and sprinkle with brown sugar.

BAKED APPLES TEL-AVIV

4 to 6 firm apples
¾ cup brown sugar
2 teasp. orange juice
¼ cup chopped walnuts
¼ cup chopped dates
¼ cup raisins
½ teasp. cinnamon

Combine orange juice, brown sugar, chopped nuts, chopped dates, raisins and cinnamon. Pare the upper portion of apples and core. Place the above mixture in the center core of each

apple, dot with butter and bake in shallow baking pan with
½ inch of water. Keep basting apples with residue during
baking at 375°F. for 50 minutes to 1 hour.

APPLE RINGS

4 to 5 tart apples   ½ cup brown sugar and a
½ teaspoon cinnamon   little flour
                Butter for frying

Core and pare apples, sprinkle with cinnamon, brown sugar
and flour. Fry in butter for 10 minutes on one side and 10
minutes on other side.

APPLESAUCE

3 lbs. cooking apples   1 teasp. cinnamon
Rind of 1 lemon, grated   6 whole cloves
Juice of 1 lemon   1 cup water
                2 cups sugar

Core apples, but do not pare. Cut up apples with skins,
place in saucepan with grated lemon rind, lemon juice, cinnamon, sugar and water and cook in covered pan until apples
are soft. Stir occasionally to blend thoroughly all ingredients.
Remove from flame and place through sieve, using a little
lemon juice to hasten the straining. Cool and serve.

Variation: Follow above directions except that apples are
cored and peeled. No straining is necessary in this instance.
If added coloring is desired, cinnamon candies will give it
a rich pink color.

RASPBERRY APPLESAUCE

2 lbs. apples (cored and   Juice of 1 lemon
    peeled)   ½ teasp. cinnamon
¾ cup sugar   ½ cup water
Grated rind of 1 lemon   1 cup raspberries

Prepare apples and place in saucepan with grated lemon rind, lemon juice, cinnamon and water. Place raspberries in separate saucepan with a little water and ¼ cup sugar. Bring to boiling point and boil 5 to 7 minutes. Remove from flame and when cool enough, place through sieve to remove seeds. Add this mixture to applesauce. Cook long enough to blend thoroughly. Remove from flame.

RHUBARB

2 lbs. red rhubarb (Do not   1 cup sugar
  remove skin)   ½ cup water
          Grated rind of 1 lemon

Cut leaves and tough stems from rhubarb. Cut in pieces about 3 inches long and cook in saucepan with ½ cup water and sugar. Add grated rind of lemon. Cook over low heat until rhubarb is reduced to sauce. Stir so that pan will not scorch. Remove from heat and cool.

RHUBARB AND STRAWBERRIES

2 lbs. red rhubarb (Do not   ¾ cup water
  remove skin)   1 cup strawberries
1½ cups sugar   (washed and cleaned)

Clean rhubarb and cut in 3 inch lengths. Combine with water, sugar and strawberries. Cook until rhubarb has been reduced to sauce and the color of the strawberries has blended with the rhubarb. It should be a lovely red hue. Cool and serve.

RHUBARB AND APPLESAUCE

2 lbs. red rhubarb   1½ cups sugar
1 lb. firm apples   Grated rind of 1 orange
          ¾ cup water

Pare and core apples and cut rhubarb into 3 inch lengths. Combine with water, sugar and rind of orange and cook until rhubarb and apples have been reduced to sauce. Remove from heat and cool. Serve when chilled.

FRESH FRUIT AMBROSIA

1 fresh pineapple	*Juice of 1 lemon or lime*
3 oranges	*1 scant cup sugar*
2 grapefruits	*½ cup grated cocoanut*

Shave outer skin of pineapple, slice off top and cut into ¾ inch slices. Core and cut into cubes. Peel oranges and grapefruits, removing membrane of each section. Pour juice of lemon or lime over top. Sprinkle with sugar. When ready to serve, combine with grated cocoanut and top with candied cherry.

PEACH COMPOTE

8 to 10 fresh, firm ripe	*2 cinnamon sticks*
peaches	*4 whole cloves*
1 cup sugar	*1 cup water*

Combine water and sugar, bring to a boil, add cinnamon sticks and cloves, and after a few minutes, drop peach slices into mixture. When tender, remove. Chill and serve as compote with whipped cream and garnished with cherry or kumquat. Excellent as garnish with entrée.

Pear Compote: Substitute large, ripe pears for peaches in above recipe.

FRENCH FRIED PINEAPPLE

1 large can pineapple	*2 eggs (beaten)*
(slices)	*Matzo meal*
	Fat for frying

Dip pineapple slices in beaten eggs, then in matzo meal. Heat fat and fry until browned first on one side and then the other. This appetizing fruit will complement any entrée—meat, fowl or fish—and depending upon the selection of entrée, use pareve margarine or oil in which to fry.

MANGOS AND SOUR CREAM

3 large mangos   *1 pint sour cream*
                4 tablesp. brown sugar

Peel and slice mangos. Serve with topping of sour cream and sprinkle with brown sugar. This is a delicacy, particularly in northern states where mangos are a rarity.

CRANBERRY SOUR CREAM MOLD

2 pkges. lemon gelatin   *1 can whole cranberries*
1½ cups boiling water   *1½ cups sour cream*

Dissolve gelatin in boiling water and chill until it reaches the consistency of raw eggs. Stir whole cranberries into gelatin mixture and fold in sour cream. Place in mold and freeze in refrigerator like any gelatin or Jello mold. Excellent with a milchig meal.

MELON BALL MOLD

1 cup cantaloupe balls   *2 tablesp. lemon juice*
1 cup watermelon balls   *¾ cup sugar*
1 cup honeydew balls   *3 cups hot water*
1 cup fresh strawberries   *1 cup cold water*
  (sugared)   *3 pkges. unflavored gelatin*
1 cup diced canned
  pineapple

Dissolve gelatin in cold water and stir into hot water. Add sugar and lemon juice. Chill until it reaches the consistency of raw eggs. Fold in melon balls, using ring mold. Freeze. When serving, place fresh strawberries and diced pineapple in center of mold. Serve with topping of mayonnaise.

DECORATIVE PINEAPPLE MOLD

1 large can sliced pineapple   1 pkge. lime Jello

Remove one end of pineapple can; drain juice. Prepare Jello as instructed on package but DO NOT USE pineapple juice as part of liquid. Pour Jello into pineapple can until it fills the can. Freeze. When ready to serve, remove other end of can and slide out onto serving platter. Cut one slice of pineapple per serving. Makes a beautiful garnish.

FRUIT CUP WITH EGGNOG

3 oranges (sectioned and skinned)
2 pears (pared, cored and diced)
1 banana (peeled and sliced thin)
1 cup seeded grapes, halved
1 cup strawberries (halved) or whole ripe raspberries or blackberries
½ cup shredded cocoanut (for garnish)
¼ cup maraschino cherries (for garnish)
2 cups eggnog (prepared)

Section fruit and mix in bowl. Spoon into parfait glasses. Pour prepared eggnog over fruit, sprinkle with shredded cocoanut and top with maraschino cherry. (A topping of whipped cream may be used before garnishing with shredded cocoanut and cherry.)

GRAPEFRUIT AND AVOCADO

3 or 4 grapefruits
2 avocados
Maraschino cherries
Mayonnaise
Whipped cream

Peel grapefruit and skin each section. Peel avocado and cut in thin wedges across the width. When stone is removed, the wedges should be the width of half the avocado. Place one section of grapefruit on a plate, then a thin slice of avocado, and follow through with the same arrangement until you have all wedges of grapefruit interleaved with avocado slices. Combine equal parts of mayonnaise and whipped cream, folding one into the other. Top with this mixture and decorate with a maraschino cherry.

BAKED BANANAS

3 or 4 bananas   ¼ *cup lemon juice*
1 cup crushed cornflakes

Peel bananas and roll first in lemon juice, then in crushed cornflake crumbs. Place in greased baking pan and bake in moderate oven of 350°F. for about 20 minutes or until crust is browned. Serve with any fruit sauce (see Page 285 for recipes).

Cakes—Traditional and General

GENERAL RULES FOR CAKE BAKING

Sift flour several times before measuring to ensure light, fluffy cakes.

When baking powder is called for in these recipes, double-acting baking powder should be used, unless otherwise specified.

Generally, cake flour is preferable to all-purpose white flour in the baking of cakes. It is just a little finer in texture and brings better results.

When baking cakes, granulated sugar is necessary for mixing, particularly for creaming with butter. Confectionery sugar is generally used for making icings for cakes or fillings in layer cakes.

When measuring brown sugar be certain that it is firmly packed. In order to keep brown sugar for baking and cooking, after opening box, remove to jar and refrigerate. Otherwise it will harden and be difficult to use. (To soften hardened brown sugar, place in top of double boiler or in warm oven for a short time.)

Supplies should be removed from refrigerator and allowed to remain at room temperature for some time before using in cakes. This will bring better results in baking.

It is wise to gather together everything required for cake baking in one area with plenty of counter space or table space, before preparing the batter for a cake. It will simplify operations to assemble all utensils, such as mixing bowls, electric or rotary beater, measuring spoons, and all of the ingredients.

Have the proper pans ready and grease them, if required, before preparing batter, so that it can be placed in the oven immediately.

TRADITIONAL HONEY CAKE
("Lekach")

4 cups sifted flour
3 teasp. baking powder
1½ teasp. baking soda
1 cup sugar
1 cup honey
½ cup oil or shortening
(melted)

¾ cup coffee (black)
4 eggs
¼ teasp. ground cloves
¼ teasp. ground nutmeg
¼ teasp. cinnamon
½ cup chopped walnuts and
seedless raisins (dark)

½ teasp. almond extract

Cream eggs and sugar; beat until light and fluffy. Combine honey with coffee. First add shortening to egg mixture, then stir in honey and coffee. Sift flour again, adding baking powder, baking soda, spices and nuts and raisins. Combine with mixture and beat until completely blended and smooth. Add almond extract. Grease a square or oblong pan about 14 x 10, pour batter into it, and bake in a moderate oven of 350°F. for 1 hour. Cut into squares and serve with a topping of whipped cream, with a little cinnamon and sugar sprinkled in while whipping.

LEBKUCHEN (Traditional)

4 egg yolks
4 egg whites (Reserve 2 egg
whites for icing)
¾ cup brown sugar
1½ cups flour
1 teasp. baking powder
1 square bitter chocolate
(grated)

1 cup confectioners' sugar
1 tablesp. grated orange rind
¼ teasp. cinnamon
¼ teasp. ground nutmeg
¼ cup chopped pecans
¼ cup chopped citron
(mixed)
1 teasp. lemon juice

¾ cup molasses

Cream egg yolks with sugar. Beat egg whites stiffly and fold into mixture. Sift flour, baking powder and add rest of spices, nuts, citron, grated chocolate, lemon juice alternately with molasses. Flour hands, and spread dough into shallow cake pan (oblong) about 1½ to 2 inches high. Bake in moderate oven of 350°F. for 35 to 45 minutes or until done. Cool and cut into small squares, icing and decorating each square with a candied cherry. Use the following icing.

ICING FOR LEBKUCHEN

1 cup confectionery sugar   A little water
A few drops of vanilla extract

Combine and make a thin coating over the lebkuchen. When firm, place candied cherry on each square.

SPONGE CAKE (Traditional)

Since sponge cake is made without butter, it is very important that egg yolks and egg whites are beaten thoroughly, particularly the egg yolks, which should be thick and lemon colored. Only cake flour should be used in making sponge cake, and flour should be sifted before measuring as well as after.

A tube pan should be used and it must be *ungreased* for the baking of sponge cake.

Results will be better if ingredients are at room temperature when preparing the sponge cake.

6 egg yolks   3½ teasp. baking powder
6 egg whites   1¼ cups sugar
2 cups cake flour   1 cup water
1 teasp. vanilla extract

Beat egg yolks until thick and light in color, adding sugar and continuing to beat. Sift baking powder with about 1 cup of the flour. Put aside. Add flour mixture and water, little by little, then the flour which has the baking powder in it. Add vanilla extract. Last, fold in stiffly beaten egg whites. Preheat oven to 325°F. and pour batter into tube pan, ungreased, and bake for between 50 minutes and 1 hour. Invert pan. When cool, remove cake to platter. Sprinkle with confectionery sugar.

ANGEL FOOD CAKE

9 egg whites (stiffly beaten)	½ teasp. cream of tartar
1 cup cake flour	Pinch of salt
1½ cups sugar	3 tablesp. water
	1 teasp. vanilla extract

Boil sugar and water. When it forms a thread, gradually pour over stiffly beaten egg whites. Add flavoring to this mixture and continue beating until it cools. Presift flour, measure, add cream of tartar and sift several more times. Gradually, fold into egg white mixture carefully. Pour batter into ungreased tube pan. Preheat oven to 325°F. and bake approximately 50 minutes to 1 hour. When finger is pressed against cake, if it springs back without leaving a dent, cake is done.

WHITE CAKE (Basic Recipe)

2 cups cake flour	1¼ cups sugar
2½ teasp. baking powder	1 stick butter, softened
3 egg whites, unbeaten	Pinch of salt
1 cup milk	1 teasp. vanilla

Sift flour, baking powder, salt and measure. Cream butter and sugar, adding unbeaten egg whites. Alternately add flour and milk and when well-beaten and smooth, add vanilla extract. Preheat oven to a moderate 350°F. and pour batter into two cake pans (greased). Bake for 30 to 35 minutes or until browned. For icings and fillings, see section on Cake Icings.

YELLOW CAKE (Basic Recipe)

2 eggs   *1 stick butter, softened*
2 cups cake flour   *Pinch of salt*
⅔ cup milk   *2½ teasp. baking powder*
1¼ cups sugar   *1 teasp. vanilla*

Cream butter and sugar and add eggs. Sift flour, baking powder and salt. Measure. Sift again and alternately add flour and milk to butter and sugar mixture. Add flavoring. Preheat oven to 375°F. Pour batter into two greased cake pans and bake for 20 to 25 minutes.

BUNDT KUCHEN

For best results with this cake, the proper type of cake pan is required. It is a round, fluted tube pan, much like a mold for freezing decorative gelatin puddings or desserts. Do not attempt to bake this unless you have this particular pan.

4 cups flour   *Rind of lemon, grated*
3 teasp. baking powder   *Rind of orange, grated*
6 eggs   *Juice of ½ orange and ½*
¾ cup butter   *lemon*
1¼ cups sugar   *12 or 15 blanched almonds*
½ cup milk   *1 teasp. vanilla extract*

Cream butter and sugar, adding eggs and constantly beating mixture. Add flavoring. Sift flour, baking powder and salt. Stir into mixture alternately with milk. Beat until batter is smooth. Place almonds at bottom of mold pan, so that they will cover the entire top when pan is inverted. Pour in batter. Preheat oven to 350°F. and bake 50 minutes to 1 hour, or until done.

MAMA'S DEVIL'S FOOD CAKE
(Light Brown)

2 cups cake flour
2 teasp. baking powder
½ teasp. cinnamon
½ teasp. ground nutmeg
½ cup milk
2 squares unsweetened chocolate

2 eggs
1 cup warm mashed potatoes
¾ cup butter (scant)
½ cup coarsely cut walnuts
4 walnut halves to garnish icing
1 cup sugar

Sift flour and baking powder, measure, and sift again. Cream butter and sugar, adding eggs. Using top of double boiler, melt chocolate in milk. When melted, remove and cool. Combine with creamed sugar; add spices and mashed potatoes. Sift flour and baking powder into mixture and beat until batter is smooth. Add nuts by folding into mixture. Place in 2 greased cake pans, baking in moderate oven of 350°F. for 50 min. to 1 hour. Use butter cream icing. See Icings.

BASIC DEVIL'S FOOD CAKE

(Prepare separately)

4 squares unsweetened chocolate
1 egg yolk, beaten
1¼ cups sugar
½ cup milk
1 teasp. vanilla extract

(Prepare separately)

2¼ cups flour
2 teasp. baking powder
1 stick butter
1 cup sugar
2 eggs
⅔ cup milk

In top of double boiler, combine chocolate, milk and sugar. When chocolate is melted and blended with milk and sugar, add egg yolk, stirring until blended. Cook until it coats spoon. Cool and add vanilla extract.

Cream butter and sugar, adding eggs, then sifted flour with baking powder and milk alternately. Combine with chocolate mixture until smooth batter is obtained. Bake in preheated moderate oven of 350°F., pouring batter into 2 well-greased cake pans. Bake for 30 to 35 minutes. For best results, fill and frost with chocolate fudge frosting. See Icings.

GOLDEN ORANGE CAKE

2 cups cake flour	5 egg yolks
3 teasp. baking powder	1 stick butter or margarine
Grated rind of 1 orange	½ cup milk
1¼ cups sugar	1 teasp. lemon extract

Cream butter and sugar, and while beating, add egg yolks beaten until lemon colored. Add grated orange rind, and flavoring. Alternately add flour sifted with baking powder, and milk. Beat until batter is smooth. Preheat oven to 350°F. and bake in greased cake pans sprinkled with flour for 45 minutes. Ice and fill layers with orange icing. See Icings.

PINEAPPLE UPSIDE-DOWN CAKE

1 large can sliced pineapple	1¼ cups sugar
1 stick butter or margarine	1 teasp. baking powder
2¼ cups brown sugar	4 egg yolks
1¼ cups flour	4 egg whites
1 teasp. vanilla extract	

The first three ingredients are prepared first and separately from the cake batter. Melt butter in heavy skillet, covering with brown sugar evenly. Place slices of pineapple on top of brown sugar, filling in empty spaces with chopped pecans or walnuts and candied cherries.

To prepare cake batter, beat egg yolks with sugar until light and lemon colored. Add vanilla extract. Sift flour and baking powder, then fold into egg yolk mixture. Last, fold in stiffly beaten egg whites.

Preheat oven to 350°F. and bake in skillet for 35 to 40 minutes. Invert skillet onto cake platter.

Peach Upside-Down Cake: substitute peaches for pineapple and proceed in same manner.

POUND CAKE

2 cups cake flour	*1 cup sugar*
10 egg whites	*1 stick butter*
10 egg yolks	*2 teasp. vanilla extract*

Cream butter and sugar, adding sugar gradually and beating continuously, so that when balance of sugar has been added and beaten, it is light and fluffy. Add beaten egg yolks to mixture and blend well. Sift flour, measure, then sift flour again so that it will be very light. Add vanilla extract to creamed mixture, then add flour gradually, beating until mixture is completely blended and smooth. Preheat oven to 325°F. Line a loaf pan with greased paper. Fold stiffly beaten egg whites into batter and pour into loaf pan. Bake for 1 hour or until browned.

MARBLE POUND CAKE

Follow recipe above, but divide the batter in half and add 2 tablespoons chocolate syrup to half the batter. Alternate layers of white and chocolate batter in loaf pan.

CHOCOLATE CAKE

2¼ cups cake flour	*Pinch of salt*
2¼ teasp. baking powder	*1 teasp. vanilla extract*
3 squares unsweetened chocolate	*3 eggs*
2 cups sugar	*1 stick butter or margarine*
	1½ cups water

Using top of double boiler, melt chocolate with 1½ cups of water. Sift flour, sugar and salt and with pastry blender, work in with butter until it is crumbly. When chocolate and water come to boiling point, remove and cool. When cool enough, add to flour and butter mixture and beat. Add eggs, and continue beating. Add vanilla extract, then baking powder. Grease 2 cake pans, and bake in moderate oven of 350°F. for 30 to 35 minutes. Fill and ice with chocolate fudge icing. See Icings.

APPLESAUCE SPICE CAKE

2 cups applesauce	½ cup chopped raisins
¾ cup butter or margarine	½ cup chopped dates
1½ cups sugar	½ cup coarsely cut walnuts
2½ cups flour	¼ teasp. cinnamon
2½ teasp. soda	¼ teasp. cloves
2 eggs	1 teasp. vanilla extract

Cream butter and sugar, adding eggs and vanilla extract. Sift flour and soda, measure, then sift again. Add rest of ingredients to creamed butter and sugar mixture, adding flour last, and blending until batter is entirely smooth. Preheat oven to 350°F. and grease 2 cake pans. Bake for one hour. Cool. Frost each layer separately with butter cream icing.

GINGERBREAD

2½ cups flour	1 cup molasses
1 cup buttermilk	1½ teasp. ginger
2 teasp. baking soda	½ teasp. cinnamon
2 eggs	½ teasp. cloves
1¼ cups sugar	1 stick butter or margarine

Mix buttermilk with soda and add to molasses. Cream butter and sugar, adding eggs. Fold in sifted flour and spices. Preheat oven to 350°F. and grease round or square cake pans. Bake for 45 to 50 minutes. Serve hot, if desired, cutting in squares and topping with whipped cream.

JELLY ROLL (Basic Recipe)

1 ¼ cups cake flour
2 teasp. baking powder
1 cup sugar
4 egg yolks
4 egg whites
3 tablesp. butter or margarine

3 tablesp. confectioners' sugar
1 tablesp. flour
Plain jelly—preferably red, such as currant, grape, strawberry, etc.

⅓ cup cold water

Combine sugar and egg yolks and beat until thick and light in color. Sift flour and baking powder several times, then add to egg mixture alternately with water until completely and thoroughly blended and smooth. Fold in stiffly beaten egg whites, while preheating oven to 375°F. Grease baking pan and sprinkle with flour. Bake for 15 to 20 minutes, and while hot, remove cake to foil or heavy waxed paper. Cut away crust and roll up cake, wrapping in either the foil or waxed paper. When cool, unroll and spread with jelly. Roll up and sprinkle generously with confectioners' sugar.

SOUR CREAM CAKE

2 cups cake flour
1 cup sour cream
½ teasp. baking soda
1 teasp. baking powder

2 eggs
1 cup sugar
¼ teasp. salt
1 teasp. vanilla extract

Beat eggs and sugar until light and fluffy. Add vanilla extract. Combine sour cream and baking soda, blending thoroughly. Sift flour, baking powder and salt, and gradually and alternately add flour and sour cream mixture to eggs and sugar. Grease 2 square or round cake pans and sprinkle with a little flour. Preheat oven to 350°F. and bake for approximately 50 minutes or until browned. May be filled with lemon custard and frosted with butter cream icing, or may be served as 2 separate cakes with any desired icing.

DATE, NUT AND ORANGE CAKE

2 cups cake flour
1 teasp. baking powder
1 teasp. baking soda
1 egg
1 cup sugar
1 stick butter or margarine
Grated rind of orange (save
  orange for juicing later)

¼ cup chopped walnuts or
  pecans
¼ cup dates (cut up and
  rolled in flour)
1 teasp. vanilla
1 scant cup sugar (save until
  cake is out of oven)
1 cup milk

Cream sugar and butter. Add egg and orange rind to sugar mixture. Sift flour, baking powder and baking soda before adding to mixture. Add alternately with milk to other ingredients, beating constantly either with electric beater or manually with rotary beater. When thoroughly blended, add nuts, dates, and vanilla extract. Grease tube pan, and preheat oven to 375°F. Bake for between 45 to 50 minutes or until browned. Remove from oven and while hot, pour 1 cup scant sugar over top, then pour juice of 1 orange evenly over sugar, covering entire cake. Allow to cool. Invert on cake plate. Garnish with candied fruit.

MANDELTORTE (Traditional)

8 egg yolks
8 egg whites
1 cup ground blanched al-
  monds
Grated rind of 1 lemon

Juice of 1 lemon
¾ cup toasted bread crumbs
1¼ cups sugar
¾ teasp. cinnamon
Pinch of salt

½ teasp. almond extract

Cream sugar with well-beaten egg yolks, continually beating until light and lemon colored. Add all other ingredients, except egg whites and salt. Beat egg whites until stiff and wet, adding salt. Fold into mixture carefully. Pour into spring form and bake in moderate oven of 350°F. for about 1 hour, or until browned. Cool in pan. Frost with butter cream icing (see Icings). Garnish frosting with blanched almonds.

COCOANUT CAKE

2 cups cake flour	¾ cup milk
1 cup sugar	Pinch of salt
3 teasp. baking powder	½ teasp. lemon extract
4 egg whites	½ teasp. almond extract
	1 stick butter

Cream sugar and butter. Add flavoring. Sift flour, baking powder and add gradually to the sugar and butter mixture. Beat egg whites and add salt, beating until stiff. Fold in. Grease and sprinkle flour on two cake pans, round or square, and preheat oven to 350°F. Bake for 35 to 40 minutes or until browned. Cool. Frost and fill with same icing:

FROSTING AND FILLING

3 egg whites	1½ teasp. lemon juice
2 cups confectionery sugar	⅛ teasp. cream of tartar
	1 cup shredded cocoanut

Beat egg whites until frothy and add 1 cup confectionery sugar. Continue beating and add lemon juice, cream of tartar, and gradually add remaining sugar. Beat until thick. Spread on each cake half and sprinkle with shredded cocoanut. Then place one half on top of other. Be generous with the frosting and filling. Decorate top with candied red cherries.

CHEESE CAKE
CRUST AND TOPPING

1 box graham crackers	3 tablesp. sugar
(rolled into crumbs)	½ teasp. cinnamon
	1 stick butter

Combine crumbs, cinnamon and sugar. Soften stick of butter and mix in. Using spring form, butter it well and line bottom and sides with graham cracker mixture. Reserve a portion of graham cracker mixture to sprinkle over top of cheese cake.

CHEESE CAKE FILLING

4 pkges. (3 oz.) of cream cheese
¾ lb. dry cottage cheese
3 eggs
2½ tablesp. cornstarch

1¼ cups sugar
1¼ cups milk
1¼ cups sour cream
1 teasp. vanilla
Pinch of salt

Beat cream cheese and dry cottage cheese together until entirely smooth, adding eggs, one at a time, and continuing to beat until thoroughly blended. Combine sugar, cornstarch and salt. Blend into cheese and egg mixture. Stir in milk and sour cream. The batter will be thick but loose. Add vanilla extract last. Pour very carefully into graham cracker lined spring form and bake in a moderate oven of 350°F. for 1 hour. Turn oven off, but allow cake to cool in oven for an hour.

CHOCOLATE TORTE

1 cup almonds, ground
9 egg yolks
9 egg whites
2 cups confectionery sugar

3 squares unsweetened chocolate, melted
12 almonds, slivered and browned (for garnish)
1 teasp. vanilla extract

Combine beaten egg yolks, flavoring and sugar and beat until light and fluffy. Add melted chocolate, ground almonds and carefully fold in stiffly beaten egg whites. Prepare beforehand well-greased and floured spring form (9 inch size) and preheat oven to 325°F. Bake for 1 hour or a little longer. Frost with chocolate icing, and garnish with slivered almonds.

DATE AND NUT TORTE

2¼ cups ground almonds
1 cup pitted dates
6 egg yolks

6 egg whites
2 teasp. baking powder
1 cup confectionery sugar

½ teasp. vanilla extract

Pour boiling water over dates and drain. Press and rub into smooth paste. Beat egg yolks until light in color, gradually add sugar and continue beating. Add date paste, vanilla, and almonds. Beat egg whites until stiff, folding in baking powder. Then fold egg whites with baking powder into the egg yolk mixture, blending thoroughly. Bake in well-greased, floured spring form for 50 minutes to 1 hour, at 325°F. Cool and top with a combination of whipped cream and 2 stiffly beaten egg whites, and a few drops of vanilla extract. Garnish with slivered almonds.

COFFEE TORTE

9 egg yolks
9 egg whites
1 cup confectionery sugar

4 teasp. instant coffee
1 teasp. vanilla
1 cup almonds, ground

Beat egg yolks until thick and lemon colored. Blend with sugar, adding ground almonds and instant coffee. Last, fold in stiffly beaten egg whites and add vanilla. Preheat oven to 350°F. and pour batter in 2 greased and floured cake pans. Bake for 35 to 40 minutes. Cool and ice with coffee icing.

HIMMEL TORTE

(Prepare separately)

(Prepare separately)

5 egg yolks
4 cups flour
Grated rind of 1 lemon
3 sticks butter
⅓ cup sugar
½ cup almonds, chopped fine

1 egg white
½ teasp. cinnamon
⅓ cup sugar

Cream butter and sugar, stirring in egg yolks and blending thoroughly. Sift flour, measure and sift again. Add grated rind and gradually add flour, stirring and beating until batter can be handled as dough. Place in 3 cake pans, well-greased. Combine egg white, sugar, cinnamon. Spread tops of cakes with this mixture and sprinkle with chopped almonds. Preheat oven to 450°F. Bake at this temperature for 10 minutes, then reduce heat to 350°F. and bake until browned. When torte has cooled, spread with raspberry jam and use following filling over jam:

FILLING FOR HIMMEL TORTE

⅓ cup sugar   3 egg yolks
2¼ cups sour cream   1¼ tablesp. cornstarch
                  ½ teasp. vanilla extract

Combine cornstarch and sugar, add sour cream and cook in double boiler, stirring continually. When it coats spoon, pour over beaten egg yolks. Heat mixture for a minute or two, or until thoroughly blended and heated. Add flavoring.

APPLE TORTE

5 egg whites   Rind of 1 lemon, grated
5 egg yolks   Juice of 1 lemon
1 cup lady finger cake   ⅓ cup chopped almonds
   crumbs   4 apples, grated
                  1 cup sugar

Cream beaten egg yolks and sugar until light lemon color. Add rest of ingredients except egg whites and almonds. Fold egg whites, stiffly beaten, into mixture. Place in greased and floured 9 inch spring form. Preheat oven to 350°F. and before placing in oven, sprinkle torte with chopped almonds, pressing them into mixture with knife. Bake for 25 to 30 minutes.

LINZER TORTE

2¼ cups flour	4 egg yolks
1 cup sugar	4 egg whites
2 sticks butter	1 teasp. vanilla extract
1 teasp. baking powder	1 lb. jar strawberry preserves
Grated rind of 1 lemon	or seedless raspberry jam
Juice of 1 lemon	(or other flavor you desire)

1 cup almonds, chopped fine

Cream butter and sugar. Add egg yolks, flavoring, lemon rind and juice and chopped almonds. Sift flour 3 times before measuring with baking powder, then once afterwards. Grease and flour a 9 inch spring form. Separate the dough, and use about ⅔ to pat on the bottom and sides of the spring form. Fill with preserves or jam. Roll out balance of dough, cutting into strips to place criss-cross on top of the jam. Bake in preheated oven of 350°F. for between 45 to 50 minutes.

MARZIPAN TORTE

(Prepare separately)	(Prepare separately)
2¼ cups flour	8 egg whites, stiffly beaten
1 stick butter	1 cup grated almonds
3 egg yolks	2 cups confectionery sugar
3 tablesp. water	Juice of 2 lemons
3 tablesp. sugar	Pinch of salt

Sift flour several times and measure. Cream butter and sugar, and add flour, beaten egg yolks and water. Blend thoroughly. Chill. Grease a 9 inch spring form and roll out ⅔ of dough, placing in bottom of form and around the sides, making it thicker on the bottom. Save the balance of the dough to make criss-cross strips on top of torte, when filled.

Using top of double boiler, heat grated almonds, salt, lemon juice and sugar, stirring continually until completely blended. Cool. Fold in stiffly beaten egg whites. Fill spring form with this mixture. Place strips on top, criss-crossing. Bake in pre-heated oven of 325°F. for about 1 hour. Garnish with citron and candied cherries.

STRAWBERRY TORTE

10 egg whites	*1½ cups sugar*
1 cup blanched almonds	*1 teasp. vanilla*

FILLING:

2 cups fresh strawberries, sugared and sliced	*2 cups whipping cream*

Beat egg whites stiffly. Add sugar, beating continually. Add vanilla extract, and fold in blanched almonds. Grease and flour 2 cake pans, preferably ones which have removable spring bottoms. Preheat oven to 325°F. and bake for between 30 to 35 minutes. Cool. Place strawberries between layers, and fill with whipped cream. Treat the top of the cake in the same manner. Garnish with a few whole strawberries.

BLITZ TORTE

1¼ cups cake flour	*¾ cup sugar*
1 teasp. baking powder	*5 egg yolks*
1 stick butter	*4 tablesp. milk*
1 teasp. vanilla	

Cream butter and sugar. Add beaten egg yolks to creamed mixture. Add vanilla extract, then alternately add flour with baking powder and milk. Blend thoroughly. Grease 2 cake pans well. Then prepare spread:

½ cup sliced almonds and 1 tablesp. sugar and ½ teasp. cinnamon	*5 egg whites*
	1 cup sugar

Beat egg whites and gradually add sugar until whites are stiff and dry. Spread on top of 2 unbaked cakes. Sprinkle top

with combined almonds, sugar and cinnamon. Bake in preheated oven of 350°F. for between 30 to 35 minutes. Use a
custard filling. See Cake Icings.

CHIFFON CAKE

2¼ cups flour	8 egg yolks
3 teasp. baking powder	8 egg whites
Grated rind of 1 lemon	½ teasp. salt
1 cup cold water	1 teasp. vanilla
¾ cup salad oil	½ teasp. cream of tartar

1¾ cups sugar

Sift flour, measure and sift again. Add sugar, baking powder
and salt to mixture. Alternately add egg yolks, salad oil, water,
lemon rind and vanilla extract and beat until batter is smooth.
Add cream of tartar to egg whites and beat until stiff but not
dry. Fold egg whites into yolk mixture. Do not stir or beat.
Grease tube pan and preheat oven to 325°F., baking for about
50 minutes. Increase heat to 350°F. and bake for another 10
to 15 minutes. Invert pan until cake cools.

Banana Chiffon Cake: Add 1½ cups mashed bananas and
omit vanilla extract and water. Follow all other directions.

Orange Chiffon Cake: Add grated rind of 2 oranges plus
the juice of 2 oranges. Omit lemon rind, water and vanilla.
Follow all other directions.

KOMISHBRODT (Traditional)
(Almond Cake Slices)

2 cups flour	½ teasp. vanilla extract
2 teasp. baking powder	½ teasp. almond extract
3 tablesp. oil	1 cup blanched almonds
¼ teasp. salt	1 cup sugar
½ teasp. cinnamon	3 eggs

Beat eggs, adding sugar and beating until light and fluffy.
Add oil and flavoring. Sift flour, measure and sift flour again

with baking powder, adding salt. Add flour to mixture, and then the almonds. Bake in preheated oven of 350°F. Grease shallow pan and pour batter into it. Bake for 45 minutes. Remove from pan and cool. Cut into ½ to ¾ inch slices about 3 inches long. Place on cookie sheet and place under broiler to brown on both sides.

AUSTRIAN BUTTER CAKE

4 sticks butter	*1½ cups sugar, sifted*
2 cups sifted flour	*¼ cup potato starch*
2 teasp. baking powder	*¼ cup cornstarch*
6 eggs	*1 teasp. vanilla extract*

Cream butter and sugar, beating until light and smooth. Sift flour, measure and sift again, with baking powder, cornstarch and potato starch. Add to creamed butter mixture, a little at a time, alternating with 1 egg each time, until entire mixture has been added. Beat well, add flavoring and pour into well-greased tube pan, spreading the batter evenly. Preheat oven to 375°F. Bake 45 to 50 minutes, or until well done. Frost with butter cream icing or chocolate icing. See Icings.

CARROT CAKE

6 good-sized carrots, scraped clean	*1 orange rind, grated*
	2 cups almonds, ground
10 egg yolks	*2 cups sugar, sifted*
10 egg whites	*2 teasp. vanilla extract*
1 cup water	

Dice carrots and cook in 1 cup of water in a saucepan. When tender remove from heat, drain, and mash or put through grinder until smooth as possible. Let cool. Beat egg yolks well, adding sugar (sifted) and beating until light. Combine carrots with orange rind and vanilla extract, adding almonds to mixture. Mix well and blend with egg mixture. Beat egg whites until stiff, but not dry, and fold into mixture carefully. Grease 9 inch spring form and bake in moderate oven of 350°F. for approximately 1 hour. Ice with butter cream icing, with almond extract. See Icings.

BANANA CAKE

2½ cups sifted cake flour	1 stick butter
1 cup sugar	3 eggs
3 teasp. baking powder	¾ cup milk
¼ teasp. salt	1 teasp. vanilla extract

Cream butter and sugar. Add eggs, beating after adding each egg, and thoroughly blend with creamed mixture. Sift flour, baking powder and salt, and alternately add to mixture with milk. Add flavoring. Grease 2 layer cake pans and bake in preheated oven of 375°F. for 30 to 35 minutes or until done. Frost and fill with butter cream frosting, adding ½ cup mashed bananas.

CARAMEL CAKE

2 cups sifted flour	3 egg yolks
3 teasp. baking powder	3 egg whites
1 cup sugar	¾ cup ice water
1 stick butter or margarine	¼ cup caramel syrup (see
½ teasp. salt	directions below)
½ teasp. vanilla extract	

Cream butter and sugar. Sift flour, baking powder and salt. Measure and sift again. Add beaten egg yolks to creamed mixture. Combine caramel syrup and ice water and add flour and syrup alternately. Beat until batter is thoroughly blended. Add stiffly beaten egg whites to batter, and pour into 2 greased cake pans. Bake in moderate oven of 350°F. for 35 to 40 minutes or until cake is done. Frost with caramel frosting. See Cake Icings.

Caramel syrup: Melt 1 cup sugar in skillet, stirring constantly. Add ½ cup hot water and continue cooking until mixture becomes syrupy. Cool and use according to above directions.

MAMA'S GRAHAM CRACKER NUT CAKE

1 lb. graham crackers   *1¼ cups sugar*
(crushed into crumbs)   *2 teasp. baking powder*
1 stick butter or margarine   *1 cup chopped pecans*
4 egg yolks   *1 cup milk*
4 egg whites   *1 teasp. vanilla extract*

Cream butter and sugar and add egg yolks, beating and blending thoroughly. Combine graham cracker crumbs with baking powder and add to mixture. Follow with milk, flavoring and then chopped pecans. Fold in stiffly beaten egg whites and pour into well-greased oblong pan. Bake in moderate oven of 375°F. for 35 to 40 minutes, or until done. Cool and frost with white icing chosen from Icings section. Or it may be topped with whipped cream sprinkled with a little brown sugar and decorated with a maraschino cherry.

LEMON CAKE

2 cups cake flour   *1 stick butter or margarine*
3 teasp. baking powder   *3 egg whites*
1 grated rind of lemon   *¾ cup milk*
¼ teasp. salt   *1 teasp. lemon extract*
1 cup sugar

Cream butter and sugar. Sift cake flour, measure and sift again with baking powder and salt. Add lemon rind to creamed mixture. Alternately add flour mixture and milk, continuing to beat. Fold egg whites thoroughly into mixture. Grease 2 layer cake pans and distribute batter evenly. Bake in preheated oven of 375°F. for 30 to 35 minutes. Cool, remove to cake platter and fill with lemon filling. Top with seven minute frosting (see Icings). Garnish with yellow gum drops.

ORANGE NUT LOAF CAKE

2¼ cups sifted cake flour   ½ teasp. salt
2 teasp. baking powder   1 cup sugar
1 stick butter or margarine 3 eggs
Grated rind of 1 orange   1 teasp. lemon extract
Juice of 1 orange   ½ cup chopped walnuts

Mix dry ingredients in a bowl. Add shortening and blend in orange rind and juice. Blend mixture with low speed electric mixer or at least 200 strokes by hand. Add eggs and chopped walnuts and beat again (with mixer or manually). Grease a loaf pan, pour in batter, and bake in slow oven of 325°F. for 1 hour and 20 minutes or until done. May be served plain or with butter cream icing.

FRUIT CAKE

3 cups cake flour, sifted   ½ teasp. cloves
2 teasp. baking soda   ½ teasp. allspice
2½ cups sugar   2 cups citron, candied cher-
1 stick butter or margarine   ries and candied pineapple
3 eggs   (all chopped)
½ teasp. salt   Grated rind of 1 orange
½ cup chopped walnuts   4 tablesp. vinegar
½ teasp. cinnamon   ¾ cup sour cream
                Juice of 2 oranges

(Reserve 1 cup sugar and juice of 2 oranges to pour over cake while hot from oven.)

Sift dry ingredients with flour and baking soda. Add citron, and candied fruits and mix well. Also add grated orange peel. Cream butter and 1½ cups sugar and beat well. Add eggs, well-beaten, and continue beating. Combine vinegar and sour cream and add to mixture, blending thoroughly, alternately

adding the dry ingredients with flour to mixture. Grease a
tube pan well and pour batter into pan, baking in moderate
oven of 350°F. for 1 hour and 15 minutes. While cake is hot,
pour 1 scant cup sugar evenly over the entire top. Pour orange
juice evenly over the sugar. Cool cake before removing from
pan. Garnish with candied cherries, half walnuts and pieces
of citron.

SPECIAL NOTE CONCERNING
PARTY CAKES

A few drops of vegetable coloring will change color of
batter to pink, blue, or green on party cakes. This same
method is applied to PETITS FOURS, where color is desired.
However, since various colored frostings are used, usually they
are baked from white cake.

Bake a two-layer white cake (basic recipe on Page 301).
Cut each layer into various shapes: circles, semi-circles,
squares, diamond-shapes (all no larger than 2 x 2 inches).

The layers may be filled with almond paste, whipped cream
or with the same fondant in which they are dipped.

Fondant may be tinted different colors by using a few drops
of vegetable coloring in each shade desired. Cakes are carefully
dipped in fondant and placed on oiled paper to dry. Use a
pastry tube for further decorations.

GEORGIA PEACH SHORTCAKE

3 cups sifted flour	*¾ cup milk*
4 teasp. baking powder	*½ cup brown sugar (dark)*
½ teasp. salt	*½ cup broken pecans*
1¼ sticks butter or marga-	*2 eggs*
rine	*½ teasp. cinnamon*

FILLING AND FROSTING

8 or 9 large ripe peaches   *1 cup whipping cream*
     ½ teasp. almond extract

Sift flour, baking powder, salt and cinnamon. Add brown sugar and blend thoroughly. Cut in butter or margarine, using pastry blender, and when mixture is crumbly, add pecans. Beat eggs with milk and add to flour mixture, stirring until completely blended.

Preheat oven to very hot (450°F.) and grease 2, 9-in. cake pans, distributing batter evenly in each pan. Bake for 20 to 30 minutes, or until shortcake is a golden brown.

In the meantime, peel peaches, dip in lemon juice to preserve color, sugar and cut into wedges. Whip cream, adding flavoring. Place whipped cream on shortcake layers, and decorate with peach wedges. Serve hot.

LEMON MERINGUE ANGEL TORTE
Meringue Shell

5 egg whites   *1 cup sugar*
¼ teasp. cream of tartar   *¼ teasp. salt*

Filling

5 egg yolks   *¼ cup lemon juice*
1 whole egg   *1 cup whipping cream*
Grated rind of lemon   *½ cup sugar*

Use glass pie plate (ovenproof) for baking shell, so that it may be used as a serving dish. Grease generously and dust with flour. Beat egg whites, adding cream of tartar and salt until foamy, shiny and double its volume. Beat in sugar, a little at a time, beating well until sugar is dissolved and meringue forms firm peaks.

Spread meringue in glass pie plate, swirling edges higher than center portion. Bake in slow oven of 275°F. for about

1 hour, or until delicately golden. Cool completely, allowing
it to remain in glass pie plate.

Prepare filling: Beat egg yolks and whole egg slightly in top
   of double boiler, stirring in lemon rind, juice and sugar.
   Stir constantly until mixture becomes thickened. Chill.
   Whip cream until stiff and fold into lemon mixture. Carefully spoon lemon filling into meringue shell. Chill at least
   1 to 2 hours before serving.

Cookies and Small Cakes

The following pages are dedicated to children all over the world. A mental picture of their eager faces and little hands clutching at Mama's apron as she takes a warm batch of gingerbread boys out of the oven . . . or when she is frosting those delectable brownies, lebkuchen, or jeweled gems . . . is refreshingly present in every recipe in this section.

Every festive holiday presents a challenge to Mama because she must be prepared to present her family and guests with just the right type of cake, cookies, snacks, and holiday treats.

CHOCOLATE FUDGE BROWNIES

3 squares unsweetened chocolate	1 teasp. baking powder
1 cup flour	1 cup sugar
3 tablesp. butter or margarine	¼ teasp. salt
	⅔ cup chopped pecans
	1 teasp. vanilla extract
2 eggs	

Melt chocolate in top of double boiler and add butter. Cool. Beat eggs and add sugar, blending thoroughly. Combine chocolate and butter mixture with egg and sugar. Add flour, baking powder and salt, by sifting into ingredients. Add vanilla extract and nuts and blend thoroughly. Bake in greased square pan, 8 by 8, in moderate oven of 350°F. for 35 to 40 minutes. Cool and cut into squares. May be frosted with chocolate fudge frosting. See Icings.

DATE BARS

1 cup flour
½ teasp. baking powder
¼ teasp. salt
1¼ cups sugar

1 stick butter or margarine
2 eggs
1 cup dates, cut fine (and floured)

1 cup walnuts, chopped fine

Grease oblong pan, about 10 x 14 inches. Cream sugar with melted butter, adding eggs, sifted flour, baking powder and salt. Flour dates so that they do not stick together and add, with nuts, to mixture. Bake in oven of 350°F. for about 20 to 25 minutes. Cut into bars about 1½ inches in width by 4 inches in length while still warm. Sprinkle with confectionery sugar.

MANDELCHEN

3 cups grated blanched almonds
¾ cup sugar

Butter (enough to knead into paste)
Grated almonds for garnish

Blanch almonds and place in oven long enough to dry out. Grind until fine. Add sugar and enough butter to make into a stiff paste. Roll thin, and cut into small round shapes. Place on cookie or baking sheet and bake in moderate oven of 350°F. for about 25 minutes. Remove from oven and roll in mixture of grated almonds and confectionery sugar.

JEWEL GEMS

2 cups flour, sifted
2 teasp. baking powder
½ teasp. salt
1 cup sugar
1 stick butter
2 egg yolks

2 egg whites
4 tablesp. milk
½ teasp. vanilla extract
Mint, peach and red jellies (in quantities required)
Silver candy decors

Cream butter and sugar, saving about 2 or 3 tablespoons sugar for mixing with egg whites. Beat in egg yolks with vanilla extract. Sift flour, salt and baking powder and add alternately with milk. Blend thoroughly. Chill until firm enough to roll with ease. Roll out on floured board to ⅛ inch thickness. Cut into ovals about 2 inches long with cookie cutter. Cut a small oval in center of cookie, reserving dough to roll into more cookies. Place about ½ teaspoon mint, peach or red jelly in center and top with another oval (cut same size with cut-out center). Press edges together to seal. Beat egg whites slightly. Brush cookies with mixture, and sprinkle with a little sugar. Decorate with little silver decors. Bake in hot oven of 400°F. for 10 minutes or until brown. Cool on cookie sheet, remove carefully and cool on racks.

WALNUT COOKIE CANES

2 cups sifted flour
½ teasp. baking powder
¼ teasp. salt
1 stick butter or margarine
¾ cup sugar
2 egg yolks
½ teasp. vanilla extract
1 square unsweetened chocolate
1 cup chopped walnuts
1 small pkge. cream cheese (3 oz.)

Sift flour, baking powder and salt together. Cream butter with cream cheese and sugar until creamy. Beat in egg yolks and flavoring. Sift in flour mixture, blend until smooth, then add chopped walnuts. Divide dough in half and pour melted chocolate into one half of dough. Roll each half portion of dough between sheets of waxed paper to ¼ inch thick rectangle. Take top sheet of paper off dough. Transfer to floured pastry cloth. Roll to about ⅜ of an inch thickness and cut into narrow strips about 6 inches long. Place on ungreased cookie or baking sheet and place the chocolate strip and white strip together, making a two-toned cane. Turn end to form cane. Bake in moderate oven of 350°F. for 10 minutes. Remove to rack. Frost with bon-bon frosting (see Icings) and decorate with broken pieces of walnuts.

COLORED POPCORN BALLS

5 cups freshly popped pop-   *½ cup corn syrup (light)*
corn (unsalted)   *¼ teasp. salt*
½ cup sugar   *Food coloring*
½ teasp. vanilla extract

Combine sugar, syrup and salt in large saucepan. Add several drops of food coloring and vanilla extract. Heat slowly until sugar dissolves. Toss in popped corn and with wooden spoon see that popcorn is evenly coated. Place saucepan on medium heat, and cook, stirring constantly, for about 5 minutes or until mixture is very sticky. Turn onto large sheets of foil. Let stand until cool enough to handle. Shape into 2 inch balls. If green balls are desired, used a few drops of green food coloring and use peppermint extract instead of vanilla; if yellow balls are desired, use a few drops of yellow food coloring with lemon extract instead of vanilla.

AYER KICHLACH

1 ¾ cups sifted flour   *½ teasp. salt*
¾ teasp. baking powder   *3 eggs, beaten*
½ teasp. vanilla extract

Sift flour, baking powder and salt. Add eggs and flavoring and knead well. Turn out on floured board and roll to about ¼ inch thickness. Sprinkle with sugar and prick dough with fork. Cut into rectangles, diamonds, and rounds, twisting dough in center. Bake on lightly floured cookie sheet in moderate oven of 350°F. or until lightly browned—approximately 35 minutes.

KICHLACH OR KICHEL

1 cup flour *3 tablep. sugar*
3 eggs *½ teasp. vanilla extract*

Sift dry ingredients into bowl. Make a well in center, dropping eggs into it. Add vanilla extract. Form into a doughy substance. Drop from teaspoon onto a greased cookie or baking sheet and bake in moderate oven of 325°F. approximately 20 to 25 minutes, until dough becomes puffed and browned.

Variation: For mohn or poppy seed kichels, add 2 to 3 tablespoons poppy seeds.

KICHEL (Variation)

1 cup flour *½ cup salad oil*
1½ tablesp. sugar *3 eggs*

Beat eggs, sugar, oil and flour very thoroughly until light, fluffy and well-blended. Using well-greased baking sheet, drop mixture with teaspoon, leaving at least 4 inches between each kichel. Bake in moderate oven of 325°F. for about 20 minutes, or until puffed and browned.

BOWKNOTS (Cruchiki)

4 egg yolks *Grated rind of 1 lemon*
2 cups cake flour *½ cup sour cream*
Pinch of salt *½ teasp. vanilla extract*
½ cup sugar *Fat or oil for frying*

Cream sugar and egg yolks. Add grated lemon rind, sour cream and flavoring, stirring continually. Gradually add flour and salt mixture, and continue stirring until batter is smooth and doughy. Turn out on floured board, and cut into strips about 2 to 2½ inches wide, ⅛ to ¼ inch thick, and about 4 to 5 inches in length. Cut a slit in the center lengthwise. Put one end through this slit, forming a bowknot. Use deep frying pan, heating at least 2 inches of hot oil or fat. Drop bowknots into hot fat until browned, turning so that they will brown evenly. Using slotted spoon, remove from pan and place on platter with paper toweling to absorb grease. Sprinkle with confectionery sugar when serving. These may be placed in oven for reheating and sprinkled with sugar for serving.

LITTLE HAMANS (Traditional)

3½ cups sifted white flour	3 tablesp. butter or marga-
1 teasp. baking soda	rine
¾ cup brown sugar	½ teasp. ginger
¾ cup molasses	¼ teasp. cloves
½ teasp. salt	¼ teasp. cinnamon
2 tablesp. water	½ teasp. allspice

Combine shortening with molasses and sugar, and add a little cold water to make it easier to stir. Dissolve baking soda in 2 tablespoons of water and combine with flour and other ingredients (spices). Form ball of dough and place in the refrigerator for at least 1 hour to chill.

Roll out on floured board to a thickness of between ¼ and ½ inch. Use a gingerbread man cutter, then shape a tri-cornered Haman hat and place on gingerbread man on floured cookie sheet. Bake in moderate oven of 350°F. for about 20 to 25 minutes.

When cool, prepare the same type of frosting as for Lebkuchen ... 1 cup confectionery sugar, a little water, about ½ teaspoon vanilla extract, and frost lightly, sprinkling with poppy seeds. If eyes, nose, mouth are desired, use cookie press decorator with vegetable coloring and decorate each in different colors.

PFEFFERNUESSE

3 cups sifted flour	*Grated rind of lemon*
1 teasp. baking soda	*½ teasp. cinnamon*
½ teasp. salt	*½ teasp. anise seed*
¼ cup butter	*2 teasp. ground cardamom*
4 egg yolks	*½ teaspoon cloves*
4 egg whites	*½ teasp. nutmeg*
1½ cups confectionery sugar	*¼ teasp. pepper*

ICING

1 cup confectionery sugar   2 tablesp. water
½ teasp. vanilla extract

Cream butter and sugar and add well-beaten egg yolks and grated lemon rind. Sift flour, baking soda and all spices, including salt and pepper, gradually adding to creamed mixture. Fold in stiffly beaten egg whites and chill in refrigerator for about 1 hour. Shape into balls about 1 inch in circumference and allow to remain at room temperature overnight. When ready to bake, brush with icing of confectionery sugar, water and vanilla extract. Place on ungreased baking sheet. Bake in moderate oven of 350°F. for 20 minutes or until done. Roll in confectionery sugar while still warm. Keep in covered cookie jar to retain freshness. They have a harder crust than most other types of cookies.

FRUIT AND NUT COOKIES

2 cups sifted flour	*1 stick butter or margarine*
2 egg yolks	*½ teasp. salt*
2 egg whites	*½ cup candied citron and*
½ teasp. baking soda	*cherries*
¾ teasp. cream of tartar	*½ cup chopped walnuts*
1 cup sugar	*½ teasp. vanilla extract*

Cream butter and sugar and add egg yolks, continuing to beat until light and fluffy. Sift flour, baking soda, cream of tartar and salt. Gradually stir in dry ingredients, blending thoroughly. Fold in stiffly beaten egg whites, adding vanilla extract to mixture. If required, add more flour for easy handling of dough and roll out on floured board to about ⅛ inch thickness. Sprinkle with candied cherries, citron and nuts and cut in various shapes with cookie cutter. Place on greased baking sheet and bake in hot oven (400°F.) for 10 to 12 minutes or until done. Place in cookie jar, but use waxed paper between cookies to retain freshness.

ANISE COOKIES

1½ cups sifted flour   ¾ cup sugar
2 eggs   ¼ teasp. salt
½ teasp. baking powder   1 teasp. anise seed, rolled fine
            ½ teasp. lemon extract

Beat eggs until thick and fluffy, adding sugar. Sift flour, baking powder, salt and anise, and add to mixture. Add lemon extract. Drop from teaspoon on greased cookie sheet and bake in moderate oven of 350°F. for from 10 to 12 minutes, or until done. Frost with thin icing of confectionery sugar and a little water and sprinkle with a few anise seeds.

ALMOND COOKIES

3 cups sifted flour   3 teasp. baking powder
4 eggs   1 cup sugar
1 cup sour cream   ¾ cup blanched almonds
½ teasp. baking soda   (ground)
            ½ teasp. vanilla extract

Cream sugar with eggs, beating until creamy and add vanilla. Combine sour cream and baking soda; add to mixture. Add ground almonds and blend thoroughly. Sift flour and baking powder and blend in to make a soft dough. Roll out dough on floured board to about ¼ inch thickness and using cookie cutter, cut into round shapes, diamond shapes, and triangles. Combine ground almonds with a little brown sugar and sprinkle on top of cookies. Bake in moderate oven of 350°F. until brown—about 15 minutes.

SUGAR COOKIES (Basic Recipe)

2 cups sifted flour	Grated rind of lemon
2 teasp. baking powder	2 eggs
1½ cups sugar	Juice of 1 lemon
¾ cup butter or margarine	½ teasp. salt
½ teasp. vanilla extract	

Cream butter and sugar, adding eggs and beating continually. Add lemon rind and juice and vanilla, blending thoroughly with mixture. Sift flour, baking powder and salt. Stir in gradually, until mixture is firm enough to roll out on a floured board. Divide dough into 2 parts, and roll out to about ⅛ of an inch thickness. Using cookie cutter, cut into round, square, diamond shapes, etc. Sprinkle with a little sugar and chopped nuts. Place cookies on a greased, floured baking sheet and bake in moderate oven of 375°F. about 10 to 15 minutes or until browned around edges. Cool and store in cookie jar.

TROPICAL COOKIES

1 cup flour	1 cup freshly shredded co-
1½ cups brown sugar (light)	coanut
½ teasp. baking powder	½ teasp. almond extract
¼ teasp. salt	4 eggs

Beat eggs until lemon colored and fluffy, adding sugar and continuing to beat. Sift flour, baking powder, salt and add to mixture, blending thoroughly. Add cocoanut and flavoring and blend. Drop from teaspoon on greased baking sheet, leaving about 2 inches between cookies. If desired, shredded cocoanut may be sprinkled on top of each cookie. Bake in moderate oven of 350°F. for about 15 minutes or until done. Garnish with candied cherry.

FESTIVE COOKIES (Basic Recipe)

1 egg	½ cup sugar
1 cup sifted flour	1 teasp. baking powder
⅓ cup butter	¼ teasp. salt

1 teasp. vanilla extract

Cream butter and sugar, adding egg and continuing to beat. Add vanilla extract. Sift flour, baking powder, salt and stir into creamed mixture. Using cookie cutter, make 6 point stars of David, round cookies, triangles, round cookies with hole cut out of center, hearts, etc. Place on greased baking sheet. Bake in moderate oven of 350°F. for 8 to 10 minutes. Remove from oven and cool. Decorate as described below.

Variation: Dropped cookies. Drop by teaspoonfuls about 2 inches apart on greased baking sheet. Baking time: 15 minutes, in 350°F. oven.

Frosting for decorating cookies with variations:

Combine 3 or 4 cups confectionery sugar, a little at a time, with 5 tablespoons melted butter. Blend thoroughly, reserving about 2 cups of the sugar. Beat in 1 egg white and continue beating until completely blended, gradually adding balance of sugar. Add 1 teaspoon vanilla extract.

Use a portion of this with a few drops of coloring for one batch of cookies. Sprinkle with cake decor of little colored candies and silver balls. For a bright glaze, powdered sugar, a few drops of food coloring and a few drops of hot water may be combined. This will serve as a border over the frosting on some cookies. Other cake decors consist of sparkling sugar in various colors, or chocolate bits sprinkled over frosting.

A pastry tube may be employed with colored frostings to decorate other cookies festively. Candied cherries in red and green may be utilized. Blue frosted cookies and silver balls make an attractive combination.

CUPCAKES (Iced)

1¼ cups flour
2 teasp. baking powder
⅔ cup sugar
3 tablesp. butter or margarine (melted)

1 egg
¼ teasp. salt
1 teasp. vanilla extract
½ cup milk

Beat egg well and add milk, melted butter and flavoring. Sift flour, baking powder, sugar and salt. Add to mixture of egg, milk, etc. Blend thoroughly. Grease muffin tin and pour in batter until ⅔ full. Bake in moderate oven of 375°F. for about 20 to 25 minutes. May be frosted with butter cream icing, chocolate icing, etc.

CHOCOLATE CUPCAKES

1¼ cups flour
1 teasp. baking powder
1 egg
½ cup milk

¾ cup brown sugar
1 stick butter
1 square unsweetened chocolate (melted)

½ teasp. vanilla extract

Cream butter and sugar and add beaten egg and melted chocolate. Sift flour with baking powder, and add alternately with milk to mixture. Add flavoring. Bake in greased muffin tins in moderate oven of 350°F. for 25 to 30 minutes. Ice with chocolate fudge icing. See Icings.

CHOCOLATE CUPCAKES (Variation)

1 square unsweetened choc-	*¾ cup sour cream*
olate	*1 teasp. baking soda*
1 egg	*½ teasp. vanilla*
1 stick butter or margarine	*1¼ cups sugar*
2 cups flour	*¾ cup hot water*

Melt chocolate in top of double boiler with hot water. Cream butter and sugar. Add egg. Combine sour cream and baking soda. Cool chocolate mixture and blend with creamed mixture. Fold in sour cream. Add flour, stirring and beating until batter is smooth. Add vanilla extract. Grease muffins tins and fill ⅔ full with batter. Bake in moderate oven of 350°F. for about 15 or 20 minutes or until browned. Remove and cool. Frost with chocolate icing.

SOUR CREAM COOKIES

1½ cups sifted flour	*½ cup sour cream*
½ teasp. baking powder	*1 egg*
½ teasp. baking soda	*½ teasp. nutmeg*
⅔ cup sugar	*½ teasp. lemon extract*
1 stick butter	*½ teasp. salt*

Sift dry ingredients and cut in butter with pastry blender. Add beaten egg, sour cream and lemon extract, beating continually, and chill dough in refrigerator, after thoroughly blended. Roll out to about ¼ inch thickness. Cut in various shapes with cookie cutter. Sprinkle with chopped nuts, if desired. Bake in hot oven of 425°F. for 8 to 10 minutes.

OATMEAL COOKIES

2 cups rolled oats (quick	*¾ cup brown sugar*
oats)	*1 stick butter*
1½ teasp. baking powder	*1 egg*
½ teasp. lemon extract	

Sift baking powder into dry ingredients. Melt butter and add to mixture. Then add beaten egg and blend thoroughly. Add flavoring. Grease baking sheet and drop batter from spoon about 2 inches apart. Bake in moderate oven of 350°F. for 10 to 15 minutes.

Variation: ½ cup chopped nuts and an additional egg may be added to mixture. Substitute 1 teaspoon almond extract for lemon extract.

MOHN COOKIES (Poppy Seed Cookies)

½ cup sugar
1 cup flour
1 teasp. baking powder
1 stick butter or margarine
½ cup hot milk
½ teasp. nutmeg
¼ cup seedless raisins
1 cup poppy seeds
½ teasp. almond extract

Cream butter and sugar. Soak poppy seeds in milk. Alternately add sifted flour and baking powder with nutmeg to creamed mixture with milk and poppy seeds. Blend well. Add raisins and almond extract. Drop *from teaspoon* on greased baking sheet about 2 inches apart and bake in oven of 350°F. for 25 minutes.

WALNUT ROCKS

2 cups flour
1 cup brown sugar
1 teasp. soda dissolved in
    1 tablesp. hot water
1 stick butter or margarine
2 eggs
½ cup chopped raisins
½ cup broken walnut pieces
½ teasp. cinnamon
½ teasp. vanilla extract
Pinch of salt

Cream butter and sugar. Add eggs. Roll chopped raisins in a little of the flour. Add flour, soda and hot water, salt, cinnamon, flavoring and raisins. Add nuts last. Blend thoroughly. Grease baking sheet, and drop with teaspoon about 2 inches apart. Bake in moderate oven of 350°F. for 20 to 25 minutes.

MACAROONS (Plain)

1½ cups sugar   ⅔ cup almond paste
6 egg whites   ¼ teasp. almond extract

Blend almond paste, sugar and flavoring. Slowly add unbeaten egg whites, blending until thoroughly mixed. Mixture
should be smooth. Drop from tip of spoon 1 or 2 inches apart
on baking sheet covered with brown paper. Bake in slow oven
of 300°F. for 20 minutes.

CHOCOLATE MACAROONS

3 egg whites   ⅔ cup sugar
2 squares unsweetened choc-   ½ cup grated almonds
   olate, grated   ½ teasp. vanilla extract

Combine sugar, chocolate and almonds. Add flavoring and
fold in stiffly beaten egg whites. Grease cookie sheet and place
brown paper over it. Drop mixture by teaspoon about 2 inches
apart and bake in moderate oven of 325°F. for 20 to 25
minutes. Remove from paper upon taking from oven.

MAPLE NUT MACAROONS

2 egg whites   1½ cups pecans, ground
         1½ cups brown sugar (light)

Add sugar to unbeaten egg whites and blend in ground
pecans. Form into small balls and place on greased baking
sheet about 2 inches apart. Bake in slow oven of 300°F. for
15 minutes or until done.

MAPLE SQUARES

1¼ cups flour   1 egg
1¼ cups brown sugar (dark)   ⅓ cup chopped pecans
1 teasp. baking powder   Pinch of salt
4 tablesp. butter   ½ teasp. vanilla extract

Heat sugar and butter in saucepan. Stir constantly until sugar is completely dissolved. Cool. Beat in egg, sift and measure flour and baking powder, and add to mixture. Add a pinch of salt and fold in nuts. Add flavoring. Grease 8 x 8 inch square pan and pour batter into it. Bake in moderate oven of 350°F. for 20 to 25 minutes. Cut in squares and cool. If frosting is desired, use caramel icing. See Icings.

GINGER SNAPS

1 egg	*½ teasp. ginger*
1 cup flour	*3 tablesp. butter*
¼ teasp. baking soda	*3 tablesp. sugar*
	¼ cup molasses

Cream butter and sugar and add egg and molasses. Combine ginger, flour and soda and add to mixture. Roll out to about ⅛ inch thickness. Using cookie cutter, cut in rounds and bake in moderate oven of 350°F. for 15 minutes, or until done.

MERINGUE KISSES

4 egg whites	*½ teasp. lemon juice*
1 cup sugar	*1 teasp. vanilla extract*
	¼ teasp. salt

Beat egg whites with salt until foamy. Add ½ cup of sugar gradually to this mixture and continue beating until egg whites form peaks. Add lemon juice and flavoring. Beat until stiff. Fold in the balance of the sugar, a little at a time. Grease baking sheet and sprinkle flour over it. Drop mixture from spoon and space about 2 to 3 inches apart. Bake in slow oven of 275°F. for about 45 to 50 minutes. Remove from oven. Cool. Remove top and fill with desired filling: ice cream, crushed fruit with whipped cream, etc. Replace top. Serve. (A few drops of vegetable food coloring may be added to mixture, if desired.)

MERINGUE KISSES (Variation)

3 egg whites	½ teasp. vanilla extract
1¼ teasp. white vinegar	½ teasp. almond extract
¾ cup sugar	Multi-colored candy sprinkles
Pinch of salt	

Beat egg whites, adding vinegar and a dash of salt. It should double its volume. Beat in vanilla and almond extract. Add sugar, a little at a time, beating continually until sugar is completely dissolved and meringue stands in firm peaks. Test meringue: it should be smooth and not gritty.

If a variation in color is desired, use a few drops of red vegetable coloring in half of mixture to tint a delicate shade of pink.

Drop by teaspoonful on cookie sheet lined with brown paper about 1 inch apart, and decorate with a sprinkling of multi-colored tiny candy sprinkles. Bake in slow oven of 250°F. for about 50 minutes, or until crisp. Cool on brown paper placed on wire rack. Keep tightly covered, so it will remain fresh and crisp.

DATE AND NUT KISSES

3 egg whites	½ cup pecans, coarsely cut
1 cup sugar	½ cup dates, cut in pieces
¼ teasp. vanilla extract	

Beat egg whites and add sugar gradually, beating until stiff. Carefully add dates, nuts and flavoring. Drop from teaspoon on greased baking sheet about 2 inches apart and bake in moderate oven of 300°F. for 30 to 35 minutes.

CHOCOLATE KISSES

5 egg whites	1 square unsweetened chocolate, grated
¾ cup sugar	
½ teasp. vanilla extract	

Beat egg whites until very stiff, adding sugar gradually and continuing to beat; then add chocolate and vanilla extract. Beat until mixture is stiff and forms peaks. Bake on well-greased and floured baking sheet about 2 inches apart, dropping from spoon. Oven should be at 250°F. Bake for 45 to 50 minutes.

CHOCOLATE CHIP NUT COOKIES

2 cups sifted flour	1 pkge. (8 oz.) semi-sweet
2 teasp. baking powder	chocolate bits
1 stick butter or margarine	1 cup chopped walnuts,
½ cup brown sugar	coarsely cut
½ cup granulated sugar	2 eggs
½ teasp. salt	1 teasp. vanilla extract

Cream sugar, both brown and white, and butter. Add eggs (well-beaten) to mixture and blend thoroughly. Combine nuts and chocolate bits and add to mixture. Add flavoring. Sift flour, baking powder and salt and add to mixture, blending thoroughly. Drop from end of teaspoon on greased baking sheet about 2 inches apart and bake in moderate oven of 325°F. for 20 to 25 minutes, or until done.

APPLE BARS

2 cups sifted flour	¼ teasp. nutmeg
1 cup sugar	1 stick butter or margarine
½ teasp. cinnamon	3 full cups sliced firm apples

1 teasp. vanilla extract

Combine sifted flour, salt and sugar and cut in butter with pastry blender until it becomes crumbly. Press all but about ¾ of a cup full into the bottom of a well-greased square pan about 8 x 8 inches and bake in oven of 350°F. for about 15 minutes. Spread apple slices over this cake mixture and sprinkle with cinnamon and nutmeg. More seasoning may be added, if desired. Sprinkle with reserved crumbs, covering the entire top of the apples. Place in oven and increase heat to 375°F. and bake for 30 to 35 minutes or until apples are done. Cool. Slice into 2 x 4 inch bars.

FUDGE INDIANS

½ cup sifted flour	1 square unsweetened choc-
½ teasp. baking powder	olate
¾ cup sugar	3 tablesp. butter or marga-
1 egg	rine
½ cup chopped pecans	1 teasp. vanilla extract
¼ teasp. salt	

Sift flour, salt and baking powder together, measure and sift again. Melt chocolate and butter in top of double boiler. Combine sugar and well-beaten egg, and continue beating until creamy. Cool melted butter and shortening a little, then blend with egg and sugar. Stir in flour and blend thoroughly. Last, add vanilla and fold in nuts. Using square pan of 8 x 8 inches, grease well and pour in batter. Bake in moderate oven of 350°F. for 30 minutes or until brown and standing slightly away from the sides of the pan. Remove from oven and cool. Frost with chocolate fudge icing. See Icings.

CREAM CHEESE KIPFEL

1 cup sifted flour	1 stick butter or margarine
1 pkge. (3 oz.) cream cheese	½ teasp. salt
3 tablesp. sugar	½ teasp. cinnamon
Grated rind of 1 lemon	½ teasp. lemon extract

Using pastry blender, combine all ingredients except nuts, sugar, lemon rind and cinnamon, and chill overnight in the refrigerator. Roll out on pastry cloth or floured board to about ⅛ inch thickness. Cut into 3 inch squares. Combine nuts, sugar, lemon rind and cinnamon. Place a small amount on each square and fold over, sealing edges firmly. Place on floured baking sheet and bake in moderate oven of 375°F. for 15 to 20 minutes or until browned. Sprinkle with brown sugar.

MOLASSES COOKIES

2 cups flour	*½ cup molasses*
1 stick butter or margarine	*1 cup brown sugar (light)*
1 square grated chocolate	*½ teasp. cinnamon*
½ teasp. baking soda	

Cream butter or margarine, adding sugar and molasses and blending thoroughly. Beat until light and fluffy. Sift flour, soda and cinnamon into mixture and blend completely. Add grated chocolate and mix thoroughly. Chill dough in refrigerator for several hours. Roll out half of the dough at a time on floured board, until about ⅛ inch thick. Cut with cookie cutters of various shapes and place on greased baking sheet. Bake in moderate oven of 350°F. for 12 to 15 minutes, or until done. Cool. Ice with butter cream icing and decorate with cake decors.

PEANUT BUTTER COOKIES

2 cups sifted flour	*¾ cup brown sugar*
1 teasp. baking soda	*2 eggs*
¼ teasp. salt	*¾ cup peanut butter*
¾ cup butter or margarine	*(smooth)*
¾ cup white sugar	*½ teasp. vanilla extract*

Cream butter and white and brown sugar thoroughly. Add eggs, flavoring and sifted flour with baking soda and salt. Blend thoroughly and add peanut butter. Blend and knead. Roll out to a thickness of about ¼ of an inch. Using cutter, make rounds and place on greased baking sheet. Bake in hot oven of 400°F. for between 10 and 12 minutes.

SPICED HONEY BARS

1 cup sifted flour   *¼ teasp. ground nutmeg*
4 oz. honey (strained)   *¼ teasp. ground cloves*
1 cup confectionery sugar   *¼ cup raisins, chopped*
3 tablesp. lemon juice   *½ teasp. lemon extract*
4 oz. blanched almonds (cut   *¼ cup citron, cut fine*
in half lengthwise)

Combine sugar, honey and almonds in saucepan over low
heat and bring to a boil. Remove and cool. Sift in flour, with
spices and lemon juice, adding flavoring, raisins, and citron.
Knead dough and cover. Chill in refrigerator overnight. Roll
out on floured board about ¼ to ½ inch thick. Grease square
pan about 8 x 8 inches and bake in moderate oven of 375°F.
for 25 minutes. Cut into bars about 2 x 5 inches. Frost with
butter cream icing, when cool. See Icings.

HONEY LEBKUCHEN

3 cups sifted cake flour   *½ cup shredded candied cit-*
¼ teasp. baking soda   *ron*
½ cup honey   *½ cup shredded candied or-*
½ cup brown sugar   *ange peel*
½ teasp. cinnamon   *1 cup blanched almonds,*
⅛ teasp. nutmeg   *slivered*
⅛ teasp. cloves   *½ teasp. vanilla extract*
2 tablesp. water   *Whole candied cherries for*
1 egg   *garnish*

Sift flour, baking soda and spices 3 times. Combine honey,
water and sugar and boil for about 5 to 7 minutes. Cool mixture and add egg, flour, and combination of citron, orange
peel and almonds. Add vanilla. Press dough into square cake
form and wrap in waxed paper. Refrigerate overnight. Roll
onto floured board to about ¼ inch thickness. Cut into 3 x 3
inch squares and place on greased baking or cookie sheet.

Bake in moderate oven of 350°F. for about 15 minutes. When cool, frost with a mixture of confectioners' sugar and a little milk, making a thin paste. Garnish each square with a candied cherry.

CHEESE COOKIES

¼ lb. pot or cream cheese	1 teasp. baking powder
¼ lb. salt butter	2 eggs
½ glass sugar	1 glass flour
1 cup chopped walnuts	

Have the cheese and butter at room temperature. Blend well and add sugar, eggs, and flour with which the baking powder has been mixed. When all ingredients have been blended well, knead on floured board. Store in refrigerator overnight.

Grind chopped nuts with rolling pin. Divide dough into sections and roll each section into a thin layer. Cut with cookie cutter or use top of juice glass to cut out rounds. Dip each round in the chopped nuts and bake on ungreased cookie sheet at moderate temperature of 350°F. for approximately 20 minutes.

TAIGLACH

1 teasp. baking powder	3 eggs
2 cups sifted white flour	3 tablesp. cooking oil
¼ teasp. salt	⅓ teasp. ground nutmeg
¾ teasp. ground ginger	½ cup candied cherries
⅔ cup brown sugar	(chopped)
1½ cups honey (dark)	1 cup chopped walnuts

Sift flour, baking powder and salt into bowl. Making a well in center, drop in eggs and oil and work into dough. Cut into 1-in. strips about ½-in. thick, place on greased cookie or baking sheet and bake in moderate oven of 350°F. until browned—approximately 15 to 20 minutes.

Cook mixture of honey, brown sugar, nutmeg and ginger

for 15 or 20 minutes, stirring constantly. Drop baked pieces of dough into mixture, together with nuts, and cook for about 15 minutes, or until dough is saturated with honey mixture. Nuts will adhere to dough. Turn out on wet board and when cool enough to handle, shape into balls and roll in additional nuts and candied cherries. Do not dispose of honey mixture; serve with taiglach as dessert. For an artistic effect you may wish to double this recipe, and make a decorative pyramid of taiglach, which will adhere to each other. Sprinkle with additional candied cherries and shredded cocoanut, if desired.

Cake Icings and Fillings

THE BAKING OF A CAKE WHICH IS APPEALING AND PALATABLE is an art derived from following recipes carefully as well as practice. Keep trying, even if the first or second one does not exactly live up to expectations. The next cake will turn out better.

The fluff, the decorations, the trimmings will bring out the best in a cake. The use of cake decors ... little colored candies, silver balls, glittering sugar in various colors, multi-colored gum drops, cinnamon hearts or candies, pastry tube and vegetable food coloring ... tends to enhance a plain cake and turn it into a festive dish.

When cakes are ready to be frosted, place the bottom layer on a serving plate with the flat surface facing up. Frost this layer first, replace the top layer, and ice the entire cake. If the cake displays a tendency to slide when top is being frosted, use toothpicks to control it. Unless directions are given to the contrary, cakes should be completely cooled before they are frosted and filled.

There are two types of icings popularly used for cakes: uncooked and boiled. Naturally, the most appealing to the busy housewife and mother is the uncooked icing which takes less time. But do not forego the pleasure of partaking of some of the delicious boiled icings. Some of them have been favorites for generations.

BON-BON ICING (Boiled)

A candy thermometer is necessary to make this icing just right.

2 cups confectionery sugar   1 cup hot water
  (10-X)   ¼ teasp. salt
2 cups sugar (granulated)   1 teasp. vanilla extract
¼ teasp. cream of tartar   Red vegetable food coloring

Combine granulated sugar, hot water and cream of tartar in saucepan. Stir constantly over low heat until sugar dissolves completely. Continue cooking until candy thermometer reads 226°F. Remove from heat. Cool to 125°F. and beat in confectionery sugar, adding salt and flavoring, and continuing to beat until smooth and syrupy. This icing is white. In order to color half of the icing, pour about half of the mixture into another bowl or saucepan and blend in several drops of red food coloring. It will color the mixture a beautiful, delicate pink shade.

ORANGE GLAZE (Boiled)

¾ cup corn syrup (light)   ¾ cup orange juice

Heat in small saucepan to boiling point. Simmer for about 5 to 7 minutes. Cool.

BUTTER CREAM ICING (Uncooked)

1 cup sifted confectionery   2 teasp. cream
  sugar (10-X)   1 teasp. vanilla extract
3 tablesp. butter   Pinch of salt

Cream butter until soft. Sift in confectionery sugar and blend with butter, adding cream a little at a time, dash of salt and vanilla extract until it may be worked into a smooth paste. Add either cream or more sugar to reach desired consistency.

Variation: For various colored butter cream frostings... place some of the butter cream icing in a little cup, add the desired food coloring and blend.

PLAIN ICING (Uncooked)

1 ¼ cups confectioners' sugar   *1 teasp. butter*
2 tablesp. hot milk   *½ teasp. flavoring*

Combine hot milk and butter, adding sugar gradually and blending thoroughly. Add vanilla or lemon extract. Blend until right consistency to spread.

CHOCOLATE ICING

1 ½ cups confectioners' sugar   *4 tablesp. butter*
3 squares unsweetened choc-   *¼ teasp. salt*
    olate   *⅓ cup milk*
2 eggs   *1 teasp. vanilla*

Place large bowl over pan of ice cubes and blend sugar, eggs, milk, salt and flavoring thoroughly. Melt chocolate and butter in top of double boiler. Cool a little and add to sugar mixture, beating until the desired consistency is reached. Will fill and ice 1 two-layer cake.

LEMON ICING (Uncooked)

1 ½ cups confectioners' sugar   *Grated rind of 1 lemon*
Juice of 1 lemon (strained)   *1 tablesp. boiling water*

Add grated rind and lemon juice to boiling water and stir mixture into confectioners' sugar, gradually. If mixture is too thin, add a little more sugar, until it reaches consistency desirable for spreading over cake. May also be used as a filling.

ORANGE ICING (Uncooked)

1 ½ cups confectioners' sugar   *½ teasp. lemon juice*
Grated rind of 1 orange   *1 tablesp. orange juice*
1 egg yolk (beaten well)

Add beaten egg yolk to sugar and blend. Add rest of ingredients, and beat until it reaches right consistency for spreading. May also be used as a filling for cake.

FROSTING GLACÉ (Uncooked)

1 cup confectioners' sugar   *1 teasp. lemon juice*
⅛ teasp. cream of tartar   *1 egg white*

Beat egg white until frothy but not stiff. Add half of the sugar to this mixture, 1 tablespoon at a time, beating continually until completely blended. Add lemon juice, cream of tartar and balance of sugar, beating until mixture is thick. This should not be used as a filling.

BUTTER ICING (Uncooked)

Vanilla Flavored: 1½ cups confectioners' sugar, 3 tablespoons butter, 3 tablespoons milk or cream, ½ teaspoon vanilla extract. Cream butter and sugar. Add milk or cream and flavoring, blending until the right consistency to spread is reached. If required, add a little more sugar or milk or cream to obtain right consistency.

Mocha Flavored: 1½ cups confectioners' sugar, 3 tablespoons butter, 1½ teaspoons cocoa (dry), 1 tablespoon hot strong coffee, ½ teaspoon vanilla extract. Blend as above.

Lemon Flavored: 1½ cups confectioners' sugar, 3 tablespoons butter, 1 teaspoon grated lemon rind, 1 tablespoon lemon juice (strained), 1 tablespoon water. Blend as above.

Orange Flavored: 1½ cups confectioners' sugar, 3 table-spoons butter, 1 teaspoon grated orange rind, 1 tablespoon orange juice (strained), 1 tablespoon water. Blend as above.

Caramel Flavored: 1½ cups brown sugar, ⅓ cup butter, 2 tablespoons cream, ½ teaspoon vanilla extract. Cream butter and add sugar, a little at a time. Add flavoring and only enough cream to obtain desired consistency.

Chocolate Flavored: 1½ cups confectioners' sugar, 3 table-spoons butter, ½ teaspoon vanilla and 1 square unsweetened chocolate. Melt chocolate in top of double boiler and blend with mixture.

WHITE FROSTING (Boiled)

2 cups granulated sugar	3 egg whites
4 tablesp. corn syrup	Pinch of salt
¾ cup water	1 teasp. vanilla extract

Combine sugar, corn syrup, water and salt, and cook until mixture forms a soft ball when a few drops are tested in cold water, or until candy thermometer reads 239°F. Remove from heat. Beat egg whites with electric or rotary beater, and while beating, slowly pour in hot syrup. Add vanilla, continuing to beat mixture until it forms peaks. Quickly spread on cake. If icing begins to harden, beat in a few drops of hot water.

Variation: If colored icing is desired, a few drops of vegetable coloring added to mixture will accomplish this feat.

Chocolate Icing: Add 2½ squares of bitter chocolate to sugar mixture while cooking.

Chopped Citron Icing: Fold in chopped citron and candied cherries when mixture has been beaten and is ready to be used.

Coffee Icing: Substitute strong black coffee for water. Flavoring should be omitted.

Mocha Icing: Add ½ cup strong black coffee and 3 tea-spoons cocoa. Omit water as well as flavoring.

Lemon Icing: Fold in grated rind of 1 lemon and strained lemon juice, just prior to frosting cake.

Marshmallow Icing: Add 1 cup of half-melted marshmallows to mixture and blend with beaten egg whites and hot syrup, just before icing is ready to be used on cake.

Peppermint Icing: Flavor with peppermint (only a few drops) instead of vanilla.

Cocoanut Icing: Sprinkle tinted cocoanut over cake after it is iced.

Strawberry Icing: Crush strawberries and fold into beaten mixture just before it is ready to use.

SOUR CREAM FILLING

1¼ cups sour cream	*2 eggs*
¾ cup sugar	*½ teasp. vanilla extract*

Beat eggs until thick. Gradually add sugar. Continue beating mixture and add sour cream. Place in top of double boiler and stir constantly until thick. Cool mixture and add flavoring.

CREAM FILLING

1 cup scalded milk	*2 tablesp. flour*
½ cup sugar	*½ teasp. vanilla extract*
1 egg	*Pinch of salt*

Combine all ingredients except flavoring, egg, and milk in top of double boiler. Slowly stir in milk and cook until mixture is thickened. Beat egg slightly. Add a little of the hot mixture to egg and return to top of double boiler. Blend for about 5 minutes. Cool and add flavoring.

Pineapple filling: Add ½ cup drained crushed pineapple and substitute lemon juice for vanilla.

Cocoanut filling: Add ½ cup shredded cocoanut to filling just before spreading on cake.

Butter cream filling: Add 2 tablespoons butter to hot mixture and blend before spreading.

Creamy custard filling: Chill mixture and fold in ½ cup whipped cream.

Banana filling: Add 1 mashed banana to filling and substitute lemon juice for flavoring.

Chocolate filling: Add 1 square bitter chocolate and ¼ cup sugar to ingredients.

Butterscotch filling: Substitute brown sugar for white sugar and add 1 tablespoon butter to mixture.

Coffee filling: Substitute ½ cup strong black coffee for ½ cup milk in recipe.

LEMON FILLING

½ cup water	Pinch of salt
½ cup sugar	Grated rind of ½ lemon
1 egg, slightly beaten	3 tablesp. lemon juice
2 tablesp. flour	1 tablesp. butter

Combine flour, sugar and salt and add water to mixture in top of double boiler. Stir constantly, until mixture thickens. Cover and cook for about 5 to 7 minutes. Stir some of the hot mixture into the slightly beaten egg, then return mixture to double boiler. Blend thoroughly for about 2 or 3 minutes. Remove from heat and cool. Add butter and lemon rind. Cool completely and add lemon juice.

Orange filling: Follow directions for above, but substitute orange rind and orange juice for the lemon rind and juice.

Orange or lemon cocoanut filling: Add ½ cup shredded cocoanut to filling, when cool.

CARAMEL FILLING AND ICING

¾ cup buttermilk   1 stick butter
½ teasp. baking soda   1½ cups white sugar
½ cup brown sugar   1 teasp. vanilla extract

Combine buttermilk and baking soda, and add brown and white sugar and butter (creamed). Cook until it forms a soft ball when a little is tested in a cup of cold water. Cool. Add flavoring. Beat until of creamy consistency and use to fill and ice cake.

BANANA ICING (Uncooked)

1 ripe banana, mashed   2 cups confectionery sugar
3 tablesp. butter or marga-   ½ teasp. lemon juice
  rine

Combine banana and lemon juice. Cream butter, adding sugar and banana mixture alternately and continuing to beat until mixture is light and fluffy. Do not use as a filling.

JAM FILLING

2 egg whites   1 cup strawberry jam, or
                                      other desired flavor

Beat egg whites, adding jam and continuing to beat until stiff enough to spread.

PRUNE AND NUT FILLING

¾ cup strained, cooked and   ¼ cup pecans, chopped fine
  pitted prunes   ½ cup apricot jam
              1 teasp. lemon juice

Chop prunes and combine with balance of ingredients.

SEVEN-MINUTE ICING (Boiled)

1 cup granulated sugar   *3⅛ tablesp. cold water*
1 egg white, unbeaten   *¼ teasp. cream of tartar*
             1 teasp. vanilla extract

Place ingredients, with the exception of flavoring, in top of double boiler. Beat with rotary beater until thoroughly blended. Place over water which is boiling rapidly, and continually beat mixture until icing stands in peaks. Add flavoring and remove from heat, placing in a pan of ice cubes and continuing to beat. Ice top and sides of cake. May be used as a filling, if desired, but quantity must be increased.

FOUR-MINUTE ICING (Uncooked)

1¼ cups sugar   *Pinch of salt*
3¼ tablesp. cold water   *3 egg whites, unbeaten*
½ teasp. cream of tartar   *1 teasp. vanilla extract*

Place ingredients, with the exception of flavoring, into a bowl. Set in a pan of hot water and beat constantly for 4 minutes. Add flavoring.

Variation: Lemon extract, almond extract, grated orange rind or grated lemon rind may be substituted for above flavoring. A few drops of vegetable food coloring may be added. Nuts—chopped or whole—may be sprinkled over top of icing on cake.

CHOCOLATE FUDGE ICING (Boiled)

1 cup sugar   *2 tablesp. butter*
1½ squares bitter chocolate   *⅓ cup cream*
             ½ teasp. vanilla extract

Melt chocolate in top of double boiler, adding milk and sugar. Stir occasionally, and when a few drops placed in cold water form a soft ball, remove from heat. Add butter and flavoring, place in pan of ice cubes and after allowing to stand a few minutes, beat with rotary or electric beater until the right consistency is reached. Double the recipe if it is going to be used as filling as well as icing.

CHOCOLATE ICING

2 cups confectioners' sugar
2 squares bitter chocolate
½ cup heavy cream

2 egg whites (beaten until stiff)
½ teasp. vanilla extract

Melt chocolate, adding cream in top of double boiler. Cool and add flavoring. Beat egg whites until stiff and add sugar, little by little, beating to blend. Combine chocolate mixture with egg whites, folding into one another. Beat until thoroughly blended and spread on cake. May be used as a filling. This recipe should be ample for top, sides and filling.

MAPLE ICING (Boiled)

1 ½ cups maple syrup
2 egg whites (beaten until stiff)

Boil syrup until it spins a thread and add gradually to stiffly beaten egg whites. Continue to beat mixture until the consistency is right for spreading. May be used only as icing.

SYRUP ICING AND FILLING

3 egg whites
1 teasp. vanilla extract
1 ¼ cups light corn syrup

Combine egg whites and syrup in large bowl. Using electric mixer, beat until thoroughly blended, then continue beating at high speed for about 10 to 15 minutes, until mixture is stiff enough to spread. Add flavoring. May be used as icing and filling for cake.

CUSTARD FILLING (Boiled)

1 cup scalded milk   *2 egg yolks*
⅔ cup sugar   *1 tablesp. cornstarch*
              ½ teasp. vanilla extract

Combine sugar and cornstarch and add hot milk. Beat egg yolks slightly. Pour mixture over eggs and cook in top of double boiler, stirring until thick. Cool and add flavoring.

Chocolate Custard Filling: Add 2 squares bitter chocolate to above mixture in double boiler.

FUDGE NUT FILLING (Boiled)

1 cup brown sugar   *1 stick butter or margarine*
2 squares bitter chocolate   *½ cup heavy cream*
              ½ cup chopped walnuts

Combine cream, sugar and butter and boil until mixture is thick, stirring often. Stir until cool and add melted chocolate and nuts.

ORANGE FILLING (Boiled)

2 egg whites (beaten until   *Juice of 2 oranges*
stiff)   *Grated rind of 1 orange*
              1 cup confectioners' sugar

Boil sugar with orange juice and grated rind until syrup spins thread. Pour gradually on stiffly beaten egg whites, continuing to beat until mixture is almost cool.

Lemon Filling: Substitute juice and rind of 1 lemon for orange rind and juice.

FLUFFY FRUIT FILLING (Uncooked)

1 cup sugar
2 egg whites
Grated rind of 1 lemon

1 cup desired fruit filling
(mashed berries, grated
peaches, apricots, etc.)

Beat egg whites with rotary or electric beater. Add sugar gradually and continue beating until meringue forms peaks. Add lemon rind and desired fruit by folding into mixture. Beat until thoroughly blended.

WHIPPED CREAM FILLING (Uncooked)

1 cup whipping cream
⅓ cup confectioners' sugar

½ teasp. vanilla, lemon, or
almond extract

Beat cream with rotary or electric beater until it begins to thicken. Gradually add sugar, continuing to beat until cream holds its shape. Blend in flavoring and use as filling.

Variation: Chopped nuts may be added to above filling.

SEA FOAM ICING

1 cup brown sugar (light)
2 egg whites
2½ tablesp. water

½ cup corn syrup (light)
¼ teasp. cream of tartar
Pinch of salt

1 teasp. vanilla extract

Place ingredients with exception of flavoring in top of double boiler. Beat continually until mixture stands in peaks. Remove from heat, add flavoring and beat over a pan of ice cubes until thick enough to spread over cake. This may not be used as a filling.

HONEY ICING (Boiled)

½ cup honey   *3 egg whites, unbeaten*

Combine in top of double boiler, beating with rotary beater until thoroughly blended. Continue beating over rapidly boiling water and cook from 5 to 7 minutes, or until icing will stand up in peaks. Use only as icing.

LEMON ICING (Uncooked)

1 cup confectioners' sugar   *Grated rind of 1 lemon*
1 egg yolk   *Juice of 1 lemon*
                ¼ teasp. salt

Beat egg yolk, adding rind and juice of lemon and salt. Beat until smooth. Gradually add sugar, continuing to beat until it reaches spreading consistency. If a little more sugar is required, add it, continuing to beat mixture.

Variation: Lime juice and rind may be substituted for lemon. If more color is desired, a few drops of green vegetable coloring may be added.

SPICE ICING (Uncooked)

1 cup confectioners' sugar   *¼ teasp. nutmeg*
¼ cup raisins   *¼ teasp. cloves*
1 tablesp. cocoa   *¼ cup heavy cream*
¼ teasp. cinnamon   *½ teasp. vanilla extract*

Combine confectioners' sugar with a little of the cream. Add spices and raisins and blend with mixture, adding balance of the cream. More sugar may be added if required. Add flavoring. Spread over spice cakes or cupcakes.

Pies, Pastry and Strudel

TO LEARN MAMA'S ART OF MAKING FABULOUS PIES WITH A flaky crust that literally melts in one's mouth, one must have patience and not lose hope if perfection is not attained with one's first attempt. All directions should be carefully followed; the most delicious, eye-appealing filling will not excuse a tough pie crust.

The most successful types of home baked pies are turned out in glass pie pans, since the bottom of the pie will brown more readily. However, the busy housewife may achieve excellent results with the new type aluminum pie plates which may be discarded after use.

Suggestions for preparations: Before you start to bake, prepare pastry board, rolling pin, pastry blender (wire), or blending fork, scissors (for cutting dough around pie crust), knives, and pastry cloth. All-purpose flour is satisfactory for pies and should be used in all recipes except where otherwise indicated.

Two fundamental rules: Handle dough as little as possible.
Chill after mixing.

FLAKY PASTRY

2¼ cups sifted flour   ⅔ cup shortening (*butter or*
5 tablesp. ice water   *margarine*)
                    ½ teasp. salt

Sift flour and salt and cut in shortening with pastry blender until the mixture is crumbly. Pour a little water into mixture, work dough, and sprinkle on a little more water until dough holds together. Chill. Divide dough into two parts and form round balls. Place on floured board, and roll, in one direction only, until ⅛ inch thick. Keep rolling from center, using as little flour on board and rolling pin as possible. Fold rolled crust in half, place on pan directly in center, and unfold half, fitting carefully in pan. Cut slits in bottom to allow steam to escape. Roll out top crust in same manner. Place desired filling on bottom pie crust. Moisten edges of pie crust by brushing with milk. Cover with top crust, cutting slits the same as in the bottom pie crust. Press edges together, brushing entire top crust with milk. Flute pie crust edges by pressing between thumb and forefinger. Bake in hot oven (425°F. to 450°F.) for about 10 minutes, reducing heat to 375°F. and baking from 30 to 45 minutes longer, depending upon the filling. The crust should be a golden brown.

For 1-pie crust: Use half of the above recipe.

Criss-cross strips on top: Use full recipe. Roll out in the same manner but cut top pie crust into strips about ½ inch wide. Place strips on top in criss-cross fashion. Place one strip all around edge, fluting after sealing.

MUERBE TEIG
(For Filled Pies and Tortes)

2¼ cups flour	4 tablesp. sugar
¾ cup butter	Grated rind of lemon
2 egg yolks	Juice of lemon
	4 tablesp. ice water

Using pastry blender, combine flour and butter until crumbly. Beat egg yolks and sugar well, combining with ice water. Add lemon juice and grated rind to egg mixture and blend with flour. Pat into 2 pans to a ¼ inch thickness. For filled pies, cut excess from around edges, sealing and fluting. Cut slits in bottom to allow steam to escape.

BLAITER TEIG
(Better Known as "Puff Paste")

1½ cups cake flour   *1¼ cups ice water*
1 lb. butter

Chill all ingredients. Divide butter into 3 equal parts, cutting a pound square into 3 oblong divisions. Place 2 parts in wax paper in the refrigerator, working the other portion into the flour with a pastry blender until it is crumbly. Add ice water, a little at a time, and as soon as it makes a smooth paste, turn out on floured board, kneading only enough to form a ball of dough. Pat and roll to ¼ inch thickness, keeping paste a little more wide than long with square corners. Lay the second oblong pat of butter on paste, sprinkling with a little flour. Fold the paste over butter in jelly roll fashion. Again, pat and roll out to ¼ inch thickness, placing the third oblong pat of butter on paste, and rolling up again in jelly roll fashion. When paste becomes soft, chill in refrigerator for a couple of hours. Place in hot oven of 500°F. and turn frequently so that it rises evenly. When well-risen, reduce heat to 350°F. for 45 minutes. This paste dough is used for pies, patty shells, tarts.

GRAHAM CRACKER SHELL

2 cups graham cracker   *¼ cup confectioners' sugar*
crumbs   *½ cup melted butter*

For use in tortes, grease sides and bottom of a spring form. Mix crumbs, confectioners' sugar and butter well and press onto sides and bottom of form. Chill in refrigerator for 2 or 3 hours.

GRAHAM CRACKER CRUST
(Bottom Crust Only)

1 cup graham cracker crumbs   3 tablesp. brown sugar
¼ cup melted butter

Mix ingredients well and press into bottom and sides of well-greased pie pan. Fill with desired filling.

CORNFLAKE CRUMB PIE SHELL

2¼ cups cornflake crumbs   ½ cup melted butter
¼ cup sugar   ½ teasp. cinnamon

Blend ingredients together and reserve ¼ cup of mixture to sprinkle over top of filling. Press the balance into a well-greased pie pan—bottom and sides. Chill for several hours.

MERINGUE TOPPING FOR PIES

2 or 3 egg whites (beaten   4 tablesp. confectioners'
until stiff)   sugar
¼ teasp. cream of tartar

Add cream of tartar and sugar gradually to stiffly beaten egg whites, beating until completely blended and meringue stands up in peaks. Spread meringue topping over pie and bake in oven of 300°F. for about 15 minutes, or until meringue turns a tinged brown.

LEMON MERINGUE PIE

Rind of 1 lemon   1¼ cups sugar
Juice of 1 lemon   1 cup boiling water
¼ cup cornstarch   2 tablesp. butter
3 egg yolks

Using recipe for Flaky Pastry (see Page 358), bake bottom pie shell. Combine cornstarch and sugar, adding boiling water gradually, stirring constantly over low heat in sauce-pan. Add butter and egg yolks, beaten, to mixture. Continue to stir. Place over double boiler, cooking until thick and stirring constantly. Add lemon rind and juice. Blend thoroughly. Remove from heat and cool. Fill pie shell and top with meringue.

MAMA'S APPLE PIE

3 to 4 cups apples, pared, cored and sliced (add more if desired)
1 cup sugar
½ cup brown sugar
1 teasp. cinnamon

½ teasp. nutmeg
½ cup raisins
4 tablesp. butter
1 tablesp. lemon juice
Recipe Flaky Pastry (see Page 358)

Line pie plate with Flaky Pastry, cut slits in bottom and sprinkle bottom with a little brown sugar and cinnamon. Place apples in pie pan, sprinkle with combination of sugars and cinnamon, nutmeg and raisins. Pour lemon juice over top and dot with plenty of butter. Place top crust over filling, sealing and fluting edges, and cutting slits in top crust. Brush with milk and sprinkle with sugar. Bake in hot oven of 425°F. until crust is golden brown (45 minutes to 1 hour).

PUMPKIN PIE

2½ cups cooked pumpkin, strained
1 cup brown sugar
½ teasp. cloves
½ teasp. ginger

1 teasp. cinnamon
3 eggs
1 cup cream
½ cup milk
Grated rind of 1 lemon

Combine ingredients, adding lightly beaten eggs and gradually adding cream and milk. Mixture should not be too thin. The pumpkin should be able to absorb all liquids. Use a little less liquid if you find you have too much. Add grated lemon rind. Place one crust in pie plate and brush with egg white. Pour in mixture. Bake in hot oven of 425°F. for about 15 minutes. Reduce heat to 275°F. and bake for 45 minutes. Cool and serve. May be topped with whipped cream.

RHUBARB PIE (With Strawberries)

2 lbs. rhubarb (cut in 1-inch pieces)

2 cups strawberries (washed and cut in half lengthwise)

3 tablesp. cornstarch

2 cups sugar

Grated rind of lemon

1 tablesp. lemon juice

Combine cornstarch and sugar. Line pie plate with Muerbe Teig (see Page 359), fill with rhubarb and strawberries, sprinkle with grated lemon rind and lemon juice, and pour on cornstarch-sugar mixture evenly. Cover with top crust of Muerbe Teig, slit, seal and flute edges. Bake in hot oven of 425°F. for 35 minutes, then reduce to 325°F. for 20 or 25 minutes more, or until crust is golden brown.

BANANA CREAM PIE

4 egg yolks

4 tablesp. cornstarch

2 cups scalded milk

¼ teasp. salt

1 teasp. vanilla extract

4 bananas (cut into ¼-inch slices)

⅔ cup sugar

Bake pie shell. Combine cornstarch, sugar and salt, adding milk slowly and stirring constantly in top of double boiler. Add beaten egg yolks, gradually, to mixture, continuing to stir until mixture is thick. Remove and add flavoring. Cool. Place mixture and sliced bananas in alternate layers in pie shell and top with whipped cream.

CHOCOLATE WHIPPED CREAM PIE

3 egg yolks
3 egg whites
1 cup sugar
2 squares semi-sweet choco-
    late (grated)

1 teasp. vanilla extract
1 cup whipping cream
2 tablesp. confectioners'
    sugar
3 tablesp. milk

Combine egg yolks and sugar and beat until creamed. Add flavoring, grated chocolate and milk. Blend thoroughly. Fold in stiffly beaten egg whites. Line pie plate with Flaky Pastry (see Page 358), seal and flute edges. Pour chocolate mixture into pie plate and bake at 450°F. 15 to 20 minutes. Reduce heat to 325°F. and bake for 30 minutes longer. Whip cream, mixing in confectioners' sugar and use to top pie.

CARAMELIZED APPLE PIE

1 tablesp. honey (hot)
⅔ cup brown sugar

3 tablesp. butter (melted)
1 cup broken pecans

Combine above ingredients, and place on the bottom and sides of a deep pie dish. Using Flaky Pastry recipe (see Page 358), prepare two crusts. Place bottom crust over the ingredients on bottom of pie plate. Prepare the following:

3 cups apples, pared and
    diced
¾ cup sugar
1 teasp. cinnamon

½ teasp. nutmeg
3 tablesp. butter
Grated rind of lemon
1 tablesp. lemon juice

Combine sugar, cinnamon, nutmeg and apples. Place in pie plate, sprinkle with grated lemon and lemon juice, dot with plenty of butter and sprinkle with a little more cinnamon and sugar. Cover with top crust, seal and flute edges. Brush with milk, particularly the edges. Slit top crust in 6 or 7 places. Bake in hot oven of 400°F. for about 15 minutes.

Reduce heat to 325°F. and bake 35 to 40 minutes longer until crust is golden brown. Cool for ½ hour, return to oven for a few moments to loosen caramelized mixture on bottom. Invert so that caramelized side is on top.

CHIFFON PIES

Before proceeding, prepare pie shell using ½ the recipe for Flaky Pastry (see Page 358).

LEMON CHIFFON PIE

5 egg yolks
5 egg whites
1 tablesp. unflavored gelatin
¼ cup cold water
Rind of 1 lemon, grated
Juice of 1 lemon
1¼ cups sugar

Soak gelatin in cold water for about 5 minutes. Beat egg yolks well, adding lemon juice, a pinch of salt and half of the sugar. Cook in top of double boiler until mixture coats the spoon. Remove, add lemon rind and softened gelatin. Mix all ingredients together well. When mixture is completely cool, fold in stiffly beaten egg whites to which remaining sugar has been added. Pour into pie shell, refrigerate and chill. Top with whipped cream to which 1 tablespoon confectioners' sugar has been added.

Orange Chiffon Pie: Follow above directions but substitute orange rind and juice for lemon.

STRAWBERRY CHIFFON PIE

1 tablesp. unflavored gelatin
¼ cup cold water
1¼ cups sugar
1½ cups crushed strawber-
ries and juice
2 egg whites
½ cup whipped cream

Soak gelatin in cold water for about 5 minutes. Combine boiling water, 1 cup sugar, strawberries, and a pinch of salt.

Add softened gelatin and stir until dissolved. Cool. When mixture begins to thicken, fold in whipped cream. Beat egg whites until stiff, adding ¼ cup of sugar, and fold into strawberry mixture. Pour into baked pie shell and chill in refrigerator until ready to serve. Garnish with a dab of whipped cream topped with a whole strawberry.

CHOCOLATE CHIFFON PIE

1 tablesp. unflavored gelatin	*1 cup milk*
¼ cup cold water	*¾ cup sugar*
2 squares bitter chocolate	*1 cup whipping cream*
	1 teasp. vanilla extract

Soak gelatin in cold water for about 5 minutes. Combine chocolate, sugar, milk and a pinch of salt in top of double boiler. When melted and completely blended, remove from heat and add gelatin, stirring to blend thoroughly. Cool and add flavoring. Refrigerate. When mixture begins to thicken, fold in stiffly beaten whipped cream. Pour into pie shell and chill until ready to serve. Top with a dab of whipped cream.

CUSTARD PIE

3 eggs	*Pinch of salt*
1½ cups scalded milk	*½ teasp. grated nutmeg*
⅓ cup sugar	*½ teasp. vanilla extract*

Line pie plate with bottom crust of Flaky Pastry (see Page 358). Bake in hot oven at 450°F. for about 10 minutes. Remove from oven and after preparing the following, pour into hot baked crust: beat eggs and add sugar, nutmeg and salt. Stir in scalded milk and blend thoroughly. Add vanilla. Bake for 35 minutes at 300°F. or until knife inserted in custard comes out clean. Cool pie at room temperature for several hours before serving.

Cocoanut Custard Pie: Add ½ cup shredded cocoanut and proceed as directed above.

PECAN PIE
(The Favorite of The South)

1 cup broken pecans	Pinch of salt
¾ cup brown sugar (dark)	1 teasp. vanilla extract
1 stick butter or margarine	1 cup heavy cream
4 eggs	1 tablesp. confectioners'
1 cup corn syrup (dark)	sugar

Prepare pie shell from ½ recipe for Flaky Pastry (see Page 358). Cream butter and sugar and add balance of ingredients (except cream and confectioners' sugar), blending thoroughly. Pour into pie shell and bake in hot oven of 425°F. for 15 minutes. Reduce heat to 350°F. and bake 30 minutes longer. Cool. Whip 1 cup heavy cream, adding confectioners' sugar, and top pie before serving. Garnish with half pecans or sprinkle with broken pecans.

DEEP DISH APPLE PIE

3 lbs. apples (cored, peeled and diced)	2 tablesp. butter or margarine
1 cup dark raisins	1 teasp. cinnamon
1½ cups sugar	½ teasp. ground nutmeg
½ cup brown sugar	1½ recipe Flaky Pastry
3 tablesp. flour	Rind and juice of 1 lemon

Roll Flaky Pastry out to about ¼ inch thickness and line bottom and sides of oblong, glass baking dish (about 9 x 12 inches) with pie crust. Flute edges. Combine flour, lemon juice, apples, raisins, sugar, spices, saving a little white and brown sugar, mixed with spices and a little flour to sprinkle over top. Fill baking dish, sprinkle with sugars and spices, dot generously with butter. Cut half-inch strips for lattice top crust and crisscross, binding, sealing and fluting edges. Bake in hot oven of 425°F. for 45 to 50 minutes or until done.

DUTCH APPLE PIE

3 cups apples (peeled, cored
and diced)
1 cup granulated sugar
1 teasp. cinnamon
½ teasp. cloves
3½ tablesp. flour
1 cup thick sour cream
Grated rind of lemon
Streusel topping
½ recipe Flaky Pastry

Streusel Topping:
½ cup flour
3 tablesp. butter
6 tablesp. sugar
½ teasp. cinnamon
(Mix by rubbing with finger
tips until small crumbs are
formed. Sprinkle over top
of Dutch Apple Pie)

Roll out pastry to ¼ inch thickness and line pie plate,
fluting edges. Brush with milk and make slits in bottom.
Place apples in pie shell. Combine sugar, flour, cinnamon and
cloves. Add sour cream to mixture and blend thoroughly. Pour
mixture over apples, including grated rind of lemon. Top with
streusel topping. Bake in hot oven of 450°F. for 15 minutes.
Reduce heat to 350°F. and bake 35 to 40 minutes longer.
May be served hot or chilled. Dutch Apple Pie à la mode is
a delectable dessert; vanilla ice cream is excellent with it.

LEMON FLUFF PIE

½ recipe Flaky Pastry
Grated rind of lemon
Juice of 1 lemon
3 tablesp. butter or marga-
rine

3 egg yolks
3 egg whites
1 cup sugar
1¼ cups milk
2 tablesp. flour

Line pie pan with pie crust. Cream butter, adding sugar
and beating until well blended. Add flour and beaten egg
yolks. Beat well, and add rind and juice of lemon. Slowly and
gradually add milk to mixture, blending. Fold in egg whites,
which have been stiffly beaten. Pour into shell and bake in

hot oven of 425°F. for 10 minutes. Reduce heat to 325°F. and bake 35 minutes longer.

EGGNOG WHIPPED CREAM PIE

5 egg yolks	½ recipe Flaky Pastry
⅔ cup sugar	5 egg whites
Pinch of salt	⅓ cup sugar
1 tablesp. unflavored gelatin	1 teasp. grated nutmeg
¼ cup cold water	1 teasp. vanilla extract
½ cup hot water	1 cup whipping cream

Bake pie shell. Over double boiler, combine slightly beaten egg yolks, sugar, salt and hot water, stirring constantly. Cook until thick enough to coat spoon. Soften gelatin in cold water for about 5 minutes. Pour hot custard over gelatin and blend thoroughly. Cool. When it begins to thicken, fold in mixture of stiffly beaten egg whites, blended with sugar and nutmeg and flavored with vanilla extract. Pour mixture into baked pie shell. Chill in refrigerator. Just before serving, whip cream. Top pie with whipped cream sprinkled with grated nutmeg.

PINEAPPLE WHIPPED CREAM PIE

1 cup crushed pineapple, drained	¼ teasp. salt
	½ cup sugar
Grated rind of lemon	1 cup cream
Juice of 1 lemon	½ teasp. vanilla extract
4 egg yolks	½ recipe Flaky Pastry
4 egg whites	1 cup whipping cream

Prepare pastry and line pie pan, fluting edges. Combine beaten egg yolks with grated lemon rind, stirring in cream pineapple, and vanilla. Add lemon juice to mixture and stir until thick. Beat egg whites until stiff, gradually adding sugar and salt. Fold into mixture and pour into pie shell. Bake in oven of 325°F. about 20 minutes or until pie crust is browned and mixture is firm and lightly browned. Whip cream and top pie, when cooled.

CHERRY TARTS

For shells: Use recipe for Muerbe Teig (see Page 359). Invert a large muffin tin and fit dough about ¼ inch thick over each reversed cup, rolling edges of tarts and shaping. Prick bottom and sides with fork. Bake in hot oven of 450°F. for 15 minutes.

3 cups pitted cherries	*1 cup water*
1 tablesp. cornstarch	*6 baked tart shells*
⅓ cup confectioners' sugar	*Few drops red vegetable*
¾ cup granulated sugar	*coloring*

Mix 2 cups of cherries with confectioners' sugar and allow to stand for about an hour. Combine remaining cherries with water in saucepan and cook until tender. Press through sieve and add to mixture of sugar and cornstarch. Cook until mixture is clear. Add a few drops of red vegetable coloring. Arrange cherries which have been standing in confectioners' sugar in baked shells and pour hot strained cherries over them. Cool. When serving, garnish with whipped cream and a whole cherry.

ICE CREAM TARTS

Bake shells as directed in Cherry Tarts. Cool. Fill with desired ice cream flavor. With rotary beater, whip 3 egg whites, slowly adding 3 tablespoons confectioners' sugar and when it stands in peaks, cover each ice cream tart with a thick layer of meringue. Place in hot oven of 400°F. for 5 minutes. Serve upon removing from oven.

FRESH FRUIT TARTS

Bake shells as directed in Cherry Tarts.

Strawberries: Prepare 4 cups strawberries but crush only 2 cups, adding 1 cup sugar. Sprinkle confectioners' sugar over whole strawberries and allow to stand until sugar has been absorbed by berries. Cook crushed berries and press through a sieve. Add 1 tablespoon cornstarch mixed with a little sugar and cook until mixture is clear. Place whole strawberries in tart shells, pouring over hot mixture. Allow to cool. Serve with topping of whipped cream and a whole strawberry.

Blackberries: Sprinkle 3 cups blackberries with 1 cup sugar. Chill for about an hour. Serve in tart shells with a topping of whipped cream.

Blueberries: Prepare in the same manner as strawberries, using the hot glazed sauce to pour over fresh berries.

CREAM HORNS OR CORNUCOPIAS

Use recipe for Blaiter Teig or "Puff Paste" (see Page 360). Brush with egg white and water and sprinkle with a little sugar. Cut heavy brown paper in the form of cornucopias and wrap paste around paper in strips which overlap each other. Chill for several hours before baking. Bake as directed for puff paste. When done, remove from oven. Remove paper and chill. Fill with following mixture:

4 egg whites   *1 cup confectioners' sugar*
              ½ teasp. vanilla extract

Whip egg whites until stiff, then gradually add confectioners' sugar. Continue beating until meringue stands in peaks. Add vanilla extract and beat again. Fill horns with this mixture, and sprinkle with confectioners' sugar.

Alternate filling:

MARSHMALLOW MERINGUE FILLING

2 cups marshmallows	¼ teasp. salt
2 egg whites	⅓ cup sugar
1½ tablesp. milk	¼ teasp. vanilla extract

Heat marshmallows and milk over low flame, stirring. Remove from heat and add flavoring. Continue to fold over and over until mixture is light and fluffy. Add salt to egg whites and beat until stiff, gradually adding sugar. Continue to beat until egg whites stand in peaks. Add marshmallow mixture. Use as filling for horns, sprinkling with confectioners' sugar.

Alternate filling:

BUTTER CREAM AND MERINGUE

2 cups confectioners' sugar	1 teasp. vanilla extract
3 tablesp. butter	2 egg whites
	2 tablesp. cream

Cream confectioners' sugar and butter, adding a little flavoring to moisten. Add a little cream and continue beating. When it has reached spreading consistency, fold in stiffly beaten egg whites. Fill horns.

CHOUX PASTE (Cream Puff Shells)

1½ cups sifted white flour	5 eggs
1½ cups water	¾ cup butter
	½ teasp. salt

Combine butter with water and salt, and bring to boiling point. Add flour, all at once, stirring over flame with large spoon. When mixture leaves sides of pan and forms ball, remove from heat. Add eggs, one at a time, beating and blending thoroughly after each addition. Fill rounded tablespoons with mixture and place on greased baking sheet about

2 inches apart. Bake in hot oven of 450°F. for 10 to 12 minutes. Reduce temperature to 375°F. and bake for 30 minutes longer, or until puffs hold shape and become golden in color. Cool on wire rack. When cool, slit side so that cream filling may be inserted.

WHIPPED CREAM FILLING
(For Cream Puffs)

1 cup whipping cream   ½ cup confectioners' sugar
½ teasp. vanilla flavoring

Whip cream, and add confectioners' sugar slowly while beating until all the sugar has been added. Add flavoring. Insert into cream puffs. Sprinkle with confectioners' sugar and serve.

Variation: May be filled with generous helping of any flavor ice cream and the top sprinkled with confectioners' sugar.

Variation: May be filled with *Butter Cream and Meringue,* see Page 372.

Variation: May be filled with *Marshmallow Meringue Filling,* see Page 372.

Variation: Chocolate Butter Cream and Meringue Filling. Add one tablespoon cocoa to Butter Cream and Meringue Filling recipe, Page 372.

FRENCH FRIED CHOUX PASTE
(Puff Shells)

Prepare same recipe as for Choux Paste. Heat a French fryer with deep oil or melted shortening until hot. Using 1 rounded tablespoon batter, drop into fat and fry until crust has formed and it is golden brown. This should take from 10 to 12 minutes. Remove with slotted spoon. Drain and cool. Slit top and place desired filling, replacing tops. Sprinkle with confectioners' sugar.

NAPOLEONS

Prepare dough from recipe for Blaiter Teig (Page 360). After chilling dough, bake in 3 sheets, pricking before baking. Place in hot oven of 500°F. and turn frequently, baking for 45 minutes.

Fill with cream, and frost—see recipes below.

CUSTARD FILLING

3 egg yolks   *½ cup sugar*
1 cup scalded milk   *1 tablesp. cornstarch*
                    ½ teasp. vanilla extract

Combine cornstarch and sugar, adding hot milk. Pour over slightly beaten egg yolks and cook in top of double boiler, stirring constantly until mixture coats spoon. Remove from heat. Cool and add flavoring. Use this filling between sheets (two) for Napoleons. Ice the top sheet with the following:

PLAIN ICING (Uncooked)

1½ cups confectioners'   *1 teasp. lemon juice*
sugar   *¼ teasp. vanilla extract*
¼ teasp. cream of tartar   *3 tablesp. cream*

Blend sugar with a little cream, add cream of tartar, lemon juice and flavoring. Mix until it reaches spreading consistency, and frost top sheet of Napoleons. With a pastry tube, add a border of chocolate icing:

1 sq. bitter chocolate   *1¼ cups confectionery sugar*
3 tablesp. boiling water   *¼ teasp. vanilla extract*

Melt chocolate in top of double boiler, adding hot water, and stirring until smooth. Remove from heat and add flavor-

ing and confectionery sugar, stirring until smooth. Decorate
top and cut into pieces 2½ x 5 inches.

SOUR CREAM PIE

1½ cups sour cream · *4 egg whites*
1 tablesp. cornstarch *1 teasp. cinnamon*
1 cup sugar *½ recipe Flaky Pastry*
½ cup raisins *(Page 358)*
4 egg yolks

Bake pie shell. Beat egg yolks and combine with sour cream,
sugar, cornstarch and cinnamon. Cook in top of double boiler
until mixture thickens. Add raisins. Pour filling in pie shell.
Beat egg whites until stiff, add a pinch of salt, and beat until
blended. Cover filling in pie shell with meringue. Bake in
slow oven of 300°F. for 15 minutes.

STRAWBERRY PIE

4 cups strawberries (cleaned *¾ cup granulated sugar*
   and cut in half) *2 tablesp. tapioca*
2 egg yolks *1 recipe Flaky Pastry*
½ cup confectioners' sugar *(Page 358)*

Line pie plate with bottom crust and sprinkle with tapioca.
Sprinkle confectioners' sugar over berries. Combine beaten
egg yolks with granulated sugar and pour over strawberries.
Pour into pie plate and cover with crust, being certain to slit
the bottom crust and to cut 5 or 6 slits into top crust. Seal
and flute edges. Brush with milk and sprinkle with sugar. Bake
in hot oven of 425°F. for 35 to 40 minutes.

Blueberry pie: Substitute blueberries for strawberries. Add
   1 tablespoon lemon juice.

Cherry pie: Substitute pitted cherries for strawberries. Add
   1 tablespoon lemon juice.

BANBURY TARTS

Recipe for Flaky Pastry	*1 egg*
¾ cup chopped nuts	*¾ cup chopped raisins*
Rind of 1 lemon, grated	*¾ cup sugar*
Juice of 1 lemon	*2 tablesp. butter*
	1 tablesp. water

Line large muffin tin with dough rolled to ¼-inch thickness. Roll edges of tarts and flute. Mix ingredients and place generous portion in each muffin tin. Bake in hot oven of 450°F. until crust is golden brown. Top with whipped cream, when cool.

MINCE MEAT PIE

2 lbs. boiled tongue, chopped	*1 cup currants*
(or chopped beef chuck	*1 teasp. ground nutmeg*
may be substituted)	*1 teasp. cinnamon*
4 cups chopped apples *	*Rind of 1 lemon, grated*
1½ cups boiled cider	*Rind of 1 orange, grated*
1½ cups molasses	*1 cup citron, chopped fine*
2 cups brown sugar (dark)	*1 cup pecan nutmeats,*
1 cup seeded raisins (dark)	*chopped* *

Combine ingredients and place in Dutch oven. Cook over low heat, simmering for at least 2 hours. Seal in sterilized glass jars and store in refrigerator until ready to bake pies. Two pies may be baked with the above ingredients.

STRUDEL

This flaky delicacy originated with the Jews in Vienna, and is certainly the aristocrat of desserts. There is an art to turning out excellent strudel. Also, it may have a variation of fillings, each one more delicious than the next.

* Add chopped apples and nutmeats when ready to bake pies.

STRUDEL DOUGH (Stretched Dough)

3 cups flour
1 egg
¾ cup ice water
1 teasp. baking powder

2 tablesp. oil (and 2 tablesp. oil to brush on stretched dough)
1 tablesp. sugar
¼ teasp. salt

Combine sifted flour, baking powder, sugar and salt in a large bowl. Make a well and drop egg in center, adding oil. Add ice water gradually, until dough is manageable. Use pastry blender and handle the dough very little, combining ingredients and turning it out on floured board for kneading. When dough is elastic, place on floured board, letting it stand covered for about ½ hour. Work oil into dough, sprinkle flour over large board and place dough in the center. Using floured rolling pin, roll out as thin as possible. Place both hands under the pastry and working from center to outer edges, stretch without tearing the dough.

Place a thin layer of desired filling or fillings in vertical rows on dough, leaving 2 inches between rows. Starting from the left, continue to roll the dough over filling, until all the filling is encased in the dough. Trim the edges. Brush the strudel with a light covering of oil. Cut to fit a large, greased, shallow baking pan and bake in oven of 375°F. for between 50 minutes and 1 hour.

ROLLED STRUDEL DOUGH

2½ cups flour
2 eggs
1½ tablesp. sugar

4 tablesp. melted shortening or oil
¼ teasp. salt
1¼ cups ice water

Sift flour, sugar and salt in mixing bowl. Make a well and drop eggs and melted shortening or oil in center. Stir to blend, adding ice water a little at a time to make dough firm. When manageable, turn dough onto floured board and knead. Using a floured rolling pin, roll out very thin. Roll from edges to center, working around dough. Spread filling as for stretched dough, roll up and brush top with oil, trimming any thick edges. Bake in greased baking pan at 375°F. for between 45 and 55 minutes, or until browned and crisp.

APPLE

2 cups thinly sliced apples
½ cup chopped nuts
½ cup seedless raisins
1 teasp. cinnamon
½ cup small pieces mixed citron
½ cup sugar
Rind of 1 orange, grated

Mix and blend together, sprinkling a little oil or melted butter over top. Use to fill strudel dough and follow baking instructions above.

DRIED FRUIT

½ cup cake crumbs
1 cup dried prunes, chopped fine
1 cup dried apricots, chopped fine
4 tablesp. honey
⅓ cup sugar
Rind of 1 lemon, grated
1 teasp. lemon juice
1 teasp. orange juice
½ cup chopped pecans
½ cup raisins
2 teasp. oil or melted shortening
½ teasp. cinnamon

Cover dried fruit with boiling water and soak overnight. Drain and chop. Combine dried fruits with grated lemon rind, fruit juices, pecans and raisins. Heat honey, pour over dried fruit mixture, and sprinkle with sugar and cinnamon. Sprinkle dough with oil or melted shortening and cake crumbs. Spread filling over dough and follow baking instructions above. Slice while hot.

CHEESE

2 cups dry cottage cheese 4 egg yolks
1 cup sour cream   4 egg whites
⅓ cup sugar   ½ teasp. cinnamon
2 tablesp. butter   ¼ cup raisins
    ½ cup bread crumbs

Cream butter and egg yolks. Press cottage cheese through sieve, and add to egg mixture. Blend sugar into mixture, adding sour cream. Fold in stiffly beaten egg whites. Sprinkle strudel dough with a little sugar, cinnamon and bread crumbs, and roll over cheese mixture. Brush with melted butter. Follow baking instructions for strudel dough.

NUT AND PRESERVES

1 cup preserves (any flavor) ½ teasp. cinnamon
½ cup nuts, chopped fine 2 tablesp. sugar
½ cup seedless raisins   Melted butter

Combine and use to fill strudel dough. Brush with melted butter before placing in oven. Bake according to instructions for strudel dough.

CHERRY

3 cups strained cherries 1 stick butter, melted
 (cooked and pitted)   ½ cup bread crumbs
    1 cup sugar

Sprinkle bread crumbs over strudel dough, cover with cherries, sprinkle with sugar and pour on part of the melted butter, saving half to be brushed on the outside of the strudel dough. Roll, brush melted butter over top, and bake in 375°F. oven for 50 minutes.

MANDEL (Almond)

¾ cup blanched almonds,   3 egg yolks
  ground   ⅓ cup sugar
Grated rind of 1 lemon   ¼ teasp. cinnamon
1 teasp. lemon juice   ⅓ cup butter, melted

Beat egg yolks with sugar, add cinnamon, grated lemon
rind and lemon juice. Mix with ground almonds. Brush
strudel dough with butter; spread ingredients over dough.
Pour melted butter over the mixture. Roll and brush top with
melted butter. Bake in oven of 375°F. for 50 minutes.

MARASCHINO CHERRY AND COCOANUT

¼ cup maraschino cherries,   ¼ cup seedless raisins
  chopped fine   ¼ cup currants
¼ cup mixed citron,   ½ cup bread crumbs
  chopped fine   2 tablesp. orange juice
½ cup sugar   2 tablesp. lemon juice
1 egg white   ½ cup shredded cocoanut
½ cup walnuts, chopped fine   1 stick melted butter

Spread melted butter on strudel dough and sprinkle with
bread crumbs. Combine nuts, raisins (mixed with orange and
lemon juice), and the rest of the ingredients (mixing shredded
cocoanut with egg white). Spread over strudel dough. Brush
with melted butter and bake in preheated oven of 375°F. for
1 hour.

PRUNE

2 cups stewed prunes, pitted   1 lemon rind, grated
½ cup cake crumbs   Juice of 1 lemon
½ cup seedless raisins   ¼ cup currants
1 cup sugar   1 stick butter, melted

Chop prunes. Brush melted butter on strudel dough.
Sprinkle with cake crumbs and sugar and distribute balance

of the ingredients evenly over the dough, leaving about 1 inch clear around the edges. Roll, trim edges, and bake in 375°F. oven for 50 minutes. Brush top with melted butter.

APRICOT

Follow the ingredients and directions above, substituting apricots for prunes.

LIVER

2 cups chopped calf's liver (precooked)
½ cup diced onions

3 tablesp. chicken fat
½ teasp. salt
3 tablesp. matzo meal

Brown onions and combine with rest of ingredients. Spread filling over rolled dough, brush top of dough with chicken fat, and bake.

KASHA

3 cups cooked groats
1 medium-sized onion, diced
½ cup melted shortening

Brown onion and combine with groats. Sprinkle rolled dough with melted shortening, spread filling over it, and bake. Brush with shortening several times during baking process.

POPPY SEED

1 cup poppy seeds, ground fine
1 cup sugar
½ cup grated apple

½ cup seedless raisins (light)
Rind of 1 lemon, grated
Melted shortening

Combine poppy seeds, ½ cup sugar, raisins, and lemon rind. Brush dough with melted shortening, spread filling over it, and sprinkle with grated apple, rest of sugar, and melted shortening. Roll and brush top with melted shortening, and bake in hot oven of 400°F. for 1 hour.

RAHM (SOUR MILK)

2 cups sour milk (thick) ½ cup raisins
1 cup sugar   ½ cup chopped nutmeats
½ cup fine cake crumbs ½ teasp. cinnamon

Sprinkle sour milk over dough. Then spread balance of ingredients over dough in the following order: cake crumbs, ½ cup sugar, raisins, chopped nuts. Sprinkle with sugar and cinnamon mixture, roll and brush top with melted shortening or oil, and bake in hot oven of 400°F. for 45 to 50 minutes, or until crusty and brown.

QUICK APPLE STRUDEL

This does not compare with the sensational apple strudel made as it should be made, but many people will forego that pleasure for something which may be prepared much more quickly. This is merely a "fill-in" or substitute for the real thing.

1½ cups white flour, sifted 3 tablesp. sugar
4 cups apples, chopped fine ⅔ cup milk
2 teasp. baking powder ¼ cup butter or margarine
     Pinch of salt

FOR APPLES

⅓ cup sugar mixed with ¼ cup chopped nuts
¼ teasp. cinnamon

Sift flour, baking powder and dry ingredients. Cut in shortening, adding milk to make soft dough. Knead on floured board and pat to about ½ inch or a little less in thickness. Brush with melted butter, cover with chopped apples, sprinkle with sugar and cinnamon mixture and roll like jelly roll. Bake on greased baking sheet in hot oven of 425°F. about 30 minutes. Cool. Glaze with confectionery sugar icing and sprinkle with chopped nuts.

Preserving and Pickling: Fruits; Catsup, Relishes, Preserves and Jellies

PRESERVING FRUITS, PICKLING ANYTHING FROM CATSUP TO cucumbers into luscious dill pickles, has always been part of the Jewish way of life. Remember the large granite crock and the pungent odor of spices wafting through the room where it was kept in a cool spot? One never knew whether it would be dill pickles, a delectable platter of marinated herring, or what the mysterious crock would bring forth with which to surprise and delight the family. Mama always kept it in constant use, piquing the family interest!

The modern age has precluded much of this expectancy by placing competent delicatessens throughout large cities. Nevertheless, whether or not one takes advantage, at one time in one's life, of attempting to preserve and pickle one's own supply of fruits, pickles, etc. . . . the directions are here for your use.

PRESERVES AND JELLIES

Helpful suggestions in preparing preserves and jellies:

1) Making preserves and jellies in small quantities produces better quality and color in finished products. Do not attempt to preserve more than one quart of fruit at a time. Additional quantities may be made but not cooked at the same time.

2) Sugar is not only a sweetening agent but a preservative, and it is wise to use sugar when preserving and making jellies.

383

3) A jelly bag is a necessity. Large sugar or flour bags may be washed, thoroughly boiled, and used for this purpose. Or, any good-sized porous cotton bag may be used.

4) Paraffin may be eliminated if pint jars which have covers with rubbers or if self-sealing type jars are used. However, these jars must be sterilized and when contents are poured into them, they must be hot. Using prongs, handle only the outside of the jars when ready to pour in jams or jellies.

5) Pectin is contained in quantity in only certain types of fruits and is responsible for producing the best jellies. Those fruits rich in pectin are:

Sour Apples	*Crabapples*
Currants	*Huckleberries*
Wild Cherries	*Blackberries*
Quinces	*Plums*
Grapes (Unripe)	*Cranberries*
Green Gooseberries	

6) You can make pectin from fruits rich in this substance. It may be stored in sterilized jars for use in the making of jams and jellies.

7) The finished jelly should be clear, bright in color, and of the consistency of a gelatin, but firm.

8) When ready to combine juice of fruit and sugar, measure one cup of juice for each cup of sugar.

   a) Measure juice into the preserving kettle and allow it to come to a boil for a few minutes.

   b) Add the sugar.

   c) If you have a jelly thermometer, it should reach 239 to 240°F. before jelly may be removed from heat. Another indication to guide you in knowing when to remove from heat is that juice drops will combine and fall in number, rather than in "one" drop.

9) A "*MUST*": Fruit should be fresh in order to obtain the best results in preserving. It is better to have "underripe" than overripe fruit for preserving.

10) Since jelly is usually placed in a small container for serving, it is suggested that self-sealing glass jars (the smaller type) be used when making it. They require less time and effort. All you need do is sterilize them, handling them with prongs, and be sure they are hot when jelly is poured into them.

11) How to use paraffin (with small-sized glasses): sterilize glasses by placing in cold water, and boiling for 15 minutes. Keep hot until ready for use. Set glasses on wet cloth. Fill with jelly, allowing about ½ inch at the top of the glass. Have melted paraffin ready and pour 1 or 2 tablespoons of paraffin over the top of the jelly. Allow to set for a few minutes, then place a little waxed paper or foil over the paraffin.

PECTIN

*20 tart, sour apples (include   1 qt. water
skin and cores—slice thin)*

Place apples and water in large kettle and bring to boiling point. Cover and allow to boil rapidly for about 15 minutes. Strain through 3 or 4 thicknesses of cheesecloth (DO NOT PRESS OR SQUEEZE) and allow to drip until all juice has come through. Set aside juice. Take pulp and measure an equal amount of water and allow to boil again for about 15 minutes. Strain through cheesecloth (3 or 4 thicknesses), extracting the juice. Combine the two extractions of juice in a wide pan, so that the juice is no more than 1 or 2 inches deep in the pan and boil for about half an hour or a little more, or until juice has been reduced to half its volume.

This mixture may be used in the making of jellies or jams where fruit is being used which is not rich in pectin, or it may be placed in hot sterilized jars (which have been standing in hot water), sealed and stored for future use.

RED RASPBERRY JELLY

3 qt. red raspberries   *1 cup sugar to every cup
                                    juice*

Wash carefully, place in kettle and mash berries. Place a little water in the kettle and heat to boiling point. Cook until berries are soft. Place in jelly bag and strain. If firm jelly is desired, one unpeeled tart apple may be added to every quart of berries (slice apple). Add 1 cup of sugar for every cup of juice, and bring to a boil. Test jelly by dropping on a cold plate. If drop jells, remove from heat, skim and fill hot, sterilized glasses or jars (which are self-sealing) or seal with paraffin.

GRAPE JELLY

Try to select underripe grapes for this jelly.

6 lbs. grapes   *¾ cup sugar to every cup of
1 cup water*   *juice
                             3 cups diced apples*

Wash grapes and apples and remove stems. Place in kettle with water and boil until seeds start coming from the grapes. Press through sieve and place residue in jelly bag to strain. Measure ¾ cup of sugar for every cup of juice. Set aside sugar and place juice separately in a kettle. When it comes to a boil, add sugar and cook until a few drops, placed on a cold plate, will jell. Pour into hot sterilized glasses or jars and seal.

GUAVA JELLY

2 qt. guavas   ½ cup lime or lemon juice
1 cup sugar to 1 cup juice

Use underripe guavas for best results. Slice them thin and place in a kettle with very little water. Bring to a slow boil and continue cooking over low heat until guavas are soft and tender. Place in jelly bag, and allow to strain through. Measure juice, reserving 1 cup of sugar for every cup of juice. Bring juice to a boil and cook for 5 to 10 minutes before adding sugar and lime or lemon juice. Cook until it jells when tested. Remove and pour into sterilized glasses or jars and seal.

CURRANT JELLY

3 qt. currants   1 cup sugar for each cup of
3 cups water   juice

Select ripe but not overripe currants. Wash and do not remove stems. Place in kettle with water and allow to boil until currants are almost white. Strain through colander and pour into jelly bag, allowing it to strain until all juice is extracted. Measure juice and reserve an equal amount of sugar, to be added after juice has boiled for about 5 minutes. Combine juice and sugar and boil for about 5 minutes. When it jells, skim top and pour into sterilized glasses or jars and seal.

FRUIT JELLY (With Pectin Added)

2 qt. berries   1 cup pectin
2½ cups sugar   ½ cup water
2 tablesp. lemon juice

Place berries in kettle and mash. Add water and slowly bring to boiling point. Allow to boil until berries are soft. Pour into jelly bag and strain until all juice has been extracted.

Combine juice, lemon juice, sugar and pectin and bring to
boiling point. Continue to cook until it jells. Pour into hot,
sterilized glasses or jars and seal.

WILD FRUITS

Follow the instructions for making jellies from regular fruit.
Generally, wild fruits make excellent jellies. Remember the
hard and fast rule of making only "fresh" fruit into jellies.
This has a definite influence on good results.

TART CHERRY JELLY

2 qt. tart cherries   1 cup sugar to every cup of
¾ cup apple pectin   juice

Place cherries in kettle with very little water and bring to a
boil. Cook until tender and pour into jelly bag, allowing to
drip until all juice has been extracted. Measure juice and an
equal amount of sugar. Combine juice, apple pectin and
sugar. Bring to boiling point and continue boiling until mixture jells when tested. Remove from heat and pour into sterilized glasses or jars and seal.

BLACK RASPBERRY JELLY

3 qt. black raspberries   1 cup sugar to every cup of
¾ cup water   juice
                3 sliced, tart apples

Place berries in kettle with apples and mash. Heat to boiling point and cook until tender. Pour into jelly bag and strain.
Boil juice for about 5 minutes and measure for equal part of
sugar. Continue to boil with sugar until it jells. Pour into hot,
sterilized glasses or jars and seal.

APPLE JELLY

5 lbs. apples (tart)
Water

*One cup of sugar to every
cup of juice*

2 teasp. lemon extract

Wash apples, but do not remove peel or cores. Cut into pieces and place in kettle with just enough water to cover. Cook until soft. Pour into jelly bag and allow to drip. Measure juice and sugar and cook juice for 5 minutes. Then add sugar and cook until it jells. Add flavoring. Pour into hot, sterilized glasses or jars and seal.

PEACH JELLY

1 qt. peaches
½ cup apple pectin

*1 cup sugar to each cup of
juice*

1 tablesp. lemon juice

Cut peaches, leaving peels. Cover with water and bring to a boil. Cook until fruit is tender. Place in jelly bag and allow juice to drip. Measure and add apple pectin and lemon juice. Bring to boiling point and add sugar. Continue boiling rapidly until it jells. Skim and pour into hot, sterilized glasses or jars and seal.

QUINCE JELLY

Quinces should be divided into two parts. The perfect part of the fruit should be preserved and the imperfect parts and parings, including the cores, should be used to make quince jelly. Take the parings (after coarsely rubbed with towel), cores and imperfect parts of the fruit and place in kettle. To every 2 parts of fruit, add 1 part water. Cook over low heat for 1 to 2 hours, or until tender. Place in jelly bag and strain. Add 1 cup of sugar for every cup of quince and bring to boiling point. Then continue cooking until it jells. Pour into hot, sterilized glasses or jars and seal.

MINT JELLY

This jelly is most popular because it is used to accompany meats which have an extraordinarily strong taste, such as lamb, venison, etc. Those persons having gardens probably have sprigs of mint growing therein. Others may secure mint sprigs at the vegetable market easily.

2 qt. snow apples	*1 cup sugar to each cup of*
Green vegetable coloring	*juice*
¼ cup fresh mint leaves	*1 tablesp. lemon juice*

Wash apples and cut in large pieces, with peelings and cores. Place in kettle, add only enough water to cover and cook over low heat until apples are soft and tender. Mash and place in jelly bag, allowing to drip until all juice is strained. Bring juice to boiling point and add sugar. Continue boiling and add mint leaves and cook until it jells. Add lemon juice and vegetable coloring. To secure clear mint jelly, strain into hot, sterilized glasses or jars and seal.

PRESERVES

Preserves, differing from jellies only in that the pulp is included, must be made with fruit which is as near perfect as possible. Sugar is added in the amount of 1 cup sugar to each cup of pulp. Pectin has the same effect as in jelly, that of making the finished product more firm.

GRAPE PRESERVES

2 qt. Concord grapes	*1 cup sugar to 1 cup grape*
Very little water	*pulp*

Wash and pick grapes carefully, removing stems. Heat water and grapes to boiling point and continue cooking until seeds are loosened. Press through sieve. Measure pulp and sugar. Combine in kettle and cook over low heat, stirring frequently to prevent scorching. Pour into hot, sterilized glasses or jars and seal.

GRAPE CONSERVE

2 qt. Concord grapes
2 oranges
2 lemons

1 cup sugar to each cup of
conserve
Small amount of water

Wash and stem grapes and place in kettle with very little water. Bring to boiling point. When seeds are loosened, press through sieve and add oranges and lemons (cut fine). Measure sugar and pulp, add, and bring to boiling point. Continue boiling until thick. Pour into hot, sterilized glasses or jars and seal.

RED TOMATO PRESERVES

4 lbs. red tomatoes
4 lbs. sugar

Ginger root (a few pieces)
Grated rind of lemon
Juice of lemon

Scald tomatoes and peel. Cover with sugar and allow to stand overnight. Drain syrup and place in kettle, boiling until thick, and skim. Add lemon rind, juice of lemon and ginger. Then add tomato pulp. Cook over low heat until mixture is clear. Pour into hot, sterilized glasses or jars and seal.

STRAWBERRY PRESERVES

2 qt. strawberries
4 tablesp. lemon juice

1 cup sugar to 1 cup strawberries (cooked)

Select only firm, good strawberries. Wash, hull and place layer of strawberries, layer of sugar in kettle and let stand overnight. Lift strawberries carefully into colander and place over kettle, allowing juices mingled with sugar to drip into kettle. Cook over low heat until boiling point is reached and boil about 3 or 4 minutes. Add strawberries strained in col-

ander and balance of sugar mingled therewith. Cook for about
3 or 4 minutes. Allow to stand overnight and again strain
over colander. Boil juice for about 3 minutes, and add berries
and lemon juice. Bring to boiling point and boil about 3 to 4
minutes longer. Pour into hot, sterilized glasses or jars and
seal.

SOUR CHERRY PRESERVES

2 qt. sour cherries, stoned   *1 cup sugar to 1 cup fruit*
and stemmed

Wash fruit, pit and stem. Measure 1 cup of sugar for each
cup fruit. Place fruit in kettle with very little water. Stir
frequently to avoid burning. Cook for about 15 minutes and
add sugar. Cook for 10 minutes longer or until mixture is
thickened and sugar is entirely absorbed. Pour into hot, sterilized glasses or jars and seal.

RASPBERRY PRESERVES

1½ qt. raspberries   *1 cup sugar to each cup rasp-*
berries

Clean raspberries carefully, using only perfect berries. Measure raspberries and sugar. Cook with very little water until
soft and tender. If seedless preserves are desired, press through
sieve thoroughly, getting every bit of pulp, except seeds. Place
in kettle with sugar and cook until mixture is thick. Pour into
hot, sterilized glasses or jars and seal.

YELLOW TOMATO PRESERVES

4 lbs. yellow finger tomatoes   *2 lemon rinds, grated*
4 lbs. sugar   *2 lemons, juice only*
Ginger root (a few pieces)

Grind tomatoes, peel and all. Cover with sugar and place
in kettle. Bring to a boil over low heat. When mixture is thick

and clear, add grated rind of lemon and juice, and ginger root. Cook until lemon and ginger have been absorbed. Pour into hot, sterilized glasses or jars and seal.

PICKLED WATERMELON RIND

Peel outer green rim of watermelon. Then cut into 1 inch pieces the parts of watermelon rind which are not too ripe, and the red pulp bordering the rind.

2 qt. watermelon rind (cut in pieces as instructed above)
6 cups sugar
6 lemons, sliced and seeded
1 cup grated pineapple
¼ cup stick cloves

Place in kettle all ingredients except cloves and grated pineapple, and allow to boil slowly over low heat for about 2 hours or until mixture is thick and clear. Add cloves and grated pineapple and allow to cook for about 15 minutes. Pour into glasses, hot and sterilized, or sterilized jars and seal.

PICKLED WATERMELON RIND (Variation)

2 watermelon rinds, cut into 2-inch strips (not green rind, but inner rind)
3 lbs. sugar (½ white and ½ brown)
3 cups vinegar
1 cup water
2 lemons, sliced thin
¼ cup cinnamon sticks and cloves
½ teasp. salt

Boil strips of watermelon rind until tender and clear in water with salt. Drain. Chill in ice water and dry with toweling. Boil vinegar, water and sugars until it forms into a light syrup. Add spices, tied in bag, watermelon rind and lemon slices. Boil until clear. Remove bag of spices. Pour mixture into hot, sterilized jars and seal. Allow to stand for at least a couple of weeks before using.

APPLE BUTTER

4 lbs. apples	2 cups apple cider
1 lemon rind, grated	1½ cups sugar
Juice of 1 lemon	1 teasp. cinnamon
	1 teasp. allspice

Without peeling or coring, cut apples into small pieces. Add lemon rind and using apple cider instead of water, cook mixture over low heat until apples are soft. Press through sieve and boil juice until reduced in volume. Add pulp, lemon juice, sugar and spices and cook over low heat until thick enough to spread. Stir to keep from burning. Pour into hot, sterilized glasses or jars and seal.

FRUIT CONSERVE

1 qt. raspberries	1 qt. currants
1 qt. gooseberries	Sugar

Wash fruit carefully and measure out an equal amount of sugar. Cook fruit, with very little water, for about 15 to 20 minutes. Stir occasionally to prevent burning. Add sugar and cook for at least 10 minutes or so, or until mixture thickens. Pour into hot, sterilized glasses or jars and seal.

GREEN TOMATO PRESERVES

2 qt. sliced green tomatoes	1 lemon rind, grated
10 sticks cloves	1 lemon, sliced thin
1 stick cinnamon	1 cup sugar to 1 cup tomatoes

Place sliced green tomatoes, grated lemon rind, lemon slices, and spices in kettle and cook for 10 minutes. Add sugar and cook until mixture is thick and clear. Pour into hot, sterilized glasses or jars and seal.

PLUM BUTTER (Lacqua)

Povidle (another name for *Lacqua*) is used in the making of Hamantaschen and as a filling for cakes and cookies eaten during Purim.

1 qt. plums   *1 cup sugar for each cup of*
1 teasp. lemon juice   *plum purée*

Wash plums, cut in half and pit. Cook fruit with no extra water other than that from washing plums. When soft, press through sieve. Measure sugar, and combine all ingredients in kettle to cook over low heat. Stir continuously until mixture becomes thick. Pour into hot, sterilized glasses or jars and seal.

ORANGE MARMALADE

12 oranges (juice of 12 or-   Grated rind of 1 lemon
anges—peel of 3 oranges)   4 cups liquid (including
Juice of 1 lemon   juices and water)
4 cups sugar

Juice oranges and reserve for later use. Cut orange rinds into thin strips, add a little water and let stand overnight. When ready to make marmalade, bring to slow boil in covered saucepan, and continue cooking over low heat until strips are tender. Add juices and sugar, including grated lemon and lemon juice. Cook over low heat for approximately 10 or 15 minutes or until it meets the jelly test—dropping from teaspoon on cold plate. If drops mass together, marmalade is done. Pour into hot, sterilized glasses or jars and seal.

RHUBARB CONSERVE

2 qt. red rhubarb   Very little water
Rind and juice of 1 orange   6 cups sugar
Rind and juice of 1 lemon   1 cup grated walnuts

Boil rinds of orange and lemon for 5 to 7 minutes. Place through food grinder. Leaving skins on, cut rhubarb into

2 inch pieces, wash, and combine with orange and lemon peel. Add juices of orange and lemon with ½ cup water, adding sugar and stirring so that it is completely dissolved. Bring to boiling point and cook rapidly, stirring continually. When mixture becomes thick, add grated walnuts and continue boiling until thickened still more, or about 15 to 20 minutes. Remove from heat and pour into hot, sterilized glasses or jars and seal.

DAMSON PLUM CONSERVE

1 qt. damson plums   *1 cup mixed walnut and pe-*
3 cups sugar   *can nuts*
1 stick cinnamon   *Rind and juice of ½ orange*
              Rind and juice of ½ lemon

Wash and cut plums, pitting. Add all other ingredients, except nuts, and cook over low heat in a covered saucepan with very little water. Cook for about 15 minutes or until mixture is thick. Add chopped nuts and pour into hot, sterilized glasses or jars and seal.

RHUBARB AND STRAWBERRY CONSERVE

1 qt. red rhubarb   *Rind and juice of 1 lemon*
1 qt. strawberries   *Very little water*
Rind and juice of 1 orange *6 cups sugar*
              1 cup grated pecans

Boil rinds of orange and lemon for 5 to 7 minutes. Place through food grinder. Leaving skins on, cut rhubarb into 2 inch pieces and wash. Wash and hull strawberries, using only perfect ones, firm and ripe. Bring rhubarb, strawberries, rinds of orange and lemon to boiling point. Add sugar and stir until completely dissolved. Continue to boil rapidly, stirring to prevent burning, until mixture becomes thick. Add grated pecans and continue cooking for about 15 minutes

more. Remove from heat and pour into hot, sterilized glasses
or jars and seal.

BEET PRESERVES (Boorekes)

5 lbs. beets (young beets)   *3 oz. dried ginger root*
Rind and juice of 3 lemons   *1 cup blanched almonds*
4 lbs. sugar   *(ground)*

Wash and peel beets. Slice very thin. Cover with water
and cook over low heat until tender. Add ginger root,
blanched and sliced very fine, together with sugar, grated
lemon rind and juice. Cook over low heat slowly until mixture becomes thick and clear, about 1 hour or a little longer.
When almost done, add blanched, ground almonds, cook
just a little more and remove from heat. Pour into hot, sterilized glasses or jars and seal.

SUGAR SUBSTITUTES

Honey or corn syrup may be substituted for sugar.

         1 cup honey equals 1 cup
            sugar
         1 cup corn syrup equals 1 cup
            sugar

When substitutes are used, one must remember that the
cooking time of jellies and preserves must be prolonged. Also
remember that sugar, besides being a sweetener, is a preservative. Sugar is preferred at all times except where health reasons may dictate otherwise.

PICKLED PEARS

8 lbs. Seckel pears   *1 cup water*
2 cups vinegar   *6 sticks cinnamon*
4 cups sugar   *2 tablesp. cloves*

Peel pears, but leave stems on. Place in pickling crock,
spreading sugar between layers of pears and covering with

vinegar and water. Cover and allow to stand overnight. Drain
and tie spices in cloth bag. Heat over low flame and when
mixture is clear, add pears and boil until tender, but not soft
and crumbly. Place pears in self-sealing jars (sterilized) and
cover. When jars are ⅔ full, add liquid to jar and seal.
Note: It is wise to cook only enough pears to fill one jar at a
   time. Add more when that is done.

PICKLED PEACHES

8 lbs. large firm peaches	*¼ cup mixed cinnamon*
4 lbs. sugar	*sticks and cloves*
2½ cups cider vinegar	

Pare peaches. Boil vinegar, sugar and spices (tied in a little
cloth bag) until mixture is clear. Add only enough peaches
to the liquid to fill one jar at a time and cook until tender,
but not crumbly. Using slotted spoon, lift peaches out of
kettle, place in hot, sterilized jars, and when jar is almost full,
pour hot liquid into jar and seal.

PICKLES, RELISHES AND CATSUP

Pickling, though almost a lost art, still is pursued by women
who have the facilities for storing and turning out quantities
of pickles, relishes and catsup with which to supply their own
families.

1. A large stone crock should be utilized in preparing
pickles.

2. Cucumbers used for pickling must be fresh, and pickled
at once, in order to have the right type of taste and flavor
when pickled.

3. The brine used in pickling consists of:

   1 cup of salt to 5 cups of water

4. When fermentation in the large stone crock stops and pickles are done, they should be placed immediately in quart self-sealing jars, covered with brine, and sealed.

PRESERVATION OF CUCUMBERS

Cucumbers may be purchased fresh for pickling and stored to be made later into whatever type of pickles are desired. Wash them carefully, place in a large, stone crock, and cover with brine.

Brine: For every quart of water, use 1 cup of salt. Boil and keep skimming until mixture is clear. Cool before pouring over cucumbers.

DILL PICKLES

50 cucumbers	Brine:
Dill	*3 qt. water*
Horse-radish root	*1 cup cider vinegar*
10 cloves of garlic	*½ cup salt*
5 teasp. mustard seed	

Soak cucumbers overnight in cold water. Drain, wash and dry and place in large stone crock, alternately with mustard seed, dill blossoms, garlic and a small piece of horse-radish root. Cook brine, skimming and cooking until mixture is clear. While hot, pour over cucumbers in stone crock, and weight board down with heavy object. Allow to ferment. When fermentation stops, place pickles in 2-quart self-sealing jars (hot and sterilized) and pour in brine to cover. Seal.

SWEET AND SOUR PICKLES

25 cucumbers (small)	*½ cup water*
1½ cups vinegar	*¾ teasp. pickling spices*
1 cup sugar	*1 small bunch dill*

Soak cucumbers overnight in a brine—¼ cup salt to every quart water. Drain and dry. Combine vinegar, sugar and water and boil until mixture is clear. Add cucumbers and simmer in kettle. When the bright green color leaves cucumbers, remove from heat. Place a few of the mixed pickling spices and dill at the bottom of each large quart jar, add pickles, and cover with hot sauce, placing a little dill on top. Seal.

CUCUMBER PICKLES
(Sometimes called "Bread and Butter" Pickles)

25 small cucumbers	*1 qt. vinegar*
½ cup ground mustard	*1 pt. water*
1 cup sugar	*½ cup salt*

Soak cucumbers in cold water. Mix salt, sugar and mustard together, and gradually add vinegar to dissolve mustard. Place cucumbers in stone crock, and pour mixture over cucumbers so that all cucumbers are covered. If the mixture is not enough to cover, make another quantity. Additional pickling brine may be added from day to day to crock to keep it full. Cover with heavy object and weight down. These pickles should be ready for use within two or three weeks.

CONTINENTAL PICKLES

2 qt. sliced cucumbers	*2 teasp. mustard seed*
4 qt. water	*2 cups brown sugar (light)*
1 qt. vinegar	*1 teasp. celery seed*
½ cup salt	*2 tablesp. pickling spices*
1 large onion, sliced	*½ teasp. turmeric*

Wash cucumbers well and cut off ends. Slice thin, but do not peel. Dissolve salt in water and pour over pickles and onions. Allow to stand for several hours. Drain. Combine mustard seed, sugar, celery seed and mixed pickling spices (tied in a bag) with vinegar and bring to boiling point. Add onions and cucumbers and again bring to boiling point. Add turmeric last, stirring into mixture. Place in hot, sterilized, self-sealing jars. Do not seal until liquid becomes cool.

SWEET PICKLES

25 large cucumbers
2 qt. boiling water mixed
 with ⅓ cup salt

1 small bunch dill
1 onion, sliced thin
3 cups sugar
1½ cups cider vinegar

Wash and drain cucumbers. Pour hot salted water over cucumbers and add dill. Let stand overnight; then drain and dry. Cut pickles into ½ inch slices and place in sterilized jars, placing a few slices of onion in each jar. Combine sugar and vinegar and boil until it becomes syrupy. Cool and pour over pickles in jars. Seal.

MIXED PICKLES, CAULIFLOWER, AND PEPPERS

1 qt. small white onions
1 qt. tiny cucumbers (whole)
1 qt. large cucumbers (cut in ½-inch slices)
1 large cauliflower (with flowerettes separated)
1 green pepper, sliced
1 red pepper (cut into pieces)

¼ cup horse-radish root, diced
⅛ lb. yellow mustard seed
3 qt. cider vinegar
¾ cup salt to 1 qt. water
2 lbs. brown sugar
½ oz. turmeric
Dash of red pepper

Combine tiny cucumbers, sliced cucumbers, flowerettes of cauliflower, green pepper, red pepper, onions (whole but peeled) and place in crock. Pour over it the mixture of salt and water. Let stand overnight. Drain. Combine the rest of the ingredients listed above and bring to boil. Pour over pickles and let stand in crock for at least 2 days. Pour into hot, sterilized self-sealing jars. Seal.

DILL GREEN TOMATOES

25 green tomatoes (firm)   *2 teasp. mustard seed*
Dill   *1½ qt. water*
Horse-radish root   *½ cup cider vinegar*
5 cloves of garlic   *¼ cup salt*

Soak tomatoes overnight in cold water. Drain, wash and dry, and place in large stone crock, alternately with mustard seed, dill blossoms, garlic, and a small piece of horse-radish root.

Cook brine, skimming and cooking until mixture is clear. While hot, pour over tomatoes in crock, and weight board down with heavy object. Allow to ferment. When fermentation stops, place tomatoes in large 2-quart jars (self-sealing type) which are hot and sterilized and pour brine to cover. Seal.

SWEET DILL PICKLES

25 dill pickles   *3 lbs. sugar*
1 pt. cider vinegar   *¼ cup mixed pickling spices*

Drain pickles and soak in cold water overnight. Drain. Cut in half, lengthwise. Combine vinegar, sugar and spices (tied in bag) and bring to boiling point. Add pickles and continue boiling for 2 or 3 minutes. Place in hot, sterilized jars, fill with hot liquid and seal.

RIPE CUCUMBERS—SWEET AND PICKLED

25 ripe cucumbers   *2 sticks cinnamon*
6 lbs. sugar   *2 tablesp. cloves*
2 qt. vinegar   *4 tablesp. mustard seed*

Peel cucumbers and cut in half lengthwise, scraping out seeds in center. Sprinkle with salt and let stand overnight. Drain and dry. Combine sugar and vinegar and bring to boiling point. Add mustard seed, spices (tied in bag) and cucumbers to mixture. When they are glazed, remove from heat. Place in hot, sterilized jars, pouring liquid, which has cooled, over them. Seal jars.

PICKLED BEETS

2 qt. boiled beets	¼ teasp. pepper
2 tablesp. brown sugar	1 onion, sliced
1 teasp. salt	1 qt. vinegar

Slice boiled beets and place in stone crock, spreading sliced onions between layers of beets, sprinkling with salt and pepper and sugar and covering mixture with vinegar. Let stand for about 1 week.

PICKLED ONIONS

2 qt. small white onions	1 cup sugar
1 qt. vinegar	2 tablesp. mixed pickling
½ cup salt	spices

Pour boiling water over onions and allow to stand for about 2 to 3 minutes. Drain and cover with cold water and peel. Place in salted water overnight. Rinse and drain. Tie spices in bag, and boil with sugar and vinegar. Remove bag of spices, add onions, and bring to boiling point. Pour onions and hot liquid into hot, sterilized, self-sealing jars.

PICKLED CAULIFLOWER

6 large heads cauliflower	3 cups sugar
3 qt. vinegar	1½ cups salt
⅓ cup mixed pickling spices	

Separate flowerettes of cauliflower. Sprinkle with salt and allow to stand overnight. Place in sieve or colander and rinse with cold water. Boil vinegar and sugar, tie spices in bag and add cauliflower. Let cauliflower boil for 3 or 4 minutes. Place in self-sealing jars, pouring liquid over flowerettes, and seal.

SAUERKRAUT

2 or 3 large cabbages   *2 teasp. salt to each quart jar*
Cold water

Shred cabbage very fine. Fill large jars with cabbage, and when half full, press down hard and add 1 teaspoon salt. Then fill other half of jar, and add additional salt. Cover with cold water, and adjust covers loosely. As water evaporates, pour a little more water in each jar. Continue this procedure for about a week. Then seal jar and store for further use.

CUCUMBER RELISH

6 green cucumbers	*1 green pepper, chopped*
3 cups vinegar	*3 cups celery, chopped*
1 cup sugar	*3 tablesp. salt*
2 tablesp. grated horse-radish	*1 tablesp. pepper*
1 onion, chopped	*1 pimento, chopped fine*

Peel cucumbers, slice and chop fine. Add celery and sprinkle with salt. Let stand overnight in cloth bag which is porous. Rinse in cold water and drain. Add rest of ingredients and place in hot, sterilized jars. Seal.

CHILI SAUCE

12 large tomatoes	*¾ cup sugar*
1½ cups vinegar	*3 large onions*
	1 tablesp. salt

Scald tomatoes. Peel them and chop. Peel onions, cut in quarters, and place through coarse grinder. Boil tomatoes and onions in mixture of vinegar, sugar and salt. Stir continually while cooking. Pour into hot, sterilized jars and seal.

CATSUP (Tomato)

20 tomatoes

8 apples

1½ pt. vinegar

2 cups sugar

3 tablesp. salt

½ teasp. cinnamon

3 green peppers

6 onions

½ teasp. cayenne pepper

Combine tomatoes, green peppers, sugar and onions and when soft, strain through coarse sieve. Add rest of ingredients and simmer over low heat until mixture is thick. Pour into hot, sterilized jars and seal.

APPETIZERS, HORS D'OEUVRES, FANCY FINGER SANDWICHES, HOT CHAFING DISHES, FANCY MOLDS, SALADS, PUNCHES, MAIN DISHES, ETC.

TODAY, BUFFET SERVING HAS ALMOST COMPLETELY REPLACED formal dinners, with the exception of elaborate, catered dinners and weddings. When more than a small number of people gather in one's home, buffet serving is the answer. It is truly a delight, especially to the hostess, since much of the preparation can be made beforehand and many of the dishes are in the form of molds, which may be unmolded onto platters just prior to serving.

In this section an attempt will be made to supply information which will be helpful when serving buffet style. All of these items have proved to be a success in this type of serving. The recipes for hors d'oeuvres, finger-type sandwiches, beverages for large groups, fruit molds, vegetable molds, salad molds, fish, poultry, and meats, sandwich loaves, appetizers of all types, chafing dish specialties, etc. will be set forth in such a manner that it will be simple for the hostess to select any one or any number of them for an attractive buffet.

Important points to remember when serving buffet style:

1) The table must be appealing to the eye.

2) Plates, silverware and napkins must be placed in a conspicuous but not obstructive spot.

3) Enough space should be left around the buffet table to permit people to secure their food without crowding one another.

4) The hostess should be ever-present (even if servants have been employed) to see that her guests are satisfactorily accommodated.

5) The table should be laden with only a reasonable portion of the food, and platters replenished from the kitchen when the supply has been depleted. In doing this, the food, such as finger sandwiches, does not have an opportunity to dry out.

6) A floral arrangement is desirable, but it should be dainty so as not to take up too much space.

7) The buffet table should be set up in the dining area with card tables, set with place cards, in another area. If, however, the gathering is very informal, allow the guests to determine their own seating.

CHOPPED HERRING

4 schmaltz herrings	*1 apple (cored and peeled)*
Vinegar	*1 large onion, grated*
Water	*1 tablesp. sugar*
4 hard-boiled eggs	*½ teasp. pepper*
	2 hard rolls

Soak herring overnight. Drain, skin and bone. Either chop by hand or place through food chopper, together with eggs and apple. Grate onion and add to mixture, together with sugar and pepper. Remove crust from rolls, utilizing the inner parts. Soak in equal amounts of vinegar and water. Put bread through food chopper, or chop into mixture by hand. Garnish with grated hard-boiled egg yolks, pieces of pimento and sprigs of parsley.

SARDINE APPETIZER

2 cans California sardines in   2 hard-boiled eggs
    tomato sauce   ½ cup chopped walnuts
1 large onion   ½ teasp. salt
                ¼ teasp. pepper

Sauté onion with butter or margarine until well browned. Chop hard-boiled eggs, add sauted onions, and chop into mixture. Bone sardines, chop fine, and add to mixture. Season and add chopped nuts. Chill and serve cold.

SWEET AND SOUR SAUCE
FOR MEAT BALLS

This may be served in chafing dish as a hot hors d'oeuvre. Mix regular hamburger ingredients (placing a little cinnamon in the meat) and form small meat balls. In a saucepan, place two bottles of chili sauce, one jar of grape jelly and one lemon, sliced thin. When jelly liquefies, remove lemon slices. Keep stirring. When hot, place meat balls into mixture and simmer for about an hour in the sauce. Pour into chafing dish and serve.

WHITEFISH SPREAD

3 smoked whitefish   8 oz. cream cheese
            1 tablesp. cream

Skin and bone whitefish. Combine cream cheese with a little cream to make it easier to mix. Mix mashed whitefish with cream cheese until it reaches spreading consistency. A little more cream may be added if necessary. Garnish with sprigs of parsley or chopped chives.

JEWISH EGG ROLLS

Filling:

2 lbs. cooked veal (chopped)
1 cup chopped celery
1 cup chopped green onion
½ cup chopped water chestnuts

1 tablesp. soy sauce
1 teasp. sugar
½ teasp. salt
1 egg
Shortening

Combine ingredients thoroughly and refrigerate. Prepare batter as follows:

Batter:

1½ cups flour
¾ cup cornstarch
½ teasp. salt

2 eggs
¾ cup water (adding a like amount gradually to beaten batter)

Sift flour, cornstarch and salt together. Beat eggs, adding water. Combine this mixture alternately with flour mixture, blending with rotary beater, and adding more water until mixture is smooth and thin enough to fry into regular blintze pancakes. Using a 6 to 7 inch rounded skillet, heat shortening and fry pancake on one side. Turn skillet over clean toweling with browned side up. Place 1 heaping tablespoon of meat filling into blintze. Fold up, as a blintze (only this will be in miniature form), and fry in deep fat until brown. These may be served on platter over a warmer, chafing dish fashion, on buffet.

CHEESE BLINTZES (Miniatures)

Follow the above instructions for batter, but use cheese filling, Page 132.

CHOPPED CHICKEN LIVER

1 lb. chicken livers	*3 tablesp. chicken fat*
3 hard-boiled eggs	*1 teasp. salt*
1 large onion (boiled)	*¼ teasp. pepper*

Cook chicken livers until medium to well done. Place in chopping bowl and chop together with boiled onion and hard-boiled eggs. Season, add chicken fat and chop until consistency of paste. Garnish with grated hard-boiled egg yolks, parsley and chopped chives.

BOLOGNA APPETIZER

1 large roll bologna	*1 cup corn syrup (dark)*
	1 cup cloves

If a rotisserie with spit is at hand, place spit through bologna (after skinning), brush with corn syrup, cut and score diagonally and stud with cloves. Allow it to brown and become crisp. Use to decorate table, then cut into small pieces and serve on party picks.

HOT COCKTAIL FRANKFURTERS

Using small frankfurters, simmer slowly for about 10 or 15 minutes. For a flavorful sauce, melt 1 jar of currant jelly with 1 jar chili sauce, adding a lemon, sliced thin. Remove lemon when jelly has liquefied. Place frankfurters into this mixture in chafing dish.

KISHKE APPETIZER

2 feet of beef casing
1 cup flour
1 cup crushed corn flakes (without sugar topping)
1 cup matzo meal
½ cup Cream of Wheat

2 sweet potatoes, grated
1 large onion, grated
1 tablesp. parsley flakes
½ teasp. paprika
Chicken fat
Salt

Clean derma, place well-mixed ingredients above into derma and sew ends. Boil in water with 1 large onion for about 2 hours. Place in the oven, with a little chicken fat, basting with chicken fat, and bake at 400°F. for about ½ hour, or until browned. Cut into 2 or 3 inch slices. Serve.

KNISHES, see Page 182

PECAN TREAT

Combine one 3 oz. package of cream cheese with 1 teaspoon anchovy paste. Cut pecan in half and fill.

LOX, BAGEL AND CREAM CHEESE

12 miniature bagels
½ lb. lox
12 small onions, pickled

12 stuffed olives (or black olives, if desired)
1 pkge. cream cheese (6 oz.)
2 tablesp. cream

Cut bagels in half and place softened cream cheese (which has been mixed with cream) on each half. Place a generous portion of lox on top of cream cheese and cover. Place an onion and an olive on each party pick and stick through bagel to keep both ends secure.

CRACKER APPETIZERS

1 pkge. cream cheese (3 oz.)   1 tablesp. cream
1 tablesp. anchovy paste

Combine and mix ingredients. Spread on crackers of various sizes and shapes. Sprinkle with grated egg yolk. Slice pimento-filled olives and garnish.

Variation: Substitute pimento cheese spread and garnish with slices of stuffed olive.

Variation: Use flat anchovy fillets on various-sized crackers and sprinkle with grated egg yolk and a little paprika.

BLACK CAVIAR (Imported)

Place caviar on various sizes (small) of toast, either rounds, diamond-shaped, or squares. Sprinkle with grated egg yolk and garnish with a little piece of pimento or tomato.

RED CAVIAR

Spread on toasted rounds, diamonds or squares and garnish with a slice of black olive.

CELERY APPETIZERS

Fill cavity of celery stalks (cut to about 3 or 4 inches in length) with mixture of cream cheese, a little cream and anchovy paste. Sprinkle with paprika and chopped chives.

CHEESE RUGELACH
(Bagelach)

2 cups dry pot cheese	*2 eggs*
3 tablesp. butter (melted)	*Recipe of stretched strudel*
3 tablesp. sugar	*dough*
¼ teasp. salt	*¼ teasp. cinnamon*

Combine cheese, eggs, sugar and seasoning, and blend thoroughly until smooth. Cut strudel into strips about 4 to 5 inches wide. Place 1 tablespoon of mixture in the center of strip, roll dough and place on greased baking sheet, allowing 2 to 3 inches between each one. Cut rolls into 4 to 5 inch lengths, and bend to form bagels, but do not pinch ends together. Brush with melted shortening or butter and bake in hot oven of 425°F. for 10 to 15 minutes, decreasing heat to 350°F. for 20 minutes more. Should be nicely browned before taken from oven. Remove from baking sheet when cool.

HORSE-RADISH APPETIZERS

Combine horse-radish with equal part of butter. Mash together, adding lemon juice to taste. Cut rounds of pumpernickel, whole-wheat and rye bread. Place mixture between two slices. Make small square sandwiches as well as diamond shapes, and serve as appetizers.

PÂTÉ DE FOIE GRAS SANDWICHES

Cook goose liver, and sauté with onions in goose fat. Chop until fine. Mash into paste with 3 chopped hard-boiled eggs, adding additional goose fat to soften. Spread on small toasted rounds of rye or whole-wheat bread.

PINWHEELS

If properly displayed, pinwheels make an excellent addition to the buffet table.

Cut crusts from loaf of bread. Slice bread. Spread with either of the following spreads:

Pimento cheese (creamed type)
Jelly (red or dark red)
Peanut butter (moistened with a little cream)

Roll each slice of bread immediately upon spreading. Cut in ¼-inch slices. Place on dish and cover with waxed paper or foil to keep fresh. These should be made directly before using, and replenished in the same manner, unless stored in such a way that bread does not dry out. May be garnished with fancy pick to fasten end.

DEVILED EGGS

See Page 145. Garnish by sprinkling with paprika and a sprig of parsley.

DEVILED EGG SALAD

6 hard-boiled eggs	½ teasp. dry mustard
1 stalk celery	3 tablesp. mayonnaise
6 small sweet pickles, diced	1 teasp. sugar
1 pimento, diced	Paprika for garnish
Chopped chives for garnish	

Dice eggs, celery, sweet pickles, pimento and combine. Add mayonnaise and dry mustard (combined beforehand) and blend with other ingredients. Sprinkle with paprika and chopped chives. May be served on thin pieces of toast of various shapes.

DATE AND NUT BREAD SANDWICHES

Using one 3 oz. package of cream cheese, moisten with a little cream, and add ¼ cup nuts, chopped fine (walnuts or pecans). Spread on date and nut bread, top, cut in half-rounds. Garnish with walnut or pecan.

RADISHES

Radishes may be made into rosebuds by cutting green stalk off end. With a sharp knife, cut through ⅛ inch petal straight down, but not quite down to bottom of radish, repeating on each side of radish until four petals have been cut. Use to garnish finger sandwiches, salads, molds, etc. They may also be used to garnish a tossed salad.

SALMON-STUFFED CUCUMBER SLICES

Use one small can of red Alaska salmon and flake salmon. Combine with mayonnaise, lemon juice, grated onion, chopped hard-boiled eggs, diced pimento, and mash until soft, being certain that salmon is thoroughly mashed. Remove seed pulp from ¼ inch slices of cucumber. Fill with salmon salad and place on round, square, or diamond-shaped pieces of pumpernickel, wheat or white bread. Toasted bread may also be used.

PORCUPINES

For this attractive means of serving, make use of one or more large grapefruits or any object which has holes to hold party picks. Fill the picks with such items as squares of sharp cheese, rolled anchovies, stuffed olives, etc. and stick them all over grapefruit. Your selection of tidbits should be guided, of course, by whether the buffet consists of milchig or flaishig foods.

THE PARTY PICK AND ITS SURPRISES

Anchovy fillets: Roll around stuffed olive, pickled onion or small sweet pickle and place on pick.

Cauliflower: Place pickled flowerettes on the end of party pick.

Pickled cocktail onions: Place on party pick with stuffed olive.

Dates: Pit and fill cavity with softened cream cheese and half pecan.

Gefilte fish balls: Place small balls on party picks.

Nova Scotia: Wrap around black olive, pickled onion or sweet pickle and place on pick.

Lox: Wrap around sweet pickle or black, stuffed olive, putting pick through both.

Bologna: Cut in squares and place cocktail onion and olive on pick, thus making "Bologna Shish Kebob."

Salami: Cut in squares and place cocktail onion and olive on pick, thus making "Salami Shish Kebob."

Tongue: Wrap one slice of tongue around small sweet pickle and spear.

Mushrooms: Sauté in butter, and combine with pickled onion and stuffed olive on pick.

TONGUE OR CORNED BEEF SALAD CANAPÉS

Using ⅛ pound tongue or corned beef (smoked and cooked), grind in food chopper and combine with about 1 tablespoon grated horse-radish, pickle relish, dash of Worcestershire sauce. Place on toasted rounds, squares or long thin shapes, and garnish with grated egg yolk and a slice of stuffed olive, or pieces of pimento.

CELERY STUFFED WITH AVOCADO

Cut celery stalks about 4 inches in length. Stuff with mixture of mashed avocado, a little lemon juice and a dash of mayonnaise. Sprinkle with paprika.

EGG AND ONION SPREAD

Bring a large onion to boiling point and cook about 2 minutes. Place through food chopper. Chop 3 hard-boiled eggs and place through food chopper. Mix with salt, pepper, and a little chicken fat.

KIPPERED HERRING SPREAD

Remove bones from kippers and mash. Add a little vinegar and mayonnaise. Spread on rounds, squares, toasted bread strips. Garnish with slice of stuffed olive.

MARINATED HERRING SHISH KEBOBS

On party picks, place a piece of marinated herring, a small pickled onion, stuffed olive, square of pickle, piece of marinated herring, square of tomato and marinated button mushroom.

CHEESE AND NUT BALLS

Soften 1 large package of cream cheese with a little cream, add ¼ cup of chopped pecans and chopped ripe olives and combine. Form into balls. Roll in mixture of chopped pecans. Place on picks.

HORS D'OEUVRE BUTTERS

Anchovy: Use anchovy paste, combined with a little lemon juice and a little cream cheese.

Chives: Chop chives and add a little lemon juice.

Eggs: Yolks of hard-boiled eggs, mashed, mixed with a little lemon juice, salt and pepper, and a dash of tabasco (if desired).

Mint: Minced mint leaves with a little lemon juice added.

Olive: Finely chopped green or black olives mixed with a little onion juice.

Parsley: Minced parsley, combined with a little onion juice.

Peanut butter: Combine ½ cup peanut butter with 1 tablespoon honey.

Salmon: 2 tablespoons mashed salmon with a little lemon juice.

Sardine: Mashed sardines, a little lemon juice and a little onion juice.

DUNKS

"Dunks" derive their name from the fact that they are served in a bowl and surrounded with potato chips and/or crackers of different dimensions which are dunked into the spread and used to scoop it up.

SOUR CREAM-CHEESE DUNK

Soften cream cheese and combine with a larger portion of sour cream. Season with salt and pepper. If desired, chopped chives may be added to this combination very effectively.

SOUR CREAM AND PIMENTO
CHEESE DUNK

1 *pt. sour cream*	1 *jar pimento cheese (spreading type)*
1 *tablesp. catsup*	

Combine sour cream with pimento cheese and add catsup. Makes a tangy, zesty dunk.

SOUR CREAM AND ANCHOVY
PASTE DUNK

1 *pt. sour cream*	2 *teasp. anchovy paste*
	2 *tablesp. chopped chives*

Combine. Makes a very tasty dunk and is most popular at parties because of the salty taste.

THREE DECKER FINGER SANDWICHES

Using pumpernickel, whole-wheat and white bread, cut off crusts and slice. Then make the following three spreads: cream cheese (softened with cream) mixed with chopped nuts and olives; salmon salad, see Page 193, chopped cucumbers, lettuce, tomatoes, radishes, and pickle relish, mixed with a little mayonnaise. Butter the bread and place the cucumber combination on the white bread, the salmon salad on the whole-wheat slice, the cream cheese on top of the whole-wheat slice, and top with the pumpernickel. Cut into 3 sections so that you have finger sandwiches about 1½ by 4 inches. Arrange on plate and cover with plastic wrap, foil, or a dampened cloth.

Variation: Bread may be cut into various small shapes and served three decker, two decker or open faced.

STUFFED PICKLES

Candied dill pickles	*1 teasp. milk or cream*
1 small pkge. cream cheese	*¼ cup chopped nutmeats*

Cream cream cheese, adding a little milk to moisten and soften. Add chopped nuts and blend. (Chopped chives may be added to this mixture, if so desired.) Using grapefruit core remover, remove center of candied dill pickles. Substitute the cream cheese filling, and slice. Serve as garnishes for sandwiches, etc.

HOT TUNA CHAFING DISH

2 cans tuna (large size)	*½ cup diced sweet pickles*
1 can button mushrooms	*2 cups potato chips*
½ cup diced pimentos	*3 cups white sauce*
1 stalk celery, diced	*½ cup green onions, chopped*
3 hard-boiled eggs, diced	*fine*

Combine ingredients, adding white sauce (medium) last. Place in chafing dish and keep hot for serving.

HOT SALMON CHAFING DISH

1 large can red salmon (flaked)

Use same ingredients as above but substitute salmon for tuna. Serve hot.

MISH-MOSH IN CHAFING DISH

1 lb. chicken livers　　　　*Pepper*
Giblets of chicken　　　　*Button mushrooms*
Chicken broth (for making　　*1 onion, diced*
　hot sauce)　　　　　　*Worcestershire sauce*
Salt　　　　　　　　*3 tablesp. flour*

Sauté chicken livers and onions. Have giblets cooked and ready for use. Dice into small pieces. Combine liver, onion and giblets and set aside. Heat chicken broth and a little pareve margarine in a saucepan. When hot, add seasoning, Worcestershire sauce and flour, stirring so that it will not form lumps. When thickened, add liver, onion, giblets and mushrooms. Place in chafing dish and serve hot. Goes well on slices of toast.

TUNA FISH MOLD
(Prepare in Large Fish Mold)

2 cans tuna　　　　　　*4 hard-boiled eggs, diced*
2 pkges. lemon Jello　　　*(save four slices for gar-*
　(Follow directions but　*nish)*
　eliminate 1 cup liquid to　*¼ cup sweet pickles*
　allow for strained chili　*¼ cup stuffed olives, diced*
　sauce)　　　　　　*(save a few for garnish)*
1 cup chili sauce (before　*3 tablesp. diced celery*
　straining)　　　　　*3 tablesp. chopped chives*
　　　　4 tablesp. vinegar

Scald tuna if necessary. Flake. Prepare Jello, straining chili sauce and vinegar and pouring into Jello mixture. Refrigerate

Jello mixture until it reaches the consistency of raw eggs. Dice hard-boiled eggs, pickles, olives, and celery and chop the chives. Arrange sliced eggs and sliced stuffed olives left for garnishing on bottom of fish mold, placing a stuffed olive in the eye impression of the fish and a strip of red pimento for the mouth. Place flaked tuna on bottom of mold and follow with the diced ingredients. Pour Jello over mixture and refrigerate. *Suggestion:* when ready to serve, combine the strained part of the chili sauce with a little mayonnaise for a delicious thousand island dressing with which to garnish mold.

MAMA'S FABULOUS SANDWICH LOAF

Bread:

1 sandwich loaf of bread (firm)—Have baker remove crusts and cut lengthwise into three sections.

Salmon salad:

Prepare following salmon salad, being careful to drain and bone salmon
4 hard-boiled eggs, diced
2 large cans red salmon

1 tablesp. lemon juice
2 tablesp. mayonnaise
1 small onion, grated
¼ cup diced sweet pickles and olives
1 pimento, diced

Frosting:

1 large pkge. cream cheese
1 tablesp. cream
Few drops of vegetable food coloring (red)

8 candied cherries, with stems affixed

Prepare salmon salad by mashing salmon until fine, adding mayonnaise to make this a simple task, and all diced ingredients. Lightly butter layers of bread in between (not the top of bread), placing salmon salad between layers. Place plastic wrap or foil around it so that it will remain fresh. Before serving, prepare frosting. Cream the package of cream cheese so that it is soft and pliable. Add cream and a few drops of vegetable coloring, which will make it a delicate pink. When ready to serve, frost the sandwich loaf and garnish with candied cherries. Prepare yourself for plaudits on this delectable loaf.

POTATO SALAD MOLD

12 to 15 medium-sized pota- toes	1 cup mayonnaise
½ cup chopped green pepper	2 teasp. salt
½ cup chopped sweet red pepper	1 teasp. basil
	1 teasp. dry mustard
⅓ cup salad oil	¼ teasp. pepper
4 tablesp. vinegar	6 hard-boiled eggs
½ cup chopped celery	3 tablesp. milk
	1 onion, grated

Cook potatoes with jackets on until tender, but not too soft. Drain and peel while warm. Cube and place in large mixing bowl. Combine oil, vinegar, salt, pepper, basil, mustard, and onion and pour over potatoes, seeing that it is completely blended.

Reserve 2 egg yolks and set aside. Chop eggs and combine with green and red peppers and celery and add to potatoes. Add milk to mayonnaise and fold into potatoes, blending thoroughly.

Press entire mixture into a large tube-type angel food pan, pressing down with spoon so that top is even all around. Chill in refrigerator, covering top so that potato mixture does not dry out. Loosen mold by inserting thin blade knife around the tube pan and invert over serving platter. When ready to serve, press egg yolks which had been reserved through a sieve, and sprinkle over top of mold, garnishing further with sprigs of parsley and thin strips of pimento.

TOMATOES FILLED WITH
COTTAGE CHEESE

8 to 10 large steak tomatoes   ½ cup chopped chives
1 lb. cottage cheese (creamed   ¼ cup chopped pimento
   type)   Stuffed olives for garnish

Scoop tomatoes. Combine cottage cheese with chives and pimento and pile high in scooped tomatoes. Garnish with sliced stuffed olives. Excellent for buffet serving, and most filling.

MIXED FRUIT AND SALAD
GREENS SALAD

1 quart mixed honeydew,   3 oranges, peeled and sec-
   cantaloupe and watermelon   tioned
   balls   4 cups salad greens, broken
1 avocado, sliced in strips   in pieces

(Salad Dressing)

½ cup salad oil   ½ teasp. salt
4 tablesp. vinegar   ¼ teasp. pepper
2 teasp. sugar   ⅛ teasp. dry mustard
        ⅛ teasp. paprika

Combine fruits and salad greens, tossing to intermingle. Serve in large salad bowl. Mix salad dressing ingredients together in a jar with tight fitting lid and shake well. Drizzle some over salad, and serve balance of dressing on the side.

FRUIT BALLS

Prepare fruit balls from cantaloupe, honeydew, and watermelon and include pineapple chunks. Scoop out half of a large watermelon and scallop edges. Arrange fruit in this shell and garnish with sprigs of mint leaf.

RIBBON SANDWICHES

Use 4 slices of bread in any desired combination. Spread inside layers lightly with butter and fill with 3 different sandwich spreads. Then cut into 3 sections.

Suggested fillings:

Cream cheese
Pickle relish
Tomato sardines—remove bones and mash fine, using a
   food chopper
Tuna fish—mash tuna and combine with mayonnaise, a
   little onion juice, and egg yolks (pressed through sieve)

COCKTAIL FRANKS IN BLANKETS

24 cocktail frankfurters   *24 thinly sliced pieces of*
Mustard relish   *bread*

Boil frankfurters and brush lightly with mustard relish. Wrap piece of bread around frankfurter with pick fastener underneath. Broil for about 5 to 8 minutes, or until bread has been browned, but not scorched. Serve hot.

EGGS AND THEIR VARIOUS USES

In addition to the regular deviled eggs, the egg yolk may be removed, after slicing hard-boiled eggs lengthwise. Substitute chopped chicken liver, chopped herring, or other types of fillings such as tuna fish salad or salmon salad. Garnish with sliced stuffed olives, sprigs of parsley, etc.

FINGER SANDWICHES

Although finger sandwiches and ribbon sandwiches are made very attractive by varying the shapes and the type of bread, they can be even more festive if they are garnished with slices of stuffed olives, half pecans or walnuts, candied cherries, thinly sliced cucumbers, sprigs of parsley, or various decorative shapes of pimento.

PLATTERS

Platters should be used to display foods to their best advantage. Do not arrange food in only one pattern. Place sandwiches at various angles on the plate and intermingle the shapes and sizes, in order to achieve variety. Or, use these sandwiches to surround a startling center offering. For a surprise effect, combine foods on the same platter which one would not expect to find side by side.

ROAST TURKEY

Preparation of a large turkey, preferably in the 20 pound or over category, provides the means of serving a large number of people. Professional kosher caterers have facilities for pre-slicing a turkey, making it convenient for people to partake of it (cold) from the buffet table.

ROAST CHICKEN

This may be served to very good advantage, if the white meat is sliced, placed attractively on platters and garnished with spiced fruit, sprigs of parsley and other kindred foods.

ROAST BEEF

This all-time favorite makes an excellent addition to the buffet. Sliced thin, it provides the makings for delectable sandwiches, or complements any serving plate filled with other delights.

CHICKEN SALAD or TURKEY SALAD

This item is very popular at buffets, especially with the hostess, since it can be made to go a little further with a large crowd. By dicing and adding other ingredients, the bulk increases and is able to accommodate many more people.

CHICKEN SALAD MOLD

2 cups diced chicken   *4 tablesp. vinegar*
2 pkges. lemon Jello   *2 hard-boiled eggs, diced*
3 cups water   *¼ cup chopped sweet pickles*
¾ cup strained chili sauce   *and stuffed olives*
                 4 tablesp. diced celery

Combine Jello, vinegar, water, and strained chili sauce and place in refrigerator until it reaches the consistency of raw eggs. Remove and place chicken, chopped eggs, pickles, olives and celery in mold. Pour Jello over mixture and refrigerate until ready for use. Garnish with sprigs of parsley and pickled pears.

SHERBET PUNCH

3 qts. ginger ale   *Garnish with cherries, berries*
1 qt. sherbet (any desired   *and sprigs of mint leaves*
flavor)

PARTY PUNCH

Frozen orange juice   *Freeze molds of different*
Frozen lemon juice   *shapes, adding maraschino*
Grape juice   *cherries, sections of oranges*
Ginger ale   *and lemon slices (halved)*
                                and float in punch

FRESH FRUIT PUNCH

12 lemons
12 oranges
12 grapefruits
1 large bottle grape juice
1 large bottle ginger ale

Berries, cantaloupe balls, honeydew balls, watermelon balls (floating on top of punch), cherries with stems.

The Art of Canning

In Mama's and Grandma's era canning and preserving, or "putting up" vegetables, as it was called, was a means of survival. In the northern climes the distances were often too great to hazard going out in the blizzards and heavy storms to buy fresh fruits and vegetables. It was vital to have supplies in the storeroom, with many jars of food on hand for the family.

There are two methods of canning which will be discussed below: by hot pack and by pressure cooking.

The most important facet to canning, however, is STERILIZATION, of jars, utensils, rubber capping bands, lids. This should be done both before and after foods have been cooked and placed in jars. Long-handled prongs, like those used for barbecues, are excellent for handling jars, lids, and other sterilized utensils used in canning.

To sterilize jars, place them on their side in a large kettle of cold water and bring water to the boiling point. Boil for 10 minutes, being certain that jars are completely submerged. Rubbers, lids, measuring cups, spoons, self-sealing caps, and all other utensils should also be completely submerged in boiling water.

Be very careful when selecting fruits and vegetables; only firm, freshly picked or purchased foods should be used for canning. Vegetables should be cooked in boiling water, while fruit is cooked in boiling syrup. While still hot, they are placed in hot sterilized jars. In turn, the jars are processed by placing them in a water canner which has a rack on the bottom to hold the jars; the caps or lids should be loosely fitted, and boiling water cover the jars to a depth of 2 or 3 inches above the tops. When the processing of sterilized jars has been completed, remove the cover of the water canner, tilting so that steam will not scald hands and face, and take out jars with prongs.

The jars should be completely sealed and then kept at room temperature for 10 days, at which point they should be checked very carefully to see that there has been no food spoilage. In fact, it is an excellent idea to test all jars before using, even if they are new. The tops may be faulty or the rubbers defective. To test: fill with water, adjust rubbers or lids (be they self-sealing glass tops, screw tops, or even vacuum-seal lids), and invert. If water seeps out, the jar is imperfect and should be discarded.

SYRUP FOR CANNING OF FRUIT

1 part water to 2 parts sugar
1 part water to 4 parts sugar
1 part water to 8 parts sugar

Depending upon the amount of sweetness desired and on whether the fruit tends to be sour or particularly sweet, the above schedule of syrups is outlined for use. Where fruit contains a great deal of sugar, the first syrup is recommended. For sour fruit, the latter is preferable.

HOT PACK CANNING

Fruits and vegetables are cooked in an open kettle for a short time in either boiling water (vegetables) or boiling syrup (fruit).

Time Table for Processing

* Peaches, apricots, other fruits in peach family	*20 minutes*	*boiling water canner*
Pears, all types	*20 minutes*	*boiling water canner*

* Peaches are easier to peel if you drop a few of them at a time into boiling water and, when skins loosen, dip them in cold water.

Time Table for Processing

Plums	15 minutes	boiling water canner
Berries (raspberries, loganberries, blueberries, huckleberries)	18 minutes	boiling water canner
Cherries	15 minutes	boiling water canner

NOTE: At least ½ to 1 inch should be left at the top of each jar when you seal it. Altitudes must be considered in canning: if time is 20 minutes or less, 1 minute must be added for each 1,000 feet above sea level; if time is longer than 20 minutes, 2 minutes should be added for each 1,000 feet above sea level.

Canning of Strawberries

For every pint (2 cups) of strawberries, use ½ cup sugar and let stand in an open preserving kettle. When juice begins to flow, heat to boiling point and cook rapidly for about 3 minutes. Cover and let stand overnight. Drain berries and pack in hot, sterilized jars. Leave cover fitting loosely and place in boiling water bath for 8 to 10 minutes. Remove jars, seal them, and place them on their sides, rolling every day for about 7 days. Store in a cool, dark, ventilated place, and protect them from the light by wrapping them in paper and using a curtain.

Tomatoes

Pour boiling water over tomatoes until skins loosen. Place in cold water, core and peel. May be canned whole. Cook them in boiling water to which ½ teaspoon salt per pint has been added. Pack while still hot, and process jars for 10 minutes. Be sure to leave at least 1 inch at top of each jar and to add 1 minute for each 1,000 feet above sea level.

PROCESSING IN PRESSURE COOKER

According to the advice of Government bulletins, all non-acid vegetables require higher temperatures for sterilization and should be processed by the pressure cooker method. Below is a list of non-acid vegetables:

Vegetable	Time	Pressure
Asparagus, peas, greens, beets, carrots	55 minutes (qt.) 35 minutes (pt.)	10 lbs.
Snap beans	25 minutes	10 lbs.
Lima beans	1 hour	10 lbs.
Pumpkin, squash	1 hour & 20 minutes	10 lbs.
Sweet potatoes	1 hour & 35 minutes	10 lbs.

Cook vegetables and place in hot, sterilized jars along with water in which vegetables were cooked. If more is required, pour boiling water to which salt, sugar, or other seasoning has been added, over vegetables. Seal the jars and arrange them on the rack in pressure cooker not too close together. Add boiling water level with the rack on bottom. Follow the manufacturer's instructions on the use of pressure cooker. DO NOT REMOVE FROM PRESSURE COOKER until the required time has elapsed and the pressure has been reduced to zero and the cooker turned off.

Continental and Israeli Dishes

MANY RECIPES HAVE NOT BEEN INCLUDED BECAUSE OF THE difficulty in securing specific herbs and spices called for. The following recipes have been adapted to the American taste.

CARNATZLACH—HAMBURGERS
(From Rumania)

2 lbs. ground beef chuck	½ teasp. paprika
3 eggs	1 clove garlic, minced
1 grated onion	½ teasp. salt
1½ teasp. poultry seasoning	Dash of pepper
3 grated carrots	4 tablesp. flour

Combine meat with all ingredients, reserving the flour and paprika. Form meat into rolls about 3 inches long and roll in flour, sprinkling with paprika. Broil first on one side, then the other and serve when browned completely.

KOENIGSBERGER KLOPS
(German origin)

1 lb. ground beef	1 tablesp. Worcestershire sauce
1 lb. ground veal	Vegetable stock (about 4 cups)
3 eggs, well-beaten	
3 slices bread (soaked and pressed dry)	½ teasp. pepper
1 large onion, grated	1 bunch parsley (minced)
1 grated lemon rind	1 teasp. salt
1 lemon, juiced	Dash of pepper
1 tablesp. capers	

Combine ground meat with beaten eggs. Brown onion with fat or oil. Add onions, bread, seasoning, lemon juice and rind, paprika, and Worcestershire sauce to meat mixture. Form into balls, and drop into boiling vegetable stock. Cover saucepan and simmer for about 20 minutes, or until meat is done. Remove meat balls from saucepan. Taking 3 tablespoons flour and combining with shortening or fat, make a gravy of the vegetable stock, adding capers and parsley. Place meat balls back in gravy and heat thoroughly. Serve hot.

WIENER SCHNITZEL
(German origin)

8 veal shoulder steaks (½ inch thick)
1 cup matzo meal

3 eggs, beaten
Shortening
1 teasp. salt

½ teasp. paprika

Pound steaks with mallet. Dip in matzo meal, which has been mixed with seasoning. Dip steaks in egg batter, then in matzo meal again. Heat skillet and melt shortening. Brown well on one side. Turn over, cover skillet, reduce heat and simmer for 45 minutes. Sprinkle with paprika and added salt and pepper, if desired. Garnish with parsley.

SHASHLICK (Far Eastern origin)

3 lbs. shoulder lamb (cubed and marinated)
Whole finger tomatoes or tomato wedges
Small pickled onions

Whole button mushrooms
Cubed pieces of green pepper
Clove of garlic
Seasoned salt
Dash of pepper

Skewers

Rub lamb with clove of garlic. Arrange meat on skewers alternately with tomato, pickled onions, button mushrooms and green pepper. Season. Broil either over charcoal broiler or under regular broiler for 15 minutes, or until well browned on all sides.

ORIENTAL LAMB (Chinese origin)

3 lbs. lamb (cut in pieces)	*1 large onion, sliced thin*
4 tablesp. oil	*⅛ teasp. ginger*
3 tablesp. soy sauce	*1 bouillon cube*
1 cup bean sprouts	*½ teasp. salt*
1 small can crushed pine-apple (include juice)	*2½ tablesp. cornstarch*
	2 tablesp. water

Brown lamb in oil, adding 1 tablespoon soy sauce. To this mixture, add bean sprouts, crushed pineapple, onion, soy sauce, ginger, bouillon cube and seasoning. Simmer over low heat until meat is tender. Combine cornstarch with water, and thicken meat mixture. When thoroughly blended, remove from heat. Serve over mounds of cooked rice.

TONGUE POLONAISE (French origin)

1 beef tongue (cooked)	*¼ cup raisins*
1½ cups tomato sauce	*2 bay leaves*
2 tablesp. grape wine (sacramental)	*1 teasp. salt*
3 tablesp. brown sugar	*2 teasp. potato starch*
	2 tablesp. water

Combine all ingredients except beef tongue, potato starch and water. Place over medium heat and bring to boiling point. Make a paste of potato starch and water and slice beef tongue. Add paste to sauce mixture. Blend thoroughly and continue to stir until it thickens. Place sliced tongue in skillet, pouring sauce over the tongue and simmer over low heat for about 15 minutes, or until thoroughly heated. Serve hot.

VIENNESE MEAT BALLS (Vienna)

2 lbs. ground beef	½ teasp. pepper
3 eggs	½ teasp. paprika
1 onion, grated	2 onions, diced
3 tablesp. dry bread crumbs	Shortening for frying
or 2 slices bread, soaked in	1 can tomato sauce
water and pressed slightly	1 cup cold water
1 teasp. salt	½ cup chopped sweet pickles

Form into meat balls, after combining meat with eggs, grated onion, soaked bread, paprika, salt and pepper. Brown diced onions in skillet, add meat balls and brown well. Combine tomato sauce and water and add to skillet. Cook over low heat for about 45 minutes. Just before removing from heat, add sweet pickles to mixture and blend thoroughly.

SWEDISH MEAT BALLS (Sweden)

2 lbs. chopped beef	3 slices cubed bread
1 bouillon cube	4 tablesp. tomato juice
1 cup boiling water	1 teasp. salt
Dash of pepper	

SAUCE

1 cup pineapple catsup	2 tablesp. brown sugar
¼ cup cider vinegar	½ teasp. dry mustard
½ teasp. paprika	1 cup bouillon
½ teasp. curry	½ teasp. salt
Dash of pepper	

Combine meat with tomato juice and season. Dissolve bouillon cube in cup of boiling water and pour over cubed bread. Add to meat mixture and form into meat balls. Brown in skillet.

Combine ingredients for sauce in separate saucepan and

drop meat balls into sauce, simmering for about 15 to 20 minutes or until completely blended and done.

VEAL SCALLOPINI (Italian)

3 lbs. veal (½ inch thick) 4 tablesp. flour
2 tablesp. parsley flakes 2 onions, diced
1 clove garlic

SAUCE

2 tablesp. sugar 1 can button mushrooms
½ teasp. marjoram (with sauce)
4 tablesp. catsup

Pound veal and press flour into meat, sprinkling with parsley flakes. Brown in shortening on both sides. Dice onions, brown, and add minced garlic. When browned, add veal and the combined sauce. Cover and simmer over low heat for 1½ to 2 hours, or until completely tender.

ANCHOVY PIZZA (Italian)

2½ cups flour 1 teasp. sugar
¾ cup water 1 teasp. salt
1 egg ⅓ cup oil
1 tablesp. yeast

Combine yeast, sugar, and lukewarm water. Make a well in sifted flour and add these ingredients. When yeast begins to rise, add balance of ingredients and let stand in a warm spot to·rise. Taking half the dough at a time, roll out to ¼ inch thickness and throw it from hand to hand, thinning and shaping into circular form as you work it. Place on a greased baking sheet and roll the edges so that a ledge is formed. Cover with tomato purée, anchovy fillets, marjoram, oregano, and sprinkle with grated mozzarella cheese. Bake in hot oven of 425°F. for 20 to 25 minutes, or until browned and cheese has melted.

ORIENTAL SWEET POTATOES
(Morocco)

6 sweet potatoes	1 tablesp. oil
½ teasp. cinnamon	1 teasp. cardamon seeds
2 tablesp. sugar	2 cloves garlic

Wash potatoes and scrape peeling. Cook with water to cover until tender. Add rest of ingredients and simmer until potatoes are glazed but not crumbly.

CHOPPED HERRING (Russian)

2 or 3 boned schmaltz herrings	1 onion (brought to boil in water)
3 slices of bread soaked in vinegar	3 teasp. sugar
	¼ teasp. pepper
1 apple (peeled and cored)	3 hard-boiled eggs

Place herring through grinder and chop fine. Place boiled onion and apple through grinder. Combine with bread, adding sugar and pepper and finely chopped hard-boiled eggs. When completely blended, it should be of fine texture. Press egg yolks through sieve, and sprinkle on chopped herring. Garnish with sprigs of parsley.

CUCUMBER SALAD
(Baghdad—Turkey)

3 large cucumbers (sliced thin)	2 green peppers (diced or in rings)
2 large onions (sliced thin)	1 clove garlic, minced

Marinade

¼ cup vinegar	¼ teasp. salt
2 tablesp. sugar	⅛ teasp. pepper
½ cup oil	

Mince garlic clove and mix with marinade. Mix rest of ingredients with marinade and serve.

POACHED FISH (Sephardic—Spanish Jews)

1 lemon, sliced	*1 red pepper*
3 lbs. fish (in 2-inch slices)	*1 teasp. salt*
1 clove garlic	*Boiling water*

To water, add sliced lemon, clove of garlic, red pepper, salt and bring to a boil. Place fish slices in cheesecloth bag and drop into boiling mixture until tender, but not crumbly. Serve with lemon slices and chopped parsley.

STRUDEL FILLED WITH EGGPLANT
MIXTURE (The Balkans)

Recipe of Stretched Strudel	*1 eggplant, cut in slices*
Dough	*2 eggs*
3 tablesp. oil	*½ teasp. salt*
1 clove garlic	*¼ teasp. pepper*

Cook eggplant in water to cover, adding chopped garlic and seasoning. Add eggs and cook until thick, stirring constantly. Place mixture about 2 inches apart on strudel dough, brush with oil, wrap, brush top with oil and bake in hot oven of 400°F. for about 25 minutes or until browned. Slice when cool.

TURKISH SWEETMEAT (Katyiff)

½ lb. fine noodles	*½ cup slivered, blanched*
½ cup honey	*almonds*
2 tablesp. butter	

Cook noodles in boiling salted water until tender. Drain and place in a square baking pan. When caked and cool, invert onto plate and cut in squares. Grease cookie sheet and arrange squares, sprinkling with nuts and pouring a little honey on each square. Melt butter and pour a little butter on each square. Bake in moderate oven of 350°F. for 30 minutes. Garnish each one with candied cherry.

ARMENIAN MOUSSAKA (Armenia)

2 lbs. ground lamb or beef	¼ teasp. pepper
1 large eggplant	¼ teasp. paprika
1 teasp. salt	1 cup toasted bread crumbs
	1 cup tomato paste

Season meat and place in a greased baking dish. Slice eggplant, arrange on top of meat, and cover with tomato paste. Cover baking dish and bake in moderate oven of 350°F. for about 25 minutes. Remove cover and sprinkle with toasted bread crumbs and brown for about 15 minutes.

PASSOVER INGBERLACH (Austrian)

2 cups matzo meal	2 eggs
1½ cups honey	2½ tablesp. ginger (pulver-
2 cups sugar	ized)
	¾ cup ground almonds

Combine honey and sugar and bring to boiling point. Continue cooking over low heat until it becomes golden in color. Combine all other ingredients, adding to honey mixture. Continue cooking over low heat, stirring constantly, until mixture becomes thickened. Turn onto wet board or foil and pat to about ½ inch thickness. Cut into squares. Place ½ pecan on each square and sprinkle with confectionery sugar.

ISRAELI DISHES
BA'MYA (Okra used as a vegetable)

1 lb. okra	1 lemon
¼ glass of water	1 can tomato sauce
½ teasp. salt	2 onions

Wash okra well and let it stand for about 20 minutes. Then mix all ingredients and bring to a boil. Reduce flame to low, cover and cook for 30 minutes.

OKRA (with meat)

Follow ingredients and directions above, but add pre-cooked meat or fowl and an additional ½ cup tomato sauce and ½ cup water. Heat and serve. Meat balls make an especially delicious dish.

EGGPLANT STICKS

1 large eggplant	*2 cups oil*
½ teasp. salt	*1 cup flour or 1 cup bread*
½ teasp. garlic	*crumbs*
2 large eggs	

Slice eggplant lengthwise into thick strips, sprinkle with garlic and salt. Dip into beaten eggs and roll in flour. Then fry in deep oil until brown on each side. Place on brown paper to drain. Serve warm as a vegetable, side dish or snack.

STUFFED EGGPLANT

1 eggplant	*½ can tomato sauce*
½ cup rice	*1 teasp. pepper*
½ cup cooked, chopped meat	*¼ teasp. garlic*
	Green pepper

Use an eggplant which is hard but smooth on the outside. Clean out the inside and fill with a mixture of the ingredients, including chopped green pepper. Cook in ½ cup of water in saucepan for 30 minutes. Or, it may also be baked. Serves 2.

STUFFED YELLOW SQUASH
(Koosa Machski)

1 large yellow squash	*¼ teasp. salt*
½ cup rice	*¼ teasp. pepper*
1 cup cooked, chopped meat	*1 green pepper, chopped*
¼ teasp. garlic	

Wash the outside of the squash well and clean out the inside. Fill with a mixture of the above ingredients. Place in a saucepan with ½ cup water and cook for 30 minutes. Or, it may also be baked.

CHICK PEA SPREAD (For Canapés)

1 can chick peas
1 teasp. salt
1 lemon

¼ cup flour
2 tablesp. olive oil
Parsley

Drain chick peas and mix with rest of ingredients with a fork. Spread on crackers or bread.

FALAFEL

Falafel is the traditional delicacy of Israel. You can see people eating it on practically every street corner, much like the hot dog in the United States.

1 can chick peas
1 teasp. sharp red pepper

¼ teasp. salt
¼ teasp. garlic

Grind chick peas well and mix with rest of ingredients. Form into balls and fry in very deep, hot oil until brown. Serve it hot inside of a *pitta*, an Israeli roll, along with a salad of your choosing.

FALAFEL (Variation)

2 cups falafel or chick peas
2 tablesp. flour
½ teasp. baking soda
1 egg
2 cloves garlic

1 teaspoon salt
¼ teaspoon pepper
Dash of turmeric
2 slices bread (soaked and
pressed dry)

Parsley

Soak chick peas overnight. Drain and place through food grinder. Combine with garlic, bread and flowerettes from a bunch of parsley and place through grinder with these ingredients. Add seasoning, flour, baking soda, and egg. Mix and form into small balls. Heat shortening in skillet and fry until completely tender and browned. Garnish with parsley and lemon slices.

LENTIL KUGEL

4 cups lentil	*2 eggs*
1 teasp. salt	*½ cup flour*
½ teasp. pepper	*½ cup oil*

Heat some of the oil in the bottom of the pan. Then mix all of the ingredients well and bake in hot oven (400°F.) until crust is brown. Slice while hot.

BAKLAVA (The Rich Cookie of the Orient)

4 cups flour	*1 cup almonds*
1 tablesp. salt	*10 sweet crackers*
½ cup oil or margarine	*¼ cup sesame seeds*
1 cup nuts	*1 cup sugar*

Mix flour, oil, salt and sugar well. Place in a flat plate for half an hour. Roll out dough, but not too thin. Spread margarine or oil over flat dough with a knife. Fold it over and spread oil as before; repeat two more times. Cover with cloth and let stand in refrigerator for one or two nights, but do not freeze.

When ready to bake, chop nuts, almonds, and crackers and sprinkle with sesame seeds and sugar. Place this mixture in a pot with oil and cook for a short time. When rich in color, remove to another pot to cool. Spread some sugar and water on dough and with a spoon, pour mixture on dough and fold it into a roll. Slice roll into individual portions and place in a greased baking pan. Bake in a hot oven (400°F.) for 1 hour.

ISRAELI FRUIT SALAD

3 cups melon balls and cubes
½ .cup dates (pitted and diced)
2 mangos, cubed
¼ cup diced figs

¼ cup black grapes
Sugar and water (equal parts)
1 cup shredded cocoanut
¼ cup slivered, blanched almonds

Combine sugar and water and bring to a boil to make a syrup. Allow to cool. Prepare and combine fruits, spooning them into individual sherbets. Pour syrup over each serving and garnish with almonds, cocoanut and candied cherry.

SUM-SUM CONFECTION

1 cup sugar
1 cup sesame seeds (sum-sum)

1 cup honey
½ cup hot water
½ cup chopped walnuts

½ teasp. salt

Using top of double boiler, combine honey, sugar and hot water. Add salt and bring to a boil, stirring to prevent scorching. Test in cup of cold water, and when it reaches soft ball stage, add chopped nuts and sesame seeds. Continue cooking for about 5 minutes, stirring. Take top of double boiler and place over direct heat, continuing to stir until color is golden brown. Turn mixture out on foil or a wet board, patting to ½ inch thickness, and cut into squares. Place half walnut on each square and sprinkle with powdered sugar.

TABLE OF WEIGHTS AND MEASURES

Weight	Commodity
1 pound	2 cups butter (packed)
1 pound	4 cups flour
1 pound	2 cups sugar (granulated)
1 pound	2¼ cups sugar (brown-packed)
1 pound	3½ cups sugar (confectionery-sifted)
1 pound	3 cups corn meal
1 pound	16 ounces
1 gallon	4 quarts
1 quart	2 pints
1 pint	2 cups
1 cup	16 tablespoons
½ cup	8 tablespoons
¼ cup	4 tablespoons
1 liquid ounce	2 tablespoons
1 tablespoon	3 teaspoons
1 teaspoon	60 drops
1 ounce	4 tablespoons flour
1 ounce	small sq. yeast (compressed)
1 ounce	1 square bitter chocolate
1 ounce chocolate	⅓ cup cocoa
1½ ounces	¼ cup raisins
¼ pound (4 ounces)	1 cup walnuts (shelled)
¼ pound (4 ounces)	1 cup almonds (shelled)
⅓ pound (5⅓ ounces)	1 cup pecans (shelled)
15 pounds	1 peck potatoes
50 pounds	1 bushel tomatoes
45 pounds	1 bushel apples
48 to 50 pounds	1 bushel peaches, plums or pears
7½ pounds	1 peck peas in pods

STANDARD SIZES OF CANNED GOODS

No. 10 can	12 to 13 cups
No. 3 can	4 cups
No. 2½ can	3½ cups
No. 2 can	2½ cups
No. 1 can	1¼ cups
8 ounce can	1 cup

Suggested Passover Menus

PASSOVER BREAKFASTS

Fresh Orange Juice
Fried Matzos, Onions and Eggs
Fruit Preserves
    Coffee   Sanka   Tea   Milk

Fruit Compote
Matzo Meal Pancakes with Strawberries (fresh,
    crushed and with confectionery sugar on them)
    Coffee   Sanka   Tea   Milk

Stewed Figs
Matzos, dipped in mixture of beaten eggs, flavored
    with lemon rind, salt and pepper and fried in
    butter (sprinkled with cinnamon and sugar)
Grape Preserves
    Coffee   Sanka   Tea   Milk

Grapefruit Sections and Avocado Slices (seasoned
    with Persian lime)
Broiled Salt Mackerel
Toasted Matzos (sprinkled with onion salt)
    Coffee   Sanka   Tea   Milk

Bowl of Berries (in season)
Creamed Finnan Haddie on Toasted Matzos
    (use potato flour to thicken sauce)
Matzo Meal Pancakes
    Coffee   Sanka   Tea   Milk

½ Canteloupe filled with Berries (in season)
Creamed Mushrooms, Onions and Diced Hard-
     Boiled Eggs on Matzos (use potato flour to
     thicken sauce)
Matzo Meal Pancakes
     Coffee   Sanka   Tea   Milk

Orange and Mandarin Sections
Omelette with Strawberry Preserves
Matzo Meal Pancakes
     Coffee   Sanka   Tea   Milk

Fruit Compote
Eggs (scrambled with mushrooms and onions)
Toasted Matzos
     Coffee   Sanka   Tea   Milk

Orange Juice
Matzo Meal Pancakes served with
     topping of poached eggs
Fruit Preserves
     Coffee   Sanka   Tea   Milk

PASSOVER LUNCHES

Matzo Meal Pancakes
Fruit Preserves
Passover Banana Nut Cake
Honeydew Melon or Berries (in season)
     Coffee   Tea   Milk

Chicken Soup with Matzo Dumpling
Broiled Chicken
Passover Beet Preserves
Lettuce and Tomatoes
Ayer Kichel (made with matzo meal)
     Tea   Black Coffee   Iced Tea

Potato Latkes
Passover Apple Kugel
Fruit Compote
Cocoanut Macaroons
    Tea   Coffee   Iced Tea

Fruit Cocktail
Breast of Beef
Potato Kugel
String Beans
Applesauce
Sponge Cake
    Hot Tea   Iced Tea

PASSOVER DINNERS

Tomato Juice
Cooked Finnan Haddie with butter
Passover Oven Rolls
Potato Kugel
Spinach
Sponge Cake
    Tea   Coffee   Milk

Gefilte Fish Appetizer
Roast Chicken with Matzo Meal Stuffing
Carrot Tzimmes with Matzo Meal Knaidlach
Fruit Compote
    Tea   Black Coffee   Iced Tea

Chopped Liver Appetizer
Cholent with Matzo Meal Knaidlach
Tossed Salad with oil and vinegar dressing
Wedge of Fruit in season or Berries, sugared
    Tea   Black Coffee   Iced Tea

Marinated Herring Appetizer
Standing Rib Roast (do not use flour paste in recipe)
Baked Potatoes
Zucchini Squash
Passover Apple Kugel
   Tea   Black Coffee   Iced Tea

Apple Juice
Passover Cheese Blintzes with Sour Cream
Matzo Meal Pancakes
Pesakdek Lemon Puffs
   Tea   Coffee   Iced Tea

Glossary of Cooking Terms

To THE PRACTICED MIND OF THE EXPERIENCED COOK, COOKING TERMS come naturally and sound familiar. This glossary is intended for those who are young in experience and knowledge of the culinary arts, as well as those experienced cooks who might accomplish these dishes and processes, but do not fully understand them. Do not feel abashed at having to refer to this glossary. Everyone has to learn to crawl before he walks. When you have studied and used this glossary, you will be well-equipped to hold your own in the company of masters in the field of home economics.

À *la mode:* This refers to desserts; a scoop of ice cream to top pie, cake, shortcake, etc.

Aspic: A gelatin made with a vegetable flavor or fruit flavor, such as tomato aspic, etc.

Au Gratin: With a crust of cheese and bread crumbs; for example, au gratin potatoes.

Barbecue: To cook or roast over hot coals slowly on a spit or grill. Usually meats thus prepared are previously marinated for zesty flavor and to assure tenderness.

Baste: This process is accomplished by periodically pouring the natural liquid or a specially prepared liquid over meats, fish or fowl while they are roasting in the oven.

Beat: To use a large cooking or wooden spoon to beat manually or to employ an automatic food mixer according to directions. This usually applies to batter, as in cakes, puddings, stuffings for meats and fowl, frostings, icings, etc.

Bisque: A thick soup made with various types of fish. Also a frozen dessert with nuts.

Blanch: To pour boiling water over food being prepared, such as almonds, to loosen the skin, so that it may be used without skins. Such foods are usually slivered, as in a compote.

Bland: This refers to foods containing no seasoning; usually recommended for people on diets or convalescing from an illness.

Blend: To mix ingredients with cooking spoon or fork. In the case of cakes, this means to handle *gently* as opposed to beating.

Borscht: A special soup, usually made with beets and served with sour cream. A favorite delicacy either hot or cold.

Bouillon: A clear broth made from meat, but strained and delicately seasoned. Used usually for people on a diet or convalescing as well as for elegant dinners.

Braise: To brown in fat before potting or roasting meat, as in "gedempte flaish."

Bread: To roll food first in a liquid, such as beaten eggs, then in bread crumbs, matzo meal or some adequate substitute. Used mostly for foods which are to be fried.

Brine: A liquid composed of salt and water and usually a tart preservative. Used for preserving meats, fish, vegetables, etc.

Broth: The liquid in which either meat, fish or fowl has been cooked.

Brown: To brown by either sautéing, roasting, frying, broiling, baking, etc. Applies to fish, meats or fowl.

Canapé: A French term referring to an appetizer which is served on daintily-shaped crackers or toast along with fancy garnishes.

Carafe: A decanter for water, coffee, wine, liquor.

Caramelize: To melt crystallized sugar (not confectioners' sugar) and cook until it is a golden brown.

Casserole: An earthenware, metal or glass covered dish to be placed in the oven for baking.

Chutney: Highly seasoned fruits and vegetables prepared in relish form. Of Oriental origin; also a sweet pickle relish combination.

Citron: Candied fruit which is widely used in recipes for holiday cakes.

Compote: A favorite dessert after a heavy meal of fowl or meat. Usually composed of prunes, apricots, peaches (all dried fruits) cooked in a heavy syrup with lemon slices.

Condiment: Spices, vinegar, salt, pepper; all types of herbs to season or flavor food.

Confectioners' Sugar: A very fine, pulverized sugar which is combined with cornstarch and used mainly for cake frostings. You may identify this type of sugar by the number of "X's" on the package, usually "XXXX" to "XXXXXX." The more "X's" the finer the texture.

Conserve: Similar to a compote, it is made with several types of fruit and heavy syrup. Raisins and nuts may be added for additional flavor.

Consommé: A clear soup usually made from more that one type of meat and highly seasoned. Of French origin.

Cream: A term used in making cake batters. Refers to either butter or a butter substitute combined with sugar, and means blending these two ingredients together well.

Crêpe: A French term signifying a thin, crisp pancake, which usually is rolled around a tasty mixture which varies from cheeses to fruits.

Croquettes: Made from finely ground or chopped meat, fish or poultry, breaded and fried, or baked in the oven.

Croutons: Very popular French garnish for soups. Toast is cut into small square shapes and used to decorate soups. May also be made from eggs and flour and dried before placing in soups.

Crown Roast: Made from beef ribs, by cutting excess meat from the bone shank so that bones stand upright like a crown. It is tied to remain thus while roasting.

Cut and fold: This term is used particularly when blending egg whites into a batter or mixture. It means cutting down into the mixture to the bottom of the bowl, and bringing the mixture up along the side to the upper part of the batter. This is done to avoid loss of air circulation.

Cut into: To use pastry blender or other type of spatula to blend butter or fat into a flour mixture.

Demitasse: Originating from the French, this is a small-sized cup, in which black coffee is served after dinner.

Devil: To mash and highly season, as in deviled eggs. In this instance, a hard-boiled egg is cut lengthwise, the yolk removed and mashed and combined with certain highly seasoned ingredients, and returned to the egg whites.

Dice: To cut into small, cubed pieces. Uniformity in size is paramount.

Drain: To remove all liquid from substance.

Dredge: To completely coat with flour, bread crumbs, or any similar item.

Escallop: A special way of baking potatoes, or vegetables, by adding cheese, bread crumbs and a white sauce with seasoning. Usually baked in a casserole with ingredients sliced and diced.

French: This term applies to lamb chops, veal chops, where meat is trimmed from the bone end, so that fancy paper trimming may be added for decorative serving. Also, to flatten meat; to cut into thin pieces, such as potatoes.

French Fry: To roll substance in butter, and fry in deep fat.

Fricassee: Pieces of meat or fowl are braised and cooked on top of stove in a highly seasoned gravy.

Fritter: A fruit or vegetable rolled in butter and fried in deep fat, such as corn fritters, etc.

Frizzle: To brown until edges curl up and become crisp, such as chipped beef.

Frost: To ice, such as a cake. To use spatula or knife and place frosting on a cake, cookies, etc.

Glaze: This applies mostly to cakes, breads, rolls, and meats and fowl. It is the coating which is applied through use of egg yolk on breads, and other substances on meats and fowl.

Goulash: A dish made of pieces of meat, cut as for a beef stew, stewed with diced vegetables and highly seasoned. Usually called "Hungarian goulash."

Grate: To reduce foods to fine particles by using a grater. Usually applies to vegetables and the rinds of fruit.

Gravy: The liquid produced from cooking meat, fish, poultry, thickened with flour or cornstarch.

Grill: To pan broil over a flame on the stove without fat; water and salt are substituted for fat. Used for people on diet.

Hollandaise: A sauce originating with the Dutch. Flavorfully seasoned with egg yolks, butter and herbs; used over fish, vegetables, etc.

Hors d'Oeuvre: Similar to a canapé; specially prepared tidbits, which are served before dinner on attractively shaped pieces of toast, colorfully garnished; sometimes served on crackers, such as caviar hors d'oeuvres.

Ice: A liquid, usually made with a fruit flavor and frozen. Served as a substitute for ice cream, since ice does not contain rich cream.

Jardinière: Derived from the French meaning "accompanied by various vegetables." As in beef jardinière—meat served with various vegetables.

Julienne: To cut into long strips—either vegetables or meat, or both.

Jus: As in prime ribs of beef au jus, this means with the natural gravy of the meat.

Kippered: A salted, smoked fish, such as kippered herring.

Knead: To fold over with fists and hands, dough which has been prepared for baking bread, rolls, etc.

Kosher: Meats, chicken, etc., prepared according to the Jewish laws on slaughtering and "kashruth."

Kreplach: A small square of prepared dough, rolled flat, folded into a diamond shape with either meat or vegetable filling; used as a garnish for soup or as a side dish.

Leavening agent: That which is used in baked foods to make them light and fluffy. Typical of these are baking powder, baking soda and yeast with sugar.

Liquor: As a term used in home economics, this means the liquid in which food is packed.

Marinade: A mixture containing vinegar, water, oil, and seasoning in which meats and fowl are placed to tenderize them before cooking.

Marinate: To allow to stand in marinade.

Marzipan: A combination of almond paste and sugar used in confections.

Mask: To cover food with a thick sauce.

Meringue: Egg whites beaten until stiff with sugar and used as a topping for pies, cakes and desserts, such as Baked Alaska.

Mocha: A combination of coffee and chocolate. A favorite for frostings and as a drink.

Mornay: Traditional white sauce recipe with cheese added.

Mousse: A frozen fruit dessert, usually made with whipped cream, either egg white or yolk and fruit flavors.

Napoleon: Originating with the French, this is made of thin pastry sheets and cream filling, usually topped with jam, fancy icing, and nuts.

Nesselrode: A dessert in pudding form, made with mixed fruits, nuts, etc. and usually frozen with ice cream.

Newburg: A cream sauce made with egg and flavored with fruit juice or sherry. Usually used in conjunction with fish.

Pan-broil: To cook in a preheated skillet, with only a little water added.

Papillote: A paper decoration for making food more attractive.

Parboil: To cook until partially done in boiling water.

Pare: To remove the skin as of an apple, potato, or fruit.

Parfait: A combination of ice cream and fruit or chocolate sauce, or both, served in tall glasses and topped with whipped cream.

Paste: A smooth mixture, soft and pliable.

Pâté de foie gras: A smooth spread made from goose livers and usually served as an appetizer. Of French origin.

Patty: A pastry shell in which to serve creamed foods, or a round patty of meat, fish, chicken, which is fried.

Peel: To remove skin or rind by cutting with a knife; removal of outer skin or rind.

Petits Fours: Attractively decorated little cakes, made with fondant and frosted.

Pilaf: Rice prepared with spices and served with meats, poultry or fish.

Pipe: To force through a pastry tube to frost cake or decorate hors d'oeuvres.

Pit: To remove stone from a fruit.

Plank: A piece of wood on which meats and fish are served, usually surrounded by mashed potatoes.

Poach: To cook food in hot liquid, such as poached eggs (in boiling water, with salt added).

Pot Liquor: Liquid in which vegetables have been boiled.

Preheat: To set temperature of oven, and allow to heat for about 15 minutes before placing food in oven.

Punch: A combination of fruit juices, sugar and sometimes wine, making a refreshing drink.

Purée: To strain through a colander, as with purée of pea, so that only the pure sauce of the pea is retained.

Ragout: A highly seasoned beef stew.

Ramekin: A small individual casserole or serving dish.

Render: To remove fat of meat, usually poultry, and cook until reduced to a liquid state.

Rice: To place food through sieve, as with potatoes, etc.

Roast: To cook meat, poultry, etc. by dry heat in the oven.

Roux: A paste mixture of flour and fat, which is the basis of cream sauces and gravies.

Sauté: To fry quickly in only a small amount of fat, using a spatula to move food around in pan frequently.

Scald: To heat milk or liquid to just below the boiling point. To pour boiling water over food.

Scallion: Green onions.

Scallop: To bake with a cream sauce, usually with bread crumbs and cheese.

Score: To cut through, as with meat, and insert cloves for decorative purposes.

Scramble: As with eggs, mixing whites and yolks together (usually with a little milk), then placing in a skillet and stirring continuously with a fork.

Sear: To brown meat quickly by exposing it to high heat, and turning rapidly.

Season: To add salt, pepper, spices, etc. to ingredients being cooked to improve the flavor.

Sherbet: An ice made with fruit flavor and either water or milk and then frozen.

Shirr: To bake in small poaching dishes, buttered and with bread crumbs added, as with eggs.

Shred: To cut into small pieces, as with cabbage in making cole slaw.

Sift: To put through a sifter to make lighter, as with flour.

Simmer: To cook slowly in small amount of liquid over low heat.

Skewer: To fasten fowl or meat with wooden or metal pin.

Smorgasbord: To have an array of appetizers, usually those made from various types of fish, arranged decoratively on a long table, and to serve it buffet style.

Soufflé: A light, fluffy baked dish, made lighter through the addition of meringue (folded in) before it is baked.

Spatula: A utensil which is flat, thin and flexible. Used most often for working with batter, particularly when using an electric mixer.

Spit: To place on thin rod and broil while rotating.

Steam: To cook by steam in a double boiler.

Steam-bake: To place baking dishes in water in the oven and bake by steam, as with custard.

Steep: To let stand in boiling water until the flavor and coloring penetrate water, as with tea.

Sterilize: To free from germs by the application of intense heat.

Stew: To simmer in liquid until tender, as with beef stew.

Stock: The liquid in which meats, fowl, fish or vegetables have been cooked.

Stuff: To fill cavity with a specially prepared mixture or stuffing.

Succotash: A combination of corn kernels and lima beans cooked together.

Torte: A rich cake of five or six thin layers, with a filling between each layer. A rich dessert made with eggs, crumbs, and nuts.

Toss: To lift repeatedly with a fork and spoon until ingredients have been properly mixed together, as with a salad.

Truss: To fasten into position, as with fowl, with skewers or twine before placing on spit or in the oven for roasting.

Welsh Rarebit: Cheese melted and mixed with other ingredients, and served over toast.

Whip: To beat either with an electric or manual type beater until stiff, as with eggs.

Index